CONSUMING BEHAVIOURS

CONSUMING BEHAVIOURS

IDENTITY, POLITICS AND PLEASURE IN TWENTIETH-CENTURY BRITAIN

Edited by *Erika Rappaport, Sandra Trudgen Dawson and Mark J. Crowley*

Bloomsbury Academic
An imprint of Bloomsbury Publishing Plc

B L O O M S B U R Y
LONDON • NEW DELHI • NEW YORK • SYDNEY

Bloomsbury Academic
An imprint of Bloomsbury Publishing Plc

50 Bedford Square	1385 Broadway
London	New York
WC1B 3DP	NY 10018
UK	USA

www.bloomsbury.com

BLOOMSBURY and the Diana logo are trademarks of Bloomsbury Publishing Plc

First published 2015

© Erika Rappaport, Sandra Trudgen Dawson and Mark J. Crowley, 2015

Erika Rappaport, Sandra Trudgen Dawson and Mark J. Crowley have asserted their right under the Copyright, Designs and Patents Act, 1988, to be identified as Editors of this work.

All rights reserved. No part of this publication may be reproduced or transmitted in any form or by any means, electronic or mechanical, including photocopying, recording, or any information storage or retrieval system, without prior permission in writing from the publishers.

No responsibility for loss caused to any individual or organization acting on or refraining from action as a result of the material in this publication can be accepted by Bloomsbury or the authors.

British Library Cataloguing-in-Publication Data
A catalogue record for this book is available from the British Library.

ISBN: HB: 978-0-8578-5611-1
PB: 978-0-8578-5739-2
ePDF: 978-0-8578-5530-5
ePub: 978-0-8578-5557-2

Library of Congress Cataloging-in-Publication Data
Consuming behaviours : identity, politics and pleasure in twentieth-century Britain / edited by Erika Rappaport, Sandra Trudgen Dawson and Mark J. Crowley.
    pages cm
Includes bibliographical references and index.
ISBN 978-0-85785-611-1 (hardcover)-- ISBN 978-0-85785-739-2 (pbk.) 1. Consumers--Great Britain--History--20th century. 2. Consumption (Economics)--Social aspects--Great Britain--History--20th century. 3. Consumption (Economics)--Social aspects--History--20th century. I. Rappaport, Erika Diane, 1963- II. Dawson, Sandra Trudgen. III. Crowley, Mark J.
    HC260.C6C66 2015
    339.4'709410904--dc23
    2014048287

Typeset by Fakenham Prepress Solutions, Fakenham, Norfolk NR21 8NN
Printed and bound in India

For Ann Rappaport and Stuart Rappaport
In memory of Albert Henry Trudgen
For Jacqueline Brooks
And in memory of Joseph Benjamin Crowley and Megan Crowley

CONTENTS

List of Illustrations   x
List of Tables   xiii
List of Contributors   xiv
Acknowledgements   xviii

1 Introduction   1
  Erika Rappaport, Sandra Trudgen Dawson and Mark J. Crowley

Part I: Gender, Sexuality and Youth: Cultivating and Managing New Consumers

2 Who is the Queer Consumer? Historical Perspectives on Capitalism and Homosexuality   21
  Justin Bengry

3 'Healthier and Better Clothes for Men': Men's Dress Reform in Interwar Britain   37
  Ina Zweiniger-Bargielowska

4 Selling, Consuming and Becoming the Beautiful Man in Britain: The 1930s and 1940s   53
  Paul R. Deslandes

5	Rational Recreation in the Age of Affluence: The Café and Working-Class Youth in London, c. 1939–65 *Kate Bradley*	71
6	Teenagers, Photography and Self-Fashioning, 1956–65 *Penny Tinkler*	87
7	Unwanted Consumers: Violence and Consumption in British Football in the 1970s *Brett Bebber*	103

Part II: In and Beyond the Nation: The Local and the Global in the Production of Consumer Cultures

8	Consumer Communication as Commodity: British Advertising Agencies and the Global Market for Advertising, 1780–1980 *Stefan Schwarzkopf*	121
9	Drink Empire Tea: Gender, Conservative Politics and Imperial Consumerism in Inter-war Britain *Erika Rappaport*	139
10	Female Credit Customers, the United Africa Company and Consumer Markets in Postwar Ghana *Bianca Murillo*	159
11	Designing Consumer Society: Citizens and Housing Plans during World War II *Sandra Trudgen Dawson*	179
12	Saving for the Nation: The Post Office and National Consumerism, c. 1860–1945 *Mark J. Crowley*	197
13	Prosperity for All? Britain and Mass Consumption in Western Europe after World War II *Kenneth Mouré*	213
14	A House Divided: The Organized Consumer and the British Labour Party, 1945–60 *Peter Gurney*	237

15 Early British Television: The Allure and Threat of America 253
   Kelly Boyd

SELECT BIBLIOGRAPHY 269

INDEX 287

LIST OF ILLUSTRATIONS

CHAPTER 3

3.1 Men's Dress Reform Party activists. *Daily Sketch*, 8 July 1937.   45

CHAPTER 4

4.1 Brylcreem hair dressing advertisement. *Picture Post*, 8 April 1939.   57

4.2 Kotalko hair grower advertisement. *Tit-Bits*, 1 March 1930.   58

4.3 Ku-bist hair fixative advertisement. *Tit-Bits*, 3 May 1930.   59

4.4 Seaside cartoon. *Tit-Bits*, 6 August 1932.   60

4.5 Image of a drum major shaving. *Picture Post*, 4 March 1939.   61

CHAPTER 6

6.1 Teenagers: Elizabeth (1957) and Irene (1965).   87

6.2 Elizabeth's college photographs, 1956.   92

6.3 Irene's album: Wholesome outdoor leisure, 1965.   97

LIST OF ILLUSTRATIONSxi

CHAPTER 8

8.1	Sell's Advertising Agency on Fleet Street, c. 1910.	127
8.2	The London Express Exchange Global Network, 1966.	131

CHAPTER 9

9.1	Drinking Empire Grown Tea, H. S. Williamson, 1931.	148
9.2	Picking Empire Grown Tea, H. S. Williamson, 1931.	149

CHAPTER 10

10.1	'Story of a successful trader' advertisement, c. 1957.	161
10.2	UAC passbook belonging to Madam Amba Otwiwa, c. 1950–60.	163

CHAPTER 11

11.1	An example of a Bauhaus-inspired house built in inter-war Chapeltown, Yorkshire, England.	181
11.2	Semi-detached Tudorbethan home built in inter-war Morley, Yorkshire.	183
11.3	Semi-detached council house built in inter-war Leeds, Yorkshire, England.	184
11.4	1930s semi-detached home in Leeds, Yorkshire.	185

CHAPTER 12

12.1	'Make Your Money Provide the Driving Power, Put it into the Post Office Savings Bank', 1942.	206
12.2	'Make Your Money Provide the Driving Power, Put it into the Post Office Savings Bank', 1942.	207

CHAPTER 13

13.1 Indexed real gross domestic product, 1938–50.   216

LIST OF TABLES

CHAPTER 13

Table 13.1   Growth of real gross domestic product, 1950–73.   214

Table 13.2a   Per cent households with domestic appliances, 1948–75.   223

Table 13.2b   Televisions per 1000 inhabitants, 1955–75.   223

LIST OF CONTRIBUTORS

Brett Bebber is Assistant Professor of History at Old Dominion University. He is the author of *Violence and Racism in Football: Politics and Cultural Conflict in British Society, 1968–1998* (Pickering & Chatto, 2012) and the editor of *Leisure and Cultural Conflict in Twentieth-Century Britain* (Manchester University Press, 2012). He teaches and writes on a variety of topics in postwar Europe, including race, migration, human rights, leisure and popular culture.

Justin Bengry is a historian of sexuality and capitalism in modern Britain. He completed a PhD in History and Feminist Studies in 2010 at the University of California, Santa Barbara, after which he was the first Elizabeth and Cecil Kent Postdoctoral Fellow in British History at the University of Saskatchewan and an SSHRC Postdoctoral Fellow in History at McGill University. Justin is currently an Honorary Research Fellow at Birkbeck College, University of London. His research has appeared in *History Workshop Journal*, *Media History* and in Brian Lewis's edited collection *British Queer History: New Approaches and Perspectives* (2013). He is currently completing a monograph titled *The Pink Pound: Capitalism and Homosexuality in Twentieth-Century Britain*.

Kelly Boyd is Senior Research Fellow at the Institute of Historical Research, School of Advanced Study, University of London. In addition to her monograph, *Manliness and the Boys' Story Paper in Britain: A Cultural History, 1855–1940* (Palgrave Macmillan 2003), she has written on the early history of television in Britain, issues of Americanization, and masculinity, most recently in *Media History*. With Rohan McWilliam, she edited *The Victorian Studies Reader* (Routledge, 2007). From 2004–10, she served as Treasurer of the Social History Society of the UK and is currently reviews editor of *Cultural and Social History*.

Mark J. Crowley is Associate Professor and Early Career Hubei Provincial 'Chu Tian' Scholar at Wuhan University, China. He has published numerous articles on nineteenth-century British Trade Unionism, Welsh Nationalism, Devolution in Wales, and women's employment in World War II. He is currently completing a monograph on women's employment in the British Post Office during World War II, and is editing (with Sandra Dawson) a volume on the Home Front in Britain and the Empire during World War II.

Paul R. Deslandes in an Associate Professor and Chair of the Department of History at the University of Vermont, where he has taught since 2004. He is the author of *Oxbridge Men: British Masculinity and the Undergraduate Experience, 1850–1920* (Indiana University Press, 2005) as well as a variety of articles and essays on the history of British education, masculinity, sexuality and the history of the body. He is currently completing a new book titled *The Culture of Male Beauty in Britain: From the First Photographs to David Beckham*.

Peter Gurney teaches British Social History at the University of Essex. Gurney has published widely on the history of consumption and working-class culture, including *Co-operative Culture and the Politics of Consumption in England, 1870–1930* (Manchester, 1996) named 'Outstanding Academic Title' in 1997 by *Choice*, journal of the American Library Association. His latest book, *Wanting and Having: Popular Politics and Liberal Consumerism in England, 1830–70*, is forthcoming (Manchester University Press, 2015).

Kenneth Mouré is Professor of History at the University of Alberta. His previous works include *Managing the Franc Poincaré: Economic Understanding and Political Constraint in French Monetary Policy, 1928–1936* (Cambridge University Press, 1991) and *The Gold Standard Illusion: France, the Bank of France and the International Gold Standard, 1914–1939* (Oxford University Press, 2002). His current research explores French experience with economic controls, black markets and consumption during and after World War II, with recent articles in *French History, French Historical Studies* and *The Journal of Contemporary History*.

Bianca Murillo is Assistant Professor of History at Willamette University in Salem, Oregon. Her research and teaching interests include modern Africa, the history of global capitalism, comparative consumer cultures, and critical race and gender studies. Her research has been published in *Africa, Enterprise & Society* and *Gender & History*, and she is a recent recipient of the prestigious 2013–14 Woodrow Wilson Career Enhancement Fellowship. Her book, *Conditional Sales: Global Commerce and the Making of an African Consumer Society* is forthcoming in 2016 with Ohio University Press.

Erika Rappaport is Associate Professor of History at the University of California, Santa Barbara. She is the author of *Shopping for Pleasure: Women in the Making of London's West End* (Princeton University Press, 2000) and numerous chapters and articles on gender, urban history, consumer culture and imperialism in *The Journal of British Studies*, *Victorian Studies*, *Gender and History* and *History Workshop*, among others. She is currently completing *An Acquired Taste: Tea and the Global History of an Imperial Consumer Culture* (Princeton University Press, 2016) a study that uses tea to explore how the histories of consumer culture and empire intersected between the seventeenth and twentieth centuries, contributing a fresh interpretation to the modern history of globalization.

Stefan Schwarzkopf is an Associated Professor in History at Copenhagen Business School, Denmark. He works on the history of advertising and other forms of persuasive communication in the commercial sphere. Schwarzkopf has a particular interest in the history and ideological underpinnings of market and consumer research.

Penny Tinkler is a senior lecturer in Sociology at the University of Manchester. She has written extensively on the history of girls and young women, popular magazines, the feminization of smoking, photography and photographic methods. Her books include: *Constructing Girlhood: Popular Magazines for Girls Growing Up in England 1920–50* (Taylor & Francis, 1995), *Smoke Signals: Women, Smoking and Visual Culture in Britain 1880–1980* (Berg, 2006) and *Using Photographs in Social and Historical Research* (Sage, 2013).

Sandra Trudgen Dawson is Acting Assistant Director of Programming and Communications, Honors Program, Northern Illinois University. She is author of *Holiday Camps in Twentieth-Century Britain: Packaging Pleasure* (Manchester University Press, 2011) and several chapters and articles on popular culture, leisure, consumption and gender history. She is currently working on *Empire at the Bedside: Commonwealth Nurses and the Making of the British National Health Service*.

Ina Zweiniger-Bargielowska is Professor of Modern British History at the University of Illinois, Chicago. She is author of *Austerity in Britain: Rationing, Controls and Consumption, 1939–1955* (Oxford University Press, 2000) and *Managing the Body: Beauty, Health and Fitness in Britain, 1880s–1939* (Oxford University Press, 2010).

ACKNOWLEDGEMENTS

Numerous personal and academic debts are accumulated when compiling a volume such as this. While each contributor has acknowledged those who have assisted in the writing process, we would like to also mention a few names. From the inception of this project, the assistance of those at Bloomsbury Academic, especially Jennifer Schmidt, Louise Butler, Molly Beck and Abbie Sharman have been invaluable. The contributors to the volume also deserve mention for their excellent essays and their patience in dealing with the endless email correspondence from the three of us living in three time zones.

    The task of completing this volume was only possible because of the unstinting support of our families, especially our spouses. Mark would like to thank Juan (Maggie) for her love, companionship, friendship and unwavering support, especially in the nine months leading up to the birth of their daughter Anna. Her arrival on 10 October 2014 comes with the hope that she, like us, will be informed and inspired by the experiences of those studied in this volume. Erika would like to thank Jordan, Andy and Ben for their good humour and help, as she has been finishing several projects at once. Sandra would like to thank Patrick and Anna for their love and support through multiple surgeries and providing the distraction she needed to be able to write.

    We would also like to acknowledge those who lived through and experienced much of the life-changing episodes examined here, our parents and grandparents whose life-spans this volume encompasses. Mark would like to dedicate this volume to his grandfather, Joseph Benjamin Crowley, who fought for Britain during World War II and his grandmother, Megan Crowley. Mark continues to be inspired by his only surviving grandparent Jacqueline Brooks, who shared with him her experiences of the Post Office Savings Bank during World War II. Sandra would like to dedicate this volume to her grandfather, Albert Henry Trudgen, a working man whose life spans the entire timeline of this volume. Born in 1895, he received few years of schooling; worked as a farm labourer; fought in World War I; took post-war work as a tin miner in Cornwall; laid roads in Scotland in the 1930s; raised a family during the depression years; endured a second war and wrote to his grandchildren every week and finally died in 1989. Erika would like to dedicate this volume to her parents, Ann and Stuart Rappaport, who experienced World War II from the relatively safe vantage point of Detroit and Los Angeles. They were the teenagers who enjoyed coffee shops and organized sports and yet acquired a critical stance on the American consumer society they were lucky enough to enjoy.

Erika Rappaport
Sandra Trudgen Dawson
Mark J. Crowley

CHAPTER ONE

Introduction

ERIKA RAPPAPORT, SANDRA TRUDGEN DAWSON AND
MARK J. CROWLEY

Writing in 1941, as Great Britain was under its greatest threat, George Orwell mused: 'We are a nation of flower-lovers, but also a nation of stamp-collectors, pigeon fanciers, amateur carpenters, coupon-snippers, darts-players, crossword-puzzle fanciers.' A harsh critic of fascist propaganda and mass commercialism, Orwell continued, '[a]ll the culture that is most truly native centres round things which even when they are communal are not official – the pub, the football match, the back garden, the fireside and the 'nice cup of tea'.[1] Orwell celebrated an Englishness defined by pleasures that he imagined were apolitical and outside of the marketplace. Similarly, Richard Hoggart, literary critic and founding scholar of British cultural studies, recalled an interwar working-class generation not yet 'assault[ed]' by the 'mass Press', 'wireless and television' and the 'ubiquitous cinema'; or, as he famously put it, the unreal 'candy-floss' world of 1950s mass culture.[2] Many casual observers and scholars likewise assumed that mass consumer society wasn't quite British, and that it arrived via young people who since the late 1950s had embraced unbridled consumerism. Hoggart, for example, described how 'middle-aged working-class' couples' homes were still 'Edwardian' with 'living-rooms little changed from the time they equipped them or took them over from their parents,' while 'young couples like to go out and buy everything new'.[3] Despite a great deal of scholarship challenging Hoggart and Orwell's account of modern Britain, it has remained a very persuasive narrative.[4] Our choice for the cover of this book might at first glance appear to reinforce the understanding of consumer culture as a foreign, 'American' army colonizing Britain's youth in the 1950s.[5] However, the essays in this volume were chosen to complicate this account and open up new questions for further research.

The cover photo is a posed portrait of Vince Taylor taken by Rick Hardy in 1958. Both sitter and photographer were part of the early British rock music world and both influenced a number of genres, including skiffle, rockabilly, glam rock and punk. The photo was taken when Hardy was in his 20s and Taylor was 19 in the 2 I's, the Soho coffee bar in Old Compton Street, which was a nursery for British rock 'n' roll and a conduit of American and European cultural influences. The coffee bar and its neighbourhood were at this time associated with a rebellious foreign masculine hetero- and homosexual consumer culture.[6] This setting and Taylor's clothing, hairstyle, sideburns and his casual yet aggressive and sexy posture provide a veritable catalogue of the new mass commodities, cultural forms and technologies which emerged in the twentieth century, many of which we explore in this volume. Taylor is holding a bottle of soda (though it is not Coca-Cola) on top of a Formica table, next to a gleaming chrome Gaggia espresso machine imported from Italy. He sits behind a jukebox that played American music, in front of a poster for Elvis Presley's new film *King Creole*, which was currently playing at the Odeon Theatre in Marble Arch. Next to the poster is a collage of photographs with a caption that reads: 'Television comes to the 2 I's'. Like the photographs that Penny Tinkler analyses in this volume, this portrait is a work of self-creation in which Taylor and Hardy used photography and specifically chosen props and setting to promote themselves as trend-setters of a new youth-oriented community. They were astute readers of the material world, much like Orwell and Hoggart.

Taylor, significantly, had a transatlantic biography. He was born Brian Maurice Holden in Isleworth, Middlesex in July 1939, but when he was seven his family emigrated to the US, first settling in New Jersey. After his sister Sheila married Joseph Barbera of Hanna-Barbera studios, the family moved to Los Angeles, where Brian attended Hollywood High School. Hanna-Barbera produced some feature films, but it was known for animation, especially the iconic children's cartoons from the 1960s and 1970s, including the *Flintstones*, the *Jetsons*, *Yogi Bear*, *Josie and the Pussy Cats*, and many others. Barbera also in a sense produced the figure of Vince Taylor. He became Holden's manager and brought him to London, where, like his more famous counterpart Tommy Steele, Taylor began his career by covering Elvis Presley songs and copying his gestures, music and clothing style. Although Taylor had a rocky relationship with his band 'The Playboys', he became quite popular, especially in Europe. His successes and failures influenced others. The Clash, for example, made Taylor's 1958 song 'Brand New Cadillac' even more famous when they covered it on their album

London Calling in 1979. Taylor's erratic drug-induced behaviour inspired David Bowie's persona Ziggy Stardust.[7] In many respects, then, Taylor and his portrait appear to be perfect examples of mass culture as a drug and as something 'alien' to traditional notions of Britishness. This volume suggests otherwise by charting the domestic and international histories that made careers such as Taylor's possible. We argue that although Vince Taylor, George Orwell and Richard Hoggart disagreed about the implications of mass consumer culture, they all saw this world as a contested arena in which the histories of identity, politics and pleasure came together.

Taylor's persona was at once a local creation born within particular urban, commercial and leisure spaces and a part of broader transnational networks and cultures that stretched across the Atlantic, English Channel and the Empire.[8] Taylor and his friends, family and colleagues were living in a new world in which the things one chose to purchase, use, think and write about and the clothing, food, shelter, social services and leisure one enjoyed increasingly came to define individual and social identities. Marketers, advertisers, corporations, political parties, voluntary and state agencies relentlessly tried to cultivate and control the consumer behaviours of men and women in the UK and its Empire. This tension between promotion and containment provides the common thread linking each of the essays in this volume. Each author examines how products, ideas and services were marketed to and understood by the British public during periods of economic instability, war, imperial crisis and decline, 'affluence' and the apparent growing cultural and economic hegemony of the USA.

Defining consumption, consumerism, or consumer society at any period is not easy, but in the twentieth century the advent of mass politics and availability of so many new goods, media and services makes this task even more complicated.[9] As many scholars have argued, commodities, the consumer and consumer culture are never constant constructs. The importance and 'value' attached to purchases, the use and display of merchandise and leisure do not carry equivalent importance. We agree with Frank Trentmann who has argued that the consumer is a historical category that needs to be interrogated and not assumed.[10] Consumption is a historical process that arises out of a shifting and often unbalanced relationship between producer, packager, purchaser and a host of intermediaries. However, we have used the idea of consumer behaviour instead of consumption or consumer society to highlight the similarities between past and present and a range of political, social, cultural and economic activities that revolve around the marketplace but do not necessarily involve purchasing. This is especially appropriate, we believe, during times of rationing, scarcity and economic crisis. It also allows us to examine the significance of women's market activities in the

African Empire that Bianca Murillo shows simultaneously could be defined as buying, selling and market research.

This volume builds upon the insights and methodologies provided by a rich scholarship that already exists on commercial and consumer practices. Some of the contributors draw upon the work of anthropologists, particularly Daniel Miller and Arjun Appadurai, who suggested that commodities have unique histories or biographies in which they shift in and out of commodity status.[11] Others return to some of the conclusions that John Benson offered in *The Rise of Consumer Society in Britain, 1880–1980*. In that seminal volume, Benson focused on organized sports, tourism and shopping to explore whether consumer culture emancipated women, consolidated national identity and created youth cultures that challenged class tensions.[12] Several of the authors have also been influenced by cultural theorists such as Dick Hebdige who charted the emergence of youth subcultures revolving around music, fashion and other 'alternative' consumer practices and yet also argued that the 'subcultural response' is neither simply affirmation nor refusal, neither 'commercial exploitation' nor 'genuine revolt'.[13]

We are equally indebted to many historical studies of early modern and Victorian consumer cultures. We recognize qualitative and quantitative differences between the 1760s, 1860s, 1930s and the 1960s, but this volume also foregrounds a number of continuities. The very fact that figures such as Vince Taylor believed they were destroying Victorian conceptions of the body, the self, the community, the nation and the marketplace illuminates the importance of this earlier history and suggests the postwar generation believed their parents still lived within the constraints of the Victorian era. Taylor's revolt was in part directed at nineteenth-century social, religious and political movements and ideologies that had set the terms of debate about how the material world impacted ideas about citizenship, the body, identity and community. Political economy, political reform, evangelicalism, imperialism and class, gender and racial ideologies informed ideas about commodities, spaces and consumer behaviours. Numerous political and social reform movements used the idea of the consumer as a citizen to effect change, but they also circumscribed many forms of consumption. The American revolutionaries, British abolitionists, temperance reformers, co-operators, free traders, tariff reformers, suffragists and anti-colonial nationalists disagreed about what constituted productive consumer behaviours, but they all envisioned consumers as political actors.[14] For example, the liberal-oriented evangelical temperance movement of the 1830s and 1840s developed a vision of the productive and moral consumer when it tried to restrain drinking among unruly, young working-class men. Like the reformers that Brett Bebber and Kate Bradley look at in this volume, the temperance community attempted to channel desires towards what they viewed as moral and profitable ends. As one Irish campaigner explained in 1840, sobriety would shift scarce funds from drink to the purchase of 'clothing, good food, all the comforts of life', and thus 'reward the grower and manufacturer' and the former drinker.[15] Temperance was part of a broadly defined rational recreation movement that sought to reform non-productive forms of masculine leisure like gambling, blood sports and visiting prostitutes by replacing these older pleasures with family-centred, hetero-social, educational and productive pastimes.[16] Working with a different notion of the working-class consumer, but one that still emphasized the difference between moral and immoral pursuits, the Co-operative movement created a variety of lasting alternatives to free market consumerism. Shopping at the Co-op remained a significant consumer experience in the twentieth century, but, as Gurney argues in this volume, its political power was eclipsed as a new individualistic notion of the consumer emerged at this time.[17] James Vernon has noted that photography and the development of the illustrated press in the mid-nineteenth century helped instil empathy between disparate groups, which laid the foundation for the idea of the society that emerged with the post-1945 welfare state.[18] Not all of these reformers and agencies agreed upon which goods or behaviours were moral and interpretations could change quickly. Nevertheless, they fashioned working men and women as potential citizens who could bring about political change. They all emphasized, in the words of Peter Gurney, how consumption was 'a vital arena in which class relationships were defined and renegotiated'.[19]

The rational citizen-consumer competed with an equally prominent understanding of consumers as gendered, passionate and sensual beings. Scholars have shown how this conception of the embodied and gendered consumer influenced the expansion of overseas trade, empire, industrialization, urbanization and retail changes. During and after the sixteenth and seventeenth centuries, the desire for porcelain, silk, tobacco, cotton, sugar, cocoa and tea, for example, reconfigured the nature of long-distance trade, propelled the development of slavery and other forced labour systems, stimulated industrialization within and beyond Europe and thereby altered the balance of power between Europe, Asia, Africa and the Americas.[20] The sensual consumer also influenced some of the most significant retail and urban changes during and after the eighteenth century. Josiah Wedgewood, for example, created new markets for mass-produced pottery through enticing new types of shops, display techniques and advertising. Wedgewood also imagined and talked about how glass and other luxurious materials could aid in the seduction of wealthy female customers.[21] During the nineteenth century, a new visual and sensual culture of advertising, exhibitions, department stores, market halls, restaurants, theatres and other urban amusements emphasized more than ever the relationship between consumerism and public display, reconfiguring public and private boundaries.[22] Victorian gender ideology increasingly defined consumerism as belonging within bourgeois women's 'domestic' sphere, even as shopping became something one did in public, and the goods one did or did not purchase had global ramifications.[23] Texts, images and spaces often also transformed commodities into everyday expressions of the imperial project, justifying empire as a comfortable and satisfying pursuit.[24] Literature and visual culture wrestled with and gave meaning to the new concepts of the self and the material world that emerged in this period.[25]

The archetype of the shopper as a middle- and upper-class woman problematized the working-class and non-white colonial consumer and it also meant that the male shopper has become an elusive figure.[26] However, as we see in this volume, economic, political and cultural changes that took place after World War I began to carve out new types of masculine consumer identities and spaces. These conditions and processes also focused attention on non-white colonial consumer behaviours.[27] The bourgeois woman was often still regarded as the ideal shopper, but with the crises created by war and depression, the onset of mass suffrage and invention of new methods of measuring and researching markets, businesses, politicians and reformers increasingly called upon and invented a range of new types of consumers: queer, male, non-white and working class.

Most of the contributors in this volume assume that consumption was especially politicized in the twentieth century – a fact well captured by a working-class mother, who, facing food shortages at the end of World War I wrote, 'I was always a bit of a Socialist but I am a rank one now and I've a vote at the next General Election. And I've a tongue and when I am waiting in mobs it is not quiet. Nothing will make my tongue wag more than want of a cup of tea.'[28] This newly enfranchised woman saw a basic standard of living as a right guaranteed by a liberal state. We ask how this understanding of the politicized consumer emerged and changed over the century. What were other significant visions of the consumer available at home and in the Empire? And what were the consequences of the promotion and containment of these various ideals?

This volume considers how various understandings of the consumer developed and were deployed in relation to particular behaviours and commodities, and how each carried assumptions about personhood, the marketplace, morality and materiality. Although interested in similar questions, the contributors do not assume a unified, stable, national or imperial culture. They break down these over-arching categories by class, sexuality, gender, period and region and focus on a variety of things, spaces and activities. Bringing together economic, business, political, social and cultural histories, this volume examines the specific institutional structures and cultural traditions that shaped British consumer behaviours and identities. This includes topics such as buying tea, watching football, and saving with the Post Office – all behaviours that Britons celebrated as a unique part of their national heritage and psyche – even when other nations enjoyed similar goods and leisure practices. The focus of this volume is on the history of saving and spending, the contemporary thinking about, and selling of, notions of pleasure and politics, together with perceptions of family, nation, colony and empire. Some essays examine nineteenth-century antecedents, but all focus on the period between World War I and the onset of neo-liberalism in the 1980s. We argue that even the simple spaces and pastimes Orwell celebrated were shaped by politics, economics and culture and were very much part of consumer society.

STRUCTURE

The volume is organized thematically in two sections that both cover the entire chronological period. The first section, 'Gender, Sexuality and Youth: Cultivating and Managing New Consumers', highlights the intersection between evolving definitions of masculinity and femininity, and the way institutions played a part in influencing and facilitating changes in consumer habits. Essays on youth culture, queer consumption and ideas of male beauty and health before World War II suggest that the new expressive body culture of the 1960s and after was not simply a natural by-product of post-war affluence. These essays bring to the first half of the century some of the sociological, ethnographic and critical cultural analyses associated with the field of cultural studies. They show how consumers forged their own distinctive identities but their attitudes and behaviours were also constrained and shaped by commercial interests, politics, family, religion, school and other institutions.[29] The second section, 'In and Beyond the Nation: The Local and the Global in the Production of Consumer Cultures', looks at how the domestic consumer culture discussed in the first section was also formed by wider political, economic and global contexts, specifically the global crises of the Great Depression, World War II, the expansion of Empire, decolonization, and the collaboration and competition with the US. This section focuses on the significance of the state, the corporation, political parties and publicity experts in shaping consumer and business behaviours and attitudes in Britain and its Empire, Europe and in the US.

The first section begins with Justin Bengry's historiographical essay reviewing how queer history has dealt with the history of capitalism and then explains how the idea of a queer market developed in the twentieth century through artwork, photography, magazines, retail shops, clubs and bars. He further posits that the gender stereotypes associated with queer consumers influenced the histories of retailing, urban culture and normative ideals of the male and female consumer. Following Bengry, Paul Deslandes and Ina Zweiniger-Bargielowska show us how ideas of male beauty, freedom and a liberated sexual and healthy self, most associated with the so-called permissive society of the 1960s and 1970s, were present in the inter-war years. They also outline the way interventions in the political and social spheres led to more attention to personal appearance by male consumers. Zweiniger-Bargielowska uses the Men's Dress Reform Party to illustrate how some men became concerned with being aesthetically appealing and physically healthy during the inter-war period. These male reformers believed that more casual clothing such as open-neck shirts and loose trousers would enable the existence of less restrictive and rigid definitions of masculinity. Deslandes expands on these themes by examining how male consumers talked and thought about their bodies, bodily practices and ideas of masculinity as revealed in many interviews conducted by Mass Observation, the innovative social research institution that began in 1937. While the focus for some men was the physical prowess extolled by muscle and fitness magazines, others appreciated the aesthetic principles prevalent in new fashions, and in advertising and male lifestyle magazines.

While the first three essayists foreground the emergence of new types of masculine consumer behaviours and attitudes and posit a kind of give-and-take between the market and the consumer, Penny Tinkler shows how working- and middle-class teenage girls used photography to articulate a sense of self that was influenced but not entirely shaped by post-war consumer society. She masterfully compares how the photographic collections of two girls from the 1950s and 1960s appear to reinforce the differences between these periods, but upon close inspection we see how, in both eras, middle- and working-class girls appropriated and/or rejected particular styles of clothing, eating and body language. In both instances, relatively limited incomes, family, education and religion also shaped the consumer behaviours of these two young women. Ultimately, Tinkler reveals how visual evidence and oral interviews can create more nuanced understandings of post-war Britain that cannot be summarized with terms such as austerity, affluence, youth culture and consumer society.

This section concludes with two essays that similarly identify the continued presence of Victorian understandings of young, working-class male consumerism. Kate Bradley explores this issue by looking at debates about coffee bars in the 1950s and 1960s while Brett Bebber explores how business understood and reacted to football hooliganism. Bradley considers how the coffee bar became a place for recreation and socialization and exposed youth to American music and European-style coffee (although this activity was often seen as American as well). Critics, however, saw the rise of café culture as a cause for moral concern, attracting a disaffected working-class youth and generating new and undesirable subcultures. Victorian-style reformers tried to control the coffee bars and new forms of working-class mass leisure by offering more respectable alternatives. Bebber also illustrates how Victorian notions of social control surfaced in the way football fans were imagined and constrained well into the 1970s. In addition to architectural changes in the stadiums and the introduction of entertainments designed to keep 'bored' working men from interacting during matches, British Rail became an instrument of the state and tried similar methods to control unruly and often violent consumer behaviours.

Opening the second section, Stefan Schwarzkopf provides a long history of British advertising to show its global influences, thereby countering the argument that British advertising was influenced and overtaken by American agencies and ideas in the twentieth century. He describes a permeable relationship between British and American advertising agencies and argues that many of the innovative aspects and practices of twentieth-century advertising actually originated in Great Britain, particularly in relationship to imperial and overseas markets. The following essays from Erika Rappaport and Bianca Murillo reinforce many of Schwarzkopf's findings as they too reveal how British advertising and marketing were already global enterprises made in Britain, the US and the colonial Empire in the 1920s and 1930s.

Rappaport's chapter picks up on the global and imperial history of British consumer culture by illustrating the way consumption, consumer practices and behaviours entered Conservative party and grassroots politics during the late 1920s and early 1930s. Through an examination of the imperial buying movement and a political and advertising campaign to encourage shoppers to buy, stock and drink only teas produced within the formal boundaries of the British Empire, Rappaport shows how the state, British planters, publicists and middle-class female intermediaries constructed a notion of the imperial consumer as critical to the stability of the economic and political crises that plagued Britain during the early 1930s. She concludes by elucidating how conservative middle-class women worked as 'middle figures' between the corporation and the working-class consumer.

Bianca Murillo takes up these questions in the Empire by focusing on how large multi-national corporations relied on African women sellers and in effect, market researchers. Murillo's female credit customers operating in colonial and post-colonial Ghana show the similarities between production and consumption and the possibilities and limitations of African women's ability to profit from a globalizing capitalist economy.

The Conservative Party's dominance in the inter-war years influenced policymaking, especially in the field of welfare and the Empire, and shaped responses to emergencies such as the Wall Street Crash and the Great Depression. The failure of the 1924 and 1929 Labour Governments to introduce the promises of Socialism had already disillusioned the electorate. Yet mounting frustration with the perceived inaction of Baldwin's Conservative Party in addressing the pressing problem of mass unemployment brought about political and attitudinal changes among policymakers of all parties during the 1930s and set the stage for a comprehensive social welfare scheme and corporatist planning.[30] This is a topic that Mark Crowley takes up in his study of how the Post Office Savings Bank (POSB) targeted working-class consumers and sought to inculcate thrifty, productive and patriotic forms of saving and spending. The same publicity experts we see in Rappaport's chapter also appear in Crowley's study. However, whereas the Empire Marketing Boarad (EMB) promoted an imperial nation, Post Office publicity fostered an island nation. This shift fitted the specific mission of each agency but it was likely also part of a broader reconfiguring of British identity and culture that was occurring at this time.[31] Crowley elucidates how the POSB tried to teach consumers to see their economic activities as having national significance.

Sandra Dawson's study also explores the relationship between the state and the consumer through examining one instance of participatory democracy that took place during World War II. She looks at the letters that consumers (many of whom were working-class women) sent to the government about their ideas and desires for post-war housing. Consumers believed their voices would be heard and their ideas and plans demonstrate just how much they had accepted the ideals of modesty, thrift and nation-building which Crowley and Rappaport also discussed. Despite the patchy welfare measures of the inter-war years, wartime Britons expected the state would assume responsibility for building homes that would respond to their needs and desires.[32]

While Arthur Marwick famously claimed that World War II brought tremendous social change and the emergence of mass consumerism, many of the authors in this volume argue that wartime and post-war austerity was connected to, and not so different from, the so-called 'affluent' society that arrived in the late 1950s.[33] Gurney, for example, demonstrates how shifts in Labour politics and the growing power of big business marginalized the political power of the Co-operative movement after the war. Even as the Co-operative movement greatly increased membership, Labour dismissed organized consumers and abandoned the co-operative alternative to capitalism in an age of presumed consumer affluence.

Kenneth Mouré's essay evaluates post-war consumption and urges a reconceptualization of the accepted narrative of affluence within a broader context of both the rest of Europe and the US. He assesses how British 'national' performance was impacted by war and post-war reconstruction and considers how and why Britain's history looks different than that of other industrialized nations. As one of the essays of the volume that offers an overview of the key economic shifts of the twentieth century, the essay concludes that Britain's economic recovery as defined by consumer spending on durable goods is problematic when compared to the behaviours of other consumer societies. Through an analysis of political and economic policies and controls, this chapter demonstrates the need for scholars to rethink the notion of a widespread affluence that shaped and expanded consumer spending.

The final essay in the volume returns to the theme of Americanization. Kelly Boyd looks at the embryonic television service of the British Broadcasting Corporation (BBC), the perceived influence of the US on British consumer culture, and the efforts made by the BBC managers to retain a sense of Britishness.[34] Boyd maintains that while the ideologies of the British and American television industries were fundamentally at odds with each other, consumer feedback was considered essential to both sides of the Atlantic when considering programming. Moreover, Boyd illustrates the collaborative relationship between the BBC and American commercial networks in the development of that programming. Americanization, so feared by anxious critics, was mediated through the lens of an assumed 'Britishness'.

Inevitably, this volume cannot provide a comprehensive account of Britain's consumer society in the twentieth century. Instead, we pinpoint approaches that integrate consumerism into twentieth-century British history. In years to come, historians will no doubt question the degree to which there was a shared Anglo-American consumer culture and they will likely pursue the suggestion made by James Belich that the so-called 'white' settler colonies provided important markets and contributed to the spread of British tastes and consumer practices during the nineteenth century.[35] Advertising shaped racial stereotypes, but more work needs to engage with how this did or did not occur in the Empire. What companies and agencies worked to create consumers; and did they, as Murillo and others have suggested, rely on local intermediaries? Beyond the US and Empire, how was British consumer culture shaped by other global relationships, such as its intense and volatile relationships with China and the European Continent? We need further work on how British consumer culture absorbed and defended against transnational entities such as the United Nations, Common Market and how nongovernmental agencies operated to control, channel and shift Britain's consumer society. Despite the clear trend towards globalization, we could also ask how local and regional tastes were maintained and even intensified in the twentieth century.[36]

We believe that this volume provides several new perspectives to the growing literature on consumer culture. We bring together scholars with diverse approaches, but all of whom are interested in how politics, pleasure and identity are inseparable categories during the twentieth century. All of the contributors are also wrestling to insert consumer culture into larger questions about the nature of British society in the twentieth century, such as the persistence of Victorian and even early modern ideals about class, gender, race and the material world. They consider the nation as a global formation and it is in this regard that they look at the nature and impact of the Depression, World War II, imperialism, Americanization, state welfare and invention of youth cultures. By no means exhaustive, the following essays argue persuasively that in the twentieth century consumer behaviours were constructed, proscribed, inflected and shaped by multiple agencies – both commercial and governmental – and that they were never static but often responded or reacted to global, regional, national and internal crises and political, economic, social and attitudinal shifts.

NOTES

1. George Orwell, *The Lion and the Unicorn: Socialism and the English Genius* (London: Secker and Warburg, 1941), p. 15.
2. Richard Hoggart, *The Uses of Literacy* (Harmondsworth: Penguin, 1957), p. 23. For a comparison of Orwell and Hoggart's critique of mass culture, see Dick Hebdige, 'Towards a Cartography of Taste, 1935–1962', in *Hiding in the Light: On Images and Things* (London: Routledge, 1988), pp. 50–2. For Orwell and Englishness, see Simon Featherstone, *Englishness: Twentieth-Century Popular Culture and the Forming of English Identity* (Edinburgh: Edinburgh University Press, 2009), pp. 14–17.
3. Hoggart, *Literacy*, p. 31.
4. Even though Avner Offer questions many aspects of this narrative, he also reproduces certain aspects of this story about consumer society. Avner Offer,

The Challenge of Affluence: Self-Control and Well-Being in the United States and Britain since 1950 (Oxford: Oxford University Press, 2006).

5. Several recent works have proposed a more nuanced account of Americanization. See, for example, Victoria de Grazia, *Irresistible Empire: America's Advance through 20th-Century Europe* (Cambridge, MA: The Belknap Press of Harvard University, 2005). For Britain, see Stefan Schwarzkopf, 'Who Said "Americanization"? The Case of Twentieth-Century Advertising from a British Perspective', in *Decentering America*, ed. Jessica Gienow-Hecht (New York: Berghahn Books, 2007), pp. 23–72; Chris Waters, 'Beyond "Americanization": Rethinking Anglo-American Cultural Exchange between the Wars', *Cultural and Social History* 4:1 (2007), pp. 451–9; Adrian Horn, *Juke Box Britain: Americanisation and Youth Culture, 1945–60* (Manchester: Manchester University Press, 2011) and Sean Nixon, *Hard Sell: Advertising, Affluence and Transatlantic Relations, c. 1951–69* (Manchester: Manchester University Press, 2013).

6. On the coffee bars, see Bradley in this volume; Markman Ellis, *The Coffee House: A Cultural History* (London: Weidenfeld & Nicolson, 2004), pp. 225–45 and Joe Moran, 'Milk Bars, Starbucks and the *Uses of Literacy*,' *Cultural Studies* 20:6 (2006), pp. 552–73. On Soho, see Frank Mort, *Cultures of Consumption: Masculinity and Social Space in Late Twentieth-Century Britain* (London: Routledge 1996) and his *Capital Affairs: London and the Making of the Permissive Society* (New Haven, CT: Yale, 2010) and Judith R. Walkowitz, *Nights Out: Life in Cosmopolitan London* (New Haven, CT: Yale, 2012).

7. Vince Taylor, http://en.wikipedia.org/wiki/Vince_Taylor. [accessed 16 September 2014].

8. For consumption as a global project, see John Brewer and Frank Trentmann, eds, *Consuming Cultures: Global Perspectives: Historical Trajectories, Transnational Exchanges* (Oxford: Berg, 2006) and Alexander Nützenadel and Frank Trentmann, eds, *Food and Globalization: Consumption, Markets and Politics in the Modern World* (Oxford: Berg, 2008). For a helpful synthetic account of the integration of late-nineteenth- and early twentieth-century markets, see Steven C. Topik and Allen Wells, *Global Markets Transformed, 1870–1945* (Cambridge, MA: The Belknap Press of Harvard University Press, 2012).

9. For a large and very comprehensive volume that introduces a variety of approaches and methodologies, see Frank Trentmann, ed., *The Oxford Handbook of the History of Consumption* (Oxford: Oxford University Press, 2012). For various discussions of the consumer as citizen in the twentieth century, see, especially, Matthew Hilton, *Consumerism in Twentieth Century Britain: The Search for a Historical Movement* (Cambridge: Cambridge University Press, 2003); Frank Trentmann, *Free Trade Nation: Commerce, Consumption, and Civil Society in Modern Britain* (Oxford: Oxford University Press, 2008); James Vernon, *Hunger: A Modern History* (Cambridge, MA: The Belknap Press of Harvard University Press, 2007) and Laura Beers, *Your Britain: Media and the Making of the Labour Party* (Harvard: Harvard University Press, 2010). For global and comparative approaches, see Kate

Soper and Frank Trentmann, eds, *Citizenship and Consumption* (Basingstoke: Palgrave Macmillan, 2008) and Matthew Hilton, *Prosperity for All: Consumer Activism in an Era of Globalization* (Ithaca, NY and London: Cornell University Press, 2009).

10. Frank Trentmann, 'Knowing Consumers – Histories, Identities, Practices: An Introduction', in *The Making of the Consumer: Knowledge, Power and Identity in the Modern World*, ed. Frank Trentmann (Oxford and New York: Berg, 2006), pp. 1–27.

11. Arjun Appadurai, 'Introduction: Commodities and the Politics of Value', in *The Social Life of Things: Commodities in Cultural Perspective*, ed. Arjun Appadurai (Cambridge: Cambridge University Press, 1986), pp. 3–63; Daniel Miller, *Material Cultures: Why Some Things Matter* (Chicago, IL: Chicago University Press, 1998); his multi-volume, *Consumption: Critical Concepts in the Social Sciences* (London: Routledge 2001) and his recent *Consumption and its Consequences* (London: Polity 2012). For a good overview of key theories, see Martyn J. Lee, 'Introduction', in *The Consumer Society Reader* (Oxford: Blackwell, 2000), pp. 3–63.

12. John Benson, *The Rise of Consumer Society in Britain, 1880–1980* (Harlow: Longman, 1994).

13. Hebdige, *Hiding in the Light*, p. 35 and his *Subculture: The Meaning of Style* (London: Routledge 1979). For other examples, see Angela McRobbie, *In the Culture Society: Art, Fashion and Popular Music* (London: Routledge 1999); Mica Nava, Andrew Blake, Iain MacRury and Barry Richards, eds, *Buy this Book: Studies in Advertising and Consumption* (London: Routledge, 1997) and Stuart Hall and Tony Jefferson, eds, *Resistance through Rituals: Youth Subcultures in Postwar Britain*, 2nd edition (London: Routledge, 2006). The University of Birmingham has established an archive of key works at the Cadbury Research Library: http://www.birmingham.ac.uk/schools/historycultures/departments/history/research/projects/cccs/index.aspx [accessed 25 September 2014].

14. See references in note 9 above and also, Timothy H. Breen, *The Marketplace of Revolution: How Consumer Politics Shaped American Independence* (Oxford: Oxford University Press, 2004); Charlotte Sussman, *Consuming Anxieties: Consumer Protest, Gender, and British Slavery, 1713–1833* (Stanford, CA: Stanford University Press, 2000) and Clare Midgley, *Women Against Slavery: The British Campaigns, 1780–1870* (London: Routledge, 1992), pp. 35–40; Lisa Trivedi, *Clothing Gandhi's Nation: Homespun and Modern India* (Bloomington, IN: Indian University Press, 2007); Lisa Tickner, *The Spectacle of Women: Imagery of the Suffrage Campaign, 1907–1914* (London: Chatto & Windus, 1989).

15. See Erika Rappaport, 'Sacred Tastes and Useful Pleasures: The Temperance Tea Party and the Creation of a Sober Consumer Culture in Early Industrial Britain', *Journal of British Studies* 52:4 (October 2013), pp. 990–1016. For evangelical influence on business practices, economic thought and British consumer culture, see Boyd Hilton, *The Age of Atonement: The Influence of Evangelicalism on Social and Economic Thought, 1795–1865* (Oxford:

Oxford University Press, 1988); Leonore Davidoff and Catherine Hall, *Family Fortunes: Men and Women of the English Middle Class, 1780–1850* (Chicago, IL: University of Chicago Press, 1987) and Deborah Cohen, *Household Gods: The British and their Possessions* (New Haven, CT and London: Yale University Press, 2006).

16. See Peter Bailey, *Leisure and Class in Victorian England: Rational Recreation and the Contest for Control, 1830–1885* (London: Routledge Kegan & Paul, 1978); Hugh Cunningham, *Leisure in the Industrial Revolution, c. 1780–1880* (New York: Croom Helm, 1980) and A. P. Donajgrodzki, ed., *Social Control in Nineteenth-Century Britain* (London: Rowman and Littlefield, 1977).

17. Peter Gurney, *Co-operative Culture and the Politics of Consumption in England, 1870–1930* (Manchester: Manchester University Press, 1996); Lawrence Black and Nicole Robertson, eds, *Consumerism and the Co-Operative Movement in Modern British History: Taking Stock* (Manchester: Manchester University Press, 2009); Peter Gurney, 'The Battle of the Consumer in Postwar Britain', *The Journal of Modern History*, 4 (December 2005), pp. 956–87 and Gurney's chapter in this volume.

18. Vernon, *Hunger*, pp. 17–19.

19. Peter Gurney, '"Rejoicing in Potatoes": The Politics of Consumption in England during the "Hungry Forties"', *Past and Present* 203 (May 2009), p. 133.

20. This literature is extensive, key works include Neil McKendrick, John Brewer, J. H. Plumb, *The Birth of a Consumer Society in England* (Bloomington, IN: Indiana University Press, 1982); Sidney Mintz, *Sweetness and Power: The Place of Sugar in Modern History* (New York: Penguin, 1985); Colin Campbell, *The Romantic Ethic and the Spirit of Modern Consumerism* (Oxford: Oxford University Press, 1987); John Brewer and Roy Porter, eds, *Consumption and the World of Goods* (London: Routledge, 1994); Ann Bermingham and John Brewer, eds, *The Consumption of Culture, 1600–1800: Image, Object, Text* (London and New York: Routledge, 1995); Kenneth Pomeranz, *The Great Divergence: China, Europe, and the Making of the Modern World Economy* (Princeton, NJ: Princeton University Press, 1991); Wolfgang Schivelbusch, *Tastes of Paradise: A Social History of Spices, Stimulants, and Intoxicants* (New York: Vintage, 1993); Elizabeth Kowaleski-Wallace, *Consuming Subjects: Women, Shopping and Business in the Eighteenth Century* (New York: Columbia, 1997); Maxine Berg and Helen Clifford, eds, *Consumers and Luxury: Consumer Culture in Europe, 1650–1850* (Manchester: Manchester University Press, 1999); Woodruff D. Smith, *Consumption and the Making of Respectability, 1600–1800* (New York and London: Routledge, 2002); Mark Overton, Jane Whittle, Darron Dean and Andrew Hann, eds, *Production and Consumption in English Households, 1600–1750* (London: Routledge, 2004); Linda Levy Peck, *Consuming Splendor: Society and Culture in Seventeenth Century England* (Cambridge: Cambridge University Press, 2005); Brian Cowan, *The Social Life of Coffee: The Emergence of the British Coffee House* (New Haven, CT: Yale University Press, 2005); John Styles, *The Dress of the People: Everyday Fashion in Eighteenth-Century England* (New Haven, CT: Yale University Press, 2007); and Jan de Vries, *The Industrious Revolution:*

Consumer Behavior and the Household Economy, 1650 to the Present (Cambridge: Cambridge University Press, 2008).

21. McKendrick, *The Birth of a Consumer Society*, pp. 118–19. John Benson and Laura Ugolini, eds, *A Nation of Shopkeepers: Five Centuries of British Retailing* (London: I. B. Tauris, 2003); Ian Mitchell, *Tradition and Innovation in English Retailing, 1700–1850: Narratives of Consumption* (Farnham: Ashgate, 2014) and Jan Hein Furnée and C. I. Lesge, eds, *The Landscape of Consumption: Shopping Streets and Cultures in Western Europe, 1600–1900* (Basingstoke: Palgrave Macmillan, 2014).

22. For an overview of literature, see Erika D. Rappaport, 'The Senses in the Marketplace: Stimulation and Distraction, Gratification and Control', in *Senses in the Nineteenth-Century Marketplace*, ed. Constance Classen (London: Berg, 2014). Also see, Geoffrey Crossick and Serge Jaumain, eds, *Cathedrals of Consumption: The European Department Store, 1850–1939* (Aldershot: Ashgate, 1999); Erika Rappaport, *Shopping for Pleasure: Women and the Making of London's West End* (Princeton, NJ: Princeton University Press, 2000), pp. 69–88; Simon Gunn, *The Public Culture of the Victorian Middle Classes: Ritual and Authority and the English Industrial City, 1840–1914* (Manchester: Manchester University Press, 2000); Rachel Rich, *Bourgeois Consumption: Food, Space and Identity in London and Paris, 1859–1914* (Manchester: Manchester University Press, 2011); Asa Briggs, *Victorian Things* (Chicago, IL: University of Chicago Press, 1989). For a good overview of key changes in the nineteenth century, see W. Hamish Fraser, *The Coming of the Mass Market, 1850–1914* (London: Macmillan, 1981). An important older book on nineteenth-century changes in British retailing is Peter Mathias, *Retailing Revolution: A History of Multiple Retailing in the Food Trades Based upon the Allied Suppliers Group of Companies* (London: Longman, 1967).

23. The most thorough discussion of gender and consumption remains Victoria de Grazia and Ellen Furlough, eds, *The Sex of Things: Gender and Consumption in Historical Perspective* (Berkeley, CA: University of California Press, 1996). Also see Maggie Andrews and Mary M. Talbot, eds, *All the World and Her Husband: Women in Twentieth-Century Consumer Culture* (London: Cassell, 2000). For Britain, the brief volume by Judy Giles is a beginning: *The Parlour and the Suburb: Domestic Identities, Class, Femininity and Modernity* (Oxford: Berg, 2004). For a fascinating new account from the point of view of the modelling industry, see Becky E. Conekin, *Lee Miller in Fashion* (New York: Monacelli, 2013).

24. For an analysis of shifting debates on consumption and empire, see Erika Rappaport, 'Consumption', in *The Ashgate Companion to Modern Imperial Histories*, eds Philippa Levine and John Marriott (Farnham: Ashgate, 2012), pp. 343–8. Important works include John MacKenzie, *Propaganda and Empire: The Manipulation of British Public Opinion, 1880–1960* (Manchester: Manchester University Press, 1984); John MacKenzie, ed., *Imperialism and Popular Culture* (Manchester: Manchester University Press, 1987); Anne McClintock, *Imperial Leather: Race, Gender and Sexuality in the Colonial Conquest* (New York: Routledge, 1995); Peter H. Hoffenberg, *An Empire on*

Display: English, Indian and Australian Exhibitions from the Crystal Palace to the Great War (Berkeley, CA: University of California Press, 2001); Piya Chatterjee, *A Time for Tea: Women, Labor and Post/Colonial Politics on an Indian Plantation* (Durham, NC: Duke University Press, 2001); Anandi Ramamurthy, *Imperial Persuaders: Images of Africa and Asia in British Advertising* (Manchester: Manchester University Press, 2003); and Joanna de Groot, 'Metropolitan Desires and Colonial Connections: Reflections on Consumption and Empire', in *At Home with the Empire: Metropolitan Culture and the Imperial World*, eds Catherine Hall and Sonya O. Rose (Cambridge: Cambridge University Press, 2006), pp. 166–90.

25. Rachel Bowlby, *Just Looking: Consumer Culture in Dreiser, Gissing and Zola* (London: Methuen, 1985); Regenia Gagnier, *Idylls of the Marketplace: Oscar Wilde and the Victorian Public* (Stanford, CA: Stanford University Press, 1986); Thomas Richards, *The Commodity Culture of Victorian England: Advertising and Spectacle, 1851–1914* (Stanford, CA: Stanford University Press, 1990); Andrew H. Miller, *Novels Behind Glass: Commodity Culture and Victorian Narrative* (Cambridge: Cambridge University Press, 1995); Tamara S. Wagner and Narin Hassan, eds, *Consuming Culture in the Long Nineteenth Century: Narratives of Consumption, 1700–1900* (Lanham, MD: Lexington Books, 2007); Krista Lysack, *Come Buy, Come Buy: Shopping and the Culture of Consumption in Victorian Women's Writing* (Athens, OH: Ohio University Press, 2008); Julie E. Fromer, *A Necessary Luxury: Tea in Victorian England* (Athens, OH: Ohio University Press, 2008); and Suzanne Daly, *The Empire Inside: Indian Commodities in Victorian Domestic Novels* (Ann Arbor, MI: University of Michigan Press, 2011).

26. Christopher Breward, *The Hidden Consumer: Masculinities, Fashion and City Life, 1860–1914* (Manchester: Manchester University Press, 1999); Brent Shannon, *The Cut of His Coat: Men, Dress and Consumer Culture in Britain, 1860–1914* (Athens, OH: Ohio University Press, 2006) and Mort, *Cultures of Consumption*. On working-class masculine consumerism, see Brad Beaven, *Leisure, Citizenship and Working-Class Men in Britain, 1850–1945* (Manchester: Manchester University Press, 2009).

27. For consumerism in the Empire, see John and Jean Comaroff, *Of Revelation and Revolution: Christianity, Colonialism, and Consciousness in South Africa*, 2 Vols (Chicago, IL: Chicago University Press, 1991); Timothy Burke, *Lifebuoy Men, Lux Women: Commodification, Consumption, and Cleanliness in Modern Zimbabwe* (Durham, NC: Duke University Press, 1996); Douglas E. Haynes, Abigail McGowan, Tirthankar Roy and Haruka Yanagisawa, eds, *Towards a History of Consumption in South Asia* (Oxford: Oxford University Press, 2010); and Bianca Murillo, *Conditional Sales: Global Commerce and the Making of an African Consumer Society* (Athens, OH: Ohio University Press, 2016). For compelling new work on Canadian consumerism, see Franca Iacovetta, Valerie J. Korinek and Marlette Epp, eds, *Edible Histories: Cultural Politics: Towards a Canadian Food History* (Toronto: University of Toronto Press, 2012); and Donica Belisle, *Retail Nation: Department Stores and the Making of Modern Canada* (Vancouver: University of Washington Press, 2011).

28. M. Todd, *Snakes and Ladders: An Autobiography*, quoted in Hilton, *Consumerism*, p. 58.
29. Sandra Trudgen Dawson, *Holiday Camps in Twentieth Century Britain: Packaging Pleasure* (Manchester: Manchester University Press, 2011); Ina Zweiniger-Bargielowska, *Austerity in Britain: Rationing, Controls, and Consumption, 1939–1955* (Oxford: Oxford University Press, 2000); and Ina Zweiniger-Bargielowska, Rachel Duffett and Alan Drouard, eds, *Food and War in Twentieth Century Europe* (Farnham: Ashgate, 2011).
30. Jose Harris, 'Political Ideas and the Debate on State Welfare', in *War and Social Change: British Society in the Second World War*, ed. Harold L. Smith (Manchester, 1986), p. 236.
31. Jed Esty, *A Shrinking Island: Modernism and National Culture* (Princeton, NJ: Princeton University Press, 2004).
32. This was before the publication of the so-called Beveridge report. William Beveridge, *Social Insurance and Allied Services* (London: HMSO, 1942). It also confirms the point made by Stephen Fielding, 'What Did the People Want? The Meaning of the 1945 General Election', *Historical Journal* 35:3 (September 1992), pp. 623–39.
33. Arthur Marwick, *The Home Front: The British and the Second World War* (London: Thames & Hudson, 1976).
34. For the BBC in wartime see Sian Nicholas, *The Echo of War: Home Front Propaganda and the Wartime BBC, 1939–45* (Manchester: Manchester University Press, 1996).
35. James Belich, *Replenishing the Earth: The Settler Revolution and the Rise of the Anglo-World, 1783–1939* (Oxford: Oxford University Press, 2009); and Gary B. Magee and Andrew S. Thompson, eds, *Empire and Globalization: Networks of People, Goods and Capital in the British World, c. 1850–1914* (Cambridge: Cambridge University Press, 2010).
36. D. Elliston Allen, *British Tastes: An Enquiry into the Likes and Dislikes of the Regional Consumer* (London: Hutchinson, 1968).

PART ONE

Gender, Sexuality and Youth: Cultivating and Managing New Consumers

CHAPTER TWO

Who is the Queer Consumer? Historical Perspectives on Capitalism and Homosexuality

JUSTIN BENGRY

In his 1902 New Year editorial, 'Beau Brummell Jr', pseudonymous editor of *Fashion*, the early men's lifestyle magazine, explicitly denied that the magazine was 'effeminate' or designed to appeal to 'young (and old) gentlemen who wear corsets and spend the morning in Bond Street getting their hair curled'. Were this true, he countered, '*Fashion* would be crowded with unpleasant advertisements, and the proprietor would be a very wealthy man'.[1] More interesting even than Brummell's derision of effeminate men was his identification of them at even this early date as prospective consumers. A generation later, in a 1925 article for the populist magazine *John Bull*, Freda Utley alerted Britons to the danger of Bond Street's 'Languid Youth'. In particular she noted his affluent consumption: a gold cigarette case and 'last-word clothes'. She described his 'vices' as 'exotic' and from the 'East', suggesting homosexual deviance.[2] And in 1963, following the John Vassall queer spy scandal, the *Sunday Mirror* continued to rely on consumerist understandings of homosexuality in its primer on 'How to Spot a Possible Homo'.[3] Such men, Lionel Crane instructed readers, could be found on London's Bond Street, Tokyo's Ginza, Rome's Via Veneto and other world-renowned, metropolitan sites of fashionable consumption.

Writing for mass audiences of mainstream publications, and relying on well-known references to gender and sexual difference, each writer identified queer men by their assumed consumer practices. I use 'queer' here to identify a range of male historical actors who felt same-sex attraction, engaged in same-sex sexual acts or whose gender expression was not conventionally associated with their biological sex. They may or may not have self-identified as homosexual, but were often classified by observers as such.[4] These commentators relied on stereotypes of elite and privileged consumption, believing that particular consumer practices, including an 'effeminate' love of fashion, characterized male homosexuality.[5] From at least the late nineteenth century, elite and effete male consumers have been coded as queer. In turn queer men, like women, have been understood as natural consumers. These assumptions have been so strong, in fact, that they have guided business practice, influenced the cultivation of male consumers, and also shaped scholarship on queer subcultures and studies of masculine consumer culture ever since.

From the late nineteenth century, interplays between legal prohibitions, the expansion of media and retailing, and demographic shifts attendant with urbanization all helped create, through processes of appeal and denial, the idea of the queer consumer. By queer consumer, I suggest the historical belief that queer men were natural consumers who enjoyed using licit and illicit goods, spaces and leisure activities in coded, homoerotic and subversive, ultimately *queer*, ways. This notion of the queer consumer was shared both by those seeking to restrain homosexual activities and those hoping to profit from them. This chapter begins to think more critically about queer consumers by providing an overview of extant scholarship, considering primarily how proprietors sold commodities to queer men, and by proposing avenues for further research.

Even as observers have long sought to identify queer men by their behaviours as consumers, only limited historical scholarship has examined the relationship between homosexuals and consumer capitalism. This is surprising given that as early as 1980, British historian and sociologist Jeffrey Weeks proposed that capitalism and sexuality were 'inextricably linked'. Building on a range of work by sociologists, social psychologists and literary theorists, Weeks insisted that capitalism creates certain sexual types, like the homosexual, at particular historical moments to regulate sexual behaviour and the body politic.[6] In the US, historian John D'Emilio also looked to capitalism for the origins of the modern homosexual. Open labour markets, he argued, separated family members from household economies. Free from the oversight of family and locality, individuals who desired their own sex could forge new identities and communities.[7]

Few historians directly expanded on Weeks's or D'Emilio's focus on capitalism, even as later research emphasized commercial spaces of the large metropolis as critical sites of homosexual identity and community formation.[8] Rather than building a history of queer capitalism, most historians have implicitly reinforced the idea that consumer practices, even if prosecuted and condemned, were themselves unremarkable. Men and women who consumed in queer ways, or proprietors who sought to profit from real or imagined queer consumers, have therefore received little scholarly attention. Frank Mort's 1996 *Cultures of Consumption* is a notable exception, embedding homosexuality in the operations of capitalism and construction of new consumer groups in late twentieth-century Britain.[9] In Mort's study, gay men play multiple roles in the capitalist project: consumers of goods and services, leisure opportunities and media; the source of homoerotic aesthetics and codes of urban gay subcultures that filtered into advertising; arbiters of taste and also media and creative professionals who helped normalize both the male and queer consumer. A longer history is yet needed, however: one extending beyond the recent past to more unfamiliar worlds of pre-decriminalization and pre-Gay Liberation experiences.

Focusing on the British but also American examples, I consider how historians have understood homosexuals as consumers and entrepreneurs. Expanding beyond homosexuals as the subject of economic interest, some scholarship also suggests business enterprise's interest in 'selling' particular understandings of homosexuality to all consumers. We must further consider how and why the historiography on lesbian consumers might differ from that of male homosexuals. This essay thus asks: What insights can be gained by interrogating rather than assuming relationships between homosexuality and consumer capitalism? Could business enterprise identify, based on the assumption of shared identities, historical consumers who did not yet even recognize themselves as a group? But first, what would it mean to *queer* the history of capitalism?

'THINKING QUEER' ABOUT CONSUMERS

Recently, historian Matt Houlbrook critiqued the drive to uncover a historical queer market.[10] Influenced in particular by Laura Doan's important new book *Disturbing Practices*, Houlbrook advocates 'thinking queer – suspending both contemporary identity categories and binary understandings of difference and normality'.[11] In his discussion of the market, Houlbrook was referring specifically to my article on the inter-war men's magazine *Men Only*, and what he characterized as the pursuit of 'an unproblematised queer consumer' that assumes 'a coherent prior existence (queer-as-being)' that could be identified and cultivated by magazine producers. He continues: 'Thinking queer we might instead consider how *Men Only* enabled particular identifications for very specific social worlds – *calling into being* temporary provisional affiliations – in a critical practice that suspends both our own categories of sexual identity and the notion of identity itself.'[12] There are two issues that must be unpacked.

First, how do we characterize queer men in the past(s)? Houlbrook contests the notion of stable identities, instead identifying 'structured processes of becoming rather than structured positions'.[13] He rightly asks us to resist the desire to uncritically read men described as 'effeminate', 'pansies', 'rouged rogues' and 'languid youth' as homosexual, or unified by any stable identity. Such men, Houlbrook suggests, cannot therefore be further named as part of a stable, shared queer consumer identity or, by extension, a market. But, second, we need to think about how the category of consumer might map onto sexual difference. Because early twentieth-century queer men did not identify as a cohesive group based upon shared sexual alterity, does this mean that marketers, advertisers and entrepreneurs could not identify these men as potential consumers? I believe they did. Other scholars argue that queer men *were* identified as different by contemporaries, including capitalists, who might use this knowledge, rightly or wrongly, to identify them as potential consumers.

US historian of marketing Blaine Branchik, for example, argues that 'American businesses have been marketing products and services to gays for more than 100 years'.[14] Branchik uses the term 'gay' loosely, but critically his focus is on consumers. Branchik identifies queer men as consumers of sexual services, leisure opportunities and various goods from small businesses, which could be influenced by their spending habits and patronage. Homosexual men emerged first as an underground subcultural 'market segment', but by the time of the Stonewall Riots and then Gay Liberation they were recognized 'as a large, identifiable *target* market'.[15] In Britain, however, Lisa Power recounts that political engagement by homosexuals as a group with consumer capitalism only appears with the explicit anti-capitalism of the Gay Liberation Front.[16] Prior to the 1970s, then, historians must grapple with a complex dissonance. Capitalists identified a potential queer market segment based on assumed similarities, stereotypes, and sexual and gender expression. But members of this group would not have identified similar links among themselves.

Houlbrook's exhortation to historicize identity, or the lack thereof, is a useful if partial intervention. It is critical that we identify from whose perspective queer consumers are being understood, whether and when they are only imagined, and when and if they become a self-aware 'subculture'. Much of this work, particularly on the transition from the imaginations of capitalists to the lived experience of gay men and lesbians, has yet to be undertaken. But even if queer identities were disparate, atomized or engaged only in 'processes of becoming', that doesn't require that capitalists recognized this complexity and contingency. That would be to assign to them a remarkable and sophisticated awareness. Instead, relying on a range of assumptions and stereotypes, capitalists interpellated a queer consumer, defined by sexual and gender otherness.

QUEER CONSUMERS AND QUEER ENTREPRENEURS

Roughly coinciding with the emergence of mass markets and new technologies for appealing to consumers, the late nineteenth century also saw the criminalization in Britain of all homosexual acts not otherwise covered by existing buggery statutes. Section 11 of the 1885 Criminal Law Amendment Act, the so-called Labouchère Amendment, criminalized any act of 'gross indecency' – all male homosexual acts short of anal penetration – whether committed in public or in private, and made them punishable by up to two years imprisonment with or without hard labour. Queer male Britons thereafter lived under a state of imposed criminality, forced furtiveness and the always-present danger of blackmail.[17] Outside a narrow range of legal and medical discourses, trial coverage and press exposés, most mainstream and commercial discussion of homosexuality and homosexuals was curtailed.[18]

Scholars have shown, however, that even during the period of criminalization, some capitalists strategically employed what US historian Lizabeth Cohen describes as a 'dual marketing approach' to speak to queer patrons without alienating mainstream consumers.[19] Much of this work has focused on the mass periodical, examining how queerness figured in arts and male fashion publications between the 1880s and 1960s. For example, historians Laurel Brake and Matt Cook have demonstrated that editors of the arts journal *The Artist and Journal of Home Culture* (1880–1902) relied upon elite knowledge of Hellenic imagery and ideals of youthful masculine beauty to appeal to queer tastes while remaining palatable to its core heterosexual audience.[20] *The Artist* used these elements to establish what Brake terms, albeit anachronistically, a '*gay* audience' as 'an important backup to its dominant address to its "artist" readers'.[21] This appeal to what she describes as a 'pink market niche' would indicate interest in queer consumers from at least the late nineteenth century. *The Artist* was not, however, the only arts publication Brake identifies as seeking a nascent queer consumer in the 1890s. Where *The Artist* relied upon literary references, *The Studio: An Illustrated Magazine of Fine and Applied Art* (1893–1964) used coded images of naked youths by photographers like Wilhelm von Gloeden and Frederick Rolfe to similarly invoke the homoerotic associations of ancient Greece and compete for the custom of the same men.[22]

While arts publications sought queer consumers by capitalizing on the beauty of others, early male lifestyle magazines pursued men concerned with their own appearance and consumption. From the turn of the twentieth century, as historians and literary scholars like Christopher Breward, Matt Cook, Brent Shannon and I have demonstrated, magazine producers increasingly realized the potential of middle-class male and also queer consumers. The earliest publications like *Fashion* (1898–1904) and *The Modern Man* (1908–15) actively cultivated male consumer desires, but in so doing could not, Shannon notes, avoid the subject of effeminate or queer consumers.[23] They were unavoidable because, as Breward asserts, after the 1895 Oscar Wilde trials, homosexuality was more readily associated with sartorial indulgence.[24] Editors of *Fashion* and *The Modern Man* needed to distinguish and insulate masculine from effeminate or even queer male consumption. A significant skill, argues Cook, was to identify suspect urban fashions when substantial overlap existed 'between recognizable urban figures and homosexual behaviour'.[25] I have argued, however, that *The Modern Man* nonetheless included coded discussions – articles on queer friendships, blackmail threats and sites for homosex – in a calculated bid to attract queer consumers.[26] Producers of the inter-war *Men Only* (est. 1935) used nude female imagery, bawdy jokes and a familiar tone to protect masculine consumption,[27] but then deployed subtle textual cues and visual codes to engage queer consumers as well.[28] Attempts to attract queer consumers were never stable, however, and these early appeals were inevitably disrupted by terminated business operations, changes to key staff or shifting editorial priorities.

Historians of fashion, gender and sexuality have further explored the aesthetics and styles associated with sexually ambiguous, transgressive and queer men.[29] As Richard Hornsey argues, 'queer desire was made visible [by] ordinary commodities that became transformed into the prosthetic extensions of their owners' criminal bodies'.[30] In late-nineteenth-century Oxbridge, for example, Paul Deslandes shows that an 'excessively feminine' décor or personal appearance that included 'bellowing waistcoat' and a 'soupcon of powder' marked the sexually ambiguous aesthete.[31] In inter-war London, Matt Houlbrook demonstrates that observers identified 'pansies' and 'dilly boys' by their brightly coloured clothes and use of rouge and powder.[32] Their gender and sexual alterity was confirmed by their purchase and use of female-gendered consumer goods. After World War II, as Sean Cole, Paul Gorman, Alistair O'Neill and I have all uncovered, some queer men identified themselves through queer-coded fashions, purchasing tight garments, low-cut trousers and unusually coloured clothes.[33] Cole pursues the link between fashion and desire further to determine how 'gay men have used their clothing specifically to attract sexual partners'.[34] They did this, he asserts, through the subtle breaking of convention and the deliberate purchase of coded garments.

Homosexual men's interest in coded styles opened spaces for queer entrepreneurs. Physique photographer cum queer retailer Bill Green, historians have noted, operated Vince Man's Shop, a boutique in London's Soho, through the 1950s and 1960s. Relying on the queer codes of erotic photography, Vince's advertisements were directed at homosexual men.[35] Another queer entrepreneur, John Stephen, learned a valuable lesson about emerging markets as a Vince sales assistant. His own early advertising initially appeared in the queer physique magazine *Man Alive*.[36] Stephen went on to fabulous mainstream success in the 1960s as the so-called 'King of Carnaby Street' based on the sale of what O'Neill terms 'drag or casual separates' originally purchased predominantly by queer consumers.[37]

Art historians too have explored the relationship between queer imagery and advertising in the cultivation of homosexual markets. Paul Jobling argues that inter-war UK underwear advertisements eroticized the male body not just for women (the primary buyers of men's undergarments), but for male consumers as well. Queer-coded images in some ads evoked cruising for sexual partners, and 'appeared at least to sublimate gay desire and to make an appeal to prospective gay customers'.[38] Richard Martin similarly identified homoerotic elements in US advertisements by 1920s illustrator J. C. Leyendecker, potentially indicating awareness of queer consumers. Alternatively, David Boyce suggests that desires of queer advertisers and illustrators may simply have seeped into their work.[39] Carole Turbin, however, argues that homosexual readings of such ads are misplaced, because 'excessive' expressions of style or colour would not have appealed to most queer consumers concerned primarily with maintaining normative expressions of masculinity.[40] Still, as Branchik demonstrates in his survey of 'gay' images in twentieth-century American advertising, representations of homoerotic situations and queer men changed alongside social, cultural, political and economic transformations.[41] Advertising, whether actively seeking queer consumers or merely reflecting creators' subjectivities, deployed doublespeak and ambiguity, insulating appeals to mainstream heterosexual consumers to avoid disrupting social norms.

Personal advertisements from men looking for companionship and sex with other men further demonstrate the readership, and therefore consumers, of some publications. H. G. Cocks identifies same-sex personal ads appearing in both specialized and mass-circulation magazines and newspapers across the twentieth century. And I have shown that from the mid-1950s until immediately prior to decriminalization, publisher Philip Dosse recognized other homosexual men as a market with sufficient disposable income to consume fashion and the arts, leisure and travel. His *Films & Filming* (1954–90) not only included content and advertisements intended for queer men, but also queer personal ads.[42] With decriminalization, competition among queer commercial magazines expanded rapidly. As Matt Cook, Stephen Jeffery-Poulter and Jeffrey Weeks have all shown, examples like *TIMM: The International Male Magazine* (1967), *Jeremy* (1969), *The International Males Advertiser* (1969, from October retitled *Spartacus*) and *Gay News* (1972) soon appeared directed more overtly at queer consumers offering, Cook notes, 'legions of advertising space' to queer-oriented British business interests.[43]

Little work has yet been undertaken on queer erotic commercial networks or their proprietors. A notable exception is recent work by Paul Deslandes on post-decriminalization gay pornography. After 1967, 'self-confidently gay and assertive entrepreneur[s]' sold magazines, erotica and pornography to a 'burgeoning community of gay men' eager to consume.[44] Many of these entrepreneurs were queer themselves and also invested in other queer business interests ranging from magazines and photos to books and travel.[45] In the US, David Johnson has demonstrated that, in the 1960s, Conrad Germain and Lloyd Spinar's mail order company Directory Services Inc. (DSI) was pivotal in creating networks that promoted collective identities. And with 14 employees by 1967, DSI was, Johnson asserts, 'arguably the largest gay-owned and gay-oriented enterprise in the world'.[46] With overlapping commercial and imperial networks, access to continental Europe and relationships with overseas territories, British history has the potential to illuminate further transnational networks of queer commerce.

QUEER COMMERCIAL SOCIABILITY AND LEISURE

Urban locations of queer sociability, like pubs and clubs, have long been regarded as the most visible indicator of a queer subculture. Matt Cook, for example, identifies their post-decriminalization expansion as 'part of the new visibility of gay life'.[47] These sites of queer commerce and visibility, however, have histories fraught by discord. In Britain after World War II, according to Hornsey, criticism of the urban queer centred on his *inappropriate consumption*.[48] His public consumption was deemed selfish, and conflicted with post-war reconstruction imperatives that emphasized social, cultural and familial, ultimately hetero-national, stability.

Even as observers feared the destabilizing effects of queer consumer practices, Houlbrook has shown that early- and mid-twentieth-century London's queer pubs and clubs were complicit in reinforcing race, gender and class hierarchies.[49] Class difference, maintained by access costs, divided queer men who socialized variously at inexpensive pubs, cafés, seedy clubs or more exclusive bars. Members-only clubs, meanwhile, appealed to white, conventionally masculine, respectable, middle-class queer men who could afford the privacy guaranteed by pricey membership dues.[50]

Locations of commercial leisure also demonstrate how homosexuality was 'sold' to wider audiences. In nightclubs, proprietors used homosexuality to signal modernity and sophistication, as with the homosexual acts and cabaret shows, or 'pansy craze', George Chauncey describes as flourishing in Prohibition-era New York. The exploitation of a queer aesthetic and presence offered heterosexual, middle-class New Yorkers the chance to participate vicariously in a sexual demi-monde, proclaiming their own modernity.[51] London's nightclubs similarly attracted urban explorers seeking the bohemian sophistication and spectacle afforded in the 1930s by brushes with the city's sexual underworlds.[52]

In addition to titillation and modernity, club proprietors also 'sold' particular representations of queer behaviours, lives and desires to mainstream, ostensibly heterosexual, consumers. They relied upon stereotypes of effeminacy to reinforce dominant perceptions of sexual deviance and uphold the hegemony of traditional gender ideologies. But there is something decidedly *queer* in these relationships between club owners and the mainstream consuming public. 'Pansy' acts performed not for queer men but for observers consuming the spectacle of urban otherness. It therefore begs the questions: who precisely is the queer consumer? And what exactly does it mean to consume queerly?

LESBIAN LIVES AND GENDERED CONSUMPTION

Scholarly work on pre-decriminalization queer consumerism tends to focus primarily on elite, urban men.[53] This is the result of several interrelated factors. Owing to stereotypes linking queer men with effeminacy, and thus also a range of associated goods and services, male homosexuals were categorically implicated in fashionable consumption. Homosexual men were often more visible due to the social and cultural resonance of their gender and legal transgressions, and were therefore also more readily identified than many lesbians as a distinct group. And, in Britain, through the 1950s and 1960s campaigns for decriminalization, the 1957 release of the Wolfenden report and ultimately homosexual legal reform in 1967, interest in legislative change positioned homosexual men at the forefront of discussions about homosexuality and public visibility. Lesbians were concerned with legal reform, to be sure, but, because only male acts were criminalized, public discussion regarding decriminalization privileged male experience and promoted queer male visibility.

Women's economic marginalization further reduced lesbians' involvement in the consumer economy and the archival record of their participation. Historian Rebecca Jennings has argued, for example, that women's unequal economic power and pressures to care for family meant that lesbian sociability remained domestically oriented. Even as venues like the noted Gateways club in London's Chelsea flourished in the 1960s,[54] British metropolitan lesbian sociability was generally non-commercial.[55] Advertisers and marketers, therefore, had less interest in identifying and courting lesbians. American author and scholar Sarah Schulman also attributes this to the lower earning power of lesbian households, which translates to lower disposable income and purchasing power. At the same time, she notes, lesbians have become adept at identifying queer subcultural codes, recognizing and sometimes even identifying with marketing directed at gay men in the absence of messages directed at them; advertisers know that 'marketing to gay men can result in sales to lesbians'.[56] This cross-gender commercial identification offers another facet of the pink pound that requires further research sensitive to gender, sexuality and marketing strategies.

Lesbians, however, were both subjects and readers of pulp fiction and nonfiction, women's and niche magazines, and consumers of other goods and services.[57] But as women they were not transgressing by consuming many of these goods and services, and therefore attracted less attention from observers. Still, there is need for work to be undertaken into consumption by lesbians who transgressed normative expectations of female behaviour and appearance: How did butch lesbians acquire non-gender conforming clothing? What of public consumption of alcohol by women not accompanied by male companions? How did female same-sex couples navigate shared consumption and their domestic economies?

CONCLUSION: SIGNIFICANCE AND DIRECTIONS FOR FUTURE RESEARCH

Even as capitalists sought queer consumers throughout the twentieth century, it was not until after the Second World War that anything resembling today's pink pound can be identified, with a clear market emerging only in the last decades of the century. Non-historians, typically economists, sociologists and business scholars, have generally been most active in describing the significance of these contemporary queer markets. Steven Kates's survey of gay men in 1990s Toronto found they valued business 'allies' and deliberately supported them financially.[58] While marketing campaigns directed at queer consumers have rapidly expanded,[59] economist M. V. Lee Badgett discredits the stereotype of the affluent gay consumer upon which they are based.[60] Building on feminist scholarship and African-American history, Alexandra Chasin finds a correlation between equality struggles and target marketing. While market forces contributed to 'hailing' into existence a cohesive and public gay and lesbian movement, the overall effect of consumer capitalism, Chasin concludes, is divisive and fragmentary.[61] Worse, argues cultural studies scholar Edward Ingebretson, consumer capitalism has the effect of containing gay men and lesbians and undermining political gains. 'Market politics,' he concludes, 'dangerously reconstitutes the pre-Stonewall closet'.[62]

Queer theorists have argued that gay participation in the consumer economy and the desire to accumulate contributes to what Lisa Duggan has termed the 'new homonormativity', a politics that sustains rather than challenges heteronormative institutions. It promises 'the possibility of a demobilized gay constituency and a privatized, depoliticized gay culture anchored in domesticity and consumption'.[63] This scholarship questions the benefit of consumer recognition to gay liberation. Domesticated and de-radicalized politics not only excludes already marginalized LGBTQ citizens, but, Jasbir Puar argues, also sustains anti-queer government agendas as 'the nation benefits from the liberalization of the market, which proffers placebo rights to queer consumers who are hailed by capitalism but not by state legislation'.[64] Puar describes the complicity between homosexuals and heteronormativity, state priorities, neo-liberal politics and the race, class and citizenship privileges they require as another form of homonormativity, which she calls 'homonationalism', with consumer capitalism playing a key role.[65]

Queer capitalism has the ability to promote visibility and liberation of some populations through public commercial validation. Queer theorists, however, counter that business enterprise privileges Anglo-American men at the expense of women, people of colour, queer elders and other economically marginalized individuals. Immersion in consumer capitalism, they argue, may also de-radicalize populations who become invested in marriage, family and the acquisition of the paraphernalia of comfortable households. Looking at the relationship between homosexuality and consumer capitalism historically, British histories of queer capitalism offer unique contributions to an increasingly vibrant and transnational field. Research linking London with other commercial centres and non-urban areas will not only contribute to a richer understanding of non-metropolitan queer experience, but also personal, professional and commercial networks. Most excitingly, a British history of queer capitalism would include imperial, post-colonial and global networks highlighting transnational differences, continuities and connections between queer identities and communities. Such research offers to expand queer histories to surpass single-city and nation-bound studies, mitigate tensions between histories of consumption and production, and illuminate the formation of collective identities, political movements and international queer networks in Britain and beyond.

ACKNOWLEDGEMENTS

I am grateful to Charles Smith for generously sharing relevant portions of his recent Loughborough PhD thesis and to Jessica Clark, Julia Laite, Brian Lewis, Bianca Murillo and the editors of this volume for their thoughtful and useful comments on drafts of this essay.

NOTES

1. Beau Brummell, Jr, 'Some New Year Remarks', *Fashion*, January 1902, p. 5 quoted in Justin Bengry, 'Courting the Pink Pound: *Men Only* and the Queer Consumer, 1935–1939', *History Workshop Journal* 68:1 (2009), p. 125.
2. Freda Utley, 'The Languid Youth', *John Bull*, 17 October 1925, p. 30. Thanks to Matt Houlbrook for sharing this reference.
3. Lionel Crane, 'How to Spot a Possible Homo', *Sunday Mirror*, 28 April 1963, p. 7.
4. On the history of the term see Jeffrey Weeks, 'Queer(y)ing the "Modern Homosexual"', *Journal of British Studies* 51:3 (2012), pp. 524–7.
5. Also see Steven Maynard, '"Without Working?": Capitalism, Urban Culture, and Gay History', *Journal of Urban History* 30:3 (2004), pp. 378–98.
6. Jeffrey Weeks, 'Capitalism and the Organization of Sex', in *Homosexuality: Power and Politics*, ed. Gay Left Collective (London: Allison and Busby, 1980), pp. 11–20. In particular, Weeks was influenced by Mary McIntosh, 'The Homosexual Role', *Social Problems* 16:2 (Fall 1968), pp. 182–92. On the multidisciplinary origins of gay and lesbian history see Weeks, 'Queer(y)ing the "Modern Homosexual"', pp. 530–1.
7. John D'Emilio, 'Capitalism and Gay Identity', in *The Powers of Desire: The Politics of Sexuality*, eds Ann Snitow, Christine Stansell and Sharon Thompson (New York: Monthly Review Press, 1983), pp. 100–13.
8. Maynard, 'Without Working?'; Christopher Breward, *The Hidden Consumer: Masculinities, Fashion, and City Life, 1860–1914* (Manchester:

Manchester University Press, 1999); Matt Cook, *London and the Culture of Homosexuality, 1885–1914* (Cambridge: Cambridge University Press, 2003); Shaun Cole, *'Don We Now Our Gay Apparel': Gay Men's Dress in the Twentieth Century* (Oxford: Berg, 2000); Richard Hornsey, *The Spiv and the Architect: Unruly Life in Postwar London* (Minneapolis, MN: University of Minnesota Press, 2010); Matt Houlbrook, *Queer London: Perils and Pleasures in the Sexual Metropolis, 1919–1957* (Chicago, IL: University of Chicago Press, 2005); Frank Mort, *Cultures of Consumption: Masculinities and Social Space in Late Twentieth-Century Britain* (London: Routledge, 1996).

9. Mort, *Cultures of Consumption*, esp. pp. 164–70, 175–82.
10. Houlbrook, 'Thinking Queer: The Social and the Sexual in Interwar Britain', in *British Queer History: New Approaches and Perspectives*, ed. Brian Lewis (Manchester: Manchester University Press, 2013), p. 141.
11. Ibid., p. 148. See Laura Doan, *Disturbing Practices: History, Sexuality, and Women's Experience of Modern War* (Chicago, IL: University of Chicago Press, 2013).
12. Houlbrook, 'Thinking Queer', p. 141. Emphasis in original.
13. Ibid., p. 143.
14. Blaine J. Branchik, 'Out in the Market: A History of the Gay Market Segment in the United States', *Journal of Macromarketing* 22:1 (2002), p. 86.
15. Ibid., p. 90. Emphasis in original.
16. See Lisa Power, *No Bath but Plenty of Bubbles: An Oral History of the Gay Liberation Front, 1970–1973* (London: Cassell, 1995), pp. 171–80.
17. Jeffrey Weeks, *Coming Out: Homosexual Politics in Britain from the Nineteenth Century to the Present* (London: Quartet Books, 1977 and revised ed. 1990); Jeffrey Weeks, *Sex, Politics, and Society: The Regulation of Sexuality since 1800* (London: Longman, 1981); Sean Brady, *Masculinity and Male Homosexuality in Britain, 1861–1913* (Basingstoke: Palgrave Macmillan, 2005); H. G. Cocks, *Nameless Offenses: Homosexual Desire in the Nineteenth Century* (London: I. B. Tauris, 2003); Hornsey, *The Spiv and the Architect*; Houlbrook, *Queer London*; and Brian Lewis, ed., *British Queer History: New Approaches and Perspectives* (Manchester: Manchester University Press, 2013).
18. For popular histories see Hugh David, *On Queer Street: A Social History of British Homosexuality, 1895–1995* (London: Harper Collins, 1997); Patrick Higgins, *Heterosexual Dictatorship: Male Homosexuality in Postwar Britain* (London: Fourth Estate, 1996).
19. Lizbeth Cohen, *A Consumer's Republic: The Politics of Mass Consumption in Postwar America* (New York: Knopf, 2003), p. 331.
20. Laurel Brake, '"Gay Discourse" and *The Artist and Journal of Home Culture*', in *Nineteenth-Century Media and the Construction of Identities*, eds Laurel Brake, Bill Bell and David Finkelstein (Basingstoke: Palgrave Macmillan, 2000), pp. 271–94; Matt Cook, *London and the Culture of Homosexuality*, pp. 127–9.
21. Brake, 'Gay Discourse', pp. 271–2. Emphasis mine.

22. Ibid., p. 286.
23. Brent Shannon, *The Cut of His Coat: Men, Dress, and Consumer Culture in Britain, 1860–1914* (Athens, OH: Ohio University Press, 2006), pp. 91–127.
24. Christopher Breward, *The Culture of Fashion: A New History of Fashionable Dress* (Manchester: Manchester University Press, 1995), p. 247.
25. Cook, *London and the Culture of Homosexuality*, pp. 31, 40.
26. Bengry, 'Courting the Pink Pound', pp. 125–8.
27. Jill Greenfield, Sean O'Connell and Chris Reid, 'Fashioning Masculinity: *Men Only*, Consumption and the Development of Marketing in the 1930s', *Twentieth-Century British History* 10:4 (1999), pp. 457–76.
28. Bengry, 'Courting the Pink Pound'.
29. See Shaun Cole *'Don We Now Our Gay Apparel'*; Christopher Breward, *The Culture of Fashion*, esp. pp. 246–8.
30. Hornsey, *The Spiv and the Architect*, p. 138.
31. Paul Deslandes, *Oxbridge Men: British Masculinity and the Undergraduate Experience, 1850–1920* (Bloomington, IN: Indiana University Press, 2005), p. 74.
32. Houlbrook, *Queer London*, esp. pp. 139–41 and Matt Houlbrook, '"The Man with the Powder Puff" in Interwar London', *The Historical Journal* 50:1 (2007), pp. 145–71.
33. Justin Bengry 'Peacock Revolution: Mainstreaming Queer Styles in Post-War Britain, 1945–1967', *Socialist History* 36 (2010), pp. 55–68; Nik Cohn, *Today There are No Gentlemen: The Changes in Englishmen's Clothes Since the War* (London: Weidenfeld and Nicolson, 1971); Cole, *'Don We Now Our Gay Apparel'*; Alistair O'Neill, *London: After a Fashion* (London: Reaktion, 2007).
34. Cole, *'Don We Now Our Gay Apparel'*, p. 6.
35. See Bengry, 'Peacock Revolution' and Justin Bengry, *'Films and Filming*: The Making of a Queer Marketplace in Pre-decriminalization Britain', in Lewis, *British Queer History*, pp. 253–4.
36. See Bengry, 'Peacock Revolution'.
37. O'Neill, *London: After a Fashion*, p. 130. On John Stephen also see Jeremy Reed, *The King of Carnaby Street: A Life of John Stephen* (London: Haus Publishing, 2009).
38. Paul Jobling, *Man Appeal: Advertising, Modernism and Men's Wear* (Oxford: Berg, 2005), p. 131.
39. See David Boyce, 'Coded Desire in 1920's Advertising', *The Gay and Lesbian Review* 7:1 (2000), pp. 26–30, 66; Richard Martin, 'Fundamental Icon: J. C. Leyendecker's Male Underwear Imagery', *Textile and Text* 15:1 (1992), pp. 19–32; Richard Martin, 'Gay Blades: Homoerotic Content in J. C. Leyendecker's Gillette Advertising Images', *Journal of American Culture* 18:2 (1995), pp. 75–82; Richard Martin, 'J. C. Leyendecker and the Homoerotic Invention of Men's Fashion Icons, 1910–1930', *Prospects* 21 (1996), pp. 453–70.

40. Carole Turbin, 'Fashioning the American Man: The Arrow Collar Man, 1907–1931', *Gender & History* 14:3 (2002), pp. 479–80.
41. Blaine J. Branchik, 'Pansies to Parents: Gay Male Images in American Print Advertising', *Journal of Macromarketing* 27:1 (2007), pp. 38–50.
42. H. G. Cocks, *Classified: The Secret History of the Personal Column* (London: Arrow Books, 2009). For the US see Martin Meeker, *Contacts Desired: Gay and Lesbian Communications and Community, 1940s–1970s* (Chicago, IL: University of Chicago Press, 2005). For personal ads in *Films & Filming* see Bengry, '*Films & Filming*', pp. 255–8.
43. Matt Cook, 'From Gay Reform to Gaydar, 1967–2006', in *A Gay History of Britain: Love and Sex Between Men Since the Middle Ages*, ed. Matt Cook (Oxford: Greenwood World Publishing, 2007), p. 189. See also Stephen Jeffery-Poulter, *Peers, Queers, and Commons: The Struggle for Gay Law Reform from the 1950s to the Present* (London: Routledge, 1991), p. 97; Weeks, *Coming Out*, pp. 180–1.
44. Paul Deslandes, 'The Cultural Politics of Gay Pornography in 1970s Britain', in Lewis, *British Queer History*, pp. 267–96.
45. Rupert Smith, *Physique: The Life of John S. Barrington* (London: Serpent's Tail, 1997).
46. David Johnson, 'Physique Pioneers: The Politics of 1960s Gay Consumer Culture', *Journal of Social History* 43:4 (2010), p. 878.
47. Cook, 'From Gay Reform to Gaydar', p. 189.
48. Hornsey, *The Spiv and the Architect*.
49. Houlbrook, *Queer London*, pp. 68–92.
50. Ibid., esp. pp. 82–5.
51. George Chauncey, *Gay New York: The Making of the Gay Male World, 1890–1940* (London: Flamingo, 1994), esp. pp. 301–29.
52. Houlbrook, *Queer London*, p. 159.
53. Histories of British lesbianism include: Doan, *Fashioning Sapphism*; Jill Gardiner, *From the Closet to the Screen: Women at the Gateways Club, 1945–85* (London: Pandora, 2003); Emily Hamer, *Britannia's Glory: A History of Twentieth-Century Lesbians* (London: Cassell, 1996); Rebecca Jennings, *Tomboys and Bachelor Girls: A Lesbian History of Post-war Britain* (Manchester: Manchester University Press, 2007); Rebecca Jennings, *A Lesbian History of Britain: Love and Sex between Women since 1500* (Oxford: Greenwood, 2007).
54. Gardiner, *From the Closet to the Screen* and Rebecca Jennings 'The Gateways Club and the Emergence of a Post-Second World War Lesbian Subculture', *Social History* 31:2 (2006), pp. 206–25. For the US, see Elizabeth Lapovsky Kennedy and Madeline D. Davis, *Boots of Leather, Slippers of Gold: The History of a Lesbian Community* (New York: Penguin Books, 1993).
55. Jennings, *Tomboys and Bachelor Girls*, pp. 76–106.
56. Sarah Schulman, *Theatre, AIDS, and the Marketing of Gay America* (Durham, NC: Duke University Press, 1998), pp. 112, 117.

57. On lesbian pulp fiction see Katherine Forrest, ed., *Lesbian Pulp Fiction: The Sexually Intrepid World of Lesbian Paperback Novels, 1950–1965* (Berkeley, CA: Cleis Press, 2005). For nonfiction see Martin Meeker, 'A Queer and Contested Medium: The Emergence of Representational Politics in the "Golden Age" of Lesbian Paperbacks, 1955–1963', *Journal of Women's History* 17:1 (2005), pp. 165–88; Kaye Mitchell, '"Who is She?" Identities, Intertextuality and Authority in Non-Fiction Lesbian Pulp of the 1950s' in *Queer 1950s: Rethinking Sexuality in the Postwar Years*, eds Heike Bauer and Matt Cook (Basingstoke: Palgrave Macmillan, 2012), pp. 150–66.
58. Steven Kates, *Twenty Million New Customers! Understanding Gay Men's Consumer Behavior* (New York: Haworth Press, 1998).
59. Grant Lukenbill, *Untold Millions: Secret Truths About Marketing to Gay and Lesbian Consumers* (New York: Harrington Park Press, 1999); Daniel L. Wardlow, *Gays, Lesbians, and Consumer Behavior: Theory, Practice, and Research Issues in Marketing* (New York: Haworth, 1996).
60. M. V. Lee Badgett, *Money, Myths, and Change: The Economic Lives of Lesbians and Gay Men* (Chicago, IL: University of Chicago Press, 2001); Amy Gluckman and Betsy Reed, eds, *Homo Economics: Capitalism, Community, and Lesbian and Gay Life* (New York: Routledge, 1997).
61. Alexandra Chasin, *Selling Out: The Gay and Lesbian Movement Goes to Market* (Basingstoke: Palgrave, 2000). See also Rosemary Hennessy, *Profit and Pleasure: Sexual Identities in Late Capitalism* (New York: Routledge, 2000); Katherine Sender, *Business, Not Politics: The Making of the Gay Market* (New York: Columbia University Press, 2004).
62. Edward Ingebretson, 'Gone Shopping: The Commodification of Same Sex Desire', *Journal of Gay, Lesbian, and Bisexual Identity* 4:2 (1999), pp. 125–48.
63. Lisa Duggan, *The Twilight of Equality: Neoliberalism, Cultural Politics, and the Attack on Democracy* (Boston, MA: Beacon Press, 2003), p. 50.
64. Jasbir Puar, *Terrorist Assemblages: Homonationalism in Queer Times* (Durham, NC: Duke University Press, 2007), p. 62.
65. Ibid., pp. 2, 9.

CHAPTER THREE

'Healthier and Better Clothes for Men': Men's Dress Reform in Interwar Britain

INA ZWEINIGER-BARGIELOWSKA

The Men's Dress Reform Party (hereafter MDRP) was launched in 1929 in a press appeal calling for 'healthier and better clothes for men'.[1] Rather than criticize the new lighter and corset-less flapper fashions of the era, this pressure group sought to emulate them and thereby liberate and modernize the male body. The party's chairman, Caleb Williams Saleeby, denounced the 'tight' and 'hard' garments forced upon men as an 'abomination' whereas women were 'fortunate in that nowadays custom regards as decent a freedom of body and exposure of skin which were formerly condemned'.[2] Alfred Jordan, honorary secretary of the MDRP, contrasted women's 'bright, airy, hygienic attire' with men's 'drab, unshapely, ugly and stuffy' clothes.[3] Likewise, Sir William Arbuthnot Lane, a prominent surgeon and president of the New Health Society, welcomed women's new habit of wearing a 'minimum of clothing', which made them 'more robust and healthy' by exposing the skin to light and air. This stood in stark contrast with men's persistent wearing of 'heavy, thick, stiff' garments, regardless of season and temperature, which was 'positively unhealthy'. Lane attributed male conservatism to the fact that man was 'essentially a vain animal' who sacrificed 'on the shrine of his vanity when no consideration of health or comfort would have the slightest effect'.[4]

The MDRP, a middle- and upper-middle-class pressure group of doctors, eugenicists and health campaigners, has received attention from fashion and cultural historians.[5] Not all dress reformers supported the party but the cause of reform resonated in physical culture circles, which also appealed to a lower-middle- and working-class clientele. Thus, it is more appropriate to talk of a wider men's dress reform movement. This movement built on late-nineteenth-century reform efforts which were revitalized by the dramatic transformation of female fashions in the 1920s. Young urban women now exposed their legs and wore loose-fitting lighter garments in contrast with the cumbersome, restrictive attire of earlier generations.[6] Dress reformers condemned conventional male office and evening attire and argued that light fabrics, exposed legs and loose-fitting garments, were appropriate for men as well as women, at work as well as play. Because of their identity-bending, dress reformers were frequently dismissed as deviants and cranks. However, the movement was part of a broader campaign which posited forms of consumption, including dress, food and physical activity as critical to health and well-being. Like the rhetoric of mass culture advertising, this movement believed that healthy forms of consumption and leisure could fundamentally change the person.

The MDRP was small, but its campaign and the ridicule it engendered provide a way to explore attitudes to male, and indeed female, consumerism in the early twentieth century. Scholars such as Christopher Breward, Frank Mort, Laura Ugolini and Paul Deslandes in this volume have dispelled the myth that men do not care about clothes or are oblivious to fashion change.[7] Clothes nearly always serve as a marker of gender, but, as recent studies of masculinity have demonstrated, masculinity is complex, contested and multivalent.[8] Masculinity is not only constructed and affirmed in relation to women, in the economic sphere, and in all male groups, but also mapped on the body.[9] R. W. Connell has introduced the concept of 'hegemonic' masculinity and George Mosse has proposed a 'positive stereotype', embodied by an economically independent, heterosexual, physically fit white man. This normative masculinity is defined in contrast to 'subordinate' masculinities or 'countertypes', which represented failed or deviant masculinities such as homosexual, racially 'other' or physically deformed men.[10]

Dress reformers sought to subvert normative or hegemonic masculinity through fashion, an arena that had been strongly gendered as feminine. They strove to liberate men from the constraints of conventional male attire, which had been criticized as unhygienic for decades. By holding up women as an example, men's dress reformers destabilized conventional gender hierarchies. Given that shorts were commonly worn by boys and that more colourful, flamboyant styles evoked effeminacy and sexual deviance, critics denigrated reformed dress as emasculating, and dress reformers provided an easy target for derision and ridicule. Dress reformers could easily be dismissed as deviants or cranks but they can also be understood as utopian visionaries whose comprehensive hygienic regimen envisaged a healthy and beautiful man who had liberated himself from outdated conventions and embraced an egalitarian gender order.

The MDRP emerged from a clothing sub-committee of the New Health Society (hereafter NHS), launched by Lane in 1925, and it had close links with the Sunlight League, established under Saleeby's chairmanship in 1924. *New Health* and *Sunlight*, the journals of these two societies, provided a forum to promote the case for reform, and the party was able to use office facilities in the NHS's headquarters in Bedford Square, central London.[11] These new pressure groups, founded in the wake of the carnage of World War I, advocated healthier lifestyles based on dietary reform, exposure to sunlight, outdoor recreation and hygienic dress in response to extensive anxieties about health and fitness, particularly among the urban masses.[12] They were part of a wider life reform and physical culture movement, which emerged in the final decades of the nineteenth century. The promoters of bodily disciplines to cultivate beauty, health and fitness advocated a wide range of practices including gymnastics and exercise, vegetarianism, fasting, sun-bathing, nudism, meditation and dress reform. This flourishing self-help culture was inspired by a critique of the artificiality of modern lifestyles and activists aimed to restore the body to more natural living conditions, including more hygienic clothes.[13]

The Victorian female dress reform movement, which condemned tight corsets and cumbersome long skirts as damaging to health and restricting women's mobility, is well known.[14] Yet the movement to reform men's clothing was not a phenomenon of the 1920s. Indeed, men such as Edward Carpenter and George Bernard Shaw wore reformed dress such as loose shirts, knee-breeches and sandals in the late nineteenth century.[15] Saleeby had already advocated looser, more hygienic clothes for men in his health advice manual published in 1908.[16] This advice was replicated by leading physical culture promoters such as the Danish hygienist Jørgen Peter Müller and the Russian wrestler George Hackenschmidt, who extolled the virtues of lighter, loose clothing and sandals in the 1900s.[17] *Health and Strength*, Britain's leading physical culture magazine, juxtaposed the confined conditions of offices and shops with their 'abominable clothes (particularly collars!)' with the 'glorious refreshment' of outdoor exercise.[18]

The campaign against conventional male attire gained new impetus in the 1920s. In 1924 a cartoon in the satirical magazine *Punch* evocatively captures the gender imbalance of the revolutionary transformation in women's appearance while men's clothes had changed little. Captioned, 'Manners and Modes: A Masculine Protest', this image shows a fashionably dressed woman, wearing a short skirt, horrified at the sight of a man in shorts.[19] Saleeby called for lighter, looser clothes in 1926. In a subsequent broadcast Saleeby described men's case as 'really pitiful'. He advocated sports shirts made from artificial silk rather than wool and shorts for tennis, hoping that he would 'live to see shorts at Wimbledon'.[20] Müller, who was 'horrified' by the 'number of layers under which "over-civilised" man has concealed himself', restated his arguments in the 1920s when he extolled the 'ideal' of wearing 'as few clothes as possible'. Müller condemned hats as an 'absurdity' and considered sandals as 'undoubtedly the best form of footwear'. He also acknowledged that it took a 'great deal of courage to face a crowded street like this'.[21]

The editor of *Health and Strength*, Hopton Hadley, contrasted women's 'healthier and more rational' designs with the 'modern day masculine costume' which left 'much to be desired'. He deplored the fact that men were 'swaddled in tight garments' and lamented that 'nothing' was 'attempted to find a solution'. Hadley commended Lane for raising the topic because in the 'matter of health and rational dress woman has left man far behind' and he called for men to 'revolt and make tailors servants instead of masters'.[22] A correspondent, N. Winch, drew attention to the excessive weight of men's clothes. According to a survey of department stores, this typically amounted to 12 lb 11 oz, whereas women's garments weighed only 3 lb 4 oz. Winch deplored that men were 'wrapped up like a mummy' in their multiple layers of everyday clothes. Winch's reform efforts 'encountered very obstinate opposition' with tailors dismissing him as a 'hopeless crank'. He insisted that 'crank' was a 'name applied by an ignorant person to a pioneer' and detailed his lighter, simplified wardrobe.[23] Other readers expressed their support and suggested modified attire such as wearing shorts during the summer months.[24]

Though often satirized, the press also gave space to supporters of the movement. In 1927, Dean Inge of St Paul's Cathedral called for 'very drastic reform' of men's clothes in the *Evening Standard*, a popular London paper.[25] Edward Shanks, also writing in the *Evening Standard*, contrasted men's clothes unfavourably with female attire. Shanks advocated an 'ideal costume' of shirt and shorts but he also acknowledged the power of conformity, noting that 'few of us are comfortable when we are conspicuous'. He wore reformed dress at home, 'even at the risk' of being thought of as a Boy Scout, but adopted a conventional style in town because he was 'too careful' of his 'mental comfort'. While Shanks lamented that men including himself were 'conservative' and 'timid', he challenged them to 'boldly' follow the 'example of our sisters who have taken some ten inches off their skirts in as many years'.[26]

Alfred Jordan was a rare pioneer who was neither conservative nor timid and defied these conventions. Jordan maintained that clothes were essentially an 'ornament', but accepted that dress was a 'necessary evil'. The central question was 'how to dress with the least detriment to health'. Jordan considered overcoats, waistcoats and hats 'unnecessary' and advocated open-neck shirts and shorts for daily wear. Shorts for tennis were an 'obvious' reform and he went on to condemn evening wear as 'hideous' and 'health-destroying'. The article is illustrated with photographs of Jordan in reformed town attire of open-neck shirt, shorts and jacket, which he wore 'for all but strictly professional purposes' from the mid-1920s.[27] This image was reproduced in a subsequent article in the *Evening Standard* in which Jordan singled out the 'evil collar stud' and held up the example of the Prince of Wales, pictured in shorts and a jumper.[28]

The relationship between clothes and health became a growing concern of the NHS. In 1927 the society appointed a clothing sub-committee, chaired by Saleeby, which ultimately led to the launch of the MDRP.[29] Signatories to the press appeal cited at the beginning of this chapter include Jordan, Saleeby, Dean Inge, Leonard Williams, a physician and leading activist in the NHS, and the actor Ernest Thesiger.[30] Other prominent activists, serving on the party's organizing committee, were the psychologist and early historian of masculine fashion John Carl Flugel and the sex-reformer Norman Haire. The party was also open to women and female activists included the eugenicist physician Stella Churchill and novelist Barbara Cartland.[31]

The first major event organized by the party was a rally in July 1929 at which activists wore reformed dress, mostly opting for shorts, an open-collar shirt and jacket. Saleeby opened the proceedings by stressing that there were no 'fixed conclusions' about reformed styles but there was general agreement that men's clothes were 'too tight', 'cumbersome', 'ugly' and 'far from clean'. He read a sympathetic letter from the founder of the Boy Scouts, Sir Robert Baden-Powell, who was 'interested' in the subject as demonstrated by the 'dress of the Boy Scouts which apparently largely meets your ideas'.[32] This was not the only time Saleeby held up his 'old friend' Baden-Powell as a model for dress reformers. Saleeby rejected allegations that shorts undermined men's 'dignity and prestige', claiming that '[n]o man living can want to look better, or to command more respect, than the Chief Scout'. The article pictured Baden-Powell in scout uniform as well as the Duke of York wearing shorts and an open-neck shirt. In a quote, Baden-Powell declared that he had 'all his life' lived 'in shorts and without collar-studs, whenever possible'.[33] By making shorts part of the Scout uniform, Baden-Powell was able to appear in this attire without opprobrium on many formal occasions throughout the inter-war years.[34]

In his 1930 book *The Psychology of Clothes*, Flugel argued that men, in contrast to women, exhibited a 'remarkable lack of enthusiasm'. He termed men's shift away from 'brighter, gayer, more elaborate, and varied' attire in the late eighteenth century 'The Great Masculine Renunciation'. He attributed this to the social consequences of the French Revolution.[35] At the rally, Flugel deplored that styles had 'fallen hopelessly into a rut of convention' which had 'utterly failed to keep pace with present-day tendencies and aspirations'. He attributed this stagnation to a 'spurious feeling of strength and support' which men derived from their stiff, tight clothes. Declaring his motto to be 'Lighter and Brighter Clothes', Flugel called for 'clothes fit for heroes to wear' as a 'supplement' to 'homes fit for heroes to live in'.[36] Flugel's argument in favour of dress reform thus complemented the inter-war architectural emphasis on light and sunny living-space.[37] To conclude the rally of dress reformers, Jordan reported the party's 'marvellous' progress demonstrated by letters from across the country which gave a boost to 'our great health-crusade' aimed to reverse years of 'swaddling' which had wrought 'havoc with a man's physique'.[38]

The party was controversial of course. Initial responses ranged from endorsement and sympathy to unbridled hostility. *Health and Strength* welcomed the MDRP. Noting that Müller had for 'many years' advocated lighter, looser clothes, '[a]ll keen physical culturalists' were urged to 'give their earnest support to this new effort to achieve sane innovations in male attire'.[39] Following the launch of the MDRP, Edward Shanks restated the case for reform in the *Evening Standard*.[40] Another commentator doubted that the 'happy change' would take place because men feared losing their dignity symbolized by that 'tent-peg of our industrial civilization', the collar-stud. In a plea for 'formality' a third piece deplored contemporary men's 'untidiness' and 'sloppiness' with their 'baggy trousers and wide open collars'. To counter the rise of the 'sandal-sporters' and 'no-hat-wearers', this article held up the styles of the 1840s as an ideal.[41]

Dress reformers were faced with a dilemma. As the trade journal *Men's Wear* put it, those who did not 'practice what they preach[ed]' showed a 'lack of courage' while men in reformed clothes were 'dismissed contemptuously as cranks'. *Men's Wear* claimed that the MDRP rally had fallen 'as flat as the proverbial pancake' and it maintained that reform campaigns were 'likely to do more harm than good' because a 'radical departure' in style was 'in danger of being killed by ridicule'. Claiming that a gradual, evolutionary approach was more constructive, the article concluded that styles were already changing with the rise of motoring and increased sports. *Men's Wear* subsequently belittled the campaign as a '"silly season" topic' and maintained that '[a]ppearance and dignity' counted 'every whit as much' as 'comfort'.[42] The National Federation of Merchant Tailors labelled the MDRP 'dress quacks' who had no right to interfere with tailors' position as the 'custodian of good taste and style'.[43] The *Tailor and Cutter* castigated dress reformers for '"monkeying" with men's attire'. Noting that the MDRP was made up of 'middle-aged and elderly gentlemen', their 'definite desire' to 'dress like boys' was 'odd'. The magazine saw the advocacy of the kilt as an alternative to shorts as a 'polite form of advocating skirts for men'. It insisted that the 'normal man' was 'comfortable' in trousers.[44]

While *Men's Wear* was worried about the economic impact of the MDRP, George Orwell was more concerned with the political implications of the movement. He mocked the 'short, pink and chubby' middle-aged, middle-class socialist dress reformers in *The Road to Wigan Pier* for wearing pistachio-coloured shirts and shorts. This vignette is preceded immediately by George Orwell's lament about the 'prevalence of cranks' among socialists and communists, ideologies which drew 'towards them with magnetic force every fruit-juice drinker, nudist, sandal-wearer, sex-maniac, Quaker, "Nature Cure" quack, pacifist and feminist in England'.[45] Such ridicule, however, was powerful. Laura Ugolini has highlighted the 'often unspoken pressures towards conformity' in dress codes during this period illustrated by the example of an early-twentieth-century physical culturalist who was labelled a 'crank' and exposed to derision and ridicule because he did not wear a hat.[46]

Ridicule notwithstanding, the MDRP embarked on an extensive publicity campaign. Apart from public lectures by leading activists, the party participated in exhibitions including the New Health Society's Exhibition, the Lancashire Cotton Fair and the International Hygiene Exhibition in Dresden. The party embraced the new mass media of the inter-war years: radio, film and television. Flugel participated in a radio debate on dress reform in autumn 1929. The party circulated a film of an exhibition match between tennis stars Brame Hillyard and Bunny Austin, wearing shorts. The MDRP's summer rambles, during which men wore short-sleeved shirts, shorts and sandals, were shown in newsreels. The party's 1937 Coronation design competition was among the first events televised, although only 50,000 were actually able to receive the transmission.[47]

Reformed styles were detailed in a report by the party's design committee which restated the demand for lighter, looser clothes in more colourful and diverse styles and shorts instead of trousers. Other suggestions included the so-called Byron collar worn with a hanging tie, which met all 'needs of aesthetics, convenience and hygiene'. Blouses or tunics were advocated as an alternative to shirts and an 'ideal' evening costume, consisting of a white silk or satin blouse, black knee-breeches and silk stockings, closely resembled reform designs from the 1890s. According to fashion historian Barbara Burman the clothes 'appeared fussy or amateur in cut'. They were either too 'pedantic' or too 'soft' and 'flamboyant', and thereby reminiscent of women's clothes, to generate mainstream acceptance.[48]

The MDRP's endeavour to transform evening wear provided an easy target for derision and ridicule. A *Punch* cartoon of 1929 showed two men wearing knee-breeches, dark stockings and white blouses confronted by a stout, older man in a one-piece romper suit cut above the knee. The caption reads, 'What our dress-reformers have to put up with. The man who goes one better'.[49] Evening wear provided an occasion for the party's call for diversity, but bizarre, effeminate styles and examples of cross-dressing did not offer a practical alternative to conventional dinner jackets. Jordan attended the party's 1931 summer revel in a knee-length tunic, cape and sandals.[50] A photograph in the *Tailor and Cutter* shows a man wearing a woman's dress with a short skirt at an MDRP event.[51] *Men's Wear* derided the winner of the first prize at another competition as a 'creation – there is no other word for it – of purple coat and shorts, heliotrope low-necked blouse with purple piping and a purple tie'. Ernest Thesiger won the second prize with a blue blouse, worn with dark blue trousers, combined with a large pouch attached to a cummerbund. A crimson Russian peasant shirt with matching trousers received the third prize. There were also 'blanket-like' Roman togas and *Men's Wear* speculated why so many styles were derived from ancient Rome or Russia, which 'might look quite well in their own age and place', but which did 'not suit the ascetic leanness of the present-day intelligentsia or the plump swagger of the intellectual *bon viveur*'.[52]

The campaign achieved its highest profile in a 1937 Coronation design competition which represented the MDRP's most spectacular failure. The widely publicized event offered a prize of 50 guineas for the best design. This was not actually awarded because the judges were not enthusiastic about the entries. A dark-blue chiffon velvet evening suit, worn with a blue cummerbund won the second prize. The third prize was awarded for an evening suit with a short cape lined with white silk. *The Times* quoted a former editor of the *Tailor and Cutter* who dismissed the designs as 'fancy dress or carnival clothes' which were 'neither very original nor beautiful, and certainly not practical'.[53] Under the headline, 'Chiffon Velvet Dictatorship', the *Tailor and Cutter* claimed that the winning entries courted 'ridicule' and maintained that the reform cause aroused the 'antipathy of the conservative

English character'.[54] This competition was the last major event of the MDRP and little was subsequently heard of the party.

The MDRP is easily ridiculed, but this episode provides a highly distorted impression of the wider dress reform movement. It is important to distinguish between historical costume, gender-bending, and plain silly clothes and the moderate reform agenda of more comfortable and hygienic clothes. This tension was apparent in the earliest days of the MDRP. Leonard Williams, one of the signatories to the original appeal, put the case for moderation at the party's first rally in 1929.[55] Williams advocated gradual reform because 'any serious attempt to promote a revolution in the matter would certainly provoke the kind of ridicule which kills causes'. There was 'not necessarily anything wrong' with 'conventional' clothes, provided that the 'evils' of 'overclothing' and 'constriction' were avoided. Williams warned against 'excess of zeal' because dress reform was a 'very delicate matter' in which 'shock tactics' were 'bound to fail'.[56] Subsequently, he no longer played a prominent role in the party. This perspective was echoed by *New Health* which acknowledged the 'shyness and conservatism of the

Figure 3.1. Men's Dress Reform Party activists. Far left, Caleb Williams Saleeby in a conventional suit, and third from left a man wearing a dark blue chiffon velvet evening suit. Far right, Alfred Jordan in his preferred reformed outfit consisting of an open-neck shirt, shorts and sandals. The other men are wearing a range of dress reform styles. *Daily Sketch*, 8 July 1937. Reproduced by kind permission of the Syndics of Cambridge University Library NPR.C.35.

average man' and urged 'Dress Reformers to coax rather than attempt to stampede him into better ways'.[57]

Dress reformers aimed to liberate men from formal business attire which was condemned as uncomfortable, old-fashioned and unhealthy. *Health and Strength* condemned men's office wear as a 'white man's burden' imposed on clerical workers by employers whose expectations of dress codes were drawn up by 'hoary-headed old fogeys who attend board meetings dressed like early Victorians'.[58] One bank cashier decided to 'test the idea', spending an entire 'day without a collar'. He did not have the 'courage' for shorts, but wore a tennis shirt open at the neck and dispensed with hat and gloves. He received some 'chaff' from the manager who threatened to take him off the counter, but was mollified when told that the cashier was at the office early because he had saved time getting dressed. The cashier felt 'fresher' at the end of a long day and looked forward to another experiment, even at the risk of being 'mistaken for a belated tennis player' who having slept on the courts was 'trying to steal unobtrusively through the business day'.[59] The MDRP issued practical suggestions for employers and some outfitters were sympathetic towards dress reform ideas.[60]

Men's clothes were changing in the direction of lighter, more streamlined and washable garments. Middle-class men's town attire became more relaxed in the 1930s. Hats were no longer obligatory and stiff collars fell out of use among younger men. Generational differences were important, as illustrated in a photograph which shows an older, formally dressed man walking down a London street next to two younger men, one hatless, whose lighter, loose clothes and unbuttoned jackets suggest an 'easy informality'.[61] It is impossible to establish to what extent the dress reform movement contributed to these changes.

By contrast, the party registered some success in its campaign to reform leisure wear, swimming costumes and uniforms. The MDRP held up the design of a new uniform for soldiers as a 'complete vindication' and activists argued that 'more serious thought' should be given to civilian uniforms. The party welcomed reports that bus and train conductors were given permission to wear tennis shirts under their uniforms in the summer. Male musicians were another group who received attention. Much was made of the adoption of reformed evening dress consisting of a 'soft white silky' shirt and 'black Palm Beach jacket' by the members of the BBC orchestra during the 1932 proms season. After 'repeated representations', postal workers were finally allowed to wear open-neck shirts in 1934. Jordan considered the party's efforts in this area as '[p]erhaps the best influence' of the MDRP.[62]

Particularly younger men and women adopted shorts and open-neck shirts for hiking, cycling and general leisure wear.[63] Jordan welcomed this outfit which had 'done more than any other recent reform to improve the health and appearance of the young of both sexes'.[64] A leading promoter of this casual camp attire was the Duke of York (later George VI) who wore an open-neck shirt, shorts and jumper at his annual Duke of York camp from the late 1920s. The widely publicised camp, which brought together 400 young industrial workers and public school boys, had become a newsreel fixture by the 1930s. Indeed, George VI attended his camp in the same attire, just weeks after the coronation in 1937.[65]

The success of hiking shorts stands in some contrast to continued resistance to tennis shorts, which were one of the MDRP's key reform demands. The gender reversal in tennis attire was particularly striking as illustrated poignantly in *Punch*. A turn-of-the-century scene shows a dishevelled, flushed woman wearing a full skirt defeated by a man who acknowledged that, 'you would have beaten me, Miss Browne, if you were not handicapped by your skirts'. This image contrasted with a scene from the early 1930s when a woman in a sleeveless blouse and short skirt chastised an over-heated and demoralized man: 'You'd give a much better game if you left off those silly trousers.'[66] The revolution of female tennis attire of the 1920s was not replicated for men who, according to Catherine Horwood, had become 'fossilized into a parody of their Edwardian forebears'. Shorts became more common in the 1930s, but British tennis champion Fred Perry never wore shorts at Wimbledon and male conservatism prevented their universal adoption until after World War II.[67]

To allow for maximum exposure to sunlight, the MDRP advocated a topless male bathing slip or trunks as hygienically superior to the full-length suit worn in the 1920s. In 1932 the party launched a 'university' bathing slip, combining Oxford and Cambridge colours, which apparently sold well.[68] The MDRP targeted individual seaside resorts and in 1933 it claimed credit for the fact that a 'majority' had dispensed with the 'obligation for men to wear a "regulation" [full-length] costume'.[69] This transition was not completed before the war and men swam and sun-bathed in either the full-length suit or trunks until the end of the 1930s.

The greater flexibility with regard to weekend, holiday and beach wear in contrast with formal work attire made no sense to a writer in *New Health* who deplored the 'irrationality' of conventions which allowed clothes for sports or the seaside which would 'label one a harmless lunatic' in the office. Another absurdity was that shorts were obligatory for football, but unacceptable for tennis or cricket. This commentator attributed the 'meek, shy conservatism', symbolized by the standard suit and collar, to the 'emasculated salary-slave docility of our modern commercialized "manhood"'.[70] Interestingly, this reformer blamed the consumer and not the market or other factors for steadfastly holding on to traditional male fashion.

By bringing the question of men's clothes to public attention, the MDRP contributed towards the emergence of somewhat more relaxed styles, even if these were not based on MDRP designs. The party failed in its campaign to revolutionize men's clothes because formal attire was identified closely with middle-class professional men's need to maintain their dignity. The party undoubtedly touched a raw nerve and the intensity of the reaction points to the significance of dress codes in maintaining normative masculinity. Ridicule functioned as a defence mechanism which reassured conventionally dressed men of their hegemonic position. The dress reform movement is further important because dress reformers embodied an alternative masculinity which was able to embrace female precedents in fashion change and did not shy away from ridicule. Not surprisingly, this representation was far from the mainstream. Nevertheless, the MDRP and dress reformers generally deserve credit for the growing popularity of open-neck shirts and shorts, an outfit which was adopted by hikers, cyclists and campers in the inter-war years. This dress code embodied a new – and, importantly – mainstream ideal which was embraced particularly by younger men and women from across the social spectrum. Indeed, the image of fit and healthy men and women in identical clothes enjoying outdoor leisure activities became a prominent representation of modernity in the 1930s.

NOTES

1. *The Times*, 13 June 1929, p. 18; *Sunlight*, June 1929, p. 13; *New Health*, June 1929, p. 30, July 1929, p. 56.
2. *New Health*, April–May 1926, p. 28.
3. *Sunlight*, December 1927, pp. 11–15.
4. Sir William Arbuthnot Lane, *Secrets of Good Health* (London: William Heinemann, 1927), pp. 138–40; Sir William Arbuthnot Lane, *Blazing the Health Trail* (London: Faber & Faber, 1929), p. 110.
5. Barbara Burman and Melissa Leventon, 'The Men's Dress Reform Party, 1929–1937', *Costume* 21 (1987), pp. 75–87; Barbara Burman, 'Better and Brighter Clothes: The Men's Dress Reform Party, 1929–1940', *Journal of Design History* 8:4 (1995), pp. 275–90; Joanna Bourke, 'The Great Male Renunciation: Men's Dress Reform in Interwar Britain', *Journal of Design History* 9:1 (1996), pp. 23–33.
6. Elizabeth Wilson and Lou Taylor, *Through the Looking Glass: A History of Dress from 1860 to the Present Day* (London: BBC Books, 1989); Elizabeth Ewing, *History of Twentieth Century Fashion* (London: Batsford, 1992); Catherine Horwood, *Keeping Up Appearances: Fashion and Class between the Wars* (Stroud: Sutton, 2005).

7. Christopher Breward, *The Hidden Consumer: Masculinities, Fashion and City Life, 1860–1914* (Manchester: Manchester University Press, 1999); Frank Mort, *Cultures of Consumption: Masculinities and Social Space in Late Twentieth-Century Britain* (London: Routledge, 1996); Laura Ugolini, *Men and Menswear: Sartorial Consumption in Britain, 1880-1939* (Aldershot: Ashgate, 2007).
8. John Tosh, '"What Should Historians Do with Masculinity?" Reflections on Nineteenth-Century Britain', *History Workshop* 38 (Autumn 1994), pp. 179–202; Martin Francis, 'The Domestication of the Male? Recent Research on Nineteenth- and Twentieth-Century British Masculinity', *Historical Journal* 45:3 (2002), pp. 637–52; Patrick F. McDevitt, *May the Best Man Win: Sport, Masculinity and Nationalism in Great Britain and the Empire, 1880–1935* (New York: Palgrave Macmillan, 2004); Paul Deslandes, *Oxbridge Men: British Masculinity and the Undergraduate Experience, 1850–1920* (Bloomington, IN: Indiana University Press, 2005).
9. Christopher E. Forth, *Masculinity in the Modern West: Gender, Civilization and the Body* (Basingstoke: Palgrave Macmillan, 2008).
10. R. W. Connell, *Masculinities* (Berkeley and Los Angeles, CA: University of California Press, 1995), pp. 76–8; George L. Mosse, *The Image of Man: The Creation of Modern Masculinity* (New York, Oxford: Oxford University Press, 1996), pp. 5–6.
11. *New Health*, August 1929, p. 24; October 1929, p. 30.
12. For a full discussion see Ina Zweiniger-Bargielowska, *Managing the Body: Beauty, Health, and Fitness in Britain, 1880–1939* (Oxford: Oxford University Press, 2010); Joanna Bourke, *Dismembering the Male: Men's Bodies, Britain and the Great War* (London: Reaktion Books, 1996).
13. Zweiniger-Bargielowska, *Managing the Body*, pp. 1–6.
14. Stella Mary Newton, *Health, Art and Reason: Dress Reformers of the 19th Century* (London: J. Murray, 1974); Elizabeth Wilson, *Adorned in Dreams: Fashion and Modernity* (London: Virago, 1985); Valerie Steele, *The Corset: A Cultural History* (New Haven, CT: Yale University Press, 2001).
15. Newton, *Health, Art and Reason*, pp. 135–48; Wilson, *Adorned in Dreams*, pp. 208–27.
16. Caleb Williams Saleeby, *Health, Strength and Happiness: A Book of Practical Advice* (London: Grant Richards, 1908), pp. 52–72.
17. George Hackenschmidt, *The Way to Live: Health and Physical Fitness* (London: Health & Strength, 1908), Jørgen Peter Müller, *My System: 15 Minutes Work a Day for Health's Sake* (London: Anglo-Danish Publishing Co., 1905). These best-selling manuals remained in print until after World War II.
18. *Health and Strength*, September 1905, p. 71.
19. Reprinted from *Punch* in Bourke, *Dismembering the Male*, p. 202.
20. *New Health*, April–May 1926, p. 28; June 1928, p. 53.
21. Jørgen Peter Müller, *My Sun-Bathing and Fresh-Air System* (London: Athletic Publications, 1927), pp. 48, 50, 53–4.

22. *Health and Strength*, 6 February 1926, p. 123; 5 March 1927, p. 243.
23. Ibid., 2 April 1927, p. 360.
24. Ibid., 30 April 1927, p. 461; 4 June 1927, pp. 575, 578.
25. *Evening Standard*, October 1927, reprinted in *Sunlight*, December 1927, p. 32.
26. *Evening Standard*, September 1927, reprinted in *Health and Strength*, 1 October 1927, p. 335.
27. *Sunlight*, December 1927, pp. 11–15.
28. *Evening Standard*, 4 April 1929, p. 18.
29. *New Health*, August 1927, p. 34; August 1928, p. 31.
30. *The Times*, 13 June 1929, p. 18; *Sunlight*, June 1929, p. 13; *New Health*, June 1929, p. 30, July 1929, p. 56.
31. *New Health*, August 1929, p. 24; October 1929, p. 30, June 1933, p. 19.
32. *Sunlight*, September 1929, p. 31; *New Health*, August 1929, p. 24.
33. *New Health*, September 1929, pp. 20–1.
34. Tim Jeal, *The Boy-Man: The Life of Lord Baden-Powell* (New York: Morrow, 1990), illustrations.
35. John C. Flugel, *The Psychology of Clothes* (London: Hogarth Press, 1930), pp. 110–12.
36. *Sunlight*, September 1929, pp. 32–3.
37. See Sandra Trudgen Dawson in this volume.
38. *Sunlight*, September 1929, pp. 34–5.
39. *Health and Strength Annual*, 1930, p. 65.
40. *Evening Standard*, 13 June 1929, p. 7.
41. *Evening Standard*, 14 June 1929, p. 7; 15 June 1929, p. 8.
42. *Men's Wear*, 13 July 1929, p. 45; 22 June 1929, p. 401; 29 June 1929, p. 437.
43. *The Times*, September 1929, p. 7.
44. *Tailor and Cutter*, 28 June 1929, p. 517.
45. George Orwell, *The Road to Wigan Pier* (London: Victor Gollancz, 1937), pp. 161–2.
46. Ugolini, *Men and Menswear*, pp. 47–8.
47. *New Health*, December 1929, p. 36; March 1930, p. 64; May 1930, pp. 45–6; July 1930, p. 50; August 1930, p. 36; September 1930, p. 36; April 1933, p. 37; June 1933, p. 19; *Sunlight*, June 1930, pp. 84–5; Summer 1932, pp. 189–91. See also Boyd in this volume.
48. *Sunlight*, December 1929, pp. 23–9; Burman, 'Better and Brighter Clothes', pp. 284, 288.
49. Reprinted in Burman and Leventon, 'The Men's Dress Reform Party', p. 79.
50. *New Health*, August 1931, p. 36.

51. Reprinted in Bourke, *Dismembering the Male*, p. 205.
52. *Men's Wear*, 2 July 1932, p. 8.
53. *The Times*, 26 April 1937, p. 11, 8 July 1937, p. 21.
54. *Tailor and Cutter*, 16 July 1937, p. 947.
55. *Sunlight*, September 1929, p. 34.
56. Letter in *New Health*, August 1929, p. 56.
57. *New Health*, November 1932, p. 25.
58. *Health and Strength*, 29 April 1933, p. 490.
59. *Health and Efficiency*, September 1929, p. 451.
60. *New Health*, November 1929, p. 66; September 1932, pp. 16–17.
61. Image in Burman, 'Better and Brighter Clothes', p. 283; Horwood, *Keeping Up Appearances*, pp. 126, 132.
62. *New Health*, August 1930, p. 36; November 1932, pp. 22–3; *The Times*, 2 December 1932, p. 19; *Sunlight*, Summer 1932, pp. 189–90; Spring and Summer 1934, pp. 285–7.
63. Horwood, *Keeping Up Appearances*, pp. 92–4.
64. *Evening Standard*, 4 April 1929, p. 18; *New Health*, September 1929, p. 20; *The Times*, 19 October 1934, p. 10.
65. Ina Zweiniger-Bargielowska, 'Keep Fit and Play the Game: George VI, Outdoor Recreation and Social Cohesion in Interwar Britain', *Cultural and Social History* 11:1 (2014), pp. 111–29.
66. Reprinted in Catherine Horwood, '"Anyone for Tennis?": Male Dress and Decorum on the Tennis Courts in Inter-war Britain', *Costume* 38 (2004), p. 101.
67. Horwood, *Keeping Up Appearances*, pp. 82–6.
68. *The Times*, 9 August 1932, p. 6; *New Health*, April 1933, p. 37.
69. *The Times*, 4 March 1933, p. 9; *Sun-Bathing Review*, Winter 1933–4, pp. 13–14; Spring 1934, pp. 22–3.
70. *New Health*, May 1930, pp. 21–2.

CHAPTER FOUR

Selling, Consuming and Becoming the Beautiful Man in Britain: The 1930s and 1940s

PAUL R. DESLANDES

In response to a Mass-Observation (M-O) directive from 1939, a 25-year-old clerk from Newport in South Wales wrote the following about personal appearance: 'I try to make the best of myself because I do really think that my appearance needs all the help it can get, then for my self-respect's sake and because I want to look civilised, and because I know that personal appearance does count with other people.'[1] With these words, this M-O volunteer subject highlighted some prevailing concerns about male beauty and personal grooming. By the 1930s, Britons, like Americans, were articulating new consumer identities and embracing a belief that modern selfhood, success in life and self-respect were partially contingent on physical appearance, an attractive personality and an active engagement in the marketplace of body-oriented goods.[2] The result of a consumer culture that sold beauty products and services to men with increasing frequency, an advertising industry that relied extensively on images of attractive faces and physically fit bodies to entice customers, and a celebrity culture rooted in the theatre, the cinema and the pages of society magazines, this preoccupation was reflected in multiple ways including, for example, celebrations of the physical attributes of politicians like Anthony Eden, who served Britain as foreign secretary from 1935 until 1938.[3] More importantly, for the purposes of this chapter, it was also tellingly revealed in the hundreds of responses to requests for information about personal appearance and hygiene that M-O received in 1939. As part of M-O's attempts to construct an 'anthropology (or science) of ourselves' in the 1930s and 1940s, the responses constitute just one component of the massive volumes of information acquired by the organization through the distribution of monthly questionnaires to a National Panel of volunteers on topics ranging from eating and drinking habits to courtship rituals and sexual relations.[4]

This chapter explores these responses alongside a series of contemporaneous advertisements in an effort both to dissect the culture of male beauty in the late 1930s and early 1940s and to explicate the rituals of social hygiene that partially guided men's daily lives in this period. While care must be taken in thinking about responses to M-O's directives as unfiltered (and therefore unproblematic) descriptions of the everyday and the mundane,[5] this material, nonetheless, provides a rare point of access for understanding how men engaged with the beauty industry and used grooming rituals to perform particular visions of masculine attractiveness and, in the process, embrace distinctive (and occasionally divergent) male gender identities. The varied responses to questions about the adornment of hands, shaving rituals and hairdressing show how men conceptualized a pleasing physical appearance as a social asset that could make them appealing to others, further their careers and reveal their level of engagement with Britain's flourishing consumer culture and, by extension, inter-war modernity. The focus on men here is not accidental. Aside from reminding readers that men participated fully in the flourishing beauty culture of the period, this attention to male appearance and grooming also serves to illustrate the limits of J. C. Flugel's narrative of a 'Great Masculine Renunciation' in the modern era regarding dress and appearance and to showcase how patterns of vigorous and fashion-conscious masculine consumption identified by historians of the Victorian era not only continued but, indeed, expanded in the 1930s.[6]

When the directive first went out to volunteers in April of 1939, respondents were asked to reflect on their attitudes to personal appearance and the degree of trouble and expense they devoted to grooming rituals. Other questions focused on more specific parts of the body and the face. Assumed gendered divisions permeated the directive as men were asked to comment on their shaving routine while women were directed to answer questions about their use of makeup. In assessing desire and sex appeal, the authors of the directive questions assumed a heteronormative stance by asking women, 'What is the attitude towards make-up of your male friends, husband, or fiancé?', while men were asked to comment on the reactions of female friends to badly shaven faces, moustaches and beards. The final area of concern for M-O was hair, focusing on shampooing practices, attitudes toward untidy hair and baldness, and a question that asked both men and women: 'Do you regard a well-groomed head of hair as an asset socially, for work, for reasons of sex-appeal, of comfort, self-respect, or what?' While clearly directed by the marketing concerns of businesses that, by the late 1930s, were already appealing to M-O for information on consumers, these questions provided remarkable leeway for respondents as they sought to both reflect on their place in Britain's beauty culture and engage in a process of self-fashioning that allowed them to situate themselves both in terms of social class and shifting gender and sexual orders.[7]

Britons in the late 1930s did not, however, need to rely on M-O alone to prompt them to consider physical attractiveness or the daily rituals of personal grooming. As Ross McKibbin has noted, the British were a 'people of the press'[8] and their consumption of newspapers and magazines through the 1930s, 1940s and 1950s grew dramatically, producing numerous opportunities to view products that promised to produce allure and appeal while also holding out the possibility of literal regeneration. Advertisements in *Picture Post*, the enormously popular illustrated magazine with a circulation of nearly two million per week on the eve of World War II, and a variety of other widely read periodicals regularly peddled beauty products to Britain's voracious readers.[9] By the period under examination in this chapter, advertisements for these products were only placed in these publications following careful market research on what was likely to sell, how consumers used products and, even, the manner in which certain goods affected the psychological well-being of those who purchased them.[10] Despite the lingering effects of an economic depression in the 1920s and early 1930s, many Britons took the bait of advertisers as they expended their rising incomes on a broad range of new luxury products, including cosmetics for women and hair gels, shaving creams, razors and fitness equipment for men.

Concerns about physical appearance, one's facial countenance or dress were not, of course, unique to the post-World War I years, as John Styles, Amanda Vickery and others have noted in their discussions of the eighteenth century.[11] Nor, as Ana Carden-Coyne has reminded us, can we forget that '[b]eauty, self-artistry and new ways of self-fashioning' in the years after 1918 were undoubtedly connected to the anxieties about the restoration and reconstruction of real and imagined bodies that predominated in this era.[12] Yet, there were a variety of factors that made the 1930s and early 1940s unique. Among the most prominent were the increasingly sophisticated understandings of the satisfied psychological self that permeated responses to the M-O directives and British culture more generally.[13] Similarly, the culmination of the physical culture craze, the social prominence of eugenics discourses and the rise of new concepts of glamour and physical allure emerging out of the film industry all contributed to the creation of a vigorous culture of male (and female) beauty in this period.[14] Finally, the growth of a cult of personality that was predicated, partly, on one's appearance and a sense that masculinity was increasingly measured by one's physical fitness, digestive fortitude and ability to adhere to newly promulgated physical ideals produced a new kind of preoccupation with personal appearance and attractiveness that would have longstanding consequences throughout the twentieth century.[15]

Indeed, as Lisa Sigel has reminded us in her recent consideration of the inter-war period, the engagement with printed words and images, as well as the proliferation of mass writing on intimate matters, was absolutely vital to the production of modern (in her case, sexual) subjectivities in the years between 1918 and 1939. With reference to this point, Sigel notes: 'popular culture provided a method for the dispersal of stories about sexuality … a place to read about sexuality, a place to articulate new stories of the self, and a place to consider the paraphernalia of desire'.[16] The same might also be said, of course, for both the aesthetics of masculinity and understandings of the appealing face and body, especially as they became cornerstones in the measurement of personal worth and an important site of pleasure for many British men in the years immediately preceding and following World War II. Reading, viewing and engaging with larger popular cultural forces, then, functioned symbiotically with a broad range of consumer and grooming practices, products, and beauty and fitness regimens for men as they imbibed popular conceptions of attractiveness and constructed individuated ideas about personal appearance. With reference to the Britishness and advantageous labour practices of one shaving product, one young and politically radical newspaper reporter from Chelmsford in Essex noted some aspects of the nature of this process in 1939: 'Sometimes, having seen them advertised in, *Daily Worker*, & knowing that they advertise: "Made under British conditions in a 40-hour-week factory" I buy "KLEEN" blades.'[17]

In identifying specific advertising practices in his response, the Chelmsford newspaper reporter highlighted not only the symbiosis between male consumers, advertisers and products but also just one in a veritable smörgåsbord of innovative marketing strategies employed to entice men into buying products like Brylcreem – 'the perfect hair dressing' – and Vinolia shaving stick. While the former product, for example, was seen as an antidote for untidiness and the 'disfiguring flecks of dandruff that accumulate on coat collars',[18] (Figure 4.1) the latter 9d. stick was marketed as a pathway to sophistication by asking readers: 'Can you imagine your smooth, suave imperturbable Englishman – sophistication personified – with a bristly, badly-shaved chin? Can you imagine him retaining his smooth, suave imperturbability if his morning shave were a trial and a bugbear?' The answer to both questions was an emphatic NO and the secret to smoothness (and, perhaps, to sophistication) was revealed, unsurprisingly, to be located in a stick of Vinolia.[19]

The transformative potential of body-oriented goods was thus a routine feature of advertisements that appeared throughout the 1930s.[20] The popular magazine *Tit-Bits*, a weekly devoted to human interest and sensational stories, ran numerous items that highlighted the curative and/or aesthetic properties of certain products. In 1930, for example, Kotalko's True Hair Grower was promoted as a simple tonic that revitalized one's hair, along with happiness and hope. Testimonials, a common advertising technique also used in nineteenth-century periodicals, accompanied this enumeration of Kotalko's healing powers. A wife from Bedlington, for instance, wrote that her husband's 'teacup' size bald spot was something that they had literally thrown money at in the past. After using Kotalko her husband's hair was restored, a fact confirmed by photographic evidence. The notion that products of this sort were thus not mere luxuries but necessities worth the investment helped to further establish, at least tangentially, that male

Figure 4.1. A typical advertisement for Brylcreem, emphasising both well-styled hair and classic good looks. *Picture Post* 3:1 (8 April 1939), p. 60.

grooming was necessary to one's success (see Figure 4.2).[21] Transformative and restorative products like Kotalko could also function as prophylactics against the harsh exigencies of a fast-paced modern life. In another 1930 item, also from *Tit-Bits*, Ku-Bist Hair Fixative was promoted as an antidote against the 'wild, dishevelled locks' that no longer 'denote efficiency in any field'. This product ensured hair health, allowing the user to 'look your best' while guarding against the perils of modern technology by making hair 'speed-proof, wind-proof and practically water-proof', a notion reinforced by an image of a young man wearing flying or driving goggles (Figure 4.3).[22]

Fears about attracting the opposite sex were a regular feature as well in advertisements throughout the 1930s and 1940s. Building on the developments associated with the physical culture movement, a number of advertisers offered methods of physical transformation that promised

Figure 4.2. An advertisement for Kotalko Hair Grower focusing on the transformative potential of goods. *Tit-Bits*, 2522 (1 March 1930), p. 788.

Figure 4.3. Another hair fixative made specifically for the modern age and the modern man. *Tit-Bits* 2531 (3 May 1930), p. 269.

both weight gain and muscle growth, rendering the user a '… Superman … Admired by Women, Respected by Men'.[23] Success in life and love was thus contingent on bodily fitness, a willingness to transform physically and an engagement with an increasingly image-conscious culture. Humourists and advertisers in magazines like *Picture Post* and *Tit-Bits* preyed upon male anxieties about personal appearance, particularly as it related to musculature, physical development and the ability to attract women. In one example from a 1932 issue of *Tit-Bits*, a cartoonist lampooned both pretentiousness and masculine ugliness, especially excessive thinness. With an image that contrasted, in a seaside locale, a beautiful, lithesome woman in a modern swimming costume with a balding, beak-nosed and painfully skinny man, the caption hints at some of the judgements made about male bodies. In an effort to impress his acquaintance, the emaciated fellow boasts: 'Like all the best families, we have a skeleton in the cupboard.' In response, the object of his desire responds: 'Really, and who lets you out?' (Figure 4.4).[24]

Purveyors of goods and services also contributed to the growth of male beauty culture in the 1930s in other ways. A variety of trade publications that targeted hairdressers and men's clothing merchants discussed how to showcase new styles and trends. The anonymous author of an article on 'Gentleman's Hair Styles' in a May 1940 issue of the *Hairdressers' Weekly Journal* noted the popularity of the magazine's fashion supplement and

Figure 4.4. Having fun at the expense of the unattractive and underdeveloped man. *Tit-Bits* 2649 (6 August 1932), p. 665.

highlighted how some salon owners cut out, framed and displayed images of hairstyles from the supplement in their shop windows to attract 'the attention of clients' and mark their work as 'both up to date and thoroughly efficient'.[25]

Feature articles reinforced the messages about masculine beauty being sold in advertisements and trade publications. Essays on army recruits, footballers and actors focused not only on their occupational or professional responsibilities and obligations but also on how they got ready for their days with baths, shaves and careful attention to their hair. In a 4 March 1939 article that focused on the dressing ritual of a Drum-Major in the Coldstream Guards, his shaving routine figured prominently in the multi-step process of preparing for a ceremonial event: 'Before dressing, Drum-Major Baldwin has a shave. His cheek must be as carefully groomed as his uniform' (Figure 4.5).[26]

In several 1939 feature articles, other exemplars of masculinity and objects of erotic desire for men and women alike (Cambridge rowers and the Captain of the Wolverhampton Wanderers) were also depicted taking a foam bath or carefully grooming their hair prior to dinner.[27] These depictions and scores of others like them in publications such as *Men Only* helped to create the popular cultural context in which the M-O respondents

Figure 4.5. Grooming Rituals in the 1930s. From an article titled 'The Drum Major Gets Dressed' that appeared in *Picture Post* 2:9 (4 March 1939), p. 54.

operated, creating a sort of dialogue with products, rituals and body regimens that held out the promise of fitness, attractiveness and, ultimately, success.[28]

In the remainder of this chapter I would like to examine just a few of the narrative themes that predominated in many of the M-O responses. The first of these focuses on the connection that many volunteers made between a pleasant physical appearance, professional and romantic success, and psychological fulfilment. The second revolves around the rituals of personal hygiene and the histories of commodification and consumption as they relate to the culture of male beauty in inter-war Britain. The final one highlights the intricacies of masculine self-fashioning by illustrating how the lines of propriety and excess, masculine and feminine, and 'normal' and 'queer' were articulated in the directive responses.

Nineteenth- and early-twentieth-century advertisers and beauty experts regularly commented on the connection between one's prospects in life and physical presentation. In the late-1930s, however, a forceful language of pleasure, personal fulfilment and psychological satisfaction permeated advertisements and the M-O responses.[29] In discussing the reactions of respondents, the author of the report on the 1939 directive on physical appearance offered an assessment of the psychology of personal adornment as well as rudimentary sociological and anthropological insights:

> The ordinary motives for most of our care and adornment of ourselves lie somewhere between the rational and the irrational. Social motives are often semi-rational, for instance it may be quite rational to indulge in fashion, however crazy, if everyone else is doing it, simply because it eases one's path through society. Failure to conform with the standards

set by society is disconcerting and shocking to others who are doing their best to conform.[30]

While the 'rough ... and crude empiricism'[31] and the middle-class biases of M-O observers (who documented social and cultural trends in places like Bolton and Blackpool) and, indeed, of the National Panel participants themselves have been noted by others, the compiler of the report on physical appearance that distilled the directive responses and offered some preliminary commentaries on their significance was not fabricating the language of personal satisfaction, pleasure and fulfilment out of thin air. While a minority of respondents indicated that they were careless or paid very little or no attention to their physical appearance, most thought about it quite a bit. A 25-year-old insurance inspector, for example, noted in language reminiscent of Victorian physiognomy: 'I regard appearance as generally indicative of character.' He then proceeded, however, to link styles of clothing with the 'type of mind' of a man, noting along the way his own particular predilections with regard to style: 'I am faddy about my dress for "occasions" – dinners, dances, theatres, etc. and always like to be "just right". Am conservative as regards style and prefer to be "under-dressed" rather than "over-dressed".'[32] For a medical student from Edinburgh, satisfaction came not through the physical expression of character but rather through the joys of sexual, social and academic success: 'I suppose the chief reasons for dressing well are invariably for self-advancement – usually sexual, sometimes for business or social reasons or to impress examiners. (I have bought a pair of spectacles to impress examiners in viva voce [oral] examinations; and I don't wear green trousers on such occasions).'[33]

Some respondents were much more conscious in their attempts to link mental well-being to appearance by utilizing a more explicit language of psychological self-hood.[34] This point was made abundantly clear in the responses of a 37-year-old single man from Streatham Common in London. While he began his response by invoking the vocabulary of duty, he quickly moved on to an emphatic language of psychological fulfilment that highlighted consciousness, self-esteem and confidence:

My conscious reasons for trying to look nice are firstly self-esteem I suppose. People will take more notice of me, and look up to me more if I am neat & smart. I like to be friendly to all with whom I come in contact and neatness helps in attracting persons of both sexes towards me... . When well-groomed I feel more confident and can be more at ease with my fellows. I hate to be thought common or rough; & thus I try to look smart & keep my dignity.[35]

Here and elsewhere, as one Oxford undergraduate put it, 'self-respect is largely involved' in one's 'attitude towards cleanliness' and 'personal appearance'.[36] While invocations of self-respect and self-esteem were the most common ways to discuss the psychological benefits of a smart appearance, some even invoked Freud. In formulating his critique of the 'colourless, drab, stiff and starched' attire of the London city clerk, an engineer's draughtsman from Surrey and proponent of men's dress reform[37] noted that this uniform was 'quite out of place' in 'these days of Freudian enlightenment'.[38]

Fulfilment through a pleasant personal appearance was, however, only attainable by those who steadfastly committed to a daily grooming ritual and the use of a panoply of products. While some admitted to being a bit careless about grooming, nearly all recognized that certain social expectations for a clean-shaven face and well-coiffed head of hair existed. The Newport clerk, with whom I began, admitted to being torn between a desire to conform and a tendency 'to feel Bohemian'. In the end, however, he highlighted social expectations when he observed: 'I might record (NOT with pride!) that on occasion it has been indicated to me that I might shave oftener, that I might take more care of my hair, & c.'[39] The importance ascribed to the shaving routine in starting one's day out on the right foot was highlighted by a 29-year-old Temperance Friendly Society Secretary who indicated: 'I don't like to see badly shaven or unshaven faces and I always feel very unkempt if I haven't shaved – in fact it gives me a definite inferiority complex.'[40] In the process, he linked slovenliness with the psychological concept of the inferiority complex, developed by the Austrian psychiatrist Alfred Adler and popularized in publications like H. L. Beales and R. S. Lambert's *Memoirs of the Unemployed*, which first appeared in 1934 and sought to delineate a social psychology of unemployment.[41]

Regardless of perspective, many respondents offered careful descriptions of shaving, hairdressing and teeth-cleansing routines in outlining their morning rituals of masculine grooming; practices that were, in fact, regularly reinforced in the visual culture of the period, including in advertisements for brushless shave cream that walked potential consumers through the steps involved in correctly shaving a face.[42] Shaving routines varied depending on living circumstances, personal preferences and the desire for privacy. The 37-year-old respondent from Streatham Common noted his need for absolute privacy: 'Always lock myself in bathroom – cannot bear to be seen shaving. Not an operation for women to see.'[43] However, the Temperance Friendly Society Secretary involved his wife by relying on her to bring him a 'jug of very hot water, because I don't like to use the water from the heating system unless it is very hot'.[44] In 1939, most men involved used either traditional straight-edge razors and strops or the newer disposable razors produced by Gillette or Wilkinson (with a small minority experimenting with electric shavers). With regards to shaving creams, some opted for brushless products and sticks while others maintained the tradition of using hard blocks of soap, the lather from which was applied to the face with a brush. Many completed the process with a range of powders and aftershaves to ensure that the face recovered adequately from the punishing scraping it had just received. Respondents provided M-O, then, with as much detailed information as possible about common practices. A 30-year-old upholsterer from Nottingham noted that he shaved five times a week, using a Gillette safety razor and a 'shilling shaving stick of soap'.[45] Since his house lacked a bathroom, he shaved in the scullery, where he enacted a ritual of laying out his gear before beginning the process of washing and shaving. Men with greater means might visit the barber or hairdresser on a regular basis or retreat to private bathrooms for their daily ablutions.[46]

The appearance of the hair was of equal, or perhaps greater, concern to many of these M-O respondents, who commented on issues ranging from the fixatives and tonics they used to the frequency of their haircuts and concerns about baldness. A 28-year-old assistant buyer and salesman noted, in the first instance, his views on baldness: 'I should loathe going bald – You see I am very small – & small bald men are usually, well, shall we say unpleasant!' He then proceeded to note his use of 'solidified brillantine [sic]' and indicated his perception of a well-groomed head of hair as a social asset and marker of self-respect.[47] A clerk from Newcastle was even more explicit about products and the social meaning of hair. After delineating a routine that involved alternating between the use of an oily fixative, Vaseline hair tonic and liquid paraffin to both combat dryness and dandruff, he reflected that '[a] well-groomed head of hair looks smart, and above all other considerations, it denotes personal tidiness'. He concluded his assessment of hair care, however, with a statement that brings me to the final topic that I wish to consider in this chapter: 'Anyone who has his hair waved – unnaturally I mean, desires to be called a "Cissie", "Pansy", "Collar and Cuff", or other suitable "handle".'[48]

With this comment we are reminded that these narratives of personal grooming also allowed respondents to position themselves in the gender and social hierarchies of the day. A number of respondents walked a fine line between indicating care about their appearance and a form of vanity that at least some associated with gender and sexual nonconformity. Excess in the direction of dandyism or effeteness was seen as especially problematic, particularly in an era when undue attention to personal appearance in the form of permanently waved hair or the use of cosmetics was connected, in popular and legal cultures alike (as Justin Bengry and Matt Houlbrook have both shown), with queerness.[49] A 67-year-old retired clerk from Letchworth discussed standards of physical appearance as a kind of balancing act, a tendency to avoid extremes that could be viewed as excessive in one direction or another: 'I like to see a reasonable & moderate amount of attention paid to personal appearance, the happy mean between slovenliness & foppishness.'[50] Similarly, a 17-year-old accountant's clerk engaged in a form of aesthetic hair-splitting in offering what he termed his 'confession on appearance': 'In myself, I believe that smartness in appearance is essential, an overdressed dandy-ish effect must be abhorred.'[51] Others were even more explicit in separating what they considered to be appropriately masculine attention to physical appearance from forms of adornment and personal grooming that marked one as something less than a normal man. Many respondents saw dressing the hands with rings (other than a simple signet ring or a wedding band), for example, as beyond the pale. One 47-year-old volunteer noted that he was 'prejudiced against Englishmen wearing flashy rings'[52] while others viewed excessively manicured or 'liberally decked' hands as a sign of 'abnormality',[53] or effeminacy.[54]

While hair, hands and dress were viewed as markers of masculine conformity or deviance, facial hair could also be read as a crucial indicator of one's place in the hierarchy of men both in terms of generational positioning and the early-twentieth-century sexual order. Some viewed moustaches or beards, particularly on older and military men, as appropriate indicators of character.[55] Facial hair was contingent on circumstances and the type of face on which it appeared. A clerk from Muswell Hill, London, noted, with some humour '… Hitler's moustache is comic, Eden's is becoming.'[56] Others were decidedly more critical about facial hair on young men or when the moustache was the excessively trendy 'thin wisp'.[57] The Surrey-based engineer's draughtsman mentioned earlier stated he has 'no particular view about moustaches except that they are mostly worn by little men who are afraid of being mistaken for boys!!!'[58] A number of respondents similarly believed that facial hair could function as a compensatory gesture intended to 'insist upon the owner's manhood'.[59] Younger men who wore moustaches could be accused of trying too hard to be manly and also of sexual and gender nonconformity, as the 29-year-old Temperance Friendly Society Secretary from Peterborough noted when he observed, 'I don't like moustaches, in young men, very much. The usual small ones, to my mind, give a "nancy boy" look.'[60] Statements, such as these, highlight the diversity of meanings that could be assigned to the groomed male head and face and show just how central outward markers were to the articulation of gender and sexual subjectivities in modern consumer societies.

This was nowhere more apparent, perhaps, than in the case of one transgender respondent from London who worked as an insurance official and identified himself as 'physically female; mentally etc. male' and as '"married" in a permanent homosexual relationship with another woman', highlighting, in the process, the slippages that could occur in some self-fashionings between the masculine and the feminine and the normative and the deviant. He indicated that he was in 'a half-way position, being officially a woman, yet dressing and regarding personal appearance from a mainly masculine point of view'.[61] With such an observation, this respondent pointed to just some of the ways in which adherence to typically-male grooming practices was important (as it was in the case of the more famous transsexual man – Michael Dillon[62]) to the transition in gender presentation he was undergoing. This was especially evident in his description of hairdressing practices, which he specifically identified in relation to those of other men, effectively establishing a kind of psychic and ritualistic link with his biologically male peers: 'I have my hair cut on the average about once a month. Everyone else has his done on pay-day, so I leave mine a day or two just to show it wasn't only the shilling!' This subject's performance of masculinity also involved regular visits to the same 'man in the City' for haircuts and the regular use of brilliantine to keep his hair tidy. After providing a careful description of the types of products he used (depending on the needs of the occasion), he ends with an assertion of masculinity that highlights, implicitly, his rejection of dandyism or effeminacy: 'My use is purely utilitarian.'[63]

As the articulations of the groomed self-contained in these responses so clearly reveal, there was much more than sex appeal or professional success at stake when it came to the personal appearance of British men in the 1930s. At a time when advertisements routinely highlighted the ability of consumers to affect dramatic transformations in their looks, their confidence and their functioning in an increasingly busy modern world, it is not surprising that M-O respondents routinely linked their sense of satisfaction and fulfilment with tidily maintained hair and clean-shaven faces, manifestations of a tendency toward bodily control and management that was part of a general quest for physical fitness, national efficiency and racial soundness during the interwar years. What is, perhaps, of greater significance are the ways in which M-O subjects engaged in a multifaceted dialogic process with products, advertisements and gendered and sexualized discourses to produce aestheticized notions of the self in their responses. In weaving these narratives, respondents drew on ideas of dissatisfaction and fulfilment, conformity and deviance, neatness and slovenliness, and beauty and ugliness not only to locate their position in the masculine beauty culture of the period but also, as one noted, 'to gratify [their] desire for fitness and harmony'.[64] With this simple statement, this 31-year-old man from Colne, Lancashire, highlighted how ideas of personal pleasure, bodily health and, ultimately, psychological subjecthood could be wrapped up in the daily (and mundane) rituals of facial grooming, hair care and shaving.

NOTES

1. Respondent 1122, *Response to April 1939 Directive on Personal Appearance* (hereafter *Response*) (n.d.), Mass Observation Archives, via *Mass Observation Online* (hereafter *MOA-MOO*). http://www.massobs.org.uk/accessing_material_online.htm [accessed 29 September 2014].
2. On consumer identities, see Matthew Hilton, *Consumerism in Twentieth-Century Britain* (Cambridge: Cambridge University Press, 2003), p. 11. On the shift toward privileging personality and appearance in the US, see Warren I. Susman, *Culture as History: The Transformation of American Society in the Twentieth Century* (New York: Pantheon Books, 1984), pp. 271–85. On these issues in contemporary culture, see Susan Bordo, *Unbearable Weight: Feminism, Western Culture and the Body*, 10th anniversary edn. (Berkeley, CA: University of California Press, 2003), pp. 165–84, 245–75. On changes in the culture of appearance related to ideas about glamour, see Carol Dyhouse, *Glamour: Women, History, Feminism* (London: Zed Books, 2010).
3. Arthur Marwick, *It: A History of Human Beauty* (London: Hambledon and London, 2004), pp. 172–7. On celebrity culture and male appearance, see Marwick, pp. 161–89 and Laura Nym Mayhall, 'The Prince of Wales *Versus* Clark Gable: Anglophone Celebrity and Citizenship Between the Wars', *Cultural and Social History* 4:4 (2007), pp. 529–43.
4. James Hinton, *The Mass Observers: A History, 1937–1949* (Oxford: Oxford University Press, 2013), pp. 61–88.
5. On this, see James Buzzard, 'Mass Observation, Modernism, and Auto-Ethnography', *Modernism/Modernity* 4:3 (1997), pp. 93–122 and Nick Hubble, *Mass-Observation and Everyday Life: Culture, History, Theory* (Basingstoke: Palgrave Macmillan, 2006).
6. J.C. Flugel, *The Psychology of Clothes* (London: Hogarth Press, 1930), pp. 110–21. On masculine consumption in the nineteenth and early-twentieth centuries, see Ariel Beaujot, *Victorian Fashion Accessories* (London: Berg, 2012), pp. 115–17, 124–31; Christopher Breward, *The Hidden Consumer: Masculinities, Fashion and City Life, 1860–1914* (Manchester: Manchester University Press, 1999); and Brent Shannon, *The Cut of His Coat: Men, Dress and Consumer Culture in Britain, 1860–1914* (Athens, OH: Ohio University Press, 2006).
7. *Report by Mass-Observation on Personal Appearance, Part I: Hands, Face and Hair* (July 1939), pp. 1–2, MOA, File A 21 7.39.
8. Ross McKibbin, *Classes and Cultures: England 1918–1951* (Oxford: Oxford University Press, 1998), p. 503. For a good overview, see Adrian

Bingham, *Family Newspapers? Sex, Private Life, and the British Popular Press, 1918–1978* (Oxford: Oxford University Press, 2009), pp. 15–50.

9. For examples, see 'Give me Nufix', *Picture Post* 3:2 (15 April 1939), p. 7 and 'My first shave with a Remington – the smoothest I've ever had!' *Picture Post* 2:8 (25 February 1939), p. 8.
10. T. R. Nevett, *Advertising in Britain: A History* (London: Heinemann, 1982), pp. 150–2 and Paul Jobling, *Man Appeal: Advertising, Modernism, and Men's Wear* (Oxford: Berg, 2005), pp. 35–57.
11. John Styles, *The Dress of the People: Everyday Fashion in Eighteenth-Century England* (New Haven, CT: Yale University Press, 2007); John Styles and Amanda Vickery, eds, *Gender, Taste, and Material Culture in Britain and North America, 1700–1830* (New Haven, CT: Yale Center for British Art, 2006).
12. Ana Carden-Coyne, *Reconstructing the Body: Classicism, Modernism, and the First World War* (Oxford: Oxford University Press, 2009), p. 220.
13. Mathew Thomson, *Psychological Subjects: Identity, Culture, and Health in Twentieth-Century Britain* (Oxford: Oxford University Press, 2006).
14. Ina Zweiniger-Bargielowska, *Managing the Body: Beauty, Health, and Fitness in Britain, 1880–1939* (Oxford: Oxford University Press, 2010), pp. 36–50, 151–2. On glamour in this period, see Dyhouse, pp. 28–79.
15. Christopher E. Forth, *Masculinity in the Modern West: Gender, Civilization and the Body* (Basingstoke: Palgrave Macmillan, 2008), pp. 169–200.
16. Lisa Z. Sigel, *Making Modern Love: Sexual Narratives and Identities in Interwar Britain* (Philadelphia, PA: Temple University Press, 2012), p. 3.
17. Respondent 1264, *Response* (April 1939), MOA-MOO.
18. 'Brylcreem Makes a Tidy Difference to Your Hair', *Picture Post* 3:1 (8 April 1939), p. 60.
19. 'Difficult Chins', *Picture Post* 2:11 (11 March 1939), p. 83.
20. On this process in a colonial setting, see Timothy Burke, *Lifebuoy Men, Lux Women: Commodification, Consumption, and Cleanliness in Modern Zimbabwe* (Durham, NC: Duke University Press, 1996), pp. 17–62.
21. 'Kotalko's Triumph As a Hair Grower', *Tit-Bits* 2522 (1 March 1930), p. 788.
22. 'That Calm Unruffled Feeling', *Tit-Bits* 2531 (3 May 1930), p. 269.
23. 'Let Me Build You a Virile New Body', *Tit-Bits* 3010 (8 July 1939), p. 27.
24. 'Seaside Acquaintance', *Tit-Bits* 2649 (6 August 1932), p. 665.
25. 'Gentlemen's Hair Styles', *Hairdressers' Weekly Journal* 59:3028 (4 May 1940), p. 1003.
26. 'The Drum Major Gets Dressed', *Picture Post* 2:9 (4 March 1939), p. 54.
27. 'Training for Henley', *Picture Post* 4:1 (8 July 1939), p. 13 and 'The Wolves', *Picture Post* 3:4 (29 April 1939), p. 13.
28. Jill Greenfield, Sean O'Connell and Chris Reid, 'Fashioning Masculinity: *Men Only*, Consumption and the Development of Marketing in the 1930s',

Twentieth Century British History 10:4 (October 1999), pp. 457–76 and Jobling, *Man Appeal*, pp. 59–76.

29. One 1939 advertisement collected by M-O read: 'Be well dressed! It's your privilege. It gives pleasure to you, to your family, to your friends. And it's good policy. Whatever your position in life, your prospects are enhanced by care of your appearance.' From a report titled 'Mass Observation: Clothes for Men (May 1939)', *Topic Collection: Personal Appearance and Clothes*, MOA, 18/2/5.
30. *Report by Mass-Observation on Personal Appearance, Part I*, p. 7.
31. Bronislaw Malinowski's comment cited in Gary Cross, 'Introduction: Mass-Observation and Worktowners at Play' in *Worktowners at Blackpool: Mass-Observation and Popular Leisure in the 1930s*, ed. Gary Cross (London: Routledge, 1990), p. 4. On issues of class, see Peter Gurney, '"Intersex" and "Dirty Girls": Mass-Observation and Working-Class Sexuality in England in the 1930s', *Journal of the History of Sexuality* 8:2 (October 1997), pp. 256–90 and Hinton, *The Mass Observers*, pp. 62, 270–2.
32. Respondent 1118, *Response* (April 1939), MOA-MOO.
33. Respondent 1404, *Response* (n.d.), MOA-MOO.
34. On the relationship between M-O and the popularization of psychology, see Thomson, pp. 244–7.
35. Respondent 1129, *Response* (19 April 1939), MOA-MOO.
36. Respondent 1337, *Response* (23 April 1939), MOA-MOO.
37. Joanna Bourke, *Dismembering the Male: Men's Bodies, Britain and the Great War* (Chicago, IL: University of Chicago Press, 1996), pp. 199–209 and Zweiniger-Bargielowska, pp. 223–35 and Chapter Three in this book.
38. Respondent 1108, *Response* (n.d.), MOA-MOO.
39. Respondent 1122.
40. Respondent 1151, *Response* (n.d.), MOA-MOO.
41. On the importance of this work, see Ross McKibbin, *The Ideologies of Class: Social Relations in Britain, 1880–1950* (Oxford: Clarendon Press, 1990), p. 231.
42. 'A Better Shave Without A Brush Than You Ever Got With One', *Picture Post* 2:5 (4 February 1939), p. 76.
43. Respondent 1129, *Response* (n.d.), MOA-MOO.
44. Respondent 1151.
45. Respondent 1235, *Response* (n.d.), MOA-MOO.
46. Respondent 1200, *Response* (n.d.), MOA-MOO.
47. Respondent (Assistant Buyer/Salesman, Stanmore, Middlesex), *Response* (n.d.), MOA-MOO.
48. Respondent 1178, Response (n.d.), MOA-MOO.
49. Justin Bengry, 'Courting the Pink Pound: *Men Only* and the Queer Consumer, 1935–39', *History Workshop Journal* 68 (Autumn 2009), pp. 122–48; Matt

Houlbrook, *Queer London: Perils and Pleasures in the Sexual Metropolis, 1918–1957* (Chicago, IL: University of Chicago Press, 2005), pp. 139–66; and Houlbrook, '"The Man with the Powder Puff" in Interwar London', *Historical Journal* 50:1 (2007), pp. 145–71.

50. Respondent 1190, *Response* (n.d.), MOA-MOO.
51. Respondent 1092, *Response* (25 April 1939), MOA-MOO.
52. Respondent 1103, *Response* (27 April 1939), MOA-MOO.
53. Respondent 1161, *Response* (n.d.), MOA-MOO.
54. Respondent 1208, *Response* (n.d.) and Respondent 1225, *Response* (n.d.), MOA-MOO.
55. Respondent 1324, *Response* (n.d.), MOA-MOO.
56. Respondent 1312, *Response* (n.d.), MOA-MOO.
57. Respondent 1337, *Response* (April 23, 1939), MOA-MOO.
58. Respondent 1108.
59. Respondent 1328, *Response* (n.d.), MOA-MOO.
60. Respondent 1151.
61. Respondent 1206, *Response* (n.d.), MOA-MOO.
62. On the Dillon case, see Pagan Kennedy, *The First Man-Made Man: The Story of Two Sex Changes, One Love Affair and a Twentieth-Century Medical Revolution* (New York: Bloomsbury, 2007).
63. Respondent 1206.
64. Respondent 1194, *Response* (n.d.), MOA-MOO.

CHAPTER FIVE

Rational Recreation in the Age of Affluence: The Café and Working-Class Youth in London, c. 1939–1965

KATE BRADLEY

Rational recreation is a term scholars have used to describe the paternalist philanthropy of the nineteenth century that attempted to control and contain the working classes through constructive leisure activities that would also promote more orderly communities.[1] In the twentieth century, the expansion of domestic tourism and leisure after World War I, the introduction of holidays with pay in the 1930s, and worker affluence after 1945 made such paternalistic interventions appear futile and outdated.[2] Nevertheless, the desire to provide what was effectively 'rational recreation' continued after 1945, driven by anxieties about an affluent working class. Voluntary organizations saw mass commercial youth-oriented culture as having an egregious effect on working-class youth. Yet more specifically, they were worried about those young people who were excluded or on the fringes and who might potentially use illegal means to obtain money or resources to participate in it. The cafés, coffee stalls and canteens set up by these organizations attempted to draw these young people into the mainstream youth culture by providing a supportive environment in which non-delinquent characters could be nurtured away from 'bad' influences. For less affluent youth, they were places to socialize without having to spend money or 'do' any specific activities, a form of anti-consumption or counter-culture. By the mid-twentieth century, young people were expected to be consumers; not consuming was a cause for concern. Non-consuming youth were apart from Mark Abram's 'teenage consumers' as their participation in the supposedly affluent post-war world was limited. These non-consumers did not fit neatly into sociological and economic understandings of the 'affluent' post-war working class, and were far more likely to be researched by criminologists looking to explain aberrational behaviour.[3] They were, in the main, too young to vote, and their voices were not heard – the café and other venues offered a space for autonomy and freedom.

A youth culture around cafés, coffee and milk bars was apparent from the 1920s. As David Fowler notes, young female workers in Central London developed a vibrant 'flapper' culture based around the Lyons Corner Houses. This was part of a wider youth culture around suburban dance halls and cinemas, all readily affordable on a young worker's income.[4] Indeed, as both Bird and Walkowitz note, the Lyons Corner Houses also formed part of the heterogeneous West End leisure landscape of shoppers, same-sex couples and the Jewish community.[5] Yet not all young people were able to participate. Melanie Tebbutt provides an example of how the young un- or underemployed men of Northampton in the 1930s were welcome to while away the hours at a local café with a sympathetic owner.[6]

Innovations in catering in the mid-twentieth century had an impact on these youth cultures. The first milk bars opened in London in the mid-1930s, selling milk in a similar way that pubs sold alcohol, whilst snack bars brought in less formal, 'fast food'. Achille Gaggia's invention of a powerful and reliable espresso machine brought better coffee to the streets of Soho in the 1940s and 1950s, helping to create a vibrant subterranean world of jazz clubs and cafés in Central London, populated by young people from the suburbs.[7] The milk bars, coffee bars and cafés that young people increasingly frequented brought a whiff of foreignness: Italian sophistication through the coffee, and, as Adrian Horn argues, a trace of Americana through the music on the juke boxes. At the same time British youth created their own distinctive identities and local cultures.[8] Cafés and coffee bars were one particular space where the young congregated, giving them a hetero-social public space to conduct friendships, intimate relationships and rivalries. At the same time it put them on public display. Such coffee bars proved popular. By 1960, there were 2000 coffee bars in Britain, including 200 in the West End of London alone. This growth was fuelled by the cessation of rationing and significant numbers of Italian migrants settling in Britain.[9]

Notable critics of the milk bar like Richard Hoggart focused on the sense of a slavish, slack-jawed adherence to the new, 'feminine' and degenerate consumerism; others, like Martha Gellhorn, saw this as an alien, foreign world she could no longer enter.[10] The new groups of supposedly affluent young people who seemed adrift from the values and experiences of older generations were agonized over by academic and media commentators, and subjected to scrutiny through Labour's Youth Commission and the Albemarle Report.[11] They were also the subject of action by a range of voluntary organizations, such as the settlement movement, the Young Women's Christian Association (YWCA) and the boys' club movement, many of whom had roots in much longer traditions of 'rational recreation'.

The café and similar spaces were part of both the mundane and the spectacular ways that young people consumed in their immediate locales or further afield. This chapter focuses on London for a number of reasons. First, London was the epicentre of many well-publicised youth 'subcultures' in the 1950s, such as the Teddy Boys and the Mods. Second, London served as a destination for young people from the provinces, whether on a short trip to Carnaby Street, or to escape home towns and find somewhere to fit in. Last, organizations in London had a strong and experimental voluntary action tradition, dating from the mid-nineteenth century. A close look at young people's movements in London, whether to listen to music in a Soho café or seek out a cup of tea locally, indicates these were locations that young people deliberately chose to attend. Yet they may not always have been the most desired option. At times the use of a café reflected exclusion from other leisure spaces. Customers might be too young or too poor to go to the pub or other fashionable night-time venues, living at home without any personal space, or excluded in some way from youth clubs and organizations.[12] Some young people were barred from specific cafés and cinemas in the neighbourhood, especially if the staff of those establishments thought they might be troublesome. The young resorted to using whatever space would have them.[13]

Reformers' interest in the movements of the young around urban spaces was far from new. In the nineteenth century, reformers tackled the problem of 'constructively entertaining' destitute or orphaned children in clubs and uniformed organizations. The issue of keeping young people off the streets in London was part of a larger process of constructing space and movement within the city. The East End was 'opened' up to the middle and upper classes through the settlement movement and other voluntary activities that allowed the respectable to go to the 'dangerous' parts of the city under the banner of social work and research.[14] At the same time the West End was constructed as a space for discerning middle- and upper-class women to gain an intimate knowledge of the most sophisticated leisure spots and purveyors of fine goods.[15] Soho emerged as a Bohemian space in the late nineteenth century. By the 1920s, Soho became a centre for the queer community; the film industry in the 1930s; writers and edgy young people in the 1940s and 1950s.[16] It offered a different variety of 'danger' to that of the East End, but a disruption and a danger nonetheless. The youthful working classes were vulnerable within their own districts, some of which bordered on or formed part of this desirable centre. Yet they were also vulnerable or out of place if they were seen as unsupervised or without a 'respectable' purpose, like paid employment, in these spaces.

As Erika Rappaport writes, the promotion of tea by the temperance movement as a wholesome alternative to alcoholic drinks in early Victorian Britain was part of a broader process of addressing concerns about the impacts of industrialization and the globalization of taste on the working classes.[17] The National Temperance League supported temperance coffee bars as an alternative to the public house from 1856. By 1884, there were 667 coffee public houses.[18] The temperance agenda did not wane in interwar Britain. Hugh D. McIntosh, a British-Australian entrepreneur, opened the first milk bar in 1935 in Fleet Street as an alternative to a public house. Indeed, Canon Dick Sheppard, a well-known London cleric and temperance advocate, officially opened the bar. As in the case of Victorian coffee shops, temperance often inspired successful mass market ventures and McIntosh developed a chain of 'Black and White' Milk Bars from this original point in Fleet Street.[19] Competition came from the Griffiths brothers' National Milk Bars and the hotelier Charles Fortes's Strand Milk Bars and Meadow Milk Bars.[20] Independent milk bars were also common. All were regulated by the Milk Marketing Board, for whom milk bars were a useful way of marketing a child's drink to adults.[21] In Australia and the US milk bars encouraged the consumption of a non-alcoholic drink in a bar-like setting. In Britain this form of consumption challenged British eating habits. A *Times* article of 1935 outlined the innovation: 'The new way in Fleet Street is to go up to the open bar, order one of the drinks enumerated on a panel, receive it within a few seconds, pay 4d to the white uniformed "barmaid", enjoy the beverage, and walk out.' This was not a particularly social form of consumption.[22] Milk bars appeared threatening because they destabilized the sense of a 'traditional' café or restaurant, and catered to a more transient, less supervised clientele.

In February 1948, the Lord Mayor of London's office received a letter from an irate resident of Battersea in South London, complaining about the policing of the milk bar on Fleet Street. Fleet Street in the City of London was home to newspaper head offices and print works. The writer spoke of how, before World War II, he had frequented a Lyons tea shop for his breaks as it was close to his office and stayed open all night. That establishment now closed earlier and he was forced to use the milk bar in question or a 'small café of doubtful reputation'. The writer felt his breaks were disturbed by 'frequent scenes created by [the] motley rabble of men and women that drift into our boundaries from the West End every night, remaining until the Milk Bar closes at 4.50 a.m. and then moving on to a nearby place'. Two incidents prompted the letter: first, the writer and a colleague were accosted at knifepoint for money just outside the milk bar, and, second, 'a gang of ruffians [fighting] in the middle of Fleet Street'. The writer took additional umbrage at the sight of other print workers enjoying this spectacle whilst they took a break from work.[23]

This letter reveals the tensions that emerged when different age and social groups attempted to use the same facilities. Here, the letter-writer felt no option other than to stray into what criminologists have dubbed a 'night-time economy',[24] aimed at a more working-class audience, or, as the writer put it, the 'motley rabble'. The writer felt threatened, literally by a knife and potential robber, but also in the sense of entering a world with different rules and mores to the more 'cultured' one he inhabited. His response to this world was highly classed; he felt anxious at being within the disordered world of the working classes. Sir Hugh Turnbull, the Police Commissioner for the City of London, responded to the Lord Mayor the following month, emphasizing that the café's clientele were manual workers employed in the print trade and local markets, both of which were more nocturnal in their routines. Additionally, he noted it was 'common, particularly at week-ends, to find young people of both sexes from East London calling there for a snack on their way home from Dance Halls and such places in the West End'. The Commissioner agreed that these customers were 'inclined to be noisy and perhaps rough in manner but not more than is to be expected at cafés catering for the working class'.[25] Turnbull's response was intended to put the original letter into context and to affirm that anarchy was not breaking out on Fleet Street in the early hours. Yet it pointed equally to a 'classed' world of places, spaces and times. The letter-writer, deprived of access to a workplace canteen or a 'respectable' place to go for a snack, was the one out of place in this night-time world.

Although milk bars had originally been seen as a place for the consumption of 'healthy' drinks, by the 1950s they were associated with the more subtle processes of social and cultural change, particularly the new consumption behaviours they encouraged. Much of this debate centred on the introduction of juke boxes into cafés and other establishments and what this was doing to British society. A 1956 *Daily Mirror* article discussed the 'juke box invasion' and suggested the insertion of silent records into juke boxes to provide a break in the music. It used the language of epidemics and warfare to suggest that the British tradition of enjoying a pint or fish and chips in silence or to the sound of conversation was becoming a thing of the past, as Elvis Presley and Frank Sinatra were blasted out of the juke box. A West End café owner claimed, 'Psychologically it is interesting. People do not seem to be able to sit around a silent machine. They feel compelled to keep it going.' Critics saw this blind acceptance of juke boxes as an assault on British traditions.[26] Yet, as commercial ventures, milk bars attracted a youthful clientele who wanted a chance to socialize outside of the parental home and consume food and drinks whilst listening to the latest pop records.[27]

The milk bar model of rapid counter service began to change the shape of the more formal and 'traditional' tea and coffee houses. The Lyons Corner House chain offered a combination of sit-down restaurant for meals or simply tea and coffee. In 1954 it worked with US entrepreneur Eddie Gold to try out a new model for providing burgers and other 'American'-style fare through a 'fast-food' style ethos at its Coventry Street branch in London. This experiment was successful and developed into the Wimpy chain of cafés/restaurants.[28] Certainly the food on offer in Wimpy bars, milk bars, cafés and the like appealed to the young – but so did the more relaxed and informal atmosphere. Yet while customers enjoyed these new types of café, the popular press bemoaned its impact on the 'traditional' providers who were forced to innovate to appeal to youngsters' desire for modern and hygienic fish and chips.[29] Cafés and restaurants that embraced this new style were popular, but not beyond suspicion or criticism.

The post-war concerns about youthful public consumption began during World War II when all aspects of family, social and working lives were disrupted. Those young people who were too young to be called into the services yet too old to be evacuated were one source of concern. Their parents were engaged in war work or serving in the armed forces; schooling was disrupted; youth clubs and organizations were shut down or running a skeleton service as leaders were conscripted or members were evacuated.[30] As the war progressed, concerns about the growing appeal of 'American' ways of consumption grew as US servicemen introduced the young to chewing gum, comics, different brands of cigarettes and a sense of an exotic Americana.[31] Concerned adults looked for solutions to the 'problem' of unsupervised young people and their exposure to 'inappropriate' adults.

Eating habits also shifted because of rationing as well as fitting in meals around war work. The exigencies of war provided space for a particular section of reformist voluntary action to expand. As James Vernon argues, from the early twentieth century the canteen was seen as a hygienic and effective means of feeding a large number of people at any one time, improving nutrition and encouraging better table manners. British Restaurants, set up at the start of World War II, provided canteen-style catering for Britons. Some were run by local authorities, others by volunteers.[32] These canteens enabled charities and voluntary groups to provide an alternative to home cooking or other commercial vendors and to pass on their message about better food choices. The aim was to provide nutritious food in an environment which imparted 'better' values to its users, encouraging healthier eating and more genteel behaviour, in contrast to the 'valueless' or weaker standards of commercial offerings.

British Restaurants continued after the war in various forms as the government and organizations looked for new roles for volunteers and their services in the post-war world. Restaurants across the country altered opening hours to enable use by young people in the evenings, with varying degrees of success. In Brighton, young people went in after a trip to the cinema and 'would settle down with cups of tea, sandwiches and magazines'. In Bath organizers saw the restaurant space appealed to groups of unruly young people, many of whom avoided spending any money on food whilst there. The Pinner version used a British Restaurant space to bring in bands to entertain the youth who appeared more interested in their own conversations than the entertainment.[33] Success, defined as the regular use of the centres by young people without too much contestation by adults, depended on the quality of organization. British Restaurants were established by the Ministry of Food, but were run by local committees of volunteers. Thus each restaurant was shaped by its local context as well as the availability of appropriate volunteers. Sometimes the volunteers had expertise working with youth; in other situations volunteers were experts at providing rationed food and drink. Some were dismayed by the young people who used the café for purposeless chatter and general 'hanging about', activities that usually took place on street corners, rather than participating in 'improving' activities. These critics assumed informal, unstructured chatter had no function, or only a deleterious one.

At the end of the war, the London County Council (LCC) Youth Committee, consisting of youth workers (some from the charities sector) and representatives from local government agencies, wanted to develop a facility to provide the pleasures of a café but with suitable adult supervision. The LCC was particularly concerned about the youth in the Holborn and Kings Cross districts of Central London. Holborn youth could walk into the West End and into the presence of numerous public houses, nightclubs and general decadence. Indeed, Kings Cross was a known centre for prostitution. Social workers were concerned that, by hanging around in the same cafés as prostitutes, pimps, gamblers, the intoxicated and other dubious types, the young were vulnerable to aping their behaviour or being recruited into sex work and the like. Proximity to these cafés of 'doubtful reputation' was exacerbated by a lack of youth clubs or other facilities for the young. The proposed LCC café club, funded by the council's education and youth budgets, would be run by someone with training or experience in youth work, and 'an interest in young people, together with an ability to win their confidence'.[34] The café would offer benevolent, supervised consumption, and discreetly steer patrons away from the pleasures of other forms of consumption, serving as a form of moral rescue. The café was not for all youth, just those not otherwise involved in youth organizations or making their own, constructive, leisure activities.

This desire to police young people's informal use of these commercial social spaces continued through the 1950s and 1960s and was fuelled by university-trained social and youth workers keen to move away from more traditional methods of youth work – the formal, organized club or the uniformed organization – to try to appeal to the excluded youth or those who excluded themselves. These youngsters were known as 'unclubbables' or later 'unattached youth'. Outreach to this group was known as 'detached' youth work.[35] In late 1947, a discussion group was formed in East London, led by a probation officer and two voluntary youth workers who had met through the networks provided by the university settlement movement, which had been involved in youth work since the 1880s.[36] Discussions about the needs of 'at risk' youth led to various outreach experiments involving the spaces where the 'unclubbables' congregated as an alternative to traditional youth club environments. Having seen a number of young men spending their time at a coffee stall, the voluntary youth workers started to befriend them. The group later bought their own coffee stall, although the local council refused them a vendor license.[37] Other members of this group were, however, able to develop this idea of using the spaces and places young people used in order to reach them, most notably the Paddington YWCA London Coffee Stall Project in the later 1950s and early 1960s.[38] Again, these projects targeted marginalized youth rather than all young people.

In 1955, the Dulwich College Mission (founded in the 1880s) based in Elephant and Castle, experimented with setting up their own 'teen canteen'. This canteen took its inspiration from the Rotary Clubs of America who set up their own 'teen canteens' as an alternative to commercial milk bars.[39] The Dulwich canteen was reliant upon grants from the London Parochial

Charities foundation, as it was not financially self-sustaining.[40] The canteen appealed to young people in general but was used predominantly by boys who usually came in large groups. Generally, canteen openings passed without incident. Occasionally the manager saw the potential for violence if the youngsters brought bicycle chains and knives with them.[41] A survey undertaken by the manager found that only ten per cent of the canteen users earned more than £7 per week: for most, their leisure pursuits revolved around the canteen, going to the cinema a couple of times a week, walking around the streets and perhaps dancing.[42] A *Daily Mirror* feature about the canteen uncovered the boys' exclusion from local cafés and cinemas, and the sense that before the canteen opened they expected to be unwanted and bored.[43] These were working-class teenagers, far from the affluent, 'teenage consumers' of Abrams' imagination. The teen canteen provided a sympathetic space for them to express themselves, without the strictures of youth club activity programmes, religion or a harsh set of rules.[44]

Café experiments continued throughout the 1960s, following the high-profile experiment under the auspices of Youth Ventures Limited, a Quaker charity in Leicester and run by Ray Gosling, a young and unhappy university student.[45] Gosling had befriended various local youth, and thus was chosen to run a café for profit to finance other youth services. Whilst the project attracted much media attention, it soon failed to raise enough capital and there were tensions with the police and local criminals, as well as with the young people who used it. Although Gosling was energized by the experience and its potential to put young people in control of their lives, he felt that he was not 'strong or big or clever enough' to keep the project together.[46] The ultimate aim was to empower young people and make them responsible for the café. It failed because this aim did not match up with the expectations of the café in practice, which were far more in tune with creating a more 'respectable' endeavour. Café experiments continued. In Bethnal Green, a London Youth Committee worker and the Warden of Eastbourne House community centre used the local cafés to make connections with young people deemed not to be making good use of their time. They did this subtly, taking time to build relationships and allowing the young people to initiate conversations.[47] The youth associated with café culture and on the street corners of Bethnal Green were seen as dangerous, requiring careful handling to build trust. Eventually, social workers ascertained these young people wanted a non-commercial space to use – at least some of the time – and that they felt excluded from the existing services.[48] Social workers took over a disused church hall, enlisting the help of the youth while also encouraging them to start using local youth clubs, and working to spark interest in those considered 'hardcore'. This project was funded from LCC grants and the local borough council. For the more recalcitrant youth, social workers appealed to their interests – motorcycles and scooters. After checking the legitimacy of ownership and the licenses for the vehicles, the social workers took the group to a racing track on the outskirts of London in Cricklewood. The youths set up their own garage for working on their scooters and socializing.[49] This was a small-scale project aimed to support those deemed in greatest need rather than an attempt to change the social lives of young people on the whole.

The Bethnal Green experiment was about diverting young people from their 'problematic' use of commercial leisure spaces into more congenial non-commercial spaces. Other projects, such as the YWCA Coffee Stall in Paddington, used a commercial space to befriend young people and support them by helping them access the welfare services they needed. The Coffee Stall opened in June 1959, and the young people gradually came to accept the team running it as people who were genuinely interested in helping them rather than a 'police front'. Others thought the endeavour was a tax dodge. The stall workers soon found that it was not just 'unattached' young people who wanted to connect with them. Lonely adults from nearby bedsits 'returned night after night for coffee and a pie, a shilling for the meter, or change for a telephone call, and often found it difficult to stop pouring out their life stories'.[50] For the stall workers, this conflicted with the requirements of their project funding. Nevertheless, it demonstrates that personal consumption is primarily a social act. Buying a cup of coffee requires social interaction on both parts, and the congeniality of the exchange plays an important role in encouraging the customer to return. To go to a café to buy something to eat or drink is to force a social interaction – and generally a respectful one. Adults who viewed young people's patronage of cafés as corrupting and/or disruptive were overly narrow.

The Hoxton Café Project was likewise an attempt to try to engage with teenagers who were excluded from youth clubs and hung around the streets or used commercial cafés. The Hoxton café grew out of previous efforts, including a club based on a Thames barge at Wapping and a club in Hoxton. The café project was supported by leading figures in the East London voluntary work scene, Lady Cynthia Colville and Basil Henriques, who both served as magistrates at the East London Juvenile Court.[51] The capital outlay for the project came from the Gulbenkian Foundation, the London Parochial Charities and the LCC grants fund. Salaries were paid through an Inner London Education Authority grant.[52] The café opened every evening and provided the usual café fare. The intended clientele was the youth of the area, not adults.[53] This was not the only difference between this café and the others in the area: another was that young people's behaviour was not controlled in the café. Although the manager intervened to stop the most anti-social behaviour, the youth were generally allowed to do as they pleased in that space. The idea was to not judge behaviour as bad or to require engagement in a regimented programme (as would happen in one of the clubs in the local area). Rather, the café allowed the youth to make decisions about their own behaviour and the impact on others as staff modelled respectful behaviour. By treating the young people as adults, their behaviour improved.[54] The Hoxton café, much like the teen canteen in south London, created a safe and empathetic space where the young could act out, and like the Coffee Stall project, gain access to the public services they needed. It was also a project that needed support from charitable or local government funding, as it was not financially viable. By this point in the 1960s, the emphasis in youth work in London was less on keeping young people away from bad influences, but more on encouraging those on the margins to build up their confidence in dealing with adult society and its institutions.

The café was a space in which young working-class people's presence was contested, and, in this way, became a site for the politics of youth and identity. Where young people and their interests were embraced, some adults could find fault with juke boxes or changes in the ways in which food was prepared and served, a signal of an 'England' that was changing – yet consuming in these spaces was less threatening than not consuming. Young people's café culture – and indeed street cultures – could feel like a frightening, anarchic world to adults. This spoke to concerns about 'Americanization' on one hand, but also a generational fear of an unspecified decline. Youth café culture could be as much about rejecting 'adult' forms of sociality as about being rejected from other venues, commercial or otherwise. Going to a café in the late 1950s or early 1960s did not have the political connotations of the eighteenth-century coffee-house, but the act of carving out an autonomous space for self-expression was political in its own way – and, as the example of Gosling showed, obtaining this autonomy was a task in itself. Whilst to adult eyes the young appeared to be 'doing nothing' in the cafés, they were very much doing something – socializing, networking, participating in relationships. They were also able to inhabit a space that looked like a commercial leisure environment, but one in which *not* consuming or consuming less than a commercial enterprise would require was allowed. If not consuming set these young people apart from their peers, these simulations of the commercial youth culture provided an opportunity for them to be brought into this 'normal' world. When the least affluent teenagers refused to participate in more formal and established organizations, the need to provide 'rational recreation' was articulated by youth workers. Those in need were the least affluent working-class teenagers, typically boys, who were more likely to be excluded from the fullest range of entertainments and more likely to be hanging around without suitable adult supervision. Girls were somewhat peripheral to this but not absent. Unlike the boys, there were fewer fears about their propensity to violence and youthful energies. The post-war experiments in London are significant because they are rooted in the longer traditions of voluntary work undertaken in the capital and supported by philanthropic foundations and overseen by very well-respected and long-established figures in the field of youth social work. The contrast between deprived youth in the working-class areas of the inner cities and the affluence and bright lights of the centre of London was sharp. The evidence suggests the youth enjoyed these services and found they enriched their social lives, particularly when the 'moral' social work was kept in the background. Where the moral social work was present, it was to provide an alternative script for those excluded from mainstream youth culture and activities. It was also built on an awareness that reaching the lonely or the isolated required exploring the spaces in which they moved and engaging with them on their terms. This awareness also required rethinking the way communities were constructed. Milk bars and cafés were not merely the places where young people went to dress up and show off; they were also spaces where many had the opportunity to 'do nothing' while casually building social skills and confidence outside of the parental home or school. If reformers were concerned about the exclusion of young people from the mainstream, then the solution was to try to reach out to them through an alternative space that looked very much like this tempting commercial norm.

NOTES

1. See James Walvin, *Leisure and Society 1830–1950* (London: Longman, 1978); Peter Bailey, *Leisure and Class in Victorian England: Rational Recreation and the Contest for Control 1830–1885* (London: Methuen, 1987); F. M. L. Thompson, 'Social Control in Victorian Britain', *Economic History Review* 34 (1981) pp. 189–208.
2. See Sandra Trudgen Dawson, *Holiday Camps in Twentieth-Century Britain: Packaging Pleasure*, Studies in Popular Culture (Manchester: Manchester University Press, 2011).
3. See David Downes, *The Delinquent Solution: A Study in Subcultural Theory* (London: Routledge and Kegan Paul, 1966). Downes posed as a writer in East London cafés to meet 'delinquent' youths.
4. David Fowler, *Youth Culture in Modern Britain, c. 1920–c. 1970* (Basingstoke: Palgrave Macmillan, 2008), pp. 66–9.

5. Peter Bird, *The First Food Empire: A History of J. Lyons and Co.* (Chichester: Phillimore, 2000), pp. 99–100; Judith Walkowitz, *Nights Out: Life in Cosmopolitan London* (New Haven, CT: Yale University Press, 2012).

6. Melanie Tebbutt, *Being Boys: Youth, Leisure and Identity in the Inter-war Years* (Manchester: Manchester University Press, 2012), p. 238.

7. John Burnett, *Liquid Pleasures: A Social History of Drinks in Modern Britain* (London: Routledge, 1999), p. 89; Joe Moran, 'Milk Bars, Starbucks and *The Uses of Literacy*', *Cultural Studies* 20 (2006), p. 556; Frank Mort, *Cultures of Consumption: Masculinities and Social Space in Late Twentieth-Century Britain* (London: Routledge, 1996), p. 155; Peter Hennessey, *Having It So Good: Britain in the Fifties* (Harmondsworth: Penguin, 2007), p. 15.

8. See Burnett, *Liquid Pleasures*, p. 89; Adrian Horn, *Juke Box Britain: Americanisation and Youth Culture, 1945–60* (Manchester: Manchester University Press, 2009), *passim*; Hennessey, *Having It So Good*, p. 14.

9. Burnett, *Liquid Pleasures*, p. 89; Moran, 'Milk Bars', p. 555.

10. Richard Hoggart, *The Uses of Literacy: Aspects of Working-class Life* (Harmondsworth: Penguin, 2009); Catherine Ellis, 'The Younger Generation: The Labour Party and the 1959 Youth Commission', *Journal of British Studies* 41 (2002), p. 199.

11. Fowler, *Youth Culture*; Ellis, 'The Younger Generation'; Contemporary reflections include: Hoggart, *The Uses of Literacy*; T. R. Fyvel, *The Insecure Offenders: Rebellious Youth in the Welfare State* (Harmondsworth: Penguin, 1966).

12. Fowler, *Youth Culture*, p. 127.

13. 'There's Hope Among the Tea Cups in the Teen Canteen', *Daily Mirror*, 5 July 1955, p. 9.

14. See Seth Koven, *Slumming: Sexual and Social Politics in Victorian London* (Princeton, NJ: Princeton University Press, 2005); Jack London, *The People of the Abyss* (London: Pimlico, 2001); Seth Koven, 'The Dangers of Castle Building – Surveying the Social Survey', in *The Social Survey in Historical Perspective*, eds Martin Bulmer, Kevin Bales and Kathryn Kish Sklar (Cambridge: Cambridge University Press, 1991), pp. 368–76; Henrietta Barnett, *Canon Barnett: His Life, Work and Friends*, 2 Vols (London: John Murray, 1918); Asa Briggs and Anne Macartney, *Toynbee Hall: The First Hundred Years* (London: Routledge, 1984).

15. Erika Rappaport, *Shopping for Pleasure: Women in the Making of London's West End* (Princeton, NJ: Princeton University Press, 2000).

16. Mort, *Cultures of Consumption*, pp. 153–5.

17. Erika Rappaport, 'Sacred and Useful Pleasures: The Temperance Tea Party and the Creation of a Sober Consumer Culture in Early Industrial Britain', *Journal of British Studies* 52 (2013), pp. 990–1016.

18. Burnett, *Liquid Pleasures*, p. 87.

19. 'Will You Come Into My Milk Bar?', *Australian Women's Weekly*, 10 August 1935, p. 4.

20. 'Milk Bars March', *News Review*, 4 February 1937, p. 43.
21. London Metropolitan Archives (hereafter LMA) EO/HFE/4/203, Extract from *The Dairyman*, February 1951.
22. 'London "Milk Bar"', *The Times*, 2 August 1935, p. 9.
23. LMA COL/MH/AD/03/11/12 Mansion House Papers 1931–51, Correspondence with Police, 1947–57. Letter, 26 February 1948.
24. See Dick Hobbs, Philip Hadfield, Stuart Lister and Simon Winlow, *Bouncers: Violence and Governance in the Night-Time Economy* (Oxford: Oxford University Press, 2003). Hobbs et al. use 'night-time economy' to refer to the youth-oriented, alcohol-driven economy created by changing licensing laws in the 1990s, but there is something of this use in the night-time world of central London from the mid-twentieth century.
25. LMA COL/MH/AD/03/11/12 Mansion House Papers 1931–52, Correspondence with Police, 1947–57, Letter 17 March 1948.
26. 'Play Me Some Silence! It's the Newest Move in the Juke Box Invasion', *Daily Mirror*, 26 June 1956, p. 11.
27. Horn, *Juke Box Britain*, p. 162.
28. Bird, *First Food Empire*, p. 194.
29. 'Look What's Frying tonight!', *Daily Mirror*, 28 April 1960, p. 12. As John K. Walton notes, the process of modernizing the chip shop to shed its associations with the slums had been in progress from the early twentieth century. *Fish and Chips and the British Working Class, 1870–1940* (Leicester: Leicester University Press, 1992), pp. 98–100.
30. For a survey of these concerns, see John Welshman, 'Evacuation and Social Policy During the Second World War: Myth and Reality', *Twentieth Century British History* 9 (1998), pp. 28–53.
31. See, for example, Martin Barker, *A Haunt of Fears: The Strange History of the British Horror Comics Campaign* (Jackson, MS: University of Mississippi, 1992). Further discussion in Kate Bradley, 'Becoming Delinquent in the Post-War Welfare State: England and Wales, 1945–1965', in *Juvenile Delinquency and Western Modernity, 1800–2000*, ed. Heather Ellis (Basingstoke: Palgrave, 2014).
32. James Vernon, *Hunger. A Modern History* (Cambridge, MA: Belknap, 2007), pp. 166–80, 187–90.
33. LMA ACC 1888/91 LCSS Youth Cafe Club, Report on Evening Refreshment Centres, 16 April 1946.
34. LMA ACC 1888/91 Youth Cafe Club, 1946. Cafe Clubs. Report of the Joint Sub-Committee of the Borough Youth Committees of Holborn and St Pancras, 18 June 1946.
35. Accounts of such work includes: Barbara Ward, 'The Role of a Detached Youth Worker', in *Debate. A Collection of Professional Papers on the Future of Youth and Community Work in the 1970s* (Leicester: Youth Service Information Centre, 1969); Mary Blandy, *Harvest from Rotten Apples. An Account of Experimental Work with Detached Youth* (London: Victor

Gollancz, 1971); Alistair Cox and Gabrielle Cox, *Borderlines. A Partial View of Detached Youth Work with Homeless Young People* (Leicester: National Youth Bureau, 1977); Mark K. Smith, 'Detached, Street-based and Project Work with Young People', *Infed.org* http://infed.org/mobi/detached-street-based-and-project-work-with-young-people/ [accessed 11 July 2014].

36. M. Lloyd Turner, *Ship Without Sails: An Account of the Barge Boys' Club* (London: University of London Press, 1953), p. 3.
37. Peter Kuenstler, *Learning from Community: Oxford House in Bethnal Green, 1940–48* (London: Oxford House and the Settlements Social Action Research Group, 2004), pp. 40–1.
38. See Mark K. Smith, 'M. Joan Tash, Youth Work, and the Development of Professional Supervision', *Infed.org* http://infed.org/mobi/m-joan-tash-youth-work-and-the-development-of-professional-supervision/ [accessed 11 July 2014].
39. For example: Photographs, *The Rotarian* 66:4 (April 1945), p. 39; 'From Barracks to Youth Center', *The Rotarian* 73:1 (July 1948), pp. 39–41; 'Teen Canteen', *The Rotarian* 97:2 (August 1960), p. 45.
40. LMA ACC 1888/102 LCSS Dulwich College Mission Canteen, 'Relations with LCSS', 30 June 1958.
41. LMA ACC 1888/102, Memo 8 May 1958.
42. LMA ACC 1888/102, Memo 10 April 1958.
43. 'There's Hope Among the Teacups ... in the Teen Canteen', *Daily Mirror*, 5 July 1955, p. 9.
44. On the rules in youth clubs, see discussion in Katharine Bradley, *Poverty, Philanthropy and the State: Charities and the Working Classes in London, 1918–1979* (Manchester: Manchester University Press, 2009), pp. 110–11.
45. After this start in youth work, Gosling became a writer and broadcast journalist. See Esther Addley, 'Ray Gosling: A Writer, Film-maker and Activist with a Deep Interest in People', *Guardian*, 16 February 2010, http://www.theguardian.com/tv-and-radio/2010/feb/16/ray-gosling-writer-film-maker-activist [accessed 11 July 2014]; Robert Chalmers, 'Ray Gosling: The Outcast', *Independent*, 30 September 2012, http://www.independent.co.uk/news/people/profiles/ray-gosling-the-outcast-8181573.html [accessed 11 July 2014].
46. Ray Gosling, *Personal Copy: A Memoir of the Sixties* (Nottingham: Five Leaves, 2010), pp. 60–74; also 'Dream Boy', *New Left Review* 1 (1960), pp. 30–4; and *Lady Albemarle's Boys*, (London: Fabian Society, 1961).
47. LMA ACC/1888/091 London Youth Committee Minutes 1957–1963. 1 July 1963. Agenda item 5, Appendix A, G. H. Jones, Experiment in Bethnal Green 1961 to December 1962, p. 1.
48. Ibid., p. 1.
49. Ibid., pp. 2–3.
50. LMA ACC 1888/100 LCSS Youth Coffee Stall Project. Coffee Stall Project Report, 1960-3, pp. 1–3.

51. See Turner, *Ship Without Sail*, p. 8; *The Hoxton Café Project, Report No. 1* (London: Hoxton Café Project, c. 1963).
52. *The Hoxton Café Project, Report No. 1* (London: Hoxton Café Project, c. 1963), p. 3; H. M. Holden, *Hoxton Café Project: Report on Seven Years* (Leicester: Youth Services Information Centre, 1972), p. 6.
53. Barrie M. Biven and Hyla M. Holden, 'Hoxton: Informal Youth Work in a Cafe Setting', in *True Pretences. Psychodynamic Work with the Lost, the Angry and the Depressed*, ed. Barrie M. Biven (Leicester: Matador, 2005), p. 249.
54. Ibid., pp. 250–1, 58–9.

CHAPTER SIX

Teenagers, Photography and Self-Fashioning, 1956–65

PENNY TINKLER

The amateur photos in Figure 6.1 are from the albums of two young English women who turned 18 in the period 1956 to 1965. The first belongs to Elizabeth (born 1938) and was one of a series taken between 1956 and 1957 when she was in her late teens and attending teacher training college; Elizabeth is on the far right. The other photo belongs to Irene (born 1946) and was one of several holiday snaps taken in 1965 when she

Figure 6.1. Teenagers: (a) Elizabeth (1957) and (b) Irene (1965). Private Collection.

was preparing to go to university; Irene is on the far left. These two group portraits of teenagers seem to portray very different experiences of being young women. Irene's photo is in colour; it features a mixed-sex group of three couples, wearing drainpipe jeans and leaning into each other in a relaxed and intimate manner. In contrast, Elizabeth's black and white photo features eight young women performing with props for the camera; they wear dresses, or skirts and blouses, and low-heeled court shoes or, as in Elizabeth's case, 'sensible' flat shoes. Underlying these visible differences there are, however, important similarities. Elizabeth and Irene were both middle-class girls who lived at home and remained in education until their twenties; as a result they had very limited free time and personal income. Although an increasing proportion of teenagers stayed in education beyond the school-leaving age of 15, in 1961 only 19.6 per cent of 15- to 18-year-olds were in secondary school in England and Wales (12.5 percent in 1951), and in 1962 only 7 per cent of 19-year-olds remained in full-time education (principally higher education). Although women predominated in teacher training, they represented less than a quarter of university students.[1] Both Elizabeth and Irene came of age during a time when young people were perceived as a distinct social group, noted for consuming time and money in ways that differed significantly from their parents.[2]

Youth and consumption are interlinked histories in the 1950s and 1960s.[3] According to Donnelly, in the early 1950s young people dressed like and listened to the same music as their parents, but by the mid-1950s a distinctive youth-oriented culture that revolved largely around consumption became visible.[4] The advent of rock and pop music, jiving and the release of Bill Haley's film 'Rock Around the Clock' in 1956 have all been regarded as pivotal.[5] A widely publicised study of teenage spending by market researcher Mark Abrams claimed that there were roughly five million teenagers in Britain in 1959 (defined as single people aged 15 to 24 years), four million of whom were at work and earning comparatively high wages.[6] According to Abrams, the late 1950s witnessed a growth in 'distinctive teenage spending for distinctive teenage ends' and a proliferation of goods and services targeted at young people.[7] Although historians state that not all young people were affluent (a point acknowledged by Abrams), they agree that, in general, young people in full-time work were relatively more affluent than their predecessors and that this gave them greater consumer power and independence at an earlier age than in previous decades.[8] High profile youth subcultures contributed to the visibility and distinctive image of youth, as did the emergence of commercially available youth fashions. Although the figure of the teenager is synonymous with consumption (particularly of music and fashion) in the historiography of youth, there is surprisingly little about the diversity and detail of young people's relationship to consumer culture in this period.[9] Moreover there is little work on middle-class youth who tended to stay in school until later than their working-class peers: Osgerby goes so far as to claim that middle-class young people 'were, for the most part, external to (and often alienated from) a youth culture which was, in essence, a working-class experience'.[10] A relative decline in middle-class incomes from 1938 contributed to the blurring of working- and middle-class lifestyles, but occupation and education continued to mark social differences. In 1951, according to McKibbin, the middle class was 'predominantly a technical-scientific-commercial-managerial class'.[11] An extended education was, therefore, a recognized marker of middle-class youth.

As members of this overlooked group, Elizabeth and Irene's photos invite us to rethink the class-based nature of the so-called teenage consumer. Their experiences parallel those of another British teenager, leisure historian Peter Bailey, when he was 18 and on the brink of going to university in 1955.[12] Drawing on autobiographical reflection and his teenage diaries, Bailey presents a 'tale of adolescent bricolage' which combined the modernity of a meritocratic education system and the 'slightly deviant' modernity offered by American jazz and his identity as a jazz pianist in a local band. Because of their gender and upbringing, Elizabeth and Irene had less scope for 'deviant' self-fashioning than Bailey, but their photographic practices illuminate the subtle and fleeting aspects of their adolescent bricolage.

PHOTOGRAPHY: A LENS FOR RESEARCH

Researchers have approached the relationship between photography and consumption in four main ways. First, we have studies of how photography has helped market consumer goods and services by inducing desire and generating the 'spectacle' that has been central to consumer culture since the 1850s.[13] Second, scholars have also looked at the photographic industry, focusing both on professional photographers and the companies that dominated sales of cameras and film.[14] The launch of the Kodak camera in 1888 heralded the separation of the processes of taking photos and developing them, and facilitated the expansion of amateur photography into a mass market. Marketing then aligned photography with the performance of family, the preservation of memories, and the construction of individual identities. Third, researchers have used photography to investigate aspects of consumption. Humphrey Spender's covert photographs for Mass Observation in the 1930s and 1940s are a notable example. Spender photographed a range of everyday practices including the use of pubs, leisure pursuits and the activities of traders and shoppers in local markets.[15] More recently, interviewers use photos as prompts to explore consumer preferences and practices.[16] Finally, scholars have considered how people use cameras and photos and the meanings attached to practices such as taking, buying and collecting photos; developing them; looking at them; distributing, storing and displaying them.[17] Initially adult-focused, scholarship has more recently illuminated the diversity of young people's experiences, including how young women expressed and managed the processes of growing up.[18]

Photography is a particularly useful lens for exploring the consumer perspectives of middle-class girls in the 1950s and 1960s. Though there are no statistics on girls' camera use, the prevalence can be gauged from meshing general consumer patterns and oral and visual evidence. By the 1960s, roughly half of UK households owned one or more cameras; in 1970, one in three people aged between 10 and 70 used a camera.[19] The photo collections of middle-class girls in the 1950s and 1960s, which frequently depict friends with cameras, suggest that photography was commonplace in this group. The Bakelite Kodak Brownie 127, introduced in 1952, was very popular. In 1963 it cost 25s 9d, which was affordable by many teenage workers.[20] Cameras were frequently given as gifts. Irene's parents gave her a Brownie 127 for Christmas, while another middle-class girl – Erin – was given one when she passed the Eleven Plus entrance exam for her local grammar school. Erin recalled: 'I was so proud. It came in a box and I can just smell that box now … it had a case and a film.'[21] Girls also borrowed cameras, commissioned professional portraits at studios or in department stores, and used photo booths.[22] They took, commissioned and collected photos that recorded fleeting aspects of identities and small and ephemeral details that may once have been important but have since been forgotten. These practices make visible elusive aspects of 'adolescent bricolage'.

Unlike autobiographies and oral histories that provide an adult perspective on being a teenager, we can study girlhood photo collections to reveal girls' priorities, interests and aspects of their youthful agendas. The details of the images – the clothes, the photos' composition and location – are, to a large degree, what the photographer/sitters wanted to convey about themselves. Young people were often responsible for buying film and developing their prints; the limits imposed by cost probably led them to think carefully about what they photographed. A roll of film contained 8 or 12 exposures and, even as late as 1974, the film industry considered three films *per year* to be a high rate of usage (i.e. 24–36 exposures in total).[23] Through the compilation of an album, we can think about the decisions girls made about inclusion, captioning and presentation.[24]

I researched the photo collections that a sample of middle-class women, born between 1938 and 1946, collected during their youth in the 1950s and 1960s.[25] These collections were principally for personal use; although the intended viewers probably included friends and possibly parents, my interviewees did not recall showing their albums to others. I also used photo-interviews to tease out the meanings associated with photographic practices. To make sense of girlhood photos involved working through several moments of meaning-making: the production of the photo; its captioning and presentation; and the photo-interview in which the photographer-owners, now in their sixties and seventies, talked to me about their photos.

While there were well-established conventions for photographing families, influenced by professional and commercial photography, including the advertising of cameras and photographic films, this was not the case with peer photography.[26] However, young people's picture taking did not appear in a social or cultural vacuum. In particular they seem to have adopted codes from cinema, periodicals and other forms of popular visual culture. The lack of formal photographic conventions may, however, have given girls scope for creativity and frivolity: they pulled humorous and grotesque faces and posed in unconventional ways; they played with identities and enacted scenarios. Friend photography also constructed identities that were independent of the family and expressed different types of belonging – to friends and to a wider 'imagined community' of young people.[27] Young people's specific needs and interests may explain why some looked to popular and commercial culture for inspiration when taking photos. Some of these cultural resources were mobilized in Elizabeth and Irene's photos.

ELIZABETH'S PHOTOS

Elizabeth's college photos, taken in 1956–7, reveal the possibilities of photography to assert her identity and autonomy.[28] The photos appear in an album compiled around the time she went to university in 1960 (age 22). The album is roughly chronological; the college photos are preceded by pictures of friends taken in her early teens, and succeeded by photos from her early twenties, prior to her marriage in 1963. The photos bear the marks of having been previously displayed in another context. Sets of photos were arranged artistically but secured in place with pieces of sticky tape. Several moments of meaning-making are represented. I address the taking of the photos in 1956–7, the addition of captions across the bottom of each and their arrangement in an album in 1960. Finally I consider how Elizabeth remembered their significance in a recent photo-interview.

Figure 6.2. Elizabeth's college photographs. Private Collection.

Elizabeth's college photos hint at the tension between freedom of expression and regulation that characterized her life at this time. On one occasion, Elizabeth collaborated with two friends to produce six photos staged in the college grounds (Figure 6.2, Elizabeth appears in photos numbered 3–5). The bench photo (no. 5) and the picture of the young woman on the stairs (far right) seem conventional portraits. The other four photos were clearly not intended solely or even primarily as portraits but as staged commentaries on college life. We will never know precisely what Elizabeth and her friends thought when they took these photos, but, at the point of arranging them, Elizabeth's captions conveyed the college's exclusivity and prison-like regulations. The two seemingly conventional photos were transformed from portraits to statements; the stair photo depicted the 'open prison' that was the college. The meaning of doors was articulated: the photo of the young woman seeking entry read 'Do not cast me out'; the two friends at the main entrance were labelled 'The Swiss Guards'; while Elizabeth's appearance at the front door was captioned, 'Who's knocking at my door?' The last caption can be read in different voices, but it is tempting to adopt an imperious tone, not least because this resonates with the theme of the pictures and the tone of the 'yes' attributed to the imposing figure of Elizabeth looking down at the viewer (no. 3).

The staging, captioning and composition of the photos suggest Elizabeth was constructing herself as a rebel, if only symbolically. In the photo-interview, Elizabeth explained that leaving home was liberating, principally because she no longer lived with her violent stepfather. Her college days were not, however, free from constraints. She had no disposable income and remained financially dependent on her parents. Moreover, because her residential college were *in loco parentis*, restrictive rules regulated all aspects of her life.[29] 'It was terribly strict. If you went out in the evening you had to be back by five to ten. Which meant you couldn't even see a film to its end.' Elizabeth explained that there was 'always the threat of the personal assessment hanging over us', and a bad one led to difficulty in getting a job. While mindful of college rules, Elizabeth claims that she and her peers 'were rebellious and proud of it': 'We would question things, which was called "arguing". ... Previously young people were "seen and not heard".' It seems likely that Elizabeth's photos were underpinned by an awareness of popular discourses about a generation gap, and shaped by a desire to be part of an 'imagined community' of teenagers who asserted their distinctive perspectives and independence. It is also likely that hindsight and popular accounts of postwar youth informed Elizabeth's discussion of shifting age relations.

There was also a gender dimension to Elizabeth's symbolic rebellion. In Figure 6.1, for instance, Elizabeth and her friends posed with bottles and trays on which 'Double Diamond' – the brand name of a popular English beer – was written. Elizabeth could not explain the caption – 'We are the puffkins' – and there is no reference to 'puffkins' in print-media adverts; this may have been a private joke or reference to the portly cartoon figures that appeared in some Double Diamond promotions. The puffkin photo conveys the impression that Elizabeth and her friends were drinking beer, but Elizabeth explained that they were pretending to drink and, moreover, that this 'can't have been a college outing for us to be behaving like this'. Elizabeth did not drink alcohol at this time, but her comment suggests that it was considered unladylike for young women to make a public spectacle of themselves, especially by consuming alcohol from a bottle. Fifty years later, Elizabeth was still attuned to the rebelliousness of the pretence.

Elizabeth drew on popular and commercial culture for inspiration. An explicit example is her use of parody in the puffkin photo (Figure 6.1). She also imposed popular cultural references through captions, including clichés – 'just good friends' – and what appear to be advertising slogans – 'See Butlins and live', 'Take *your* holiday abroad' (emphasis in original). The caption of one photo – 'Still' – directly referenced the 'Running, Jumping and Standing Still Film' made by the Goons and released in Britain in 1960. There were also subtle ways in which cultural reference points were embedded in the photo collection. Elizabeth's efforts to produce and display a series of playful college photos suggests that she sought to construct herself as witty, slightly rebellious and as possessing a wry view of contemporary life including her status as a student. While it is not possible to pinpoint precisely the influences that informed this identity, the interview provided a clue to an over-arching identification. Commenting on the photo captioned, 'Standing Still', Elizabeth declared that she and her friends were 'Goon fans, of course'. This almost incidental reference seems key to understanding Elizabeth's college photos. The *Goon Show* was a British radio comedy programme, originally produced and broadcast between 1951 and 1960. The show's chief inspiration was Spike Milligan and the original 'gang' of four, including Milligan, Harry Secombe, Peter Sellers and Michael Bentine. It featured implausible storylines, weird sounds, surreal humour and the satirization of aspects of British life.[30] The Goons were not teenagers, but they were much younger than Elizabeth's parents and her college tutors and they also ridiculed the establishment associated with this generation. Imitating some of the antics of these men, Elizabeth and her friends flouted age-based systems of authority and notions of gender-appropriate behaviour.

Elizabeth's photos portray no visible markers of youth culture, but it would be misleading to assume she was external to it. Elizabeth remembers being immersed in popular music. She saw 'Rock Around the Clock' in 1956, although, contrary to press reports of frenzied young audiences, 'nobody tore up any seats or anything'.[31] Although she did not have a television at home for most of her youth – 'My mother thought it wouldn't catch on' – she watched the youth-oriented music programme, '6, 5 Special' (1957), when she was at college. She had a record player and 'heaps' of records, including those by Tommy Steele, who is credited with being the first British teenage idol following his success in 1956 with 'Caveman Rock'. Although adults may have listened to popular records, Elizabeth explained that music divided the generations; as a young woman she found it 'a matter of incomprehensibility that adults didn't know the top twenty'.

Elizabeth had little to say about her clothes, and she and her friends dressed 'sensibly', as seen in her photos. While Elizabeth could not afford to buy clothes, and relied on those her mother bought or those she made herself, this is only part of the explanation for her style. Some young women had distinctive styles, for instance, Teddy girls and some middle-class students who adopted a 'scruffy artistic and intellectual' style or one influenced by American Beat and French Bohemian fashions at this time.[32] A distinctively young female style associated with jiving was also discernible in teenage images from the late 1950s. A skirt to jive in was a quintessential element in a young woman's wardrobe in this period: 'We had taffeta skirts – that was a vogue when I was at college – with these multi-frilled underskirts that you starched in sugar. And then if you were dancing and got hot and sticky, the sugar started to stick to your legs.' Unfortunately, there are no photos of Elizabeth in her dance outfit.

Elizabeth's college photos did not feature visible markers of teenage style, but they were evidence of her search for ways to convey a distinctive, young and modern female identity. This is evident in her creative use of peer photography to express herself and critique age- and gender-based college regulations. It is also evident in her engagement with commercial culture, particularly advertising, and her emulation of the Goons' irreverent and zany outlook. We have already seen one example of how Elizabeth's photos compared to Irene's, but now I look more closely at Irene's collection. Do Irene's photos suggest a different articulation of identity and relationship to consumer and youth culture?

IRENE'S PHOTOS

In 1965, aged 18, Irene went on holiday with friends.[33] She had just finished school and was soon to start university. The holiday represented Irene's growing independence from her family as it was her first unsupervised holiday, albeit at a holiday camp run by the Methodist Church to which her family belonged (Figure 6.1). During this holiday Irene and her friends, especially her cousin Liz, took snaps that Irene later arranged in an album. The photo collection was a mnemonic device, but also a means to self-definition.

Whereas Elizabeth grew up in a period when 'the teenager' was emerging, Irene reached 18 at a time when youth was centre-stage in cultural terms. The first mass-production teenage glossy magazine, *Honey*, was launched in 1960. In 1962 the Beatles released 'Love Me Do' and by 1963 the band were attracting unprecedented crowds of young fans, a phenomenon described as 'Beatlemania'. A host of young British musicians and singers appeared in the UK pop charts, including the Rolling Stones who had their first UK no. 1 hit in July 1964. 'Ready Steady Go!' was launched in 1963 and, unlike previous music television programmes, it catered exclusively for young people.[34] Although the Teds faded from public view by 1960, the Mods and Rockers emerged and attracted extensive press coverage, especially when they 'invaded' coastal resorts or clashed in 1964.[35] Mod styles quickly influenced the newly emerged youth fashion industry, which grew rapidly in the early 1960s.

Irene and her friends seem the epitome of cool youth in the coffee-bar photo (Figure 6.1). This was partly because it was in colour, but also because it resonates with themes from contemporary commercial and popular imagery of friends – leisure, heterosociality, youthful style and physicality. Irene's pose is resonant of images from the 1950s and 1960s of Bohemians and Beatniks that appeared in newspapers, on television and in advertising targeted at young people.[36] Typically, young people were depicted sitting cross legged or with legs folded beneath them, sometimes on the floor. Their poses signified youthful rebellion because they defied the formalities of adult/traditional society and located the subject closer to the carefree experience of childhood rather than the responsibilities of adulthood. When engaged in by a young woman, the poses also transgressed codes of feminine conduct and hinted at sexual autonomy and self-definition, particularly if, as in Irene's photo, there were visible signs of physical intimacy between the sexes. The visibility of the coffee-bar sign also contributed to the image of cool teenagers. The coffee shop was the place for teenagers to meet in this period and was widely recognized by adults as a youth space.[37] Set in this context, the prominence of the words 'coffee bar' in the photo is significant as a marker of youth culture; the reference is reinforced further by the caption – 'Davey Jones' Locker (local coffee bar)'.

The coffee-bar photo is not, however, typical of Irene's holiday snaps. Her holiday was narrated through 21 photos: two professional large-group portraits of everyone at the holiday camp, and 19 other snaps, including 13 black-and-white photos taken on Irene's camera and six colour ones taken on Liz's camera. Two visual themes emerge in the album. The first is wholesome outdoor leisure in which young people go off on rambles and outings; this is conveyed in the bulk of the photos (see Figure 6.3). The second is 1960s' youth culture and emerges in only two photos: the coffee-bar photo and a picture taken of Irene and Liz ready to leave for their holiday dressed in the latest teen fashions. The photo-interview confirms the album's impression of two prominent themes and suggests a complex relationship between them. These themes correspond to two identities. First, the 'good girl', characterized by service, responsibility and application at school and at home. Second, the 'cool teenager', characterized by heterosociality, fun, leisure, self-expression (especially through style, physicality and movement), relative independence from parents and a willingness to question adult perspectives and authority.

Style is an important aspect of Irene's relationship to youth culture in the coffee-bar photo. There is, however, more to this than meets the eye; indeed, it is the product of considerable effort to construct a distinctively contemporary youthful look. As Irene explained: 'Mum used to get upset because I used to go up into the bedroom and take the stitching in down the sides [of my jeans]. And she used to say, "Have you taken those trousers

Figure 6.3. Irene's album: Wholesome outdoor leisure, 1965. Private collection.

in again?'" Irene's youthful look relied heavily on her dress-making skills as she had very limited money. Irene was not alone in this; other middle-class women that I interviewed also told tales of DIY style. Strategic consumerism was another means to engage in youth culture on a shoestring budget. A few well-chosen items of clothing – jeans, a skirt with multi-frilled petticoats – were enough to create a teenage look when it really mattered. This was an intermittent teenage look that facilitated participation in the fundamental activities of youth culture, especially dance and moments – such as the one photographed – when Irene constructed herself as a 'cool teenager'.

The cool, slightly radical pose that Irene struck in the coffee-bar photo speaks of her identification with a Bohemian culture that is critical of tradition and generational hierarchies; yet, as Irene explained, this was far from how she lived at the time. In everyday life Irene deferred to parental authority; she could not rebel because she was too religious. Although the coffee-bar photo suggested sexual sophistication, her relationships with boys were restrained. Irene believed firmly that sex was reserved for marriage and she lived in fear of getting pregnant, although she had no idea how babies were conceived.[37]

Irene's holiday was different from her everyday life when there was little time and space for commercial culture and being a 'cool teenager'. In everyday life, Irene's time was taken up with school and preparations for A-levels. She was intent on securing a place at university to study social work. Outside school lessons, Irene's time was occupied with rational recreation, including a host of communal activities, such as playing in the youth club band, being in the school choir and hockey team, learning the piano, and being a member of the Girls' Life Brigade. Her home life was framed by the Methodist Church and she went three times to church on Sunday, walking three miles each way. Irene straddled cultural worlds, but she was, nevertheless, a part-timer in youth culture. The coffee-bar photo gave visibility to Irene's identity as a 'cool teenager', but as the album and photo-interview reveal, she had other youthful identities that revolved around rational recreation and the Church; she was a 'good girl'. Irene commented that she was not a 'proper' teenager, but the coffee-bar photo is one of the few places where she succeeded in constructing and preserving this aspect of youth identity.

Elizabeth and Irene celebrated friendship and crafted identities through taking, collating and presenting photos of themselves and their friends. Their photographic practices highlight the creative consumption of young people and demonstrate its personal and historical significance. Irene and Elizabeth's use of photography was underpinned by historically specific discourses about the distinctiveness and modernity of post-war youth. This distinctiveness revolved around self-expression; an assertion of autonomy from adult authority at an earlier age than previous generations; and feeling part of an 'imagined community' of young people. Both fashioned slightly rebellious young and modern identities through an engagement with commercial and popular culture. Elizabeth's college photos referenced advertising and the humour of the Goons, while Irene's coffee-bar photo resonated with representations of 'cool' and anti-establishment youth cultures. These identities were, however, tenuous and fleeting. Elizabeth and Irene had very little personal income and experienced heavy demands on their time and energy. Their behaviour was also constrained by age- and gender-specific expectations and strictures. In one sense, both used photography to symbolically resist these curtailments. Importantly, Elizabeth's college photos and Irene's coffee-bar picture were not typical representations of their teenage identities. Their photos and the stories around them reveal co-existing and more prominent identifications, especially to family and Church, and other investments in modernity, notably education qualifications and a professional career. The college and coffee-bar photos are, however, a testimony to the ascendancy of an imagined community of (assertive) young people in British society in the late 1950s and 1960s. Personal photos suggest that rather than being on the margin of youth culture, middle-class young people, even girls with little time and money, participated in the creation of youth culture and its consumption.

ACKNOWLEDGEMENTS

I am extremely grateful to the women who participated in this study, especially Elizabeth and Irene (pseudonyms).

NOTES

1. John Davis, *Youth and the Condition of Britain: Images of Adolescent Conflict* (London: Athlone, 1990), p. 94; Ministry of Education, *Higher Education: Report*, Cd. 2154 (London: HMSO), p. 12, Table 1; Carol Dyhouse, *Students: A Gendered History* (London: Routledge, 2006), p. 87.
2. Bill Osgerby, *Youth in Britain since 1945*, (Oxford: Blackwell, 1998); Mark Donnelly, *Sixties Britain: Culture, Society and Politics* (Harlow: Pearson, 2005); Selina Todd and Hilary Young, 'Baby-boomers to "Beanstalkers": Making the Modern Teenager in Post-war Britain', *Cultural & Social History* 9:3 (2012), pp. 451–67; Catherine Ellis, 'The Younger Generation: The Labour Party and the 1959 Youth Commission', *The Journal of British Studies* 41:2 (2002), pp. 199–231.
3. Exceptions include Stephanie Spencer, *Gender, Work and Education in Britain in the 1950s* (Basingstoke: Palgrave Macmillan, 2005).
4. Donnelly, *Sixties Britain*, p. 26; Davis, *Youth*, p. 160.
5. Davis, *Youth*, pp. 160–5. See also: Simon Frith, *The Sociology of Rock* (London: Constable, 1978).
6. Mark Abrams, *Teenage Consumer Part II* (London: Exchange, 1961), p. 3.
7. Abrams, *Teenage Consumer*, p. 5.
8. Davis, *Youth*, pp. 120–2; Osgerby, *Youth in Britain*, pp. 24–6.
9. Exceptions include Bradley in this volume.
10. Osgerby, *Youth in Britain*, p. 27. See also Donnelly, *Sixties Britain*, p. 35.
11. Ross McKibbin, *Classes and Cultures: England 1918–1951* (Oxford: Oxford University Press, 2000), p. 49. Also see Jon Lawrence 'Class, "Affluence"

and the Study of Everyday Life in Britain, c. 1930–64', *Cultural & Social History* 10 (2013), pp. 273–300; Arthur Marwick, 'Class', in *A Companion to Contemporary Britain 1939–2000*, eds Paul Addison and Harriet Jones (Oxford: Blackwell, 2007), pp. 76–92.

12. Peter Bailey, 'Jazz at the Spirella – Coming of Age in 1950s Coventry', in *Moments of Modernity? Reconstructing Britain 1945–64*, eds Becky E. Conekin, Frank Mort and Chris Waters (London: Rivers Orams, 1999), pp. 22–40.

13. Thomas Richards, *The Commodity Culture of Victorian England: Advertising and Spectacle, 1851–1914* (Stanford, CA: Stanford University Press, 1990) and Anandi Ramamurthy 'Constructions of Illusion: Photography and Commodity Culture', in *Photography: A Critical Introduction*, ed. Liz Wells (London: Routledge, 2000), pp. 165–216.

14. For example: Val Williams, *Women Photographers: The Other Observers 1900 to the Present* (London: Virago, 1986); Don Slater, 'Consuming Kodak', in *Family Snaps: The Meanings of Domestic Photography*, eds Jo Spence and Patricia Holland (London: Virago, 1991), pp. 49–59.

15. Examples of Spender's photos can be viewed at http://boltonworktown.co.uk/photo-collection/ [accessed 25 September 2014].

16. Photo-elicitation is used in marketing and social science research, for example, Deborah Heisley and Sidney Levy, 'Autodriving: a Photoelicitation Technique', *Journal of Consumer Research* 18:3 (1991), pp. 257–72.

17. Penny Tinkler, *Smoke Signals: Women, Smoking and Visual Culture in Britain* (Oxford: Berg, 2006), pp. 23–4, 155–84. Alistair Thomson, *Moving Stories: An Intimate History of Four Women Across Two Countries* (Manchester: Manchester University Press, 2011); Patricia Holland, '"Sweet it is to Scan …": Personal Photographs and Popular Photography', in *Photography: A Critical Introduction*, ed. Liz Wells (London: Routledge, 2000), pp. 117–64; Jo Spence and Patricia Holland, *Family Snaps: The Meaning of Domestic Photography* (London: Virago, 1991); Marianne Hirsch, *Family Frames: Photography, Narrative and Postmemory* (Cambridge, MA: Harvard University Press, 1997); Marianne Hirsch, ed., *The Familial Gaze* (London: University Press of New England, 1999); Annette Kuhn, *Family Secrets: Acts of Memory and Imagination* (London: Virago, 2002); Annette Kuhn and Kirsten E. McAllister, eds, *Locating Memory: Photographic Acts* (New York and Oxford: Berghahn Books, 2006).

18. Penny Tinkler, 'A Fragmented Picture: Reflections on the Photographic Practices of Young People', *Visual Studies* 23 (2008), pp. 255–66; Penny Tinkler, '"Picture Me as a Young Woman": Researching Girls' Photo Collections from the 1950s and 1960s', *Photography & Culture* 3 (2010), pp. 261–82.

19. Michael Langford, *The Story of Photography: From its Beginnings to the Present Day* (London: Focal Press, 1980), p. 67; Kodak Archive, British Library, Box 43, A792, *Kodak Dealer* Spring 1972, p. 8.

20. Kodak advertisement, *Daily Express*, 3 May 1963, p. 16. According to Abrams, *Teenage Consumer*, p. 7, in 1959 the average working-class girl had

roughly 47 shillings a week spending money excluding board and lodgings, but most was spent on clothes.

21. Interviews: Irene, 20 February 2008; Erin, 21 May 2013.
22. In 1970, a Kodak survey reported that 11 per cent of all domestic photographs were taken by 8- to 16-year-olds and 53 per cent by women, although it is not possible to isolate young women in these figures. Kodak Archive, British Library, Box 43, A792, *Kodak Dealer* Spring 1972, p. 9.
23. Boots Archive, Nottingham, *Boots Film Service 1974* (n. p.). Thanks to Annebella Pollen for this reference.
24. Album titles could also be revealing, but none of my participants created these.
25. On photo-elicitation, see Penny Tinkler, *Using Photographs in Social and Historical Research* (London: Sage, 2013).
26. Spence and Holland, *Family Snaps*; Kuhn, *Family Secrets*; Martha Langford, 'Speaking the Album: An Application of the Oral-Photographic Framework', in *Locating Memory*, pp. 223–46; Hirsch, *Family Frames*; Tinkler, '"Picture Me"'.
27. Benedict Anderson, *Imagined Communities: Reflections on the Origins and Spread of Nationalism* (London: Verso, 1991).
28. All quotes from Elizabeth are from an interview, 26 February 2008.
29. Dyhouse, *Students*, pp. 126–8.
30. There were some TV shows and films, but these were less successful than the radio shows, http://en.wikipedia.org/wiki/The_Goon_Show [accessed 4 June 2013].
31. See Davis, *Youth*, pp. 160–4.
32. Adrian Horn, *Juke Box Britain: Americanisation and Youth Culture, 1945–60* (Manchester: Manchester University Press, 2009), pp. 142–60.
33. All quotes from Irene are from an interview, 20 February 2008.
34. John Hill 'Television and Pop: The Case of the 1950s', in *Popular Television in Britain: Studies in Cultural History*, ed. John Corner (London: BFI, 1991), pp. 90–107.
35. Stanley Cohen, *Folk Devils and Moral Panics. The Creation of the Mods and Rockers* (Oxford: Basil Blackwell, 1990); David Fowler, *Youth Culture in Modern Britain, c. 1920–c. 1970* (Basingstoke: Palgrave Macmillan, 2008).
36. For example: *Vanity Fair*, October (2) 1960, p. 68; *Vogue*, June 1954, p. 127; *Daily Mirror*, 9 August 1963, p. 9.
37. Horne, *Juke Box Britain*, pp. 103–4, 171–80. This was consistent with contemporary survey results. See Michael Schofield, *The Sexual Behaviour of Young People* (London: Little, Brown and Co., 1965).

CHAPTER SEVEN

Unwanted Consumers: Violence and Consumption in British Football in the 1970s

BRETT BEBBER

When football violence emerged in Britain in the mid-1960s as a social phenomenon and political problem it generated wide-ranging responses from politicians, the press, police authorities and the football industry.[1] These parties were especially worried about the problem of growing affluence among working-class men. Young labourers, thriving on the so-called British 'Age of Affluence', ostensibly had too much money and suffered from prolonged bouts of idleness and boredom.[2] Violence at football matches, these commentators contended, was a problem of consumption. Young men were not consuming football as a commodity in socially acceptable and culturally prescribed ways. Instead, as numerous sociologists and historians have since contended, various activities labelled as 'football hooliganism' centred on processes of masculine identity-formation, intersocial exploration and the reclamation of working-class meanings in Britain's most popular sport.[3] Violence became routine and often anonymous, linked to notions of territoriality, community pride and defending the home stadium from outsiders. Football supporters engaged in communal and exceptionally interactive forms of football watching, often leading to habitual battles with local police, fights with groups of rival spectators, and the destruction of private property within and around stadiums. In response, football clubs worked with local police and government authorities at the Home Office and the Department of the Environment to change the places and patterns of consumption in British football.

While changes to policing and sentencing strategies, along with the manipulation of architectural environments, have been discussed elsewhere, this chapter analyses efforts to promote forms of football consumption that avoided potentially violent activities.[4] Government and football authorities reasoned that distractions and new stimuli both inside and outside football grounds would redirect supporters' attention and potentially help avoid unwanted rowdyism. These initiatives attempted to instil disciplined attention and focus the sporting gaze in ways that reflected gendered and classed understandings of supposedly feeble-minded working-class men. Football violence disrupted not only the football industry, but sports tourism as well. British Rail, once simply a provider of regular transportation to and from matches for travelling fans, became implicated in policing the consumption of travel, as supporters extended their violent activities outside stadiums. Analysing the pricing and policing of British Rail 'special' trains (those designated for football travellers) reveals that the railway industry responded to the challenge of increased violence and criminality on trains by attempting to control the gendered consumption of sports travel.

Examining this episode in post-war British consumption reveals that conflicts over class- and gender-based consumption practices further divided consumers of leisure from producers and regulators, precisely at a time when many Britons identified consumption as a political act, and consumerism as a right.[5] Post-war Britain witnessed the rise of consumerism as a movement, helping individuals to understand their position as consumers within the market as they defended their ability to consume products and services in their own ways.[6] Football violence and the responses by football authorities, railway managers and government officials provides an aperture onto conflicts generated by anxieties about working-class men's consumption patterns and the gendered marketing of domestic sports travel, demonstrating how both public and private providers attempted to reshape those patterns to match socially constructed notions of proper masculine conduct.

FOOTBALL VIOLENCE, DISCIPLINE AND ATTENTION

Although violence at football matches appeared intermittently since the nineteenth century, it re-emerged regularly and as a serious challenge to politicians in the mid-1960s. John Clarke has shrewdly argued that a generational split occurred during this era, where younger spectators responded to commercial and professional advances in the industry by incorporating aggressive and communal spectacles into their consumption of the match, thus reclaiming leisure as their own.[7] Some supporters also imagined their rowdy activities as a rejection of the growing commercialization and modernization of the football industry, preferring the communal interaction and aggressive associations deplored by those wanting to keep order in new football stadium environments. Rather than seeing new forms of football consumption as working-class social custom, or investigating this shift in the cultural meanings of football for young working-class men, state and police authorities essentialized their behaviour as deviant and anti-social. They worked to discipline the attention of rowdy football supporters, taking part in broader processes of enhancing order, heightening individual awareness and increasing desired forms of consumption inherent to the cultural logic of late capitalism.[8]

From the mid-1960s, sociable forms of watching increasingly included violent and disruptive activities like pitch invasions, fights between supporters, violent encounters with police, damage to stadium property, throwing and spitting at footballers and other fans, and vandalism of surrounding environs, including pubs, train stations and rail cars.[9] While the origins of these activities have been debated at length, most historians and sociologists recognize that this violence was tied to notions of working-class identity, community building among adolescent men, and aggressive territoriality between home and away supporters.[10] Reviews of arrest records and witness statements have shown that the majority of offenders were white working-class labourers, usually under the age of 21, leading many to consider declining working-class affluence in the mid-1960s and increased competition for jobs and housing as factors.[11]

British politicians from both parties championed law-and-order and perceived football violence as the outbursts of a thoughtless and overly sensitive minority, rather than as an evolving form of communal leisure embodying working-class masculine values. Politicians used descriptive adjectives like 'thug' or 'hooligan' without specifically targeting labourers as the subjects of their moralizing discourses. However, clear distinctions were made between 'genuine' football supporters and the 'riff-raff' who participated in violent activities.[12] These labels coded the football environment and its spectators in class discourses. To limit violence and prevent it from tarnishing Britain's football reputation, the Home Office and the Department of the Environment under successive administrations empowered local authorities and football clubs to improve their policing and sentencing policies and recommended changes to the football terraces and spectator environments. Barriers, pens, segregated seating schemes and plans for police dogs and horses restricted spectators' mobility and sought to institute more disciplined consumption habits that were in line with notions of propriety held by 'genuine' supporters and politicians.[13]

Two government-sponsored commissions to address football violence recognized the need for controlling spectators' attention through eliminating boredom at the match. The break between halves particularly concerned a group of psychologists from the University of Birmingham who conducted the first government inquiry: 'Rowdyism is likely to break out at half time when expectant fans get bored waiting for the game to restart. Likewise the waiting period before the game when rival fans have arrived early to secure vantage points is a time when brawling on the terraces may occur.' They suggested intermittent entertainments as a possible solution.[14] A second group of investigators from Glasgow in 1969 also recommended 'some form of entertainment, both before the game and during the interval ... so that supporters had something to occupy their minds while waiting for play to commence'.[15] These analysts believed that focusing supporters' attention forward to the field through short entertainments could avoid the supposedly distracting stimuli of other spectators. Both recommendations also reinforced the perception of spectators as witless and receptive bystanders.

A committee chaired by former England national team manager Walter Winterbottom also recognized the advantages of directing attention to the field of play before and after games, especially when such tactics helped police with timing ingress and egress. On-field entertainment could promote a lengthier period of entering and leaving the field directly before and after matches, thus preventing pushing and shoving within crowded stadium hallways and stairwells. The commission noted that when clubs had adopted some form of 'pre-match entertainment', such as 'music, club information and light entertainment', spectators tended 'to arrive early and to avoid last-minute crushes'. Similar distractions like match updates and lights shows could also stop a departure rush.[16] Winterbottom's committee passed on Everton FC's suggestion that 'bringing a disc jockey to away games', including when abroad in Europe, helped promote harmony in the stands.[17]

During a reading of the Safety at Sports Ground Bill, a bill aimed at mandating changes to stadium environments to improve crowd safety, Clement Freud (Liberal) wanted to hold the junior or reserve matches before and after games to help break up the rushes on either end of the match.[18] Such efforts supposedly encouraged fans to focus on the pitch and ignore the communal activities around them. Much like today's cheerleaders and other scheduled gimmicks at any major sporting event, filling time during pauses in sporting matches aims at avoiding boredom, thus reducing opportunities for unwanted behaviours.

Government and club officials contemplated various changes to the day's entertainment structure as they sought to reorganize the fundamental ways in which spectators consumed football. Although police felt that they helped, these developments proved largely unsuccessful at curbing violence. Their implementation revealed, however, officials' perception that working-class spectators needed disciplined attention when consuming the sport to avoid predilections for violent behaviour. Restricted mobility and the addition of 'light entertainment' was thus a means to discipline unruly consumer behaviours.

RAILWAY CONTROL AND GENDERED CONSUMPTION

While officials mainly focused on behaviours within stadiums, spectator violence outside of organized stadium spaces disconcerted both police and the public. Damage to areas outside sports grounds menaced private property and threatened the railway industry. Vandalism to trains and damage to local businesses were common. In response, government officials teamed up with police and British Rail to attempt modifications to travel consumption by away supporters.

Increased vandalism on British railcars by football spectators had occurred since the mid-1960s, consistent with the general spike in crowd violence.[19] The report from the Birmingham research group led by J. A. Harrington, written with police recommendations, described the smash-ups:

> The most common types of damage to railways are damage to luggage racks and the nets, seats slashed and otherwise misused, window blinds and straps torn from fixed points, windows broken, advertisement panels and mirrors broken or defaced, electrical fittings and light bulbs removed and sometimes thrown out or smashed. Woodwork and paneling and tables are sometimes damaged, lampshades are either torn out or destroyed. Fire extinguishers are sometimes discharged in corridors or from windows, and are disposed of either by being thrown out of the train or by being stolen. Toilets suffer considerable damage with mirrors, pans, and washbasins broken and sometimes completely smashed.[20]

The report also noted the problems British Rail experienced in attempting to identify and apprehend offenders, as the damage usually occurred when trains were unmonitored. British Rail also had difficulty convincing fellow travellers to bear witness against spectators, and could not introduce stricter control measures, 'without adversely affecting the well-behaved travellers and thereby losing their goodwill'.[21]

Train vandals on football specials used different terms to describe their activities, often reinforcing the notion that their violence had no purpose. Wreaking havoc and eliciting anxious and intimidated responses from local citizens, police and other spectators provided its own reward. One fan remembered:

> It wasn't particularly an act of violence, it was a ludicrous, hysterical act. Throwing a toilet out of a train window was funny. It's a set of surreal actions, to take a toilet out of an old train and through a window ... We could walk up and down the High Street and everyone would look at us and everyone would be frightened of us and we wouldn't have to do very much, just shout and swear a bit: 'You're gonna get your fucking heads kicked in.'[22]

Such articulations reveal the hyper-masculine social settings in which many young offenders sought to express their aggressiveness among their cohort. On trips to away stadiums, football specials thus concentrated potentially vandalous travellers onto trains and into spaces where offenders became anonymous, much like pens and terraces did with large crowds within stadiums.

To prevent damage, police and government authorities sought to regulate train stations as public spaces requiring increased discipline. Train stations often hosted instances of conflict between rival groups of fans, as clever supporters ambushed adversaries at train stations upon their arrival or departure. Police gradually increased their detail as they escorted rival groups of fans to the stadium in order to mitigate conflicts between supporters.[23] When Manchester United fans arrived in Liverpool in 1970, they faced thrown stones, empty beer bottles and verbal abuse from rival supporters, despite the presence of over 50 police officers and eight mounted police. The abuse continued, with intermittent fights, along the two-and-a-half-mile route to the stadium.[24] When a match in Stoke yielded broken windows and missile damage along the route from the train station, Stoke City police found it 'necessary, therefore, to prevent any form of wild chase along the route by supporters and this was done by forming them into columns and escorting them by Mounted Branch, Dog Handlers and patrol men'.[25] Escorts subjected fans to strict discipline along these routes as they attempted to both protect and prevent them from causing damage to private property. At Luton, club officials and local police intermittently discussed having several matches moved to another nearby stadium rather than risk the long walk between the train station and their grounds.[26]

Football specials, as trains designed specifically for the transportation of football fans to away matches, also became a primary anxiety for the state and the public. British Rail and the Department of the Environment considered getting most of the troublemaking travelling supporters on the same train the primary matter of security and safety.[27] They also aimed to separate unruly supporters from other travellers. The dichotomy between 'genuine' supporters and 'hooligans' provided the basis for segregation and formed the backbone of crowd control policy. According to an internal British Rail assessment, football trains produced over £800,000 per year in revenue, with £435,000 coming from football specials and private charters. Out of a total market of £1.2 to £1.5 million, rail officials estimated losses of £200,000 to £500,000 over the course of the 1975–6 season.[28] Controlling the football market also had implications for a third group: 'normal' Saturday passengers. British Rail recognized foul language, boisterous behaviour and damage to the interiors of train coaches as deterrents to other passengers, and thus a serious threat to their financial solvency. British Rail hoped segregating passengers would prevent financial losses, but the Department of Environment also promoted the policy as its main initiative for preventing disorder on nationalized railways and eliminating violence outside stadium grounds.[29] Both groups looked to manipulate the consumptive behaviours of football travellers.

British Rail generated these policies as it faced its own struggles with maintaining revenue and actualizing any number of business plans failing to put the company on solid ground in the declining economic climate of the late 1960s and early 1970s. T. R. Gourvish's magisterial business history of British Rail in the post-war period noted two distinct problems with creating a viable and profitable rail industry in Britain after the introduction of cars, coaches, taxis and other competitors. First, 'freedom to choose and charge the traffic they carried was severely restricted by legislation designed to encourage a "public service" obligation in management'. British Rail, as the nationalized service provider, struggled with pricing indexes that satisfied both their desire for profit and the need to serve the public, particularly at acceptable price points for working-class consumers. Second, rising labour costs, despite government intervention in managing capital-labour disputes was 'the industry's most enduring financial and operating problem'.[30]

With these pressures in the foreground, British Rail faced ongoing debates about how to fulfil their public service, and how pricing related directly to marketing football specials for working-class men. By considering input from political parties and Home Office officials, British Rail composed segregated travel schemes for football specials to protect their trains using pricing. Railway planners first used incentivized price-cutting to lure working-class football supporters onto 'special' trains. British Rail and several football club representatives supported this effective tactic.[31] As one British Railway policy guideline noted, 'The fare must be sufficiently attractive to steer at least the younger football supporters from normal service trains carrying regular fare paying passengers.'[32] The British Railways Board even admitted that, 'BR is accused of undercutting, but fares have to be pitched to keep football traffic off ordinary trains'.[33]

Railway authorities believed supporters polluted the projected image of a bourgeois railway environment, and ensured that deviant working-class passengers inhabited their own trains with separate rules and increased surveillance. This policy allowed British Rail to secure the market for other 'genuine' supporters and middle-class passengers, with the non-special trains free from unwanted spectators. British Rail attempted to monopolize football railway passage by segregation along class lines, using football supporters and their deviancy to divide the market. Scrutiny of football supporters' activities could now be extended to their ventures both directly before and after matches, in a further attempt to control all of the environments inhabited by these unwanted consumers.

Additionally, British Rail and other train companies frequently demanded British Transport police presence on football specials and other Saturday trains.[34] While uniformed police were often teased and jeered, and sometimes attacked, plain clothes officers allowed surveillance to go unnoticed. Rail officials assumed the latter provided the essential dimension of continual observation of supporters' behaviour. In providing mobile and uninhibited scrutiny of the confined coaches, plain clothes officers added a concealed dimension to the contestation of power on trains.

Nonetheless, consternation about police presence gave way to further monitoring strategies, including club-appointed stewards on trains. Like stewards at matches, train stewards provided a less threatening substitute for uniformed police. As an implementation of community policing, clubs paid stewards, usually team fans, a small wage to keep order and monitor train coaches. While stewards had a long history of ushering football matches, using stewards on trains had been relatively infrequent and unsuccessful before the 1970s. In late 1969, a train operator forced all Tottenham fans off the train at Flitwick, nearly 50 miles from their London home, due to destructive behaviour. The Home Office announced thereafter that stewards would be mandatory on all trains carrying fans to away games.[35] By 1974, British Rail recommended two stewards in each train car, although this would prove difficult to implement.³⁶ Generally, supplying stewards allowed clubs and British Rail to receive a discount on their policing of travel consumption, since fewer police were required to accompany spectators. Stewards cost less to employ than British Transport police and minimized direct contact with state authorities. Assured free travel and usually a free ticket to matches, stewards could travel to away matches to watch their team, still be among other groups of supporters, and only needed to follow simple crowd monitoring procedures.³⁷

Government officials also felt stewards could be useful in addressing the ongoing problem of identifying and charging specific culprits. Just as police had trouble identifying spectators for specific transgressions in open stadium terraces, railway officials also faced extreme difficulty in pinning damage on any individual in the anonymity of a railcar. The state's highest police authority, Eric St. Johnston, commented that, 'the problem was to identify trouble-makers and to take action to prevent the known hooligans getting on trains carrying supporters'.³⁸ St. Johnston's deputy recommended that adult spectators from each club be placed alongside stewards to help, 'keep the younger ones in hand but also, when trouble arose, to give evidence to the police of the identity of those responsible'.³⁹ Accountability for criminal activity became such a problem that Home Office representatives considered a way to charge all the occupants of a given car in certain situations. In 1969, D. J. Trevelyan, a high-level Home Office representative, contacted the Director of Public Prosecutions to ascertain the feasibility of charging all occupants of a railcar subject to severe damage.⁴⁰ The Director of Public Prosecutions advised, however, that such arrests would be considered unlawful and recommended that the Home Office drop the matter.⁴¹ Stewards could nevertheless serve as witnesses should any individual eventually be charged.

Rail and football officials also tried to turn trains into environments conducive to focused attention and individual placidity similar to those attempted within football stadiums. In 1973, with a new season approaching, British Rail and the Football League announced a partnership entitled the 'Brighter Football Campaign'. The Football League agreed to pay £45,000 for 50 journeys on a train, the 'League Liner', designed specifically to 'entertain' groups in excess of 400 supporters. The 12-coach train included a discotheque, a cinema car and two music coaches offering a variety of musical styles.⁴² The train evidenced the Football League's efforts to stem football disorder outside stadiums in ways other than calling on the iron fist of law. British Rail's public relations office noted it would 'counter the falling attendances, and improve the image of football supporters'. Such amenities would increase revenue, and, the office added, exploit 'the obvious PR advantages'.[43] In addition to cinema and movie cars, individualized headsets in each seat also ensured that supporters remained seated, encouraged discreet seating and decreased the amount of communal contact and movement among supporters. As with assumptions about attention within stadiums, rail officials also implied that breaking up groups of supporters, even within very confined spaces, could possibly prevent fans from acting in concert to damage private property or provoke stewards and police, thus decreasing the amount of group violence on football specials.

Rail officials and the Football League also hoped that luxury incentives would promote a more gender-balanced crowd. Increasing female attendees, it was thought, would decrease disorder and promote the family values they hoped to associate with football attendance in the 1970s.[44] Like several other moral commentators, both British Rail and the Football League felt that the absence of women permitted a more chaotic masculine environment. To secure order and promote the peaceful controlled football travel setting, Alan Hardaker, Chairman of the Football League, and subsequent member of several Working Parties on football hooliganism, hoped 'that the added touch of luxury provided by the League Liner, together with its unusual and novel facilities, would encourage soccer supporters to bring their wives and families – and girl friends – with them when they travel to away games'.[45] Rail officials assumed that women could bring about the desired levels of attentive discipline and tranquillity. The peculiar addition of 'girl friends' to the group of wives and mothers indicated that football authorities felt that female presence, and not simply the presence of families, would lead to a calmer, more orderly disposition among groups of young male supporters. Rail authorities employed stereotypes that imagined women as calming, docile and mild-mannered. In contrast to the impressionistic stereotypes of young men as strident and destructive, women here represented a resource to quell disorder: families and the feminine presence provided the salve for this particularly infective scourge on proper masculine conduct. Women would also provide distractions for young men, assumed to be destructive in groups and when encouraged by one another. Hardaker stated 'This is what we shall be providing to encourage the younger fan to bring along his girl. The more mature in age may prefer to while away the journey chatting, playing cards, or enjoying screened entertainment.'[46] The fear of young men associating and acting collectively posed a greater threat than interaction among young men and 'their' girls.

State and club authorities also viewed alcohol as an exacerbating factor in aggressive behaviour and worked to limit its consumption. As early as 1971 British Rail considered removing alcohol from football specials altogether.

The British Transport Police Committee recommended a complete ban on intoxicants on trains due to an increased rise in attacks on British Transport police at railway stops and during travel.[47] Rail authorities briefly considered this proposal, but excited at the opportunity of securing several thousands of thirsty passengers to 15 or so away matches a year, quickly quelled any consideration of total prohibition. One BR executive noted 'that restriction on the sale of intoxicants is not desirable as a general policy and would lead to the significant loss of revenue'. In defence of his position, he quickly added, that 'as a general comment, all the evidence suggests that the hooligan element consists of young teenagers who are *not* alcoholic drinkers'.[48] Executives at British Rail acted quickly to ensure that revenues from alcohol – including that consumed by teenagers – would not decrease. A full ban on alcohol on British Rail trains materialized in 1975, but only at the behest of Denis Howell, Labour's leading authority on sport.[49]

By 1975, since most of the above implementations failed to render acceptable patterns of consumption, British Rail drastically increased prices for football supporters. Over a two-year period from 1975–6, British Rail deliberated over a policy change. Rising vandalism, a reduced British Transport police force, and club resistance to appointing and paying stewards for train duty all influenced the decision to raise travel prices.[50] More significantly, though, the public awareness of British Rail supporting and encouraging the travel of unruly supporters proved too detrimental to the company's public relations. On 30 August 1975, in an 'emergency measure', British Rail ceased to offer football specials and suspended the issue of all football travel tickets to away matches on Saturdays. The Executive Director of Passenger Travel recognized that, 'This strong action, which met with a favourable response from the media, the public and the Minister for Sport, the Football Association and the Football League, had an immediately beneficial effect in "pricing out" the potential troublemakers.'[51]

British Rail's emergency measures removed discounts for football travellers and intermittently raised prices of Saturday trains to ensure undesirable supporter groups could no longer make the journey. Authorities' distinction between 'genuine' supporters and 'hooligans', prompted renewed class discourse. 'Genuine' supporters were bourgeois supporters who could afford away game travel, embodied bourgeois values of propriety and family, and exemplified the ideal football man, representing club and country while out of their home city. 'Undesirable' supporters acted out, disrespected authority and constantly caused trouble for those regulating the rail and football industries. These distinctions were clearly made along class and gender lines. State authorities situated them at opposite ends of the football supporters' spectrum. As British Rail's headquarters commented: 'It is not in the Board's best interests to cater for the "Hooligan Market", nor to offer low fares to attract this class of football supporter.' Denis Howell, Labour Minister for Sport and the politicians leading the Department of the Environment's efforts, completely agreed.[52] The League Liner, despite its advances in spectator entertainment and control, was removed from British Rail's fleet in 1976.[53] This policy implemented a complete turnaround from the early 1970s, where undesirable fans were recruited not only for revenue, but also because they could be more easily controlled within train cars. Apparently, even the promise of public order and disciplined consumption proved too costly for British Rail.

Unsurprisingly, British Rail soon realized that it missed the lost revenue. Facing a projected loss of over £500,000 per year, British Rail hoped to recoup select supporters without either violating its agreements with government authorities or allowing excessive vandalism to dissolve its quickly restored public image. The answer to this apparent paradox was to retain the ability to offer football specials 'where commercially justified', especially for areas having a lower likelihood of violent supporter groups, and where incidents would be unnoticed by the watchdog media. British Rail would turn the 'hooligan market' over to competitors, and allow clubs to charter trains for their supporters at their own cost. Meanwhile, they set about recapturing the 'genuine' supporter market by incrementally raising ticket prices on Saturday trains and refusing travel to anyone viewed as a 'potential troublemaker'.[54] A final comment from the Executive summed up their new approach in 1976: 'The effect on revenue must be accepted as a consequence of the withdrawal of unstewarded trains. Marketing activity for additional charter business, and for genuine supporters at Awayday fares must be increased to generate compensating revenue.'[55]

The end result of these changes to rail policy for football supporters was a flexible plan that allowed British Rail to capitalize on the revenue generated by football spectating while maintaining fans' segregation, a good public image of service from a nationalized industry, and the appearance of punitive response to incidents of public disorder, a policy they maintained throughout the late 1970s and 1980s. Overall, British Rail utilized an elastic approach to pricing that discouraged unwanted consumers from travelling on their trains unless on tightly controlled football specials, often by excluding them from sports travel promotion at all.

Football violence challenged not only the ingenuity of sports governors and football clubs, but also encouraged them to police spectator conduct in ways that aimed to transform the consumptive habits and experiences of football consumption in the 1960s and 1970s. Despite multiple efforts and a variety of strategies to limit the phenomenon, new forms of physicality and aggressiveness associated with the football spectating experience persisted, rooted in processes of masculine identity-formation, community protection and belligerent territoriality. Attempts to entertain and instil disciplined attention in ostensibly idiotic working-class supporters proved futile and betrayed renewed class conflict within the football arena. The discourses of politicians and police, as well as the marketing strategies pursued by British Rail, revealed gendered perceptions of working-class families and the supposedly calming influence of women to counter the thuggery of young working-class men. Fractures of class and gender overlapped to justify policing patterns and marketing strategies that hoped to neutralize unwelcome consumers. In these two related industries, British football and sports tourism, the British government intervened not only to reconfigure and chastise unwanted patterns of consumption within each industry, but also in an attempt to promote desired patterns of consumption and secure sought-after consumers who acted appropriately.

NOTES

1. Brett Bebber, *Violence and Racism in Football: Politics and Cultural Conflict in British Society, 1968–98* (London: Pickering & Chatto, 2012), Part One; Anastasia Tsoukala, *Football Hooliganism in Europe: Security and Civil Liberties in the Balance* (London: Palgrave, 2009); Richard Giulianotti, 'Social Identity and Public Order: Political and Academic Discourses on Football Violence', in *Football, Violence and Social Identity*, eds Richard Giulianotti, Norman Bonney and Mike Hepworth (London: Routledge, 1994), pp. 9–36; Gary Whannel, 'Football Crowd Behavior and the Press', *Media, Culture & Society* 1:2 (1979): pp. 327–42; Stuart Hall, 'The Treatment of "Football Hooliganism" in the Press', in *Football Hooliganism: The Wider Context*, ed. Roger Ingham (London: Inter-Action Inprint, 1978), pp. 15–36. Football violence existed before the mid-1960s, but not with the same consistency or popularity. See Richard Holt, *Sport and the British: A Modern History* (Oxford: Oxford University Press, 1988).

2. Rosemary Wakeman, 'The Golden Age of Prosperity, 1953–73', in *Themes in European History Since 1945*, ed. Rosemary Wakeman (London: Routledge, 2003), pp. 59–85.

3. Bebber, *Violence and Racism in Football*, Introduction and Chapter 1; Giulianotti, *Football, Violence and Social Identity*; Eric Dunning, Patrick Murphy and John Williams, *The Roots of Football Hooliganism* (London: Routledge, 1984); Eric Dunning and Norbert Elias, *Quest for Excitement: Sport and Leisure in the Civilizing Process* (Oxford: Blackwell, 1986); Ian Taylor, 'Soccer Consciousness and Soccer Hooliganism', in *Images of Deviance*, ed. S. Cohen (Harmondsworth: Penguin, 1976), pp. 53–76; Ian Taylor, 'Class, Violence and Sport: The Case of Soccer Hooliganism in Britain', in *Sport, Culture and the Modern State*, eds Hart Cantelon and

Richard Gruneau (Toronto: University of Toronto Press, 1982), pp. 39–97. The term 'football violence' will be used here as a descriptive phrase, in lieu of the value-laden term 'hooliganism'.

4. Bebber, *Violence and Racism in Football*, Part Two.
5. Matthew Hilton, *Consumerism in Twentieth-Century Britain: The Search for a Historical Movement* (Cambridge: Cambridge University Press, 2003), pp. 1–3.
6. See the various articles in Matthew Hilton and Martin Daunton, *The Politics of Consumption: Material Culture and Citizenship in Europe and America* (Oxford: Berg, 2001), *passim,* esp. Introduction and Ch. 12.
7. John Clarke, 'Football and Working Class Fans: Tradition and Change', in *Football Hooliganism*, ed. Ingham, pp. 37–60.
8. Jonathan Crary, *Suspensions of Perception: Attention, Spectacle and Modern Culture* (Cambridge, MA: MIT Press, 1999).
9. Any attempt to list the activities described by the term 'football hooliganism' is difficult. See Steve Frosdick and Peter Marsh, *Football Hooliganism* (Portland, MA: Willan, 2005), Part II.
10. See the literature review in Megan O'Neill, *Policing Football: Social Interaction and Negotiated Disorder* (London: Palgrave Macmillan, 2005); Tsoukala, *Football Hooliganism in Europe*; Frosdick and Marsh, *Football Hooliganism*.
11. Bebber, *Violence and Racism in Football*, pp. 4–5, 125–9; Eugene Trivizas, 'Offences and Offenders in Football Crowd Disorders', *British Journal of Criminology* 20:3 (1980), pp. 276–88; Trivizas, 'Sentencing the "Football Hooligan"', *British Journal of Criminology* 21:4 (1981), pp. 342–9; Trivizas, 'Disturbances Associated with Football Matches', *British Journal of Criminology* 24:4 (1984), pp. 361–83.
12. Bebber, *Violence and Racism in Football*, pp. 56–9.
13. Ibid., Ch. 3.
14. J. A. Harrington, *Soccer Hooliganism: A Preliminary Report* (Bristol: John Wright and Sons, Ltd, 1968), p. 22. Hereafter, 'the Harrington report'.
15. Working Party on Crowd Behaviour at Football Matches, Report of a Meeting held at Ibrox Park, Glasgow, 16 June 1969. In National Archives UK, (hereafter NA) HO 287/1500.
16. Walter Winterbottom, 'Report of the Team Appointed to Consult Football Clubs on Safety of Grounds', June 1971, p. 15. In NA HLG 120/1618.
17. Letter from M. J. Skinner, Promotions Manager at Everton Football Club, to Denis Howell, 13 August 1975. NA AT 60/39.
18. *Parliamentary Debates, House of Commons* Vol. 867 (18 January 1974), col. 1112.
19. Supporters' organizations frequently worried about railcar damage incidents as early as the 1950s. See Rogan Taylor, *Football and Its Fans: Supporters and Their Relations with the Game, 1885–1985* (Leicester: Leicester University Press, 1992), p. 159.

20. The Harrington report, p. 45.
21. Ibid., p. 46.
22. In Andrew Ward and Rogan Taylor, *Kicking and Screaming: An Oral History of Football in England* (London: Robson Books), p. 260.
23. For example of ambitious police details, see 'Operational Order, 25 March 1975: Notts County vs. Manchester United, 19 April 1975'. NA HO 287/2053.
24. Report of incidents, Liverpool and Bootle Constabulary, 9 September 1970. NA HO 287/2051, file 4.
25. Report Re: Crowd Control, etc., Stoke City vs. Manchester United Football Club, 30 August 1975, 2. NA HO 287/2053.
26. Meeting of Denis Howell with Luton FC, 5 September 1975. NA AT 60/39.
27. Note policy priorities in British Railways Board internal memo, 2 June 1975, p. 2. In Files of the Office of the Chief Executive of Railways, NA AN 156/469, *British Railways File on Trains and Specials, 1972–1985*.
28. Memorandum to British Railways Management Group from Executive Director of Passenger Affairs, 23 February 1976, pp. 1, 4. NA AN 156/469.
29. Notes of Meeting between Denis Howell, Department of the Environment, and British Rail officials, 4 September 1974. NA AN 156/469.
30. T. R. Gourvish, *British Railways, 1948–73: A Business History* (Cambridge: Cambridge University Press, 1986), pp. 1–2.
31. British Railways Board Memo, 2 June 1975, p. 2. NA AN 156/469.
32. British Rail, Football Traffic Policy Guidelines, 14 August 1974, p. 1. NA AN 156/469.
33. British Railways Board Memo, 2 June 1975, p. 2. NA AN 156/469.
34. British Rail, Football Traffic Policy Guidelines, 14 August 1974, p. 1. NA AN 156/469.
35. Home Office Press Notice, 20 November 1969. In Taylor, 'Class, Violence and Sport', p. 89.
36. Football League/British Rail Regulation Scheme to Regulate Young 'Supporters' To Away Matches, 14 March 1975, p. 1. NA AN 156/469.
37. See British Railways Board Memo, 2 June 1975, p. 1. PRO AN 156/469.
38. Sir Eric St Johnston, Her Majesty's Chief Inspector of Constabulary, in 'Note of a Meeting Held to Discuss Hooliganism by Football Supporters', Home Office, 2 October 1969. NA HO 287/1500, file 12.
39. F. E. Williamson, Her Majesty's Inspector of Constabulary, in ibid.
40. D. J. Trevelyan, Home Office to J. F. Claxton, Dept of the Director of Public Prosecutions, 26 September 1969. NA HO 287/1500.
41. Letter from F2 Division of Home Office and Department of Public Prosecutions to D. J. Trevelyan, 2 October, 1969. NA HO 287/1500.
42. Press Release, British Railways Board, 23 January 1973, p. 1. NA AN 156/469.

43. Letter from A. E. T. Griffiths to D. Boswick, British Rail Headquarters, 1 September 1973. NA AN 156/469.
44. Brett Bebber, '"The Misuse of Leisure": Football Violence, Politics and Family Values in 1970s Britain', in *Leisure and Cultural Conflict in Twentieth-Century Britain*, ed. Brett Bebber (Manchester: Manchester University Press, 2012), pp. 129–56.
45. Press Release, British Railways Board, 23 January 1973, p. 2. NA AN 156/469.
46. Ibid.
47. Minutes of Meeting of British Transport Police Committee, 26 November 1971. NA AN 156/469.
48. Internal memo from Executive Director of Passengers to the Principal Assistant to Chief Executive, 16 February 1972. NA AN 156/469.
49. Notes of Meeting between Denis Howell, Department of the Environment, and British Rail officials, 4 September 1974. The ban took effect on 30 July 1975. NA AN 156/469.
50. For British Rail comments on reduced police presence and their battle with clubs to appoint stewards for trains, see Notes and Minutes on Football Traffic, by D. V. Ellison, Chief Passenger Marketing Manager, British Rail. NA AN 156/469.
51. Memorandum to British Railways Management Group from Executive Director of Passenger Affairs, 23 February 1976, p. 2. NA AN 156/469.
52. Ibid., p. 4.
53. See Notes of a meeting of Ministerial Working Party on Crowd Misconduct, 13 February 1976. NA AN 156/469.
54. Ibid., p. 3.
55. Ibid., p. 4.

PART TWO

In and Beyond the Nation: The Local and the Global in the Production of Consumer Cultures

CHAPTER EIGHT

Consumer Communication as Commodity: British Advertising Agencies and the Global Market for Advertising, 1780–1980

STEFAN SCHWARZKOPF

Our Age has one gigantic advantage over its predecessors: we are a people of advertisers.

— *Daily Telegraph*, 1891[1]

BRITISH ADVERTISING AND THE GLOBALITY OF EMPIRE

Britain was the first nation that turned the production of consumer culture into an industry. Well before other nations developed advertising sectors, Britain had a dense network of advertising agents who were closely connected to the coffeehouses and newspaper printers in London's

Fleet Street. Indeed, the entrepreneurial concept of the advertising agent and the business model of the advertising agency emerged first in late-eighteenth-century England. The British advertising industry enjoyed a period of continuous growth throughout the nineteenth century. By 1900, London was the world's advertising capital: the city was populated by hundreds of independent advertising agents and was home to the largest agencies in the world, some counting up to 200 employees and more than 100 clients.[2]

With regard to this industry, a particular narrative has become accepted which tells us how British advertising became side-lined by American advertising services during the twentieth century. This focus ignores how British consumer communications emerged during the nineteenth century and misses the expansion of British advertising services overseas beginning in the 1880s. By underwriting global commodity chains from the nineteenth century onwards, British advertising agencies staged successful company takeovers in Europe and, crucially, the US later in the twentieth century. This development culminated in the early twenty-first century, when British advertising and marketing communications groups began once again to shape the global market for consumer communication.

From about 1890 onwards, British advertising agencies expanded to continental Europe, the Empire and the United States. In this chapter, I will look at the expansion strategies of these firms from the 1890s to the 1980s and consider the general relevance of this kind of research for historians of modern British consumer culture. By questioning the 'Americanization' narrative, I draw attention to the uniqueness of the British historical experience and illuminate the enterprises that enable modern consumer culture. The continuities in the global expansion of these companies points at the importance of the British Empire for the making of a globalized world in which chains of commodities, finance, services and symbols shape social and cultural realities. Advertising grew with the development of print media and with the expansion of consumer industries in terms of scale, scope and global reach. Since the late nineteenth century, a globalized media and consumer culture have existed, driven by a 'cosmopolitan' advertising industry that rarely stayed within national borders. In these processes, London as a global trade centre and the geopolitical framework provided by the Empire both played early and more fundamental roles than the expansion of American marketing, which followed the path laid out by British entrepreneurs.

GEORGIAN AND VICTORIAN BEGINNINGS: 1780–1910

At the same time as Great Britain was in the process of becoming the 'workshop of the world', it also emerged as a centre of magazine and newspaper publishing.[3] In the wake of the late-eighteenth-century media and consumer revolution, a new kind of industry grew, which helped finance this great number of new publications: advertising. Although sellers had advertised their wares in news-sheets since at least the early seventeenth century, the rise of entrepreneurial capitalism necessitated a more focused approach. Importers of perfumes, for example, addressed a different public from those who sought investors for a merchant ship bound for India. The buyers of advertising space in print media, such as financiers, importers, exporters and producers of consumer goods, and the sellers of this space, i.e. the publishers, were known to use the coffee houses around Fleet Street to create the first market for the exchange of that medium.[4]

As the number of buyers of advertising space and the availability of different print media increased, a new type of entrepreneur helped both sides of the market to meet. This entrepreneur, the advertising agent, helped space buyers because he knew which print media were available, which paper had what deadline for the acceptance of advertisements, and what price the papers would charge. Agents were also able to help with the formulation of the advertising text, known as 'copy'. Print media, in turn, increasingly relied on such agents since they were willing to buy space in the papers in bulk, which gave newspapers and magazines a regular income. The agents then sold the space they had bought from the papers at a profit to advertising clients.[5]

During the nineteenth century, agents were closely connected to and at times even dependent on certain newspaper houses from which they gained commission for attracting advertisements. These agents often also traded as publishers, printers, advertisement contractors and billposters. Before World War I, advertising was therefore often understood as the business of 'space brokering', that is, the selling of newspaper space at a profit, and the main task of the agent was to facilitate the insertion of advertisements as opposed to the creation of advertising. The world's first advertising agencies that followed this model can be found in London. Scripps agency was founded in 1783, and William Tayler set up his business in 1786. The best known, and longest surviving, of the early London agencies was the firm set up by James White in Fleet Street in 1800.[6] George Reynell, a clerk at the official journal *London Gazette*, set up his agency in 1812. It remained a family business until 1993.[7] Also in 1812, Charles Barker founded another early agency that continued to trade until recently, Charles Barker & Sons Ltd.[8]

As individual agents began to take on clerks to take care of mundane tasks of delivering advertisements to newspaper desk offices, checking when and whether they had appeared, invoicing clients, and occasionally writing copy, their business model slowly evolved into what by the mid-nineteenth century became known as advertising agency. After the abolition of the newspaper stamp duty in 1855, their number increased with the same speed as new periodicals came on the market. Most of the largest British advertising agencies that still traded during the mid-twentieth century had entered business between the 1830s and the 1890s.[9] Among them were G. Street (1830), C. Mitchell (1837), Mather & Crowther (1850), Sell's (1869), Smith's (1878), T. B. Browne (1880), C. Vernon & Sons (1884), the London Press Exchange (1892), S. H. Benson's (1893), Samson Clark (1896) and Frederick Potter (1897).[10] In 1866 there were around 100 advertising-related businesses in London and by 1906 this number had grown to 500.[11]

By the late nineteenth century, Britain had become the global centre of advertising at an industrial scale. An astounding number of London agencies were internationalizing across the North Atlantic and the English Channel. The London agencies of Henry Sell and Thomas Brooks Browne had opened offices in the US, Canada and France well before American agencies made such moves to internationalize. As early as 1892, Browne's agency prided itself on its ability to give clients access to the vast American market through its offices in Canal Street in Lower Manhattan, and to the French market through its offices on the Rue du Louvre. The agency was equally able to advise them about markets in India and on advertising in Africa.[12] American agencies, in contrast, did not enter the Indian and African markets before the late 1920s.[13]

Yet London's agencies were not merely home-grown concerns. As early as 1867, Gordon & Gotch, a Melbourne-based news and advertising agency, and distributor of magazines and newspapers, opened a branch in London. Exploiting the new steamship and telegraph connections within the British Empire, this agency allowed Australian producers to place advertisements in newspapers in the UK, and British producers and sellers to seek markets in Australia and New Zealand.[14] In addition to agents from the Empire, French, German and American entrepreneurs also became attracted to London as a global commercial centre. Among the many foreigners who came to Britain during the late Victorian years and contributed to Britain's burgeoning advertising culture was Charles Garnier. Born in France in 1841, Garnier settled with his family in London during the 1870s and initially worked as an engraver. In 1890, Garnier set up his own company to make advertising signs from copper and enamelled steel. In 1912, Garnier's workshop was bought up by Henry Sell's advertising agency.[15] Numerous German commercial artists settled in London during the early twentieth century, including Charles (Karl) Holzer and Henri Henrion. Holzer arrived in London in 1900 and worked as a lithographer for various art studios. In addition to Mazawattee Tea Co., Lever Brothers used Holzer's designs to advertise Pears', Lux and Sunlight soap.[16] Henrion settled in London in 1936 and designed posters for the Ministry of Information, British European Airways, KLM and the Royal Mail.[17] Americans like Paul E. Derrick also came to London to start their careers. Derrick settled in London in 1904 and became the advertising representative for Quaker Oats in Britain. During the Edwardian years, Derrick did much to professionalize the advertising industry and infuse it with marketing management ideas.[18]

American, French and German advertising agencies developed later and at a slower pace. The first advertising agencies were set up in the US in the 1840s. In 1849, the Philadelphia-based businessman Volney B. Palmer described his outfit for the first time as an 'Advertising Agency'. Twenty years later, in 1869, Francis Wayland Ayer founded the N. W. Ayer agency in the same city.[19] In France, the most important newspapers formed a company, the Société Générale des Annonces (SGA), in 1845. Through the SGA, these papers rented their advertising space out to advertisers. Since 1865, this business was run through Auguste Havas and his agency, which consequently held a near-monopoly position in the French advertising market. In 1912, the first service-oriented advertising agency, Hémet, Jep et Carré, was set up in Paris.[20] Service advertising agencies did not exist in Germany until the 1920s.[21] In 1899, the J. Walter Thompson Co. (JWT) became the first American advertising agency to set up a subsidiary in London in order to place advertising for its clients in British newspapers. By that time, London agencies had already expanded to North America and the European continent.

Because of its surprisingly early move into international markets, Sell's agency warrants a closer analysis in order to understand how Victorian agencies operated and how they contributed to the growth of global consumer markets. Henry Sell, an avid reader, traveller and Fellow of the Royal Geographical Society, founded Sell's in 1869.[22] In 1886 Sell's became one of the first advertising firms registered as a limited liability company, allowing it to sell shares, increase its working capital and grow nationally and internationally. During the late nineteenth century, its office premises occupied numbers 166 to 168 on Fleet Street and No. 1 Johnson's Court at the rear. No. 168 became a widely known landmark of late Victorian

London because of the large gilt letters that covered the front of the building (Figure 8.1).

Sell's also ran an enamelled steel sign workshop and a publishing house, which issued the *Dictionary of the World's Press*, the Directory of Telegraphic Addresses and *Sell's Telegraphic Code*. Its clients included large British companies that pioneered branding and consumer advertising, such as Cadbury (cocoa, chocolate), Colman's (mustard, starch), Lipton's (tea), Maypole's (dairy retail), Reckitt's (household cleaner) and Fry's (cocoa, confectionary). As service providers, agencies had to be close to their clients, the national newspapers on Fleet Street, and to the various provincial papers. Hence, there existed a direct telephone line between the agency and the offices of Thomas Lipton, one of Britain's earliest pioneers in producing and distributing branded tea. By 1900, Sell's agency had opened offices in Birmingham, Liverpool, Manchester, Leeds and Glasgow, and two overseas offices in Montreal and Paris. From its offices in Paris, Sell's published the *Telegraphic Address Book of France* and organized the advertising in this publication.[23]

Like most other agencies at that time, Sell's principal source of income was space booking and the 'space farming'. Sell's agency had sole access to the top right and left corners ('ear spaces') of the *Globe*, a London evening paper. At its London offices, the agency employed dozens of people to service the account of Maypole's alone, one of Britain's largest retailers of dairy products. Before World War I, Maypole's wrote its own advertisements and sent the finished designs to Sell's agency, which then wrote orders for insertions of these adverts in hundreds of national and provincial daily and weekly papers in the areas covered by Maypole's 700 branches. A large portion of Sell's work was also dedicated to financial advertising, such as the advertisement of so-called prospectuses that specifically addressed City investors. With all of these activities combined under one roof, by 1900 Sell's counted about 120 members of staff in its various regional and international offices.[24]

Before the 1910s, Sell's business model was based on the agency buying advertising space in bulk and reselling it to clients at a profit, and on earning commission from newspapers for attracting new advertising clients. At the same time, agencies like Sell's began to build up manufacturers and retailers as profitable long-term clients by providing communications services needed for these business to increase their economies of scale. As such large clients became more important, agencies became more focused on clients' needs and presented themselves as service-oriented, trustworthy companies that conducted their business in an honourable way.[25]

From the late 1870s onwards, agencies like Mitchell's, Sell's, Mather & Crowther and T. B. Browne began to issue yearbooks, annual newspaper

Figure 8.1. Sell's Advertising Agency on Fleet Street, c. 1910.

directories and guide books in which they explained how their services differed from those of the less reputable advertising agents that still populated the environs of Fleet Street.[26] Henry Sell's 1883 handbook on the *Philosophy of Advertising*, for example, outlined how advertising policies for manufacturers who sold their goods through wholesalers and retailers would have to differ from those who sold to the public directly. The handbook also explained how advertisers could assess appropriate newspapers in terms of circulation and type of readership. Reputable agencies like Sell's, so went the message, could help advertisers in the estimation of both the quantitative and the qualitative side of their media strategy.[27] It also provided a full assessment of the costs of an advertising campaign (costing); advice on the wording and drawing up of advertisements; the production and printing of circulars, pamphlets, prospectuses and posters; the translation of advertisements into the languages of export markets; and 'colonial advertising', that is, advertising campaigns in the countries of the British Empire.[28]

The new methodological outlook and the professional attitudes set Victorian advertising practitioners apart from their German and French contemporaries and suggests that a service-oriented advertising industry appeared before the rise of American enterprise culture.[29] While the French, German and US economies continued to be regionally focused, London became the centre of a concentrated media market and a nationally integrated market for the retailing of consumer goods like soap, household cleaners, packaged and branded foods and alcoholic beverages.[30] Nationally distributed consumer brands and a heavily concentrated media market required and supported a professionalized advertising industry.

Although the total size of the British market was actually smaller than that of France, Germany and the US, its national and international integration took place at a much quicker pace. Both Britain's formal Empire and its informal Empire contributed to the emergence of a nationally integrated market for consumer goods. Unsurprisingly, it was packaged, branded and heavily advertised goods based on ingredients from the Empire, like tea (Lipton's, Horniman's, Mazawattee), cocoa and chocolate (Cadbury's, Fry's, Rowntree's), sugar (Tate's, Lyle's), rubber products (Dunlop) and palm-oil-based products, such as soap (Pears', Hudson's, Lever Brothers), which provided the mainstay of work for the early British advertising industry. As argued by Roy Church and Erika Rappaport, a lot of these products were introduced to middle- and working-class consumers by nonconformist entrepreneurs, whose aim it was to associate their name with a trustworthy product and differentiate it as 'pure' and 'unadulterated'. Advertising was the best way of branding new mass consumer products as safe and reliable.[31]

LOSS AND RECAPTURE OF GLOBAL INFLUENCE: 1910–80

From about 1910 onwards, the global power balance shifted in favour of American agencies, which came to be seen as superior in virtually all European commercial cultures. By 1920, British agencies lived – and survived – by constantly comparing themselves with their American counterparts.[32] Although only two American agencies had opened offices in London before World War I, J. Walter Thompson (JWT) in 1899 and Dorland in 1905, the 1920s and 1930s witnessed a rapid rise in the commercial and cultural influence of American agencies in Britain. After closing its subsidiary during the war, JWT re-opened it in 1919. In the same year, Erwin, Wasey & Co. came from Chicago. Three years later, in 1922, Lord & Thomas and McCann Erickson arrived, with McCann Erickson and JWT beginning to use novel statistical research methods to measure the British consumer market and open it for American goods.[33] Within a decade after re-opening, JWT grew to occupy a place among the ten largest advertising agencies in Britain. Immediately after World War II, Young & Rubicam, and Foote, Cone and Belding rounded off the presence of leading Madison Avenue agencies in London.[34]

Together with the American agencies came American products like Kellogg's cereals, Quaker Oats, Goodyear tyres, Esso petrol, General Motors cars, Kodak cameras, Frigidaire refrigerators, Palmolive soap and Wrigley's chewing gum. The tendency of American advertising agencies to follow their clients abroad and to seek additional local European advertising business led to the successful positioning of American agencies as 'masters of the global market' after 1945.[35] The strong growth of American agencies in the immediate post-war era caused a competitive shakeout, which some observers believed led to the total domination of the British advertising market. The number of American agencies operating in London rose from five in 1939 to 24 by the year 1970. Between 1957 and 1967 alone, American agencies bought 32 British agencies. In 1970, American agencies controlled some 86 per cent of the declared billings (turnover) of the top 20 British advertising agencies.[36] In the words of the London *Times* in 1969, the march of American 'super-agencies' into the British market was an example for 'yet another successful American invasion'.[37]

These figures seem to make a strong case for the Americanization theory of twentieth-century advertising. Yet this picture emerged because historians have focused too much on the three decades or so between World War I and the post-war period of austerity. These decades were an exception in that they witnessed two global wars and a period of unprecedented austerity.

The very basis of Britain's economic success, the Empire, fell apart precisely during these decades. Historians like Victoria de Grazia also ignore the way in which British agencies successfully expanded within the Empire, to continental Europe and North America both before and after World War II. In the mid-1920s, for example, the T. B. Browne agency set up a subsidiary in Sydney. S. H. Benson's, the second largest agency in Britain at that time, expanded to India in 1928. Their competitor, the Samson Clark agency, was particularly active in Australia, setting up offices in Sydney, Melbourne and Brisbane between 1925 and 1927. Mitchell's agency proudly advertised the fact that it could build brand loyalty on the five continents of the Empire. In 1927, the W. S. Crawford agency set up subsidiaries in Berlin and Paris. Other leading agencies in the Asia-Pacific region also had their direct roots in the economic connections between Britain and its colonies in that region. British and Australian entrepreneurs who arrived in Singapore in the 1920s, for instance, established the oldest advertising agencies in the Crown Colony.[38] American agencies like JWT and McCann Erickson only developed a serious presence in the Pacific region outside Australia in the 1960s.[39]

In the early 1950s, the British Colman Prentis & Varley (CPV) agency expanded to Italy where it overtook its major American rival, the JWT agency from New York.[40] The largest agency in Britain at that time, the London Press Exchange (LPE), expanded globally and finally maintained 19 international offices. Before merging with the American Leo Burnett agency in 1969, the LPE bought the New York-based agency Robert Otto Inc. and opened branch offices all across the world (Figure 8.2).[41] Even smaller agencies operating from Britain's economic periphery, like the Rex Stewart agency of Glasgow in Scotland, exploited the opportunities of the European common market and expanded to the continent by setting up subsidiaries in West Germany, Italy and France. Before merging with another London agency in 1989, this small Glaswegian agency managed to become the seventh-largest advertising agency in Europe with a staff of over 500.[42]

Advertising for branded consumer goods emerged in Britain and British advertising agencies were the first to expand internationally. It is therefore less surprising that from the 1970s onwards the global reign of American advertising came under severe pressure once again from British agencies. Between the 1960s and 1980s a new generation of British advertising creatives and a new kind of small company, which often started from scratch, like Collett Dickenson Pearce (1960), Boase Massimi Pollitt (1968), Saatchi & Saatchi (1970), Abbott Mead Vickers (1978), Lowe Howard Spink (1981) and Bartle Bogle Hegarty (1982), developed specialized skills

INTERNATIONAL ADVERTISING · MARKETING · MERCHANDISING · RESEARCH
DIRECT MAIL · PUBLIC RELATIONS

THE LONDON PRESS EXCHANGE LTD
7 St Martin's Place, London WC2, England
Telephone: TEMple Bar 2424 · *Telex:* 24243 · *Telegrams:* Instantaneous London WC2

LPE INTERNATIONAL LTD

FRANCE	**SINGAPORE & MALAYSIA**	**USA**
EDIP SA	LPE SINGAPORE LTD	LPE INTERNATIONAL INC
Paris	*Singapore*	TELPEX INC
Analyses et Recherches		*New York*
InteRPrise	**JAPAN**	
	LPE INTERNATIONAL LTD	**VENEZUELA**
GERMANY	*Tokyo*	LPE-NOVAS-CRISWELL CA
LPE INTERNATIONALE WERBE	Research Services & Market	*Caracas*
UND MARKETING GmbH	Development (International) Ltd	
Düsseldorf & Hamburg		
Telpex GmbH	**SOUTH AFRICA**	**COLOMBIA**
	LPE SOUTH AFRICA (PTY) LTD	TORO-NOVAS-CRISWELL
ITALY	*Johannesburg & Cape Town*	*Bogotá*
LPE ITALIANA SpA	Market Research Africa (Pty) Ltd	
Milan & Rome	Merchandising and Marketing	**ARGENTINA**
	Development (Pty) Ltd	LPE-ROBERT OTTO & CO SAC
PORTUGAL	**RHODESIA**	*Buenos Aires*
LPE-MORRISON LDA	LPE CENTRAL AFRICA	
Lisbon	(PRIVATE) LTD	**PUERTO RICO**
	Salisbury	LPE-ROBERT OTTO & CO
SPAIN	Market Research Africa (Rhodesia)	(PUERTO RICO) INC
LPE-MORRISON SA	(Pvt) Ltd	*San Juan*
Madrid	Merchandising & Marketing	
	Development (Pvt) Ltd	
INDIA	**ZAMBIA**	**MEXICO**
LPE-AIYARS (PVT) LTD	LPE Zambia Ltd	ROBERT OTTO & CO SA
Bombay, Calcutta, New Delhi, Madras	*Lusaka*	*Mexico City*

✲ ✲ ✲

Centralised International Advertising and Marketing Agencies

LONDON   NEW YORK
LPE INTERNATIONAL (CENTRAL SERVICE) LTD   LPE-ROBERT OTTO INC

ASSOCIATES IN 68 COUNTRIES THROUGHOUT THE WORLD

Figure 8.2. The London Express Exchange Global Network, 1966.

in seeking more visually arresting solutions for their clients.[43] The foremost among this so-called 'new wave' of British agencies was the London-based Collett Dickenson Pearce (CDP) agency.

CDP made its name for being the home of young British advertising talents like Charles Saatchi and John Hegarty. It quickly became known for producing sharp, witty, bold and memorable advertisements both in print and on television for brands such as Ford, Fiat, Parker Pens, Birds Eye food, Heineken beer, Benson & Hedges cigarettes and Hamlet cigars.[44] The new wave of creative British agencies produced advertising that was said to 'twinkle and dance, especially when placed next to typical American ads of the time'.[45] At home, both in art galleries and on the trading floor, firms like CDP and Saatchi & Saatchi challenged the global dominance of American agencies by reconnecting to the City of London as a source of capital.

Brothers Charles and Maurice Saatchi set up their eponymous agency in 1970. The Saatchis themselves, their art directors and copy-writers produced award-winning creative work for Silk Cut cigarettes and British Airways. At the same time they used a little-known American agency in London, Compton, to gain Public Company listing on the London Stock Exchange, where they raised the funds to acquire 35 marketing service companies between 1972 and 1987, including entire American advertising agency networks. Deborah Leslie has argued that the Saatchis' outlook on advertising mirrored the politics of the British Empire. During the 1980s and 1990s, the Saatchis pioneered the idea of the global brand which targeted similar consumer segments across the world regardless of national or cultural differences. Between 1985 and 1991, the agency released identical advertisements for a major brand, British Airways, in 46 national markets. In the advertisements, 'British Airways, like the British Empire, plays the role of co-ordinating and reuniting different cultures across the colonies. Individuals are draped in different-colored outfits to signify different "colors" of race. They come together at the end of the advertisement to form the smiling face of a global traveler.'[46] While many American agencies at that time still believed in using international advertising campaigns to 'bring America to the world', the Saatchis' approach used a much more generic commercial language that flattened out cultural differences.[47]

In 1975, the Saatchis employed a new Director of Finance, Martin Sorrell, who perfected the company's growth and acquisition strategy based on developing new financial instruments. In 1986, Sorrell joined a small shopping basket manufacturer, then known as Wire and Plastic Products (WPP), as CEO and once again used the stock market in London to raise capital. This capital was then used by Sorrell to acquire American advertising agencies, among them JWT in 1987, the Ogilvy group in 1989, Young & Rubicam in 2000 and Grey Global in 2005.[48]

The arrival of the Saatchi brothers and of Martin Sorrell took most American advertising professionals and industry experts by surprise. Always believing that American agencies would dominate global marketing communications, JWT and other Madison Avenue agencies resisted but failed to prevent their hostile takeovers. The vigour with which first British and then French advertising groups like Publicis bought up American agencies led industry insiders to talk about a British or European 'invasion'.[49] Of the ten largest advertising groups that today control global advertising, only two are based in the US (Omnicom, Interpublic), with the remainder organizing global marketing communications from London (WPP; Aegis), Paris (Publicis; Havas) and Tokyo (Dentsu; Hakuhodo; Asatsu). The world's largest consumer communications company today, the WPP group, which owns a portfolio of over 300 advertising agencies, PR agencies, market research companies, direct marketing companies, media buying companies, social media, and interactive and search-engine agencies worldwide, is a British company, based in London's Mayfair, and headed by a Knight of the Realm, Sir Martin Sorrell. The world's biggest advertising budgets have long left New York, Philadelphia and Los Angeles, and moved to Mumbai and Shanghai. More and more historians are puzzled how these facts can be explained through the paradigm of 'Americanization'.[50]

The story of the rise and subsequent fall of the Saatchi brothers, the 'British invasion' of Madison Avenue, and the global race between French, British, American and Japanese communication groups has been told and retold numerous times.[51] Given the argument of this chapter, it is interesting to note that the life story of the Saatchi brothers reflects the Imperial traditions of the British economy. Charles and Maurice Saatchi were born to Nathan Saatchi and Daisy Ezer, a wealthy Iraqi Jewish family in Baghdad, at a time when the British ruled Iraq. Their father was a textile merchant who in 1947 fled Baghdad for the suburbs of North London, where another Jewish businessman with Eastern European roots, Martin Sorrell, was also born. There, Nathan Saatchi rebuilt his business by purchasing two cotton mills; Charles went to study at the London School of Printing and Graphic Arts, and Maurice to the London School of Economics.[52] In the story of British advertising, Empire and immigration loom large – at least as large as small-town Englishness. Few of the leaders of twentieth-century British marketing communications were actually born in London despite the fact that the city became its dominant centre.

GLOBAL CONSUMER CULTURE, MADE IN BRITAIN

The advertising agent as professional, the advertising agency as business model, and the 'advertisement' as part of mundane consumer culture, existed first in Britain during the second half of the Georgian era. Although American agencies dominated global advertising during the five decades between 1920 and 1970, American dominance in global advertising needs to be interpreted as a mid-twentieth-century exception, an epiphenomenon of what Bacevich called the 'short American century'.[53] Elements of early-nineteenth-century British commercial culture, such as the advertising agent system, advertising-funded print media and the 'commodity spectacle'[54] helped shape American society in the first place. From the 1970s onwards, first the British and then the Japanese and the French bought large stakes in the American advertising industry and challenged the creative and communicative norms promoted by American agencies. The US is now province and periphery in a multi-polar world that, commercially speaking at least, has fewer and fewer centres. The international expansion of particular aesthetic forms and commercial techniques does not so much depend on where advertising agencies are physically based, i.e. whether they are either American, or British, or French. What matters are the roles they fulfil within a world characterized by increasingly globalized industrial networks.[55]

Historians of this modern world of the global production of advertising imagery will benefit from investigating aspects of transnational exchange processes and the factors that caused the rise of a trans-Atlantic Anglo-American advertising industry structure, which dominated the rest of the globe for most of the nineteenth and twentieth centuries. Historical research of this kind brings into closer focus the question of the geopolitical economy of capitalism.[56] The early industrialization and internationalization of British consumer communications also needs to be read as a prologue to the increasing global entanglement of national cultures produced by what Gunn and Vernon have termed Imperial Britain's 'liberal modernity'.[57] Britain's place in the global market as an exporter of consumer commodities and consumer culture was determined by the role it played in forming a global Empire. Inasmuch as Britain promoted trade in generic and branded commodities with North America, Asia and Australia, its own advertising system was also shaped by images of globalized consumer culture. Well before American advertisements featured foreign markets, foreign settings and consumers, British advertisements connected consumers both at home and in overseas markets through household brands like Lever's Lifebuoy Soap.[58]

Early British advertising agencies acted as promoters of a new type of consumption imagery within global chains of consumer goods. These chains did, of course, become restructured as *Pax Americana* replaced *Pax Britannica*. But it would be wrong to assume, as Susan Strasser has done, that prior to World War I consumer culture was radically different from that of the early twenty-first century. Once the relationship between advertising and consumer culture is seen through the prism of the enterprise as key unit of historical-sociological analysis, parallels and continuities emerge where the past might seem alien at first.[59]

NOTES

1. Quoted in H. Sell, *Philosophy of Advertising* (London: Henry Sell, 1883), p. 27.
2. T. B. Browne, *The Advertiser's ABC: The Standard Advertisement Press Directory* (London: T. B. Browne, 1901), pp. 77–103.
3. B. Clarke, *From Grub Street to Fleet Street: An Illustrated History of English Newspapers to 1899* (Aldershot: Ashgate, 2004), pp. 82–100.
4. T. R. Nevett, 'London's Early Advertising Agents', *Journal of Advertising History* 1 (1977), pp. 15–18.
5. T. R. Nevett, *Advertising in Britain: a History* (London: Heinemann, 1982), pp. 61–6; J. Treasure, *The History of British Advertising Agencies, 1875–1939* (Edinburgh: Scottish Academic Press, 1977); W. Leiss, S. Kline, S. Jhally and J. Botterill, *Social Communication in Advertising: Consumption in the Mediated Marketplace* (London: Sage, 2005), pp. 130–48.
6. White's evolved into White Bull Holmes Ltd, a recruitment advertising agency that went out of business in the late 1980s. See D. Chandler, 'White, James (bap. 1775, d. 1820)', in *Oxford Dictionary of National Biography*, eds H. C. G. Matthew and Brian Harrison (Oxford: Oxford University Press, 2004), online edition, January 2008, http://www.oxforddnb.com [accessed 4 December 2012].
7. Reynell & Son is now part of the TMP Worldwide agency network. See http://www.tmpreynell.co.uk [accessed 14 March 2014].
8. Nevett, 'London's Early Advertising Agents'.
9. 'Advertising Agents Established before the King's Accession and still in Business', *Statistical Review* (April 1935), pp. 26–36.
10. Nevett, 'London's Early Advertising Agents'; G. Miracle, 'An Historical Analysis to Explain the Evolution of Advertising Agency Services', *Journal of Advertising* 6 (1977), pp. 24–8.
11. Nevett, *Advertising in Britain*, pp. 100–2.
12. Browne, *The Advertiser's ABC* (1892), pp. 109–16, 979–83; R. B. Browne, *T. B. Browne: the First 100 Years* (London: T. B. Browne, 1984), manuscript at History of Advertising Trust (HA) Archive, Raveningham, T. B. Browne Box.
13. J. Merron, 'Putting Foreign Consumers on the Map: J. Walter Thompson's Struggle with General Motors' International Advertising Account in the 1920s', *Business History Review* 73 (1999), pp. 465–504.
14. R. Crawford, *But Wait, There's More ...: A History of Australian Advertising, 1900–2000* (Carlton: Melbourne University Press, 2008), pp. 9, 34.
15. V. Thompson, 'Garnier & Co. Ltd: Manufacturers of Vitreous Enamelled Steel Signs in Willesden since 1898' (1998), London Metropolitan Archives LMA/4418/01/005.
16. Charles Holzer Collection, HAT Archive.
17. M. Middleton, 'F. H. K. Henrion', *Graphis* 7 (1951), pp. 314–23.

18. P. Derrick, *How to Reduce Selling Costs* (London: George Newnes, 1916).
19. E. Applegate, *The Rise of Advertising in the United States: A History of Innovation to 1960* (Lanham, MD: Scarecrow Press, 2012), pp. 31–43.
20. M. Martin, *Trois Siècles de Publicité en France* (Paris: Odile Jacob, 1992), pp. 74–102, 251–61; M.-E. Chessel, 'Les Publicitaires dans la France de l'Entre-deux-guerres. Histoire d'une Professionnalisation?', *Bulletin du Centre Pierre Léon d'histoire économique et sociale* 3–4 (1997), pp. 79–89.
21. C. Ross, *Media and the Making of Modern Germany: Mass Communications, Society and Politics from the Empire to the Third Reich* (Oxford: Oxford University Press, 2008), pp. 213–22.
22. 'Death of Mr Henry Sell', *Advertising World* (August 1910), p. 200.
23. E. G. Norris, 'Notes on Sell's History' (November 1967), unpublished manuscript at HAT Archives, Sell's Collection, SL20/1.
24. 'Notes on Sell's History by Mrs Ernest Norris' (November 1967), unpublished manuscript at HAT Archives, Sell's Collection, SL20/4.
25. S. Schwarzkopf, 'Respectable persuaders: The advertising industry and British society, 1900–1939', PhD thesis, University of London, 2008.
26. Mitchell's *The Newspaper Press Directory* started in 1876. Sell's began to issue its annual *Dictionary of the World's Press* in 1885. T. B. Browne published its annual *Advertiser's ABC* from 1892, and in 1895 Mather & Crowther began *Practical Advertising*.
27. Sell, *Philosophy of Advertising*, pp. 7–13.
28. Sell, *Philosophy of Advertising*, pp. 17–21.
29. V. de Grazia, *Irresistible Empire: America's Advance through Twentieth-Century Europe* (Cambridge, MA: Belknap, 2005), pp. 226–83.
30. M. Casson and T. da Silva Lopes, 'Imitation, Brand Protection and Globalization of British Business', *Business History Review* 86 (2012), pp. 287–310; R. Church, 'Advertising Consumer Goods in Nineteenth-Century Britain: Reinterpretations', *Economic History Review* 53 (2000), pp. 621–45.
31. Church, 'Advertising Consumer Goods', pp. 627 and 635; E. Rappaport, 'Packaging China: Foreign Articles and Dangerous Tastes in the Mid-Victorian Tea Party', in *The Making of the Consumer: Knowledge, Power and Identity in the Modern World*, ed. F. Trentmann (Oxford: Berg, 2006), pp. 125–46.
32. 'Service the Secret of American "Supremacy"', *Advertiser's Weekly*, 5 November 1920, p. 182.
33. See J. Walter Thompson Co., *Population Handbook of Great Britain and Ireland* (London: JWT, 1924); J. Walter Thompson Co., *A Market Analysis of the Population Statistics for Great Britain and Ireland* (London: JWT, 1931). An overview is in S. Schwarzkopf, 'The Statisticalization of the Consumer in British Market Research, c. 1920–1960', in T. Crook and G. O'Hara (eds), *Statistics and the Public Sphere: Numbers and the People in Modern Britain, c. 1800–2000* (New York: Routledge, 2011), pp. 144–62.

34. T. Nevett, 'American Influences on British Advertising before 1920', in *Historical Perspectives in Marketing*, eds T. Nevett and R. Fullerton (Lexington, MA: Lexington Books, 1988), pp. 223–40; D. C. West, 'From T-Square to T-Plan: the London Office of the J. Walter Thompson Advertising Agency, 1919–1970', *Business History* 29 (1987), pp. 199–217; D. C. West, 'Multinational Competition in the British Advertising Agency Business, 1936–87', *Business History Review* 62 (1988), pp. 467–501; Nevett, *Advertising in Britain*, pp. 99–103.

35. de Grazia, *Irresistible Empire*, p. 203.

36. J. O'Connor and J. Crichton, *Fifty Years of Advertising – What Next? From Minor to Major Key* (London: Institute of Practitioners in Advertising, 1967), p. 13; J. Tunstall, *The Advertising Man in London Advertising Agencies* (London: Chapman & Hall, 1964), pp. 224–6; D. Jeremy, *A Business History of Britain, 1900–1990s* (Oxford: Oxford University Press, 1998), p. 481; Leiss *et al.*, *Social Communication in Advertising*, p. 372; S. Brierley, *The Advertising Handbook* (London: Routledge, 2002, 2nd ed.), p. 69.

37. 'Why Madison Avenue Moved In', *The Times*, 26 June 1969, p. 25.

38. K. Pashupati and S. Sengupta, 'Advertising in India: the Winds of Change', in *Advertising in Asia: Communication, Culture and Consumption*, ed. K. T. Frith (Ames, IA: Iowa State Press, 1996), pp. 155–81; F. A. Marteau (ed.), *Who's Who in Press, Publicity, Printing* (London: Cosmopolitan Press, 1939), pp. 343, 346; Meeting of Directors Samson Clark Ltd, 30 June 1925, 10 May 1927, HAT Archive, SAM 3/1; C. W. Frerk, 'How to Advertise in Germany', *Advertiser's Weekly*, 8 July 1927, pp. v, x; *Sydney Morning Herald*, 18 April 1931, p. 4 (Supplement); 'Advertising Association', *Straits Times*, 6 May 1948, p. 10.

39. Crawford, *But Wait, There's More*, pp. 137–41.

40. E. Bini and F. Fasce, 'Irresistible Empire or Innocents Abroad? American Advertising Agencies in Postwar Italy, 1950s–1970s', Journal of Historical Research in Marketing 7 (2014), forthcoming; S. Nixon, *Hard Sell: Advertising, Affluence and Transatlantic Relations, c. 1951–69* (Manchester: Manchester University Press, 2013), pp. 27–30.

41. *In and Out the Lane* 8 (1962), pp. 12–30, HAT Archive, LPE 3/2/8. The Figure is from *The LPE Reporter* 9 (1966), HAT Archive, LPE 3/4/4. In 2002, Leo Burnett-LPE was acquired by the French advertising agency network Publicis.

42. 'Rex Stewart Married off to Lopex in £6m Takeover', *Glasgow Herald*, 6 September 1989, p. 25.

43. S. Schwarzkopf, 'From Fordist to Creative Economies: the de-Americanization of European Advertising Cultures since the 1960s', *European Review of History* 20 (2013), pp. 859–79.

44. M. Tungate, *Adland: A Global History of Advertising* (London: Kogan Page, 2007), pp. 80–8; W. Fletcher, *Powers of Persuasion: The Inside Story of British Advertising, 1951–2000* (Oxford: Oxford University Press, 2008), pp. 137–47.

45. S. Fox, *The Mirror Makers: A History of American Advertising and its Creators* (Urbana, IL: University of Illinois Press, 1997), p. ix.
46. D. Leslie, 'Global Scan: The Globalization of Advertising Agencies, Concepts and Campaigns', *Economic Geography* 71 (1995), pp. 402–26.
47. W. O'Barr, 'The Airbrushing of Culture: An Insider Looks at Global Advertising', *Public Culture* 29 (1989), pp. 1–19.
48. D. Teather, 'Sir Martin Sorrell: Advertising Man who Made the Industry's Biggest Pitch', *Observer*, 4 July 2010, p. 38.
49. S. Caulkin, 'The Taking of Madison Avenue', *Campaign*, 9 June 1989, pp. 40–4; T. Douglas, 'The Rise and Rise of the New Brits', *The Times*, 27 September 1984, p. 14; R. Rothenberg, 'Brits Buy Up the Ad Business', *New York Times Magazine*, 2 July 1989, pp. 14–19, 26, 29, 38.
50. S. Schwarzkopf, 'The Subsiding Sizzle of Advertising History: Methodological and Theoretical Challenges in the Post-advertising Age', *Journal of Historical Research in Marketing* 3 (2011), pp. 528–48.
51. K. Goldman, *Conflicting Accounts: The Creation and Crash of the Saatchi & Saatchi Advertising Empire* (New York: Simon & Schuster, 1997).
52. I. Fallon, *The Brothers: The Rise & Rise of Saatchi & Saatchi* (London: Arrow Books, 1989), pp. 29–33.
53. A. J. Bacevich, *The Short American Century: A Postmortem* (Cambridge, MA: Harvard University Press, 2012).
54. T. Richards, *Commodity Culture of Victorian England: Advertising and Spectacle, 1851–1914* (Stanford, CA: Stanford University Press, 1991).
55. J. R. Faulconbridge, J. V. Beverstock, C. Nativel and P. J. Taylor, eds, *The Globalization of Advertising: Agencies, Cities and Spaces of Creativity* (London: Routledge, 2010), pp. 11–18; Schwarzkopf, 'Subsiding Sizzle'.
56. S. Topik and A. Wells, 'Commodity Chains in a Global Economy', in *A World Connecting: 1870–1945*, ed. E. Rosenberg (Cambridge, MA: Harvard University Press, 2012), pp. 593–813; F. Trentmann, 'Crossing Divides: Consumption and Globalization in History', *Journal of Consumer Culture* 9 (2009), pp. 187–220.
57. S. Gunn and J. Vernon (eds), *The Peculiarities of Liberal Modernity in Imperial Britain* (Berkeley, CA: Berkeley University Press, 2011).
58. A. Ramamurthy, *Imperial Persuaders: Images of Africa and Asia in British Advertising* (Manchester: Manchester University Press, 2003); B. Lewis, *So Clean: Lord Leverhulme, Soap and Civilization* (Manchester: Manchester University Press, 2008); T. Burke, *Lifebuoy Men, Lux Women: Commodification, Consumption and Cleanliness in Modern Zimbabwe* (Durham, NC: Duke University Press, 1996).
59. S. Strasser, 'The Alien Past: Consumer Culture in Historical Perspective', *Journal of Consumer Policy* 26 (2003), pp. 375–93.

CHAPTER NINE

Drink Empire Tea: Gender, Conservative Politics and Imperial Consumerism in Inter-war Britain

ERIKA RAPPAPORT

'Indian Tea Trade almost paralysed – many gardens closed – thousands of labourers unemployed. Urge Chancellor of the Exchequer immediate re-imposition six pence import duty with four pence rebate on empire produce.'[1] The Indian Tea Association (ITA), a powerful body of British planters, sent this desperate telegram to the Secretary of State in India in September of 1931. The planters believed that such a preference would help them combat mounting surpluses and steeply falling prices by excluding cheap Dutch-grown teas from Java and Sumatra from the British market. Although in the past British-grown teas had enjoyed an imperial preference, this protection had been abolished in 1929 under the free trade policies of conservative Chancellor of the Exchequer, Winston Churchill. His successor, the socialist free trader Philip Snowden refused to grant the planters' wishes.[2] The tea industry nevertheless continued to lobby for protection and it initiated a massive publicity effort known as the Drink Empire Tea campaign.

This public relations campaign was intended to teach British tea buyers and drinkers to prefer teas from India, Ceylon and British East Africa to those from the Netherlands East Indies and to regard shopping as part of their duty as imperial citizens. The campaign illuminates how the imperial consumer citizen was imagined and mobilized in political discourse, advertising and propaganda. It moreover reveals how imperial actors, ideologies and politics shaped British consumer culture during the inter-war years. As this chapter suggests, during this time national, imperial and global economic problems politicized imperial commodities in ways that had not occurred since the Boston Tea Party.[3]

The Drink Empire Tea campaign was developed in the spring and summer of 1931, just before the Labour government fell, and it began in September just as a new Tory-dominated National Government was forming.[4] Labour Prime Minister Ramsay MacDonald led the government, but imperial trade policy was also shaped by Neville Chamberlain, who became Chancellor of the Exchequer, and by his colleague conservative imperial protectionist Sir Philip Cunliffe-Lister, who served as Secretary of State for the Colonies. These men dealt with an alarming trade deficit, high unemployment and the virtual collapse in the global economy through austerity measures and by taking Britain off the gold standard. They were reluctant to adopt protectionism, however, fearing higher food prices and trade retaliations. Protectionists, many from within the Conservative Party, asked the British public to both execute an informal preference for Empire goods when they went shopping and to pressure the government to institute formal protectionism.

Instead of instituting tariffs and other forms of protection, the government promoted imperial shopping habits. The government started to support the many businesses, politicians and female grass-roots activists who were already working to create imperial consumerism. These groups all believed that cultivating consumer knowledge about the geographic origins of goods would transform preferences, tastes and politics. The imperial shopping movement was most prevalent between the International Exhibition held at Wembley in 1924 and Britain's adoption of imperial protectionism at Ottawa in 1932. Such ideas and activities were not new, but they gained urgency as the Dominions and colonies were pushing for greater political autonomy and the US was moving into what had been thought of as British markets. The Stock Market Crash of 1929 and near-collapse in global markets thereafter, coupled with the passage of the Statute of Westminster, which granted self-governance to the Dominions in December of 1931, only intensified the project.

Most scholars have studied empire shopping through an examination of the successes and failures of the Empire Marketing Board (EMB).[5] The EMB was a government-funded agency that from 1926 to 1933 was charged to create a 'National Movement with a view to spreading and fostering [the idea] that Empire purchasing creates an increased demand for the manufactured products of the United Kingdom and therefore stimulates employment at home'.[6] Under the direction of Stephen Tallents, the EMB advocated a materialistic understanding of the British Empire through publicity, education, funding scientific and economic research, and developing schemes to facilitate the production and marketing of empire goods.[7] Although generally underfunded and relatively short-lived, the Board became a school for the budding field of public relations – a place where numerous men and women learned how to sell commodities, industries, nations and empires.[8]

The EMB had promoted numerous empire goods, but it was initially reluctant to help Indian tea planters until Ceylon, East African growers and large wholesalers and retailers proved receptive. Distributors had previously resisted marking teas with an imperial label because blends came from many sources, including those outside the Empire. Moreover, it was the EMB's policy not to support one colony or region over another. Even with trade co-operation, however, the EMB did not fund the scheme.[9] Instead it agreed to give advice and display space to the Indian Tea Cess Committee, the body that had organized Indian and many generic tea promotions in Britain, the Empire and overseas markets since 1903.[10] In 1931 it relied on proven methods that included paying canvassers to speak to and distribute free commercial information, store display material and other publicity to grocers, caterers and other retailers. It distributed posters, films, radio broadcasts, pamphlets, news articles and educational materials to schools and other public institutions and advertised in trade journals and similar venues. Lecturers demonstrated and served a great deal of hot tea too.[11] All of these efforts entreated consumers, and indeed all buyers, retailers, caterers and others, to put their Empire before their pocketbook when they went shopping.

For centuries various institutions and forms of British popular culture, such as the Great Exhibition of 1851 and its many sequels, had taught visitors to enjoy looking at and thinking about the material benefits of the Empire.[12] Department stores, speciality shops and brand advertising frequently used racialized, Orientalist imagery and other explicit and implicit messages to sell a range of goods and the Empire itself.[13] World War I expanded the State's control over the economy and aided the acceptance of advertising and use of propaganda to sway public opinion. The advent of universal suffrage and development of new media such as radio and cinema politicized the consumer in new ways. As Gurney argues in this volume, over time the Conservatives rather than Labour came to articulate a powerful vision of the consumer citizen. However, in the inter-war period the conservative consumer citizen was not the individual, pleasure-seeking ideal that it would later become. Rather, this was a consumer whose first duty was to the nation. There were two critical questions: How to teach consumers to shop for the nation, and what were the boundaries of that polity – the island or the imperial nation. Although in general these questions were never resolved, tea growers living in the Empire were quite clear about these issues. They believed in an imperial nation, imperial protectionism and voluntary forms of imperial shopping as well.

After the war, many conservatives pushed for imperial protection and sought to stimulate imperial shopping habits. As Frank Trentmann has proposed, this fashioned a conservative model of the consumer as possessing a national duty to shop for the Empire.[14] Most protectionists did not advocate national tariffs, as was the case in the US, Germany and other nations. Rather, they envisioned a wider economic union surrounding the British Empire. Building on Joseph Chamberlain's Edwardian Tariff Reform League, they believed that differential tariffs and duties could solve domestic and imperial economic problems and create closer ties between the disparate entities that made up the Empire.[15] By the 1920s, differences surrounding whether and how to institute imperial preference rocked the Conservative Party, with many still reluctant to abandon free trade, while others thought this was critical both to the party and Empire's future.

Several years before the Drink Empire Tea campaign began, Lord Beaverbrook, Canadian press baron and conservative politician, and supportive business groups waged what Beaverbrook called an 'Empire Crusade'.[16] Since 1929 Beaverbrook had been using his wealth, influence and newspapers to pressure Stanley Baldwin and the Conservative leadership to adopt protectionism. Imperial preference, Beaverbrook explained, would allow the 'British people', including those in the colonies, 'to insulate themselves from the economic follies and miseries of the world'.[17] Beaverbrook even went so far as to create a separate though short-lived Party of Empire Crusaders.[18] Autarky was of course most associated with the fascist project but it also appeared in imperial Britain at the same time.

The National government resisted protectionism but it also responded to Beaverbrook and his allies by supporting a massive Buy British campaign that the EMB launched in September 1931. One of the largest government propaganda campaigns ever conducted in peacetime, the Buy British campaign used persuasion, not tariffs, to try to solve Britain's mounting trade deficit.[19] British products were defined as those grown and produced in the British Isles and secondarily those grown or manufactured in the

Empire. EMB secretary Stephen Tallents gained support for the campaign from many institutions that appear elsewhere in this volume, including government bodies such as the Ministry of Agriculture, Board of Trade and the Post Office. The Co-operative Society, BBC, Boy Scouts, Federation of British Industries, railway companies, football clubs and countless other bodies joined in as well. The campaign used press advertising and posters and sent display and informational material to countless businesses and organizations. Tallents wrote, 'We need not emphasise the dramatic effect upon the public mind which the mobilisation of a considerable proportion of advertising energy of the country to the endorsement of this single theme would achieve.'[20] The theme of the campaign was simply that people should 'Buy British'. All Britons regardless of class, region or gender were asked to think about the nation every time they made a purchase.

Both the EMB and Beaverbrook's approaches were theoretically class and gender neutral, but in practice they assumed that women, especially housewives, did the lion's share of the nation's purchasing.[21] Female consumers now possessed the vote and were a force to be reckoned with. For example, commenting on his frustration with Baldwin's reluctance to adopt imperial protectionism, Lord Beaverbrook exhorted 'The women of England ... to give comfort to the faltering politicians and show them the way to greater faith in Britain and the Empire.'[22] The British Empire Producers' Organization, a trade group representing many imperial and domestic industries, also targeted women and employed a great deal of propaganda to teach the average housewife that her shopping basket and her kitchen were imperial spaces.[23]

Many women responded to such calls and joined women's organizations and/or became paid or unpaid agents in support of Empire Buying. Conservative women's groups became dedicated to the cause. The large and powerful Primrose League, for example, defined women's shopping as a way to unite 'Home, Nation, and Empire'.[24] The pro-Empire female Forum Club hosted Buy British luncheons and meetings where businessmen were invited to inform women that 'as shoppers' they were 'employing British Labour and helping to build up the British Empire overseas'.[25] The Duchess of York pronounced that only 'Empire Products' should be used in royal kitchens, and the League of Empire Housewives' motto became 'Every Kitchen an Empire Kitchen'. Their manifesto explained: 'Our existence as a nation depends on buying as much as possible from producers at home and in the Empire.'[26] The Empire Day Medal Association also instructed children that the prosperity of the 'Overseas Dominions is indissolubly linked with the prosperity of working classes of the Home Country'.[27] Some pro-empire activists assumed that the working-class female shopper was essentially ignorant, but this perception inspired more education, advertising and propaganda. In other words, class and gender stereotypes necessitated the growth of advertising and publicity.[28]

The Buy Empire Tea campaign was hence a part of a much more widespread movement. Yet the tea industry was motivated by its particular concerns and it had in fact led, not followed, the imperial consumer movement, having invented many of the techniques used by the EMB and other businesses.[29] As Stefan Schwarzkopf argues in this volume, many of the innovations in British advertising happened first or at the same time in the Empire. This is particularly clear in the tea industry. In the 1890s Ceylon's tea planters, followed by India's, invented a means to raise funds to pay for global advertising. Through their trade associations and with the backing of the colonial state, planters imposed a duty on exported teas known as a cess.[30] Cess funds paid for publicity to open overseas markets and grew with the expansion of exports. Ceylon had first used a cess to fund its extravagant displays at the Chicago World's Fair in 1893, and India did so to erect its impressive show at the Louisiana Purchase Exhibition held in St Louis in 1904. At these events Ceylon and India competed with each other, but by the 1920s and 1930s they worked together to combat the sourcing and blending of Dutch-grown teas in British and other markets via well-known brands.

Perhaps no commodity was as thoroughly associated with the Empire as was tea in the 1930s. Until the 1890s Britons typically drank tea from China, but after the turn of the century nearly all teas consumed in the UK and colonial markets were from India and Ceylon. In 1931 tea accounted for 1 per cent of the value of the total merchandise entering world trade and over two-thirds was produced and consumed in the British Empire.[31] In the UK, tea's largest market, per capita consumption had been growing very rapidly since the turn of the century and had reached a peak of 9.6 lb per year.[32] Yet during the 1920s, unemployment and labour unrest in India and Ceylon's tea gardens brought shortages and encouraged distributors to begin importing cheaper teas from the Netherlands East Indies.[33] Soon shortages gave way to surpluses and by the mid-1920s India and Ceylon's planters tried to stop the influx of Dutch-grown teas through various legal and fiscal means, but they were often thwarted by the big brands that increasingly had multi-national interests.[34]

In 1930 and 1931 surpluses grew, prices fell and British planters turned to consumers to save their imperial industry. John Harper, a publicity expert who had worked for the Indian Tea Association developing Indian markets, directed the Drink Empire Tea campaign. Harper gained knowledge about British publicity from Gervas Huxley, the EMB employee who was the main advisor for the tea campaign and who acted as liaison between the Board and the Indian Tea Cess Committee.[35] A member of one of Britain's most famous families that straddled the worlds of science, imperial administration, fiction and publicity, Gervas was the grandson of evolutionary scientist Thomas Huxley, cousin of both Julian Huxley, the evolutionary biologist, and Aldous Huxley, the writer. Gervas married Elspeth Grant, who became best known for her autobiographical novel, *The Flame Trees of Thika* (1959), which described her memories of growing up on a coffee farm in Kenya. Despite coming from the planter class, Elspeth was a transnational figure and a modernizer who gained a degree in agriculture from the University of Reading and also studied at Cornell University in New York. She then worked as the assistant press officer to the EMB and at around the same time was made Honorary Treasurer of the Women's Institute. This was precisely the sort of female organization that most responded to the empire shopping movement. Gervas and Elspeth Huxley and John Harper also communicated with and befriended the most famous American advertising and public relations professionals: Earl Newsom, Elmo Roper and William Esty.[36] Newsom's Company would later represent Ford and General Motors, Standard Oil, CBS and Republican politicians Dwight D. Eisenhower and Richard Nixon. He also handled empire teas in the US. For decades he carried on a regular correspondence with the Huxleys and their cohort of PR experts, discussing family and politics and how to sell commodities and industries. This transatlantic cohort of publicists envisioned selling as occurring in the store, the advertisement, trade journal, newspaper and in a myriad other public settings, often in ways that the public would not recognize as selling at all. The Huxleys first practised this art while working on the Drink Empire Tea campaign.

The Tea Campaign constructed a positive image of the colonial industry, the British Empire and the idea of protectionism. Campaign agents targeted retailers and caterers, grocers and hotels. They pressured schools, government agencies, factories and even 'Public Assistance Institutions' to serve only imperial teas.[37] In these institutions poor and unemployed men and women became imperial consumers, albeit as passive recipients of aid. One of the leading promoters of Empire Tea, Sir Charles C. McLeod, emphasized all these points in a widely read and discussed speech he first gave at the Royal Empire Society in November of 1931. He explained to British consumers that they could save their own and a million tea garden workers' jobs by stopping foreign teas from entering the British market.[38] Although he may not have meant it, McLeod encouraged British workers to identify with out-of-work Indians who picked and processed their tea. The chairman of the Ceylon Association also explained how important the commodity was to their island's economy, paying for food, hospitals, schools, roads and railways.[39] 'Empire Grown Tea', a pamphlet distributed to tens of thousands of retailers, shareholders, politicians and shoppers similarly activated consumers by telling them they must 'create a demand for "EMPIRE TEA"' and 'obtain protection for such teas in the home market'. They needed to *'ask for Empire tea, recommend your friends to purchase Empire Teas and, if possible, insist on obtaining such teas'*.[40] British consumers thus had a hefty responsibility when they bought their tea.

Similar arguments occurred in the Empire, but with a subtle yet very important difference. For example, Rai Bahadur Nagendra Nath Chaudhury, a member of the Assam Legislative Council, supported tea publicity as a way to promote Indian entrepreneurship. He reminded fellow politicians that since Indians now owned a significant proportion of the tea gardens, buying empire teas supported Indian – not British – development.[41] While Indians were aware of such debates, British consumers and retailers were not, since no propaganda or publicity made the point that not all planters in India or Ceylon, or Java and Sumatra for that matter, were in fact British.

Instead publicity was vague. Canvassers explained to thousands of grocers and retailers and shoppers that tea was either from the Empire or it was not. In November 1931 alone, for example, they distributed 52,459 window bills and 118,224 leaflets to retailers in 806 towns.[42] By December, 40,000 grocers were found displaying Empire Tea materials and the major distributors such as Lipton's, Home and Colonial Stores, Maypole and the Co-operative Wholesale Society had brought out one or more Empire brands.[43] Smaller companies affixed red, white and blue labels bearing the Union Jack and other national symbols to countless tea packages.[44] Grocers' journals discussed campaign literature and store promotions, adopting and adapting many of its ideas.[45]

Politics, consumer pressure, free display material and the belief that Empire boosted sales encouraged grocers to jump on the empire bandwagon. Trade shows and trade journals told shopkeepers that '[t]he public wants empire goods'.[46] Empire displays were patriotic but also they were modern, eye-catching and 'tempting', claimed *The Grocer* in 1931.[47] Experts promised that imperial imagery and rhetoric elevated the mundane into the interesting by placing everyday commodities into compelling narratives. Scenes of exotic tropical lands and empire production engaged consumers in the human story behind the product, attracting interest and inciting consumers to fantasize about commodities.

Lewis's department store, known to serve a largely working-class clientele, transformed the main hall of their Manchester store into 'an Empire Tea Exhibition' in the spring of 1932. As one appreciative journalist put it, this exhibition invited visitors to see the 'East' as 'an annex of Manchester'. Visitors sipped Indian tea and listened to music played by a 'native' orchestra that had been brought over from India for the Wembley Exhibition, while gazing at paintings depicting staged scenes of 'old Benares' and the Taj Mahal. India was cast as a pleasant escape from a drab Manchester. 'Many people', the reporter claimed, 'took the opportunity to-day of escaping from Manchester's misty streets to a fragrant atmosphere of the colourful East, where a warm sun shone permanently on tea plantations and dark-skinned men and women.' Lewis's working-class customers could feel, taste and listen to a highly attractive, romanticized and consumer-oriented India, as 'a tourist would like to see it'.[48] This was a theatrical, sanitized, recycled India, a simulacrum of Asia that was all the more powerful in its denial of changing colonial realities. Even in the most depressed areas of Britain, workers were figured as 'white' consumers who enjoyed buying into what had primarily been an upper-class vision of the Raj. And this translated into profits. According to the firm's sales figures, Empire was popular with their customers who had apparently purchased 20 per cent more tea since they had erected their 'show' in Manchester.[49]

Films such as 'Empire-Grown Tea', the famous 'The Song of Ceylon' (1934), and beautifully designed posters replicated the themes presented in such exhibitions.[50] For example, a pair of posters by H. S. Williamson placed a white, wealthy and fashionable female consumer and a non-white tea picker both in the tea garden (Figures 9.1 and 9.2).

The similarities in colour (both posters feature the same yellow, pink and green), layout and setting used in the posters, the gender of the subjects and the text, highlighted global connections even as race and fashion mapped differences between consumer and producer.[51] This portrayal of tea's commodity chain purported to make production and consumption visible. Yet this common image of the West consuming the East suppressed men's activities, women's role as producers and the importance of non-white colonial consumers and producers in the global economy.[52] It obscured as much as it revealed, and this was just what the Empire Tea activists wanted.

Consumption was a form of work, but women were also getting paid to sell Empire.[53] Not unlike Ghana's female credit traders that Bianca Murillo describes in this volume, a handful of New Imperial saleswomen began to sell imperial commodities and conveyed market information to growers, thereby shaping how imperial business envisioned consumers. Since the 1880s, female owners, managers, waitresses, sales assistants, demonstrators, teachers, lecturers and journalists had pushed the empire's produce. In the 1920s and 1930s, however, they were increasingly showing up in the business archive in more formal capacities.[54] For example, a Mrs

Figure 9.1. Drinking Empire Grown Tea, H. S. Williamson, 1931. NA C0 956/442 Reproduced with permission of the National Archives.

Figure 9.2. Picking Empire Grown Tea, H. S. Williamson, 1931. NA CO 956/440. Reproduced with permission of the National Archives.

Lidderdale, the Secretary of the Women's Guild of Empire, was hired to work for the Empire Tea campaign. She and other similar women lectured at countless female organizations and wrote detailed reports that provide an unusually rich document of consumer reactions and her own class and gender prejudices.[55] In July of 1932, Lidderdale delivered 12 lectures to between 40 and 80 women and a handful of vicars, tea planters, reporters and grocers at the Women's Conservative and Unionist Association, the Women's Guild of Empire, the Conservative Women's Society, the Central Mission in Tottenham Court Road and the Young Women's Christian Association. She liked to organize mixed-class, all-female meetings because she assumed that Society women could influence the shopping habits of their social inferiors.[56] Much to her dismay, however, Lidderdale found that although her audiences were generally receptive to the idea of empire shopping, they were on the whole very ignorant about tea production and imperial geography. At one such lecture in Kent, she described her listeners as 'Women in good circumstances but many of them not very intelligent – it was necessary to repeat the same point again and again ... from a different angle.' Poor women were even worse; Lidderdale found they knew nothing about where their tea came from and assumed that because they 'bought tea in a local shop it must be British'.[57]

At the same time, Lidderdale learned much from her supposedly ignorant audiences. A Cardiff woman, for example, told her that J. Lyons, the huge blenders, packers and caterers, was promoting empire by showing their factory workers 'a most interesting entertainment with a lantern, showing the processes of tea making'.[58] Nevertheless, the female owner of a small general shop revealed that the Lyons' traveller who came to her store had never heard of Empire-grown Tea. The 'owner of a very nice teashop in Dorking' told the same story about a Brooke Bond traveller.[59] These large corporations controlled a huge proportion of the market. They were packaging their teas as imperial products, but the message did not always make it down the distribution chain. Lectures were places, then, where information was disseminated and gathered, a site where planters told their story through intermediaries like Lidderdale, and a place where they learned about markets.

By this time, however, professional market research was also available. For example, a survey of shopkeepers concluded, 'the movement is definitely swinging the country over to buying British in everything from coffee to collar studs'. A London grocer estimated that 90 per cent of his custom was asking for Empire goods. One leading Glasgow retailer claimed the response had been 'electrical'. A Wolverhampton shopkeeper reported a 60 per cent increase in the demand for Empire goods. The survey found, however, that public interest varied by region, gender, age, type of commodity and the wealth of the consumer. On the whole, shopkeepers felt that men were more patriotic than women and that older women more so than 'younger girls' who still preferred 'foreign' goods. Everywhere older Conservative ladies were especially 'furious at the thought that foreign tea imported by us was tax free'.[60] At the same time husbands sometimes returned foreign goods to the shop, suggesting that Empire Buying may have inspired marital conflict. Regional differences emerged as well, with the conservative Midlands leading the call to engage in Empire Buying. In Birmingham, for example, over 100 Co-operative Society outlets were showing 'only Empire goods'.[61] On the other hand, the very smallest shops that sold to the nation's poorest customers still preferred to stock non-Empire brands.[62] Politics, income, region, age and gender shaped one's consumer preferences. What is especially notable is that age and political affiliation more than gender or class seems to have shaped attitudes and tastes. Far more research would be needed here, but the young seemed to welcome foreign goods and habits in the 1930s, but when they became parents in the 1950s and 1960s they would bemoan their children's rebellious global tastes.

Despite such surveys, the long-term impact of patriotic shopping campaigns is very difficult to measure, in part because the government did adopt protectionism at the end of 1932 and the EMB was shut down soon thereafter. The ideas and methodologies the Board developed, however, did not end in 1933. Stephen Tallents moved on to the Post Office and then the BBC, and in this and other jobs he became a leading figure in British public relations. Ceylon's tea growers hired Gervas Huxley to publicise their teas, a job he kept until the mid-1960s. In 1935 he also worked in the same capacity for the newly formed International Tea Market Expansion Board, a body that publicised British *and* Dutch grown teas until 1952. His career thus demonstrates the impact of the EMB and Drink Empire Tea campaign on global publicity through periods of war, austerity and the so-called consumer boom of the late 1950s and 1960s.

While the 1920s and 1930s was a very difficult period for producers and labourers, it was nevertheless a creative moment in which diverse ideals of the consumer were debated. While business taught people to think of shopping as pleasurable and a form of individual expression, Labour and the Co-operative movement fashioned a social democratic consumer, conservative activists and imperial business created an imperial consumer citizen, who shopped and voted for the Empire. Like the social democratic consumer, the imperial consumer implicitly condemned mass culture's appeals to individual pleasure. However, the conservative consumer had a very different definition of nation than the social democratic consumer discussed by Gurney or others in this volume, although it paid lip service to labourers' concerns.

John Mackenzie argued some time ago that inter-war businessmen and politicians hotly debated what the public knew or cared about the Empire.[63] Many female shoppers and saleswomen also entered this conversation and pushed others to care about this issue. Imperial industries such as tea, Beaverbrook's Empire Crusaders and government agencies such as the EMB imagined consumers as lynchpins holding together a fragile Empire. Together, these groups formulated a vision of shopping as a social and global act. Just as today's consumer activists remind purchasers that their buying habits affect workers and suppliers across the globe, Empire Buying revealed the global history of the commodity. However, this was a decidedly gendered, class-bound and racist global vision that assumed the moral and economic superiority of the British Empire and which failed to question the violence, inequality and mistreatment of non-white colonial labourers. Even as the imperial shopping movement broadened the idea of the consumer, it also implicitly maintained the standing assumption that the most sophisticated and knowledgeable shoppers were bourgeois women.

ACKNOWLEDGEMENTS

A version of this paper was given at the Berkshire Conference of Women's Historians, Toronto, Canada, May 2014. I would like to thank Jayeeta Sharma and the other participants and audience members for their helpful comments. I would also like to thank Paul Deslandes, Kenneth Mouré, Bianca Murillo and my co-editors for their thoughts on the chapter.

NOTES

1. Indian Tea Association (hereafter ITA) to the Secretary of State for India, 4 September 1931, IOR: L/E/9/1294, file 1. 'Tea Prices: Report by the Food Council to the President of the Board of Trade', 30 July 1931. NA MAF 69/100. Ceylon's tea value fell by a third between 1929–31. Minutes of the Forty-Third Annual General Meeting of the Ceylon Association in London, 25 April 1932, *Yearbook of the Ceylon Planters' Association*, p. 48.
2. 'The Removal of the English Tea Duty', *Home and Colonial Mail* (hereafter HCM) (May 1929), pp. 721–2.
3. T. H. Breen, *The Marketplace of Revolution: How Consumer Politics Shaped American Independence* (Oxford: Oxford University Press, 2004). For empire, politics and consumption, see Erika Rappaport, 'Consumption', in *The Ashgate Companion to Modern Imperial Histories*, eds Philippa Levine and John Marriott (Farnham, Surrey: Ashgate, 2012), pp. 343–8. For Britain,

see Peter Gurney, *Co-operative Culture and the Politics of Consumption in England, 1870–1930* (Manchester: Manchester University Press, 1996); Matthew Hilton, *Consumerism in Twentieth Century Britain: The Search for a Historical Movement* (Cambridge: Cambridge University Press, 2003); James Vernon, *Hunger: A Modern History* (Cambridge, MA: The Belknap Press of Harvard University Press, 2007) and Frank Trentmann, *Free Trade Nation: Commerce, Consumption, and Civil Society in Modern Britain* (Oxford: Oxford University Press, 2008). Also see, Gurney, Crowley and Dawson in this volume.

4. 'Empire Tea: Inauguration of Notable Campaign', *HCM* (9 September 1931), p. 1; *Report of the Empire Tea Sub-Committee to the Marketing Committee*, EMB, 13 July 1931. NA CO 758/88/4; *Minute Paper on Tea*. IOR, L/E/9/1294, file 1; S. S. Murray, 'Advertising of Empire Tea in the United Kingdom', published in Bulletin No. 1., Department of Agriculture, Nyasaland Protectorate (Zomba: Government Printer, February 1932), p. 12.

5. Trentmann, *Free Trade Nation* and Kaori O'Connor, 'The King's Christmas Pudding: Globalization, Recipes, and the Commodities of Empire', *Journal of Global History* 4 (2009), pp. 127–55.

6. Michael Havinden and David Meredith, *Colonialism and Development: Britain and its Tropical Colonies* (London: Routledge, 1993), p. 150; Stephen Constantine, '"Bringing the Empire Alive": The Empire Marketing Board and Imperial Propaganda, 1926–1933', in *Imperialism and Popular Culture*, ed. John M. MacKenzie (Manchester: Manchester University Press, 1986), pp. 192–231; *Buy and Build: The Advertising Posters of the Empire Marketing Board* (London: Her Majesty's Stationery Office, 1986); David Meredith, 'Imperial Images: The Empire Marketing Board, 1926–32', *History Today* 37:1 (January 1987), pp. 285–300; Mike Cronin, 'Selling Irish Bacon: The Empire Marketing Board and Artists of the Free State', *Eire* 39: 3&4 (2004), pp. 132–43; James Murton, 'John Bull and Sons: The Empire Marketing Board and the Creation of a British Imperial Food System', in *Edible Histories, Cultural Politics: Towards a Canadian Food History*, eds Franca Iacovetta, Valerie J. Korinek and Marlene Epp (Toronto: University of Toronto Press, 2012), pp. 225–48.

7. *H. M. Treasury Committee of Civil Research: Report of the Research Co-ordination Sub-Committee* (London: HMSO, 1928), pp. 61–3. IOR Eur Mss F174/1089.

8. Jacquie L'Etang, *Public Relations in Britain: A History of Professional Practice in the Twentieth Century* (Mahwah, NJ: Lawrence Erlbaum Associates, 2004), pp. 32–9.

9. Murray, 'Advertising of Empire Tea in the United Kingdom', pp. 13–14.

10. For these earlier campaigns see, Erika Rappaport, *An Acquired Taste: Tea and the Global History of an Imperial Consumer Culture* (forthcoming, Princeton, NJ: Princeton University Press, 2016).

11. 'Empire Tea', *HCM* (9 September 1931), p. 1; *Report of the Empire Tea Sub-Committee*, 13 July 1931. NA CO 758/88/4, and *Minute Paper on Tea*, IOR, L/E/9/1294, file 1.

12. There is a huge literature on exhibitions and empire. Two important works that look at the imperial context are Peter H. Hoffenberg, *An Empire on Display: English, Indian, and Australian Exhibitions from the Crystal Palace to the Great War* (Berkeley, CA: University of California Press, 2001) and Daniel Stephen, *The Empire of Progress: West Africans, Indians and Britons at the British Empire Exhibition, 1924–25* (New York: Palgrave Macmillan, 2013).

13. John M. MacKenzie, *Propaganda and Empire: The Manipulation of British Public Opinion, 1880–1960* (Manchester: Manchester University Press, 1984); MacKenzie, ed., *Imperialism and Popular Culture* (Manchester: Manchester University Press, 1986); Anne McClintock, *Imperial Leather: Race, Gender and Sexuality in the Colonial Conquest* (New York: Routledge, 1995); Piya Chatterjee *A Time for Tea: Women, Labor and Post/Colonial Politics on an Indian Plantation* (Durham, NC: Duke University, 2001); Anandi Ramamurthy, *Imperial Persuaders: Images of Africa and Asia in British Advertising* (Manchester: University of Manchester Press, 2003).

14. Trentmann, *Free Trade Nation*, pp. 229–40.

15. For the politics surrounding protectionism, see Anthony Howe, *Free Trade and Liberal England, 1846–1946* (Oxford: Clarendon, 1997); Philip Williamson, *National Crisis and National Government: British Politics, the Economy and Empire, 1926–1932* (Cambridge: Cambridge University Press, 1992); Basudev Chatterji, *Trade, Tariffs, and Empire: Lancashire and British Policy in India, 1919–1939* (Delhi: Oxford University Press, 1992); T. Rooth, *British Protection and the International Economy: Overseas Commercial Policy in the 1930s* (Cambridge: Cambridge University Press, 1994); Andrew S. Thompson, *Imperial Britain: The Empire in British Politics, c. 1880–1932* (Harlow: Longman, 2000); Forrest Capie, *Depression and Protectionism: Britain Between the Wars* (London: George Allen and Unwin, 1983); Michael Kitson and Solomos Solomou, *Protection and Economic Revival: The British Interwar Economy* (Cambridge: Cambridge University Press, 1990); Andrew Marrison, *British Business and Protection, 1903–1932* (Oxford: Clarendon, 1996).

16. Beatrix Campbell, *The Iron Ladies: Why Do Women Vote Tory?* (London: Virago, 1987), pp. 60–1.

17. Lord Beaverbrook, *The Resources of the Empire* (London: Lane Publications, 1934), p. 11.

18. Anne Chisholm and Michael Davie, *Lord Beaverbrook: A Life* (New York: Knopf, 1993), pp. 275–82.

19. Stephen Constantine, 'The Buy British Campaign of 1931', *European Journal of Marketing* 21:4 (1987), pp. 44–59.

20. Quoted in ibid., p. 49.

21. Constantine, 'Buy British', p. 54.

22. Lord Beaverbrook, *My Case for Empire Free Trade* (London: The Empire Crusade, 1930), p. 15.

23. 'Empire Meals on Empire Day', *Empire Production and Export* 187 (March–April 1932), pp. 57–8.

24. Campbell, *Iron Ladies*, p. 61. On these sorts of female conservative organizations see, David Thackeray, *Conservatism for the Democratic Age: Conservative Cultures and the Challenge of Mass Politics in Early Twentieth-Century England* (Manchester: Manchester University Press, 2013), especially pp. 142–8. For other national examples, see the special issue of *International Labor and Working Class History* 77:1 (2010).
25. 'Women's Buy British Campaign: Intelligent Demand', *Empire Production and Export* 186 (February 1932), pp. 46–7.
26. 'Every Kitchen an Empire Kitchen', Manifesto of the League of Empire Housewives, 1927, IOR Mss Eur F174/1094.
27. 'Labour and Empire Trade', *British Empire Annual* (May 1927), p. 4. Mss Eur F174/1094. Mrs Walrond Sweet, 'How to Help the Empire in Your Shopping', *British Empire Annual* (May 1927) p. 3. Mss Eur F174/1094.
28. On the Tory view of the working-class consumer, see David Jarvis, 'British Conservatism and Class Politics in the 1920s', *English Historical Review* 111:440 (February 1996), pp. 72–3.
29. Erika Rappaport, 'Packaging China: Foreign Articles and Dangerous Tastes in the Mid-Victorian Tea Party', in *The Making of the Consumer: Knowledge, Power and Identity in the Modern World*, ed. Frank Trentmann (Oxford: Berg, 2006), pp. 125–46.
30. William Ukers, *All About Tea*, Vol. II (New York: *The Tea and Coffee Trade Journal*, 1935), p. 199; Indian Tea Districts Association Charter, February 1880. IOR Mss Eur F174/1.
31. *Imperial Economic Committee Report on Tea* (1 June 1931), p. 1. NA C0 323/1142/18.
32. Richard Stone, ed., *The Measurement of Consumers' Expenditure and Behaviour in the United Kingdom, 1920–1938*, Vol. 1 (Cambridge: Cambridge University Press, 1954), p. 145.
33. Between 1920 and 1930 acreage under cultivation in Java and Sumatra doubled, and by 1929 these teas accounted for just over 16 per cent of the British market, up from 11.4 per cent in 1925. *International Tea Committee: Fiftieth Anniversary, 1983* (London: Tea Broker's Publications, 1983), p. 2. *Imperial Economic Committee Report on Tea*, p. 11.
34. In 1933 British and Dutch growers entered into a commodity restriction scheme. Bishnupriya Gupta, 'Collusion in the Indian Tea Industry in the Great Depression: An Analysis of Panel Data', *Explorations in Economic History* 34 (1997), pp. 155–73 and 'The International Tea Cartel During the Great Depression, 1929–1933', *The Journal of Economic History*, 61:1 (March 2001), pp. 144–59.
35. Gervas Huxley, 'Suggested Empire Tea Campaign', *Minutes of the Empire Tea Sub-Committee to the Marketing Committee*, EMB, 6 June 1931. NA CO 758/88/4.
36. Gervas Huxley, *Both Hands: An Autobiography* (London: Chatto and Windus, 1970), pp. 187–94; Scott M. Cutlip, *The Unseen Power: Public Relations, A History* (New York: Routledge, 1994), pp. 662–759.

37. *Indian Tea Cess Committee Minutes* (hereafter *ITCC*), 11 March 1932, p. 6, and 8 July 1932.
38. Sir Charles C. McLeod, 'A Plea for Empire Tea', speech first given at the Royal Empire Society, 17 November 1931. IOR Eur Mss F174/854. It was also published and/or discussed in trade papers, many dailies and local newspapers. *ITCC Minutes*, January 1932, pp. 6–7.
39. Chairman's Annual Speech, Ceylon Association in London, 25 April 1932, *Yearbook of the Planters' Association in Ceylon* (1932), pp. 48–9.
40. 'EMPIRE GROWN TEA' pamphlet, 19310, IOR Eur Mss F174/854. Emphasis in original. It was reprinted and discussed in many trade journals, see for example, J. R. H. Pickney, 'Empire Tea', letter to the editor of *HCM* (26 February 1931), p. 13. On shareholder responses, see 'Labelling Teas', *HCM* (16 July 1931), p. 1.
41. Rai Bahadur Nagendra Nath Chaudhury, 'Discussion of Adjournment Motion Regarding Levy of Preferential Import Duties on Teas Entering Great Britain', *Extract from Proceedings of the Assam Legislative Council*, 2 October 1931. IOR: L/E/9/1294, file 1.
42. *ITCC Minutes*, 8 January 1932, p. 6.
43. *ITCC Minutes*, 12 February 1932, p. 6.
44. Banks and Company Printing Guard Book of Labels (1932–34), University of Glasgow Archives, BKS 11/11/3.
45. 'United Kingdom as the World's Tea Shop', *The Grocer* (28 March 1931), p. 57 and 'New Empire Trade "Push"', *The Grocer* (10 January 1931), p. 78.
46. 'The Birmingham and Midlands Grocers' Exhibition: Fine Display of Colonial and Home Products', *The Grocer* (17 January 1931), p. 54 and *The Grocers' Gazette*, (19 September 1931), n.p. NA CO 758/88/4.
47. 'The Art of Window Dressing: Let the Empire Stimulate Sales this Summer', *The Grocer* (27 June 1931), pp. 48–9.
48. *ITCC Minutes*, 13 May 1932, p. 3. Eur Mss F174/928.
49. *ITCC Minutes*, 10 June 1932, p. 2. Eur Mss F174/928.
50. *ITCC Minutes*, 8 January 1932, p. 8. Eur Mss F174/928.
51. H. S. Williamson, 'Drinking Empire Grown Tea', NA CO 956/442 and 'Picking Empire Grown Tea', NA CO 956/440.
52. Chatterjee, *A Time for Tea*; Ramamurthy, *Imperial Persuaders*.
53. Kristin L. Hoganson, *Consumers' Imperium: The Global Production of American Domesticity, 1865–1920* (Chapel Hill, NC: University of North Carolina Press, 2007) and Catherine Hall and Sonya Rose, eds, *At Home with the Empire: Metropolitan Culture and the Imperial World* (Cambridge: Cambridge University Press, 2006).
54. Mrs C. Romanne-James lived in India, had given travel talks for the BBC, and was also a paid lecturer for Empire Teas. F. M. Imandt, a journalist who had worked for the *Daily Telegraph* and the *Glasgow Herald* and who had just returned from two years travelling 'the world', also gave lectures on 'A Day in

a Tea Garden in Darjeeling'. *ITCC Minutes*, 9 December 1932, pp. 2–3. Eur Mss F174/928.
55. Ibid., 8 July 1932, p. 5.
56. Ibid., 21 October 1932, p. 2.
57. Ibid., 11 November 1932, pp. 2–3.
58. Ibid., 9 September 1932, pp. 14–15.
59. Ibid., 11 November 1932), pp. 2–3.
60. On younger women and girls and cosmopolitan consumerism, see Alys Eve Weinbaum, Lynn M. Thomas, Priti Ramamurthy, Uta G. Poiger, Madeleine Yue Dong and Tani E. Barlow, eds, *The Modern Girl Around the World: Consumption, Modernity, and Globalization* (Durham, NC and London: Duke University Press, 2008).
61. *ITCC Minutes*, 12 February 1932, pp. 6–8. Eur Mss F174/928.
62. Ibid., 10 June 1932, p. 3.
63. Mackenzie, *Imperialism and Popular Culture*, p. 7.

CHAPTER TEN

Female Credit Customers, the United Africa Company and Consumer Markets in Postwar Ghana

BIANCA MURILLO

In 1958, the *Guinea Times* published a series of advertisements featuring the stories of successful African traders.[1] Paid for by the United Africa Company (UAC), a subsidiary of the Anglo-Dutch multinational Unilever, the adverts focused on the benefits gained by local retailers 'working together' with the firm. Madam Mary Opoku, for instance, was left with little money after the death of her father, but prospered by investing in the company's textile trade (Figure 10.1). Through her relationship with the UAC, the ad reads, she gained access to the 'wise counsel and help of the Company's Managers' and as a result 'commands great respect in Kumasi – as a keen social worker, cocoa farmer, and a very wise woman'.[2] Intended for African audiences, the advertisement further described how many successful trading careers began with stock supplied on UAC credit and emphasized the importance of profit through friendship. While it is unclear whether the real Madam Mary Opoku ever existed, by the late 1950s, she would have been one of about

6000 credit customers who had secured a UAC passbook allowing her to take and resell goods on credit. Although some men were credit customers, African women dominated this system.

This chapter foregrounds the role of African businesswomen in shaping the international circuits through which companies, like the UAC, operated. While the colonial government enabled a handful of foreign firms to control the import/export market, those companies, in turn, relied heavily on African networks to facilitate the flow of consumer goods and provide valuable consumer feedback. Although credit customers offered firms a cheap method of distribution, their activities went beyond just serving company interests. Credit customers often established themselves independently from the firm in ways that altered, and sometimes even inverted, the assumed power of colonial capitalism.

However, this chapter extends beyond a quest for demonstrating African women's agency by illuminating how ideas about race and gender, as well as power relations, are constructed within transnational commercial spaces. UAC directors and management (predominantly British men) considered credit customers as fundamental parts of, yet also obstacles to, their merchandise business. Credit customers' superior market knowledge and sales skills were a constant source of anxiety and suspicion, particularly when they affected profit margins, but also because of gendered and racialized notions that figured African women as sneaky and deceptive.[3] Ultimately these attitudes, couched in debates about credit customers' 'reliability', contributed to an eventual phasing out of some of the firm's wealthier customers in the post-war years.

The relationship between the UAC and its largely female salesforce therefore asks us to reconsider simple narratives of economic exploitation and resistance that too often frame histories of consumption in colonial contexts. While my research builds on scholarship that has challenged notions about African consumer culture as either a product of processes that originated in Europe or North America or as a recent global phenomenon, it shifts attention from the circulation and meaning of 'things' and centres the relationships among 'people'.[4] Especially in colonial settings where a large distance existed between manufacturers abroad and ordinary consumers, access to goods relied heavily on everyday interactions within company offices, at wholesale depots and across credit counters. This chapter therefore demonstrates that distribution itself has an economic as well as a social history that is not separate from consumer culture and is fundamental to understanding the domestic trajectories of consumerism in Ghana, the operation of global capital, and the ways in which economic power is 'manufactured, institutionalized, and recursively inscribed'.[5]

Figure 10.1. 'Story of a Successful Trader' advertisement, c. 1957, UAC Public Relations Department. Reproduced with kind permission of Unilever from originals at the Unilever Archives, UAC/1/11/20/4.

COMPANIES, CUSTOMERS AND CREDIT

When the UAC arrived on the Gold Coast in 1929, systems of commodity distribution were already in place. The Gold Coast cocoa boom of the first decade of the century led to growth in African purchasing power, and, together with improved road, rail and port construction, there was an increase in the availability and affordability of imports throughout the colony.[6] The increase in employment and educational opportunities also stimulated consumerism among a growing African wage-earning class.[7] By 1919 imported goods were nearly double the value of the pre-war period and the next year doubled again to a value of £15 million (a figure that would not be surpassed until the 1940s). European companies like the UAC were the primary beneficiaries of growing African consumer markets. As Timothy Burke observed, these 'new modern monopoly firms', became central to the operation and structure of colonial capitalism.[8]

New thinking in Britain about imperial solidarity and economic co-operation also refocused manufactures' and exporters' attention onto African markets. During the 1920s and 1930s, domestic unemployment, industrial decline and foreign competition led to important parliamentary discussions about colonial markets as key to Britain's recovery. The rhetoric surrounding imperial preference also increased awareness of the links between Britain and its overseas possessions, as Erika Rappaport has demonstrated in this volume. Development efforts initiated by the Colonial Office further encouraged commercial connections. For instance, the Colonial Development Act of 1929 was designed to promote British capital investment throughout the empire.[9]

In West Africa, European firms enjoyed a substantial amount of autonomy with little to no state regulation before World War II. They did, however, regulate themselves through market-sharing agreements to ensure 'fair play' and the formation of trade organizations like the Association of West African Merchants (AWAM).[10] The extent to which British firms were favoured, however, is unclear. For instance, AWAM, which became companies' primary method for coordinating policy in the private sector and consulting with the colonial government, equally represented the interests of its Swiss and French members. In addition, Unilever, the UAC's parent company, was registered as a multinational with Dutch investment. Although UAC's main buying organizations were in London and Manchester, by the 1950s it had offices in Brussels, Hamburg, Milan, New York, Bombay and Osaka. UAC director and high-level management positions in Ghana, however, remained predominantly British.

While coastal cities and towns had been the main centres of retail trade, foreign firms relied heavily on credit customers to distribute and sell goods in areas where company stores did not exist. According to the UAC, the British firm F. & A. Swanzy established the credit customer system around 1850.[11] Through this system firms allowed Africans to buy bulk merchandise at wholesale, interest-free prices.[12] All credit sales were accounted for on a monthly basis and only after settling their account could a credit customer stock up on new supplies for the following month.[13] Most companies expected credit customers to put down a deposit, in the form of cash or valuables. To record account activity companies provided each of its credit customers with a passbook containing a black-and-white photograph of the holder, the selling district, rates of commission, credit limits (which could fluctuate over time) and dates when goods were supplied (Figure 10.2).[14] The term 'passbook trader' was synonymous with 'credit customers'. Long-time, trusted customers could receive as much as £300–400 worth of goods for one month without full payment, most were only able to take goods against the amount of their original deposit.[15]

By the 1930s, the UAC had subsumed the majority of firms operating on the Gold Coast through a series of purchases and amalgamations.[16] It

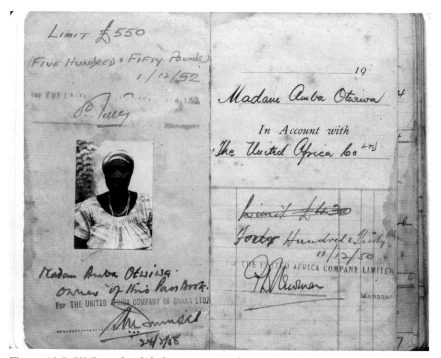

Figure 10.2. UAC passbook belonging to Madam Amba Otwiwa, c. 1950–60, UAC of Ghana Ltd, Financial Records. Reproduced with kind permission of Unilever from originals at the Unilever Archives, UAC/2/20/2/9/1.

inherited hundreds of wholesale and retail spaces, as well as thousands of credit customer accounts. Early company policies further centralized and systematized channels of distribution and improving communication. Goods ranging from textiles, tinned foodstuffs and beverages to perfumes, enamelware and sewing machines were sent to 17 district branches, also known as a district's main wholesale store. From there, goods went to UAC-owned retail stores or credit customers. Company storekeepers and credit customers sold to three constituencies: independent storekeepers, 'petty traders' and end-use consumers. Yet this system proved to be far too rigid to implement on the ground. Most district branches, for instance, operated as 'self-contained units'.[17] In other words what happened when goods arrived at district wholesale stores relied heavily on the relationships between managers, their African storekeepers and staff (including clerks and salesmen) and credit customers.

While the UAC considered its credit customers essential, the relationship between the two was never stable. For instance, during times of heightened competition, the UAC focused on securing the loyalty of long-time customers and catering to their demands. During times of scarcity, however, the company distanced itself from large credit customers as these women were often accused of 'black market trading' and received the brunt of consumer frustrations. Unlike salaried storekeepers, credit customers were not subject to regular inspections, stocktaking or audits, which made them difficult to supervise. In addition, they sold in smaller units (cigarettes by the stick and sugar by the cube), did not have fixed prices and allowed consumers to bargain. According to company managers the credit customer business prevented them from obtaining accurate statistics about sales and consumers, as well as enforcing district quotas and wartime price controls.

A FEMALE SALES FORCE

While literature on market women in Ghana is extremely rich, this scholarship often presents credit customers as merely appendages or dependent clients of European companies.[18] This portrayal has obscured the diversity of these women's business practices and how they attempted to establish independence from firms. It also flattens our understanding of credit customers themselves. Levels of education, autonomy, experience and age among women varied. The youngest UAC credit customer recorded, for instance, was a 16-year-old girl from Akuse.[19] In addition, customers specialized in different stocks, and as one UAC merchandise director described, '[credit] accounts ranged from the humble trader turning over of a few pounds a month to the biggest account of £30,000 a month'.[20] While credit customers were by no means a homogenous group, the fact that a woman held a passbook, paid a deposit and had security with a firm elevated her from other retailers. She was known within local business circles as a 'first degree trader'.[21]

A number of credit customers operated as wholesale-retailers, controlled networks of sub-distributors and had their own clients or 'second degree traders' who sold on their behalf. For instance, credit customer Mary Baiden relied on smaller retailers to move popular lines such as boneless beef, pig's feet and stockfish while she concentrated full-time on the more profitable tobacco business. Her delegation of safe selling to assistants and steady profits on smaller lines allowed her to invest further in the tobacco trade. By the early 1950s she was known in Kumasi as the 'Tobacco Queen', although she continued to deal in other types of commodities.[22] By fluctuating between wholesale and retail activity, Mary Baiden maintained the flexibility to both invest in products that would maximize her profits and collect commission on safe lines delegated to others depending on the market. In managing a number of smaller retailers, Baiden probably also provided credit herself and managed her own group of 'credit customers' – a strategy not uncommon among 'first-class traders'.

Other credit customers conducted business from multiple sites and in various districts. For instance, Accra credit customer Esther Mensah operated two different stalls in the city's largest market, Makola, and hired assistants to push handcarts around various Accra neighbourhoods displaying goods and spreading product information. She also ran a samples viewing room in her own home where she invited buyers to visit and test new lines.[23] In addition, credit customer Catherine Botchway described going between Obuasi and Dunkwa, a 40- to 50-mile distance, and operating business in both towns.[24] This strategy reached a wider number of consumers and was used to sell older stock. As former UAC customer Agnes Kwa Kwa from Cape Coast explained, if goods were not moving in the city, she would sell them in nearby rural areas. Some farmers, she says, were not aware of new trends so they would be more likely to buy, not knowing that a particular style was from 'last season'.[25]

While women's sales strategies helped UAC profit, their skills also provided them with opportunities to invest in other types of business. Not unlike Baiden who invested her retailing profits in the tobacco trade, other credit customers became property owners, transporters and moneylenders.[26] Business reputations translated into social capital and leadership positions in communities. One 'first degree trader' in Accra became a prominent member of the Market Traders' Association, the Federation of Gold Coast Women and the Presbyterian Church.[27] Some women also secretly held passbooks from different companies, a practice that firms strongly discouraged.[28] Multiple passbooks, the UAC argued, allowed credit customers to evade debt and prevented company loyalty. However, among customers the strategy allowed them to negotiate lower prices and avoid dependency on one firm.

A number of the UAC's first credit customers were from long-established trading families and had accounts with the company's predecessors.[29] Older credit customers described apprenticeships or learning the merchandise business from grandmothers, mothers and aunts.[30] This familial connection is not surprising, as passbooks could be passed down from generation to generation. Others had formal schooling and professional training. Esther Mensah, for example, went to Accra Government Girl's School in 1929, passed standard VII and trained as a nurse. In 1938, she resigned from the hospital to trade and secured herself a UAC passbook.[31] Additionally, all three Igbo credit customers whom Gloria Ifeoma Chuku interviewed in Nigeria attended primary school, and two of the three had secondary school education and trained as teachers. Chuku argued that retailing offered flexibility, which enabled many women to care for their children and tend to household responsibilities.[32]

Some of the more profitable passbook holders were wives and relatives of UAC employees. Although many began retailing before marriage, their husbands' positions no doubt played a part in their later business success.[33] Wealthy husbands and influential male relatives provided the cash deposit needed to gain a passbook and often set up female relatives with a small store and collected the profits.[34] Yet some customers purchased or inherited passbooks from other women and maintained entire households of immediate and extended family, up to 30 dependants, on their own.[35] Beauty Boye, stepdaughter of prominent Accra credit customer Esther Mensah, revealed that many of her stepmother's 'business associates never formally married'. She described that some of these women were wealthy, owned property and had built their own homes, implying that their status had intimidated potential suitors.[36] Others may have simply not seen the sense in formally marrying.[37] Credit customers served their own and company interests. Some became independent entrepreneurs and social leaders. These strategies proved especially important during the post-war period, as foreign firms increasingly became targets of public criticism and disdain.

'MARKET MAMMIES' AND TRICKY TRADERS

Historians have long demonstrated the ways in which African men and women as intermediaries, 'cross-cultural brokers' and 'middle figures' contested and negotiated the terms of empire.[38] What I find more revealing in the case of female credit customers is *how* and *when* they appear in the corporate record, and, more importantly, what these moments might reveal about how gender and race are embedded in the structuring of business practices. Unfortunately UAC's corporate documents were written almost exclusively by British men and the voices of African men and women almost never appear alongside those of their superiors.[39] However, an analysis of managers' correspondence and staff circulars suggests that the demands of successful female retailers caused discomfort among British male management. Not only did these women's public authority and economic independence challenge bourgeois ideas of femininity to which many of these men subscribed, their practices also disrupted the racial logic that figured Africans as inferior and in need of guidance. How then did company management reconcile these contradictions and make sense of their dependency on credit customers?

One way was the firm's use of pejorative stereotypes that masked credit customers' crucial role in a firm's merchandise business. Company publications often referred to credit customers as 'market mammy', 'bush mammy' and 'mammy traders'.[40] To refer to someone as 'bush', meant that they were simple and uneducated, lacking any type of sophistication. The term 'mammy' in the US South was used to describe black women, often enslaved, who worked for white families. The happy-go-lucky mammy character was known for being a loyal servant and her image was offered as evidence of the supposed humanity of the institution of slavery. Furthermore, persistent depictions throughout the twentieth-century US both represented and maintained a white fantasy of harmonious race relations.[41] While it is unclear to what extent similar meanings translated into the British colonial context, the term 'mammy' applied to credit customers negates any understanding of female credit customers as serious business associates or colleagues. This familial connotation, implying mother, also rendered invisible a capitalist relationship and the exploitative potential of such a system.

Staff narratives fluctuated between viewing such women as intimidating forces to be reckoned with and as sources of amusement. For instance, as a 1950s British-American Tobacco employee explained in his memoir, 'market mammies are powerful, apart from their sheer physical presence. Raucous, impetuous, bawdy and full of fun.'[42] As Anne Stoler reminds us, racial distinctions were fundamentally structured in gendered terms. Through these depictions of credit customers' appearance and behaviour, black femininity is then figured as an opposite to white womanhood within a racial logic that imagined European women as delicate 'domestic angels', however stereotypical those categories might be as well. British managers also seemed fascinated with what they described as market women's mix of 'matronly kindness' and 'ruthless arrogance'.[43] While male staff often remembered these women humorously, their erratic behaviour, wavering between 'kind' and 'ruthless', constructed them as objects of suspicion. The depictions further provided male staff with the power to assert that African women needed to be in some way managed.

These representations had implications for how companies understood credit customers' business practices. Managers often rendered credit customers' superior business skills as a form of trickery, or even deception. For instance, in December 1954, the General Manager of G. B. Ollivant Limited (GBO), a company owned by the UAC, circulated a letter to all stations concerning loss of sales on 110 cases of Dutch Silver Fish. Whereas the correct selling price should have been 66 shillings, a district manager mistakenly sold to local traders for 50. This 'fatal blunder', the General Manager argued, cost the company £80. Clearly irritated by the mistake, he stated, 'I can accept no valid excuse … it is a question of not looking at the goods and not showing much intelligence in trade … We cannot afford to be fooled.'[44] Credit customers' business practices are reduced to a form of trickery and the product of bad management rather than being associated with superior market skills.

In a similar case, one Goods Manager of the Swiss African Trading Company (SAT), another UAC-owned firm, described being outsmarted by two experienced credit customers during his first buying trip to Manchester. He remembered, 'I was taken around several textile factories … to select saleable materials, assisted by two "market mammies"… Of course they picked the cream of the available designs for themselves.' They left him, as he later found out when he returned to Kumasi, with what were 'second-rate styles'.[45] Because of their intimate knowledge of local style and changing consumer tastes, female credit customers, especially those dealing in textiles, were often invited as guests to England to consult on designs. Although he later recalls this incident with a sense of humour, the tone of his narrative positions the act of the women taking the best designs as an underhanded move to trick him. The same women whom the company invited to England because of their perceived skill in identifying popular designs are still presumed to be untrustworthy.

While European male management drew on preexisting racial and gender ideologies, they also constructed notions about race, gender and ability through their everyday business interactions and correspondence. In many ways the sneaky 'market mammy' maintained 'a particular set of relations of production and power', in ways that served Western capitalist agendas.[46] It also justified treatment of these women as a cheap form of disposable labour. The persistent use of the term 'market mammy' further undermined the partnership message in corporate literature. That international audiences were presented with the market mammy character instead of stories about businesswomen like Mary Baiden or Esther Mensah in the previous section suggests that the company had a stake in representing African women as in need of company guidance. Further research is needed to understand how these ideas kept women out of salaried staff and managerial positions.[47] It was not until 1952, after more than 20 years of business that the UAC hired its first African woman, Miss Martha Sylvia Dadzie, at the management level though the firm's department store division.[48]

RELIABLE WOMEN?

In the post-war period, assumptions about credit customer's race, gender and ability came to a head in discussions about corporate restructuring. World War II had brought serious commodity shortages, introduced government price controls and increased pressure on firms to ensure fairer distribution, mostly by regulating district allocations. After the war, restrictions eased and there was a substantial growth in African spending power as the price of cocoa, timber and gold (the Gold Coast's main exports) rose on the world market. This was a time of intense competition between firms who by then controlled two-thirds of the West African import/export trade. As a result, companies stepped up their merchandising strategies and attempted to restructure business. Increasing public criticisms and nationalist activities, as well as new rhetoric about economic development and colonial rule further shaped changes in policy.[49]

To gain a competitive edge, two of the UAC's initial strategies were to increase credit limits and ease pressures associated with debt collection. For instance, in March 1950, UAC General Manager Patrick Fitz-Gerald instructed district managers, 'we shall have to give our credit customers a higher limit of credit … if you are satisfied that the woman is reliable, it is to the benefit of the company to extend credit.'[50] By extending credit, the UAC hoped to secure customers' loyalty and ensure that they would not work for competing firms.[51] UAC literature consistently discussed how to gain the favour of female credit customers in order to outsmart competitors, gain loyalty and better market knowledge. For instance in February 1953, GBO's General Manager H. Schiess instructed agents in Kumasi, Sekondi and Accra (the largest Gold Coast cities) to choose ten customers with turnovers of £500 monthly and to conduct monthly interviews. The main purposes were to 'keep fully alive to local trade developments' and to gauge the 'trustworthiness' of credit customers, offering the 'right' ones more credit to expand their business.[52]

The repetitive and desperate tone of merchandise circulars suggests that station agents were in fact unable to cultivate personal relationships and trust.[53] This disconnect led to persistent complaints about aging stocks and slow-moving and unsuitable lines that cost the company 'unnecessary losses'.[54] The company also grew annoyed by 'upcountry traders' who were not satisfied with their district allocations and travelled to Accra for a better selection.[55] Well into the 1950s there was still a gap in the UAC's knowledge about local markets, consumer taste and demand – precisely those areas of operations in which credit customers were most expert.

Whether credit customers ever strategically withheld market information is unclear. However, the company increasingly considered credit customers, particularly the top-sellers, as unreliable sources of market information. In 1955 UAC directors in London and its General Manager in Accra began discussions about how to break down their power.[56] While these efforts are part of a larger shift in postwar UAC business that focused on prioritizing the firm's identity as a wholesaler, this change also stemmed from the fact that some of the more successful credit customers had become powerful independent wholesalers.[57] This, as well as the ability of top-selling customers to create alliances that forced down buying prices and pressured companies to offer better terms, had an 'undoubted effect on selling margins'.[58] According to the company, distributing passbooks to a number of smaller credit customers would in effect diffuse the power of larger ones.

In a confidential letter to the UAC's General Manager, A. C. C. Baxter, UAC Merchandise Director, wrote, among other things, 'We are seeking a larger number of new [credit] customers, many of whom will be in a smaller way of business.' He further instructed that larger customers should be 'sold smaller quantities than have been customary'. He was cautious, however: 'we are not trying to eliminate our big customers or to take their customers away from them', he claimed, 'we are seeking new customers and in doing so we shall be coming closer to people who are themselves retailers but we remain wholesalers.'[59] His careful delivery suggested that this policy might not have been popular with those actually working on the ground. While agents most likely preferred to deal with a few large customers, they also probably found it equally difficult to withhold goods from women who wielded a considerable amount of authority in their districts. Resistance and/or the inability to enforce this top-down policy is evident in a letter, three years later, reprimanding district agents for lack of compliance.[60]

The UAC's efforts to break down large credit customers should also be understood in connection with its shift to a more 'scientific approach to selling'. The London 1955 merchandise meeting established an urgent need to recruit and train a force of young African salesmen as 'researchers' to act as the company's 'eyes and ears'.[61] While this was an attempt to close the gap between the firm and everyday consumers, directors also agreed that they could not rely on large customers to develop new lines or to provide consistent consumer feedback. Instead, they needed 'objective research and the continual passing back of information on consumers' reaction to our lines, competitors' activities, [and] ideas for new lines'.[62] Corporate language renamed and reshaped cultural competence in business, a competence that many female credit customers already possessed. The discourse about the increased professionalization of selling, within the Ghanaian context, signifies UAC's inability to fully control the local market and envision female credit customers as equal business partners. After all, as A. C. C. Baxter would describe to an audience full of business students and professors at the City of London College in 1960, after 30 years in business, 'nearly all African traders' were still 'ignorant of progressive retail techniques' and needed proper guidance.[63]

ELIMINATING PASSBOOKS

Surviving in the Gold Coast merchandise business depended on skill, flexibility, energy and timing, as well as considerable knowledge about African consumers' tastes and desires. While foreign merchant firms facilitated interactions between West African markets and manufacturers abroad, credit customers mediated between companies and everyday consumers. During the post-war period, commodity shortages, heightened competition and increasing government intervention in the economy fuelled companies' anxieties about credit customers' loyalty and reliability. At the same time, African nationalists, businessmen, retailers and consumers accused companies of conspiring with the colonial government, cheating customers and cutting Africans out of trade. This conflict came to a head in 1948 as Gold Coasters organized a massive boycott of foreign firms and imported goods that ended with angry crowds burning and looting the stores and properties of mostly European-owned companies.

While the events of 1948 marked an important turning point in Ghana's struggle for independence, this chapter suggests that post-war conditions were part of a longer and larger struggle over access to goods and systems of distribution that were equally significant. While the credit customer system provided firms with a readily available and cheap labour force, credit customers' activities also prevented the UAC's ability to control the market and often affected profit margins. British managers' frustrations, however, cannot be separated from racialized and gendered assumptions about 'African women' that were (re)produced through everyday interactions and transactions that affected their ability to imagine female credit customers as business partners, regardless of propaganda that suggested otherwise. These ideas were further reinforced through international trade journals from the 1950s that depicted African women's economic activity (through images and text) as 'circumscribed by tradition', static and lacking the innovative skills necessary for developing a modern economy.[64]

After independence in 1957, the passbook system was even adopted by the Ghana National Trading Corporation (established by the country's first Prime Minister and President Kwame Nkrumah) as an attempt to regain control over merchandising and limit the dominance of foreign capital. In 1970, however, passbooks were outlawed and deemed an inefficient and outdated mode of distribution that led to market abuses. 'Market women' also became the primary scapegoats for the country's economic problems, and the state, as well as firms and consumers, blamed them for creating artificial shortages and high prices.[65] As this chapter demonstrates, however, the extent to which the elimination of passbooks should also be understood in connection to colonial and postcolonial governments' inability to address the authority of African businesswomen and the importance of female distribution networks in local and international economies deserves further attention.[66]

ACKNOWLEDGEMENTS

I am extremely grateful to panellists and participants at the Sixteenth Berkshire Conference on the History of Women (2014) and the 'Archives of Post-Independence Africa and its Diaspora' Conference sponsored by the Council for the Development of Social Science Research in Africa (2012) for their comments and suggestions on earlier versions of this chapter. The editors of this volume and UAC archivist Diane Backhouse also deserve special thanks for their assistance and advice.

NOTES

1. I use 'African' instead of 'Ghanaian' since Ghana was a multiethnic society. Where possible, I refer to retailers as they would themselves, in terms of ethnicity. However, in discussions about broader issues affecting local retailers as a group, or when ethnic designation is not clear, I use the term 'African'.
2. UAC advertisement, 'Story of a Successful Trader', *Guinea Times*, 5 April 1958.

3. Ann Stoler, *Along the Archival Grain: Epistemic Anxieties and Colonial Common Sense* (Princeton, NJ: Princeton University Press, 2010).
4. Timothy Burke, *Lifebuoy Men, Lux Women: Commodification, Consumption & Cleanliness in Modern Zimbabwe* (Durham: Duke University Press, 1996) and Jeremy Prestholdt, *Domesticating the World: African Consumerism and the Genealogies of Globalization* (Berkeley: University of California Press, 2008).
5. Brenda Chaflin makes a similar argument in her interrogation of state power in *Neoliberal Frontiers: An Ethnography of the Sovereignty in West Africa* (Chicago, IL: University of Chicago Press, 2010), p. 15.
6. Elizabeth Wrangham, 'An African Road Revolution: The Gold Coast in the Period of the Great War', *The Journal of Imperial and Commonwealth History* 32:1 (2004), pp. 1–18.
7. Emmanuel Akyeampong, *Drink, Power, and Cultural Change: A Social History of Alcohol in Ghana, c. 1800 to Recent Times* (Portsmouth: Heinemann, 1996); Philip Foster, *Education and Social Change in Ghana* (Chicago, IL: University of Chicago Press, 1965).
8. Timothy Burke, 'Fork Up a Smile: Marketing, Colonial Knowledge and the Female Subject in Zimbabwe', *Gender & History* 8:3 (1996), pp. 440–56.
9. B. R. Tomlinson, 'The British Economy and the Empire, 1900–1939', in *A Companion to Early Twentieth Century Britain*, ed. Chris Wrigley (Oxford: Blackwell, 2003), pp. 198–211; Frank Trentmann, *Free Trade Nation: Commerce, Consumption, and Civil Society in Modern Britain* (Oxford: Oxford University Press, 2009).
10. A. G. Hopkins, *An Economic History of West Africa* (New York: Columbia University Press, 1973); David Kenneth Fieldhouse, *Merchant Capital and Economic Decolonization: The United Africa Company 1929–1987* (Oxford: Clarendon Press, 1994), pp. 124–5.
11. Frederick Pedler, *The Lion and the Unicorn in Africa: The United African Company 1787–1931* (London: Heinemann, 1974), p. 107.
12. Credit customers could also receive commissions. Gloria Addae, 'The Retailing of Imported Textiles in the Accra Market', in *Proceedings of the West African Institute of Social and Economic Research Conference, March 1954* (Ibadan: University Press, 1956).
13. Pedler, *The Lion and the Unicorn*, p. 240.
14. UAC Credit Customer Passbooks belonging to Helena Quansah, Mrs Annah Manful, and Madam Amba Otwiwa, Financial Records, Unilever Archives and Records Management (hereafter UARM), United Africa Company collection (hereafter UAC)/2/20/2/11.
15. Paula Jones, *The UAC in the Gold Coast/Ghana, 1920–1965*, PhD thesis, School of Oriental and African Studies, 1983, pp. 65–71; P. T. Bauer, *A Study of Competition, Oligopoly and Monopoly in a Changing Economy* (Cambridge: Cambridge University Press, 1954), pp. 61–2; Gareth Austin, 'Indigenous Credit Institutions in West Africa, c. 1750–c. 1960', in *Local*

Suppliers of Credit in the Third World, 1750–1960, eds Gareth Austin and Kaoru Sugihara (Basingstoke: Palgrave Macmillan, 1993), p. 132.

16. See, especially, Fieldhouse, *Merchant Capital and Economic*; Pedler, *The Lion and the Unicorn in Africa*.
17. W. E. Conway, Chairman, *Report of the Commission of Enquiry into the Distribution and Prices of Essential Imported Goods* (Accra: Government Printing Department, 1943).
18. Claire Robertson, *Sharing the Same Bowl: A Socioeconomic History of Women and Class in Accra* (Bloomington, IN: Indiana University Press, 1984); Beverly Grier, 'Pawns, Porters, and Petty Traders: Women in the Transition to Cash Crop Agriculture', *Signs* 17:2 (1992), pp. 304–28; Gracia Clark, *'Onions are my Husband:' Survival and Accumulation by West African Market Women* (Chicago, IL and London: University of Chicago Press, 1994).
19. 'Youngest Credit Customer', *Gold Coast UAC News* 4:1, December 1952.
20. A. C. C. Baxter's talk at City of London College, 'The Evolution of Merchandising in Africa', 9 February 1960, UAC Corporate Planning Department: Reports, UARM, UAC/1/9/1/6/2.
21. Addae, 'The Retailing of Imported Textiles'; Ione Acquah, *Accra Survey: A Social Survey of the Capital of Ghana, Formerly Called the Gold Coast, Undertaken for the West African Institute of Social and Economic Research, 1953–1956* (London: University of London Press, 1958), pp. 68–71; Mansa Apeadu, 'She is an Important Factor in our Distributive Trade', *Ghana Trade Journal*, February 1961, pp. 14–15.
22. 'Kumasi Tobacco Queen: Mary Baiden – Thirty Years a Credit Customer', *Gold Coast UAC News* 3:10, September 1952.
23. 'Madam Esther Mensah: A Story of Rapid Success', *Gold Coast UAC News* 3:8, July 1952.
24. 'Obuasi Credit Customer for Coronation', *Gold Coast UAC News* 4:5 (April 1953). Others did the same, see 'Mrs Agatha Blewor Borti, Keta Credit Customer Tells Her Own Story', *Gold Coast UAC News* 4:4, March 1953 and 'Korforidua Credit Customer Started Young', *Gold Coast UAC News* 3:6, May 1952.
25. Interview with Agnes Kwa Kwa, Cape Coast, 1 June 2010.
26. Interview with J. F. Enninful, Cape Coast, 2 June 2010. Also see Chuku, 'From Petty Traders' and Gloria Ifeoma Chuku, 'Nzimiro, Mary (1898–1993)', in *Women in World History*, Vol. 7, ed. Deborah Klezmer (Waterford, CT: Yorkin Publication, 2000). Other West African examples include Felicia I. Ekejiuba, 'Omu Okwei, the Merchant Queen of Ossamari: A Biographical Sketch', *Journal of the Historical Society of Nigeria* 3:4 (1967), pp. 633–46; Catherine Coquery-Vidrovitch, *African Women: A Modern History*, trans. Beth Gillian Raps (Boulder, CO: Westview, 1997).
27. Addae, 'The Retailing of Imported Textiles'.
28. Interview with Issac Kofi Annan, Cape Coast, 3 June 2010.

29. 'Kumasi Tobacco Queen'; 'Oda Credit Customer Establishes Family Business', *Gold Coast UAC News* 4:3 (February 1953); J. Etson-Ansah, 'Sekondi's Ace Credit Customer', *Gold Coast UAC News* 3:5 (April 1952); Tamakloe, 'Keta Credit Customer'.

30. Etson-Ansah, 'Sekondi's Ace Credit Customer'; 'Oda Credit Customer'.

31. 'Madam Esther Mensah: A Story of Rapid Success', *Gold Coast UAC News* 3:8, July 1952.

32. Chuku, 'From Petty Traders to International Merchants', p. 10.

33. Interview with Kwesi Akumenya Cato, Accra, 13 September 2007; Background on Mary Idun Cato in Pedler, *The Lion and the Unicorn*, pp. 106–7.

34. Robertson, *Sharing the Same Bowl*.

35. Addae, 'The Retailing of Imported Textiles'; Chuku, 'From Petty Traders', pp. 9–10.

36. Interview with Beauty Boye, Accra, 21 November 2007.

37. For historical debates on marriage, financial autonomy and domestic labour in Ghana, see Jean Allman and Victoria Tashjian, *I Will Not Eat Stone: A Women's History of Colonial Asante* (Portsmouth: Heinemann, 2000).

38. Benjamin N. Lawrence, Emily Lynn Osbourne and Richard L. Roberts, eds, *Intermediaries, Interpreters, and Clerks: African Employees in the Making of Colonial Africa* (Madison, WI: University of Wisconsin Press, 2006), p. 4.

39. I approach the corporate archive as a space to investigate the negotiation of power. See Achille Mbembe, 'The Power of the Archive and Its Limits', in *Refiguring the Archive*, eds Carolyn Hamilton, Verne Harris, Michele Pickover, Graeme Reide, Razia Saleh and Jane Taylor (Boston, MA: Kluwer Academic Publishers, 2002), pp. 19–26; Antoinette Burton, 'Introduction: Archive Fever, Archive Stories', in *Archive Stories: Facts, Fictions, and the Writing of History* ed. Antoinette Burton (Durham, NC: Duke University Press, 2005), 1–24.

40. Survey of official company publications housed at UARM. For a specific example see *Statistical & Economic Review*, September 1950. Consumer Survey: Replies concerning the *Statistical & Economic Review*, 27 April 1950, UAC Public Relations Department: Statistical & Economic Review, UARM, UAC/1/11/19/89.

41. Kimberly Wallace-Sanders, *Mammy: A Century of Race, Gender, and Southern Memory* (Ann Arbor, MI: University of Michigan Press, 2009); Micki McElya, *Clinging to Mammy: The Faithful Slave in Twentieth-Century America* (Cambridge, MA: Harvard University Press, 2007).

42. Copy of Leslie Craigan, 'Craigan Takes up in Nigeria', *BAT News*, 1984, UAC Public Relations Department, UARM, UAC/1/11/14/3/9.

43. Ibid. Also see, *Old Coasters Tales*, Vols 1–2, collected, typed and collated by UAC Public Relations Department, September 1985, UARM, UAC/1/11/14/3/8.

44. Letter from General Manager H. Schiess (Accra) to all stations, 12 December 1954, G. B. Ollivant DIU: Circulars: UARM, UAC/2/10/3/4.

45. Hans Rudolf Roth, *Because of Kwadua: Autobiography of Hans Rudolf Roth* (Accra: Afram Publications (Ghana) Ltd, 2008), p. 89.
46. Ann Laura Stoler, *Carnal Knowledge and Imperial Power: Race and the Intimate in Colonial Rule* (Berkeley, CA: University of California Press, 2002), pp. 24–5.
47. Also on how these ideas resonated with African managers, even though they made up a very small group and were relegated to lower managerial staff positions. A 1953 survey reported that the UAC employed 160 African managers in its merchandise departments throughout British West Africa; European managers numbered 521. 'Africanisation of the UAC Group's Managerial Staff in British West Africa', 23 October 1953, UAC of Ghana Ltd. General Manager's Circulars, UARM, UAC/2/20/3/3.
48. 'Accra Staff Innovation: Lady Optician Joins Company', *Gold Coast UAC News* 3:11 (October 1952), p. 1.
49. A. G. Hopkins, 'Economic Aspects of Political Movements in Nigeria and the Gold Coast, 1918–1939', *Journal of African History* 7 (1966), pp. 133–52; Frederick Cooper, *Decolonization and African Society: The Labor Question in French and British Africa* (Cambridge: Cambridge University Press, 1996); Sarah Stockell, *The Business of Decolonization: British Business Strategies in the Gold Coast* (Oxford: Oxford University Press, 2000).
50. UAC of Ghana Ltd. General Manager's Circulars, 25 March 1950, UARM, UAC/2/20/3/3/4.
51. 'African and Syrian Merchandise Trading Accounts', 19 May 1953, File 32 (9), G. B. Ollivant Division: Circulars, UARM, UAC/2/10/3/4.
52. 'General Goods Trade', 4 February 1953, File 32 (7); G. B. Ollivant Division: Circulars, UARM, UAC/2/10/3/4.
53. 'Principal Merchandise Clients', 24 September 1954, File 32 (16); 'Merchandise Sales', 27 October 1954, File 32 (17), G. B. Ollivant Division: Circulars, UARM, UAC/2/10/3/4.
54. 'Aged Stocks', 15 January 1954, File 32 (11); 'Merchandise Sales', 26 February 1954, File 32 (12); 'Sales and Selling Policy', 27 October 1954, File 32 (17), G. B. Ollivant Division: Circulars, UARM, UAC/2/10/3/4.
55. 'Merchandise Clients from Up-Country Buying at Ports', 30 September 1953, File 32 (10), G. B. Ollivant Division: Circulars, UARM, UAC/2/10/3/4.
56. UAC of Ghana Ltd, Ghana: General Manager's Circular, File 57, 25 January 1955, UARM, UAC/2/20/3/3.
57. Some of the credit customers began to import directly from manufacturers, UAC of Ghana Ltd. Ghana: General Manager's Circulars, 9 December 1954, UARM, UAC/2/20/3/3.
58. A. C. C. Baxter, London to General Manager, Accra (Private and Confidential), UAC London Conference-Merchandise, 13 September 1955, UARM, UAC/2/20/3/2.
59. Ibid.
60. UARM, UAC Ghana Ltd. General Manager's Circulars, 22 October 1958, UARM, UAC/2/20/3/3.

61. A. C. C. Baxter, 13 September 1955, UARM, UAC/2/20/3/2.
62. Ibid.
63. A. C. C. Baxter's talk at the City of London College, 'The Evolution of Merchandising in Africa'.
64. Stephanie Decker, 'Corporate Legitimacy and Advertising: British Companies and the Rhetoric of Development in West Africa, 1950–1970', *Business History Review* 81:1 (Spring 2007), pp. 59–86, see especially pp. 71–2.
65. Claire Robertson, 'The Death of Makola and Other Tragedies', *Canadian Journal of African Studies* 17:3 (1983), pp. 469–94.
66. Important exceptions include Gracia Clark and Takyiwaa Manuh, 'Women Traders in Ghana and the Structural Adjustment Program', in *Structural Adjustment and African Women Farmers*, ed. Christina H. Gladwin (Gainesville, FL: University of Florida Press, 1991); Akosua Keseboa Darwah, 'Going Global: Ghanaian Female Traders in an Era of Globalization' (PhD dissertation, University of Wisconsin, 2002).

CHAPTER ELEVEN

Designing Consumer Society: Citizens and Housing Plans during World War II

SANDRA TRUDGEN DAWSON

'I can give you a few ideas that would be a great help to all the housewives', penned Mrs F. Wilkins to the Burt Committee in January 1943.[1] Responding to a newspaper advertisement asking the public for housing design ideas, Wilkins requested under-house coal-cellars with 'a shoot outside' so she didn't have to 'go out in all weathers to get a scuttle of coal'.[2] This would also 'do away with the ugly [coal] sheds that fall to pieces in a very short time', a sentiment shared with Mrs Georgina Meyor who claimed wooden sheds 'an eyesore'.[3] Wilkins also wanted a large kitchen to have enough room to 'stoop down to the oven' and to accommodate a small work table. Finally, she wished for an outside 'lavatory … as well as one upstairs' so that family members don't traipse mud from outside all over the house making more work for womenfolk. Wilkins did not anticipate a post-war gender role revolution, but she expected a post-war home designed to reduce the workload for overburdened housewives.[4] Her desires echoed scores more as citizens responded to the request by the Burt Committee for ideas and suggestions for low-cost, efficient post-war homes.[5]

The wartime public appeal appeared first in December 1942. A small notice in the *Daily Telegraph* read: 'Ideas in new methods of house-building for use after the war are invited by the Inter-departmental Committee recently appointed by the Ministries of Health and Works and Planning'.[6] After the destruction and damage to millions of homes, the response was immediate.[7] Letters arrived written on brown paper bags, postcards or scraps of precious stationery saved from before the war. Most came from individuals living in towns and cities targeted by enemy aerial bombing. While letters came from men and women, the vast majority reflected concerns about the middle- and working-class housewife. Middle-class women would no longer have servants and the working-class housewife simply wanted more comfort, less crowding and less work. Taken together, the letters reveal the way Britons imagined their post-war lives, disclosing desires and the expectation that their wishes would be fulfilled. Surprisingly, those who had lost most of their personal belongings did not wish for more 'things' or bigger homes. Rather, they desired small, efficient and well-organized homes that would reduce housework. Moreover, these letters suggest that consumers saw the state, not the market, as the means of bringing about a higher standard of living after the war.

The notion of documenting opinion and requesting consumers to vocalize desire was not new. The British Institute of Public Opinion (later Gallup) as well as Mass Observation, both established in 1937, documented the views of ordinary citizens. Other organizations and institutions surveyed housing conditions, leisure activities, political attitudes and family life. Social surveys and opinion polls abounded in the inter-war years.[8] As Britain re-structured economically to embrace the working-classes as integral to the expansion of mass consumption, consumer opinion and desire mattered.[9] However, the wartime requests from the government for ideas about how best to replace what was lost during the war signalled two important things: first, that consumer desire was deemed central to the future reconstruction of consumer markets; and, second, that the government planned to take a leading role in ensuring that those desires would be met.

This chapter examines the way wartime citizens were encouraged to design post-war consumer society. Examining the letters and designs from civilians on the home-front to the Burt Committee suggests that even before the establishment of the post-1945 welfare state, British consumers assumed and expected the government to re-build homes to meet consumer requirements and desires.[10] In addition, wartime 'wish lists' had roots in pre-war desires and home marketing pre-dating post-war consumer culture so celebrated as a product of the affluent society.

The concept of the 'ideal home' was an important aspect of consumption and production in the inter-war years throughout Europe. The Soviet Union experimented with Art Deco apartment blocks and communal living space while the Weimar Republic embraced the Bauhaus School of design that saw architects as artists and emphasized the centrality of technological innovation to modern life.[11] Plain white walls, large windows, flat roofs, balconies, terraces and roof gardens characterized inter-war architecture. The desire to design functional, hygienic, universal, democratic and economical buildings and homes inspired architects. Contemporary preoccupation with fresh air, sunshine, space, health and hygiene informed modernist schools like those founded by Adolf Loos, Walter Gropius and Le Corbusier.[12] In Britain, builders adopted many of the design features of Continental Europe including large windows and low housing densities (Figure 11.1).[13]

Home design was politicized after World War I by 'homes fit for heroes', the programme assisted by the Housing and Town Planning Act (1919) that offered generous subsidies to local authorities to build council housing for returning veterans.[14] The result was the construction of large uniform council estates and a grand social experiment in building suburban communities.[15] The 1918 Tudor Walters committee report on the 'provision of dwellings for the working classes' established the 'blueprint for inter-war local authority and, to a considerable extent, private sector suburban housing development'.[16] Between the wars, 4.3 million new homes were

Figure 11.1. An example of a Bauhaus-inspired house built in inter-war Chapeltown, Yorkshire. Author's private collection.

built. Of these, four million were suburban houses, transforming Britain from the most urbanized to the most suburbanized nation in Europe by 1939.[17]

The home was also marketed specifically as the epicentre of modern domesticity from 1908 at the *Daily Mail* Ideal Home Exhibitions in London.[18] The spectacular displays modelled the newest domestic technology, appliances and furniture, selling the idea that the home was the 'site of citizenship' and 'dutiful consumption'.[19] After World War I, citizens responded to the *Daily Mail* call for suggestions. Consumers asked for 'light and airy' houses with large windows, following the lead of the health and beauty culture of the inter-war years discussed by Paul Deslandes and Ina Zweiniger-Bargielowska in this volume.[20] The strongest plea, however, was for labour-saving appliances and designs containing features to reduce housework and maintenance in a largely servant-less world after World War I.[21] Architects and home-designers created model homes that featured kitchens with streamlined surfaces, radiators heated from a central coal fire and minimal mouldings to reduce dust. The exterior of these 'Tudorbethan' semi-detached homes, however, emphasized 'individuality' that was emphatically different from the uniformity of council housing (Figure 11.3) to appeal to aspiring owner-occupants (Figure 11.2). Nevertheless, the designs remained prohibitively expensive for many.[22] The Halifax and Abbey Road building societies advertised at the Ideal Home Exhibition from 1925, enticing consumers to save to purchase a home.[23]

From 1928, the Ideal Home Exhibition included a display of the house of the future built with 'adaptable' space. Furniture deflated and folded and could move from room to room; two double bedrooms could convert quickly into four single bedrooms; heating came from electric panels on the floor; light came from windows in the roof and on dull days, ultraviolet ray treatment was available throughout the house.[24] Many of these features came from the Bauhaus School, emphasizing function over form and technological innovation. Homes of the future exhibits at the Ideal Home Exhibitions continued throughout the 1930s and many of the ideas are reflected in the letters sent to the Burt Committee.

The aftermath of the New York Stock Market crash in 1929 created high unemployment and reduced consumer spending. British economic recovery during the 1930s was, according to many scholars, mediated by new house-building. The British building industry and building movement marketed home-ownership to working-class families. Peter Scott argues a large 'number of sophisticated marketing strategies were employed to transform the popular image of a mortgage from "a millstone round your neck" to a key element of a new, suburbanized, aspirational lifestyle'.[25]

DESIGNING CONSUMER SOCIETY

Figure 11.2. A semi-detached Tudorbethan house built in inter-war Morley, Yorkshire. Author's private collection.

Many working-class families became owner-occupants for the first time, strengthening the desire for domestic consumer goods marketed at the Ideal Home Exhibitions.[26]

Speculative builders 'identified what people really wanted and developed vast estates of semi-detached houses' built to a 'universal plan' that included three bedrooms and modern, efficient interiors (Figure 11.4).[27] The desire for home ownership came through careful industry marketing and assisted by a range of monthly women's magazines that were established in the inter-war years like *Homes and Garden* (1919), *Ideal Home* (1920), *Good Housekeeping* (1922) *Women & Home* (1926), *Women's Journal* (1927), *Woman & Home* (1929) and *Harper's Bazaar* (1929). The monthly magazines targeted middle-class women and promoted the idea of the suburban lifestyle with the 'professional housewife' in an efficient home. In the 1930s the suburban ideal expanded to include working-class families

Figure 11.3. Semi-detached council house built in inter-war Leeds, Yorkshire. Author's private collection.

and was supported by popular weekly magazines like *Woman's Own* (1932) and *Woman* (1937).[28]

The outbreak of war in 1939 halted all but essential war-related construction and closed the annual Ideal Home Exhibition. The war nevertheless enhanced desires for the perfect home. By September 1940, bombs fell nightly on London and the major port cities, destroying large housing tracts.[29] Scarcity and rationing made replacement of lost possessions impossible. Yet, Britons imagined a post-war world with practical, uncluttered homes filled with useful objects and appliances designed to make life easier. When the Burt Committee offered the opportunity to vocalize desires for post-war homes, citizen designers sent letters asking for houses planned and customized to meet specific lifecycle needs – the young family; the older couple; the single pensioner. Britons wanted individual dwellings but they did not envisage living in the same home for their whole life as their parents had done. Rather they imagined post-war life as a series of moves to purpose-built homes, designed for individual needs and requirements as they aged and entered each new stage in life. They nevertheless did not want to live far from relatives or people in different stages of life. Mrs M. M. Hooper put it this way, 'A mixture of sizes of houses ... would enable two or three generations of relatives to live *near* each other and yet enjoy independent homes' (emphasis in the original).[30] Hooper's request may have been an indirect criticism of inter-war slum clearance policies that

Figure 11.4. 1930s semi-detached house built in Leeds, Yorkshire. Author's private collection.

separated families even as it re-housed them in suburban council homes. Council estates tended to be built specifically for families with children, based on a three-bedroomed design of approximately 1000 square feet. Even private inter-war housing estates used similar floor plans for family homes offering mainly superficial additions to the exterior. Hooper wanted to keep extended families geographically close while maintaining the ideal of privacy that had grown during the inter-war years.[31]

Living close to family yet in independent homes was a luxury few Britons had enjoyed, especially during the war. The destruction of urban homes forced evacuation to rural areas and a life with distant relatives or strangers. Others rented rooms or had their spare rooms requisitioned to house evacuees or service personnel.[32] Conscription into the armed services separated families and by 1941 single women were also conscripted and forced to live in hostels close to wartime factories or in rented rooms with strangers.[33] Many of the letters received by the Burt Committee suggest that the home-front experience helped Britons rethink priorities. Few letters complained openly about wartime lodgers or communal living but some made clear that the post-war home should have toilets separate from bathrooms to better accommodate 'guests'. Still others requested architects consider the noise of the toilet in new homes. G. Falstead advised that 'when planning new houses ... it would be good to refrain from building the lavatory over the dining room as [the noise] is very embarrassing'.[34] An unsigned postcard simply said, 'Always plan a separate lavatory – when in the bathroom it is awkward for families and difficult for visitors.' Post-war homes, the postcard author continued, should have 'water pipes laid so that one or two bedrooms can have a supply for basins' and ease bathroom traffic.[35] When Mass Observation published a study of *People's Homes* in 1943, the lack of bathrooms and inadequate hot water headed the list of complaints for over 40 per cent of the survey responders.[36] As late as 1951, over two million people still lived in homes without an indoor toilet.[37]

Mothers with large families and nightshift workers were especially concerned about noise. Elizabeth Wilton worked the night shift and wrote, '[W]hat a blessing it would be if we could have sound proof homes.' Through the day, when trying to sleep, Wilton complained she could hear a cacophony of sounds made by neighbours – the wireless, piano, doors banging, the water heater, gossiping women and dogs barking.[38] M. F. Whelan, a mother of eight, wrote similarly, '[W]hy not include a sound-proof room specifically designed for children to play in when unable to go out in bad weather, and neighbours would have no cause to complain of noise.' Perhaps weary of the complaints as well as the noise of her own children, Whelan explained that a sound-proof room would 'at least ensure a little peace and quiet for mothers like myself', something she expected the state to provide: 'The country wants larger families so ... provide for them ...'.[39]

Other letters predicted smaller families and smaller homes in the post-war world. Inter-war council houses routinely contained at least three bedrooms. John Watson wrote, 'Surely what is needed [after the war] is the Bungalow built on a quarter acre ... with two bedrooms, living room and bath come spare bedroom.'[40] Watson's letter suggests post-war families would have the choice and the means to limit family size.[41] In fact live births for each married woman in Britain had fallen from an average of six to two since 1860.[42] Many letters seemed to reflect this demographic shift. Mrs M. Black wrote, 'My idea of the ideal house would be to utilize space as practical as possible.' Black wanted folding chairs and tables and an alcove fitted with a dresser for crockery and table linens, eliminating the need for extra furniture. Reflecting ideas prominent in the interwar Ideal Home Exhibition 'house of the future', Black continued, 'Kindly fit a cloakroom ... in the hall. Make it spacious so that Johnny and Mary can have hooks low down, father and mother the higher ones.' Next, Black demanded that 'the stair bannister (*sic*) ... [be] ... entirely plain. No dust crevices' and that the bathroom have tiles three-quarters of the way up the walls for ease of cleaning. The kitchen should include an electric refrigerator and an 'electric washer and combined wringer'. In a servant-less home, had these items been available before the war, Black claimed, housework 'would have been much simpler and much easier'.[43] Housewives didn't want large Victorian houses and clutter, but they did assume they would be purchasing modern labour-saving devices and indoor plumbing. To a large extent, Britons felt weary. Rationing and increased work hours made it harder to shop and cook appetising and nutritious meals, while time was also filled with queuing for goods, mending and sewing, recycling and reusing.[44]

Older and single women had their own concerns. For example, 70-year-old Mrs A. Tempest wanted to eliminate steps down to pantries: 'steps is a great trial especially for women who have had children or abdominal operations as I know from experience'.[45] Mrs M. B. Ashton, who had been 'bombed out of Battersea after being a householder for twenty-eight years', asked could they 'build some two-roomed cottages for us old people?' She thought it would be 'lovely to have our own street door and a tiny bit of garden'.[46] Forty-five-year-old Miss L. M. Barker, who had been a domestic servant her whole life, also wanted large bed-sitting rooms for single women, with 'a small garden for vegetables'.[47] While Barker clearly desired an independent living space, other Britons were anxious about the particular housing issues of older single women in reduced circumstances. Some letters expressed unease at the thought that these women would be left to live alone and wanted to ensure that post-war plans included a provision for this population. The accommodation question for the older, single woman was not new, but rather seen as part of a larger social issue stemming from the wholesale loss of marriageable young men in World War I.[48] Mrs H. E. Hambly wrote, 'I have been thinking a great deal lately about the old ladies, or ladies in reduced circumstance ... there are so many of them and nobody seems to want them.' Hambly, the present caretaker of an older single woman acknowledged 'they can be very trying and difficult at times ... but life must be very lonely for them and they cannot live alone'. Hambly suggested converting larger two-storey dwellings into 'bed-sitting rooms with gas or electric fires and rings where [single women] can sit and boil their own kettle if they wish'. Downstairs would include a communal room for company and a pleasant garden for exercise managed by a 'man and wife and an overseer'. This, claimed Hambly, would ensure adequate care of single women after the war. Additionally, the work and living situation might also appeal to a young couple before they embarked on raising a family.[49] Clearly for Hambly, care of the older, single woman, was imagined as a communal responsibility and should be planned for accordingly.

Arthur Henry also believed post-war living should be more collective and suggested 'what might be termed communal hotels or communal castles' with accommodation for at least 50 families. In what sounds very like the large-scale inter-war Holiday Camps developed by Billy Butlin and others, Henry suggested everyone pay the same rent and have access to the same facilities – a communal dining-room, a roof garden and children's playground, a concert hall or cinema, sports grounds with cricket, tennis and badminton as well as a post office, general store and school.[50] Like many Britons, Henry was frustrated with the amount of heating fuel the wartime government allotted for domestic use and remembered the relative waste of the interwar years.[51] He wrote, 'Instead of thousands of wretched small houses and bungalows using coal etc. trying to keep each compartment warm, in the above castle or hotel there would be CENTRAL HEATING and the whole place would be kept at the same temperature all year.'[52]

While Henry's castle might not appeal to all, his concern about wasteful heating is reflected in other letters. Faced with wartime shortages, rationed heating fuel and cold rooms, some Britons thought of ingenious ways to heat homes. G. F. Huneyberry suggested that a 'ventilator in the kitchen ceiling could allow warm air to pass into a room above' and heat it. Huneyberry also pointed out that 'one small pipe from the hot water boiler to the bathroom cistern' will warm the room adequately.[53] S. Cannon, stoker at a hospital with central heating wrote, 'I live in a council house where there are fourteen cottages and I guarantee that one cottage burns enough coal to heat three houses.' Cannon made his suggestion for community central heating along with his critique of the local housing authority. 'Had the council erected one fair sized boiler in the centre of those cottages and the necessary pump and radiators installed … there would be only a quarter of the fuel burnt in the course of a year.' This idea, claimed Cannon, would save fuel and be 'healthier … as it would abolish the dust that each tenant has to endure'.[54]

Other citizens wanted designs that reflected the inter-war preoccupation with sunshine and healthy living, requesting post-war homes utilize natural light and have access to outside living. Mrs Marie Budd asked that all homes have south-facing living-rooms with a French window to a veranda for eating outside in good weather. Graciously, Budd wrote, 'In our new cities, I would like everyone to be able to have free ultra violet ray treatment during the winter months and in each home a room to be a suntrap.'[55] Others asked similarly for homes with plenty of light and air so that children would be healthy and families would be happy.[56] The request for large windows and sunlight came perhaps as a result of wartime frustrations with the nightly blackouts as well as an echo of the importance of sunshine to the health movement of the inter-war years.[57]

Windows could also maintain a connection to the outside community. Mrs P. Harrison told the committee that people wanted houses with large windows. Unhappy with her pre-war council flat, Harrison spoke of the loneliness she felt. 'I am in a flat, shut in all round with no light or air' feeling like a prisoner, depressed and frustrated.[58] Like other older authors, Harrison wanted her own front door to the street and windows both to let in light and to help dispel the isolation of living alone.

H. L. White also wrote about his dissatisfaction with pre-war housing. Recently 'blitzed in Exeter', White claimed the concrete homes built after the last war were 'not satisfactory' and easily destroyed in the recent bombing. Although the concrete house won the Ideal Home Exhibition architect's design in 1928, according to White, the walls of his former home were 'always damp' because concrete 'sweats'.[59] Arthur Henry claimed the 'majority of people ARE NOT satisfied with … the jerry-built bungalow and tenements' of the inter-war years.[60] W. Page Edwards, a surveyor, reiterated this view in a list of problems. Inter-war homes were badly built, suffered from dry rot and had window casements, sashes and outside doors 'falling in pieces and refusing to function', defective damp-proofing leading to rising damp, no outlet for fumes from gas stoves, inadequate service pipes to the bath and basin and numerous other problems derived from 'flagrant breaches of bylaws'. Although Edwards admitted some problems were the result of poor production methods, most were not. 'No Town Planning Committee will satisfy the harassed housewife', Edwards claimed, 'by telling her to ignore these … problems … because she is living on a beautifully planned estate in park-like surroundings.'[61] In the post-war world, Edwards alleged, consumers, particularly housewives, would not tolerate substandard house-building. Implicit in this observation is the idea that post-war consumers would have political influence as well as the economic power to demand higher standards and better living conditions. Post-war planning and building, according to Edwards, needed to take into account the expectations of a higher standard of living for all Britons.

Significantly, however, this higher standard of living did not include car ownership. Few people requested garages in post-war planning. In 1928 the Ideal Home Exhibition showcased a home with an integral garage as an 'Attractive Home Planned for the Owner-driver' but it was an anomaly.[62] The inter-war years saw a growth in the number of personal vehicles and drivers, but the numbers were still comparatively small and the cost of a motor vehicle out of the reach of most working families.[63] Most home designs did not include garages until the 1960s. Consumers did want less commuting, however. For example, a letter from H. L. White wanted flats for small families built as close to the city centre as possible for access to shops and the dockyard – presumably for work.[64] Others, like John Watson, asked for homes with garages, but he thought that these could have multiple functions. For example, 'In the event of another war', Watson claimed, a garage 'could be used to house goats or rabbits etc.'. In fact, Watson noted that while he hoped this was a 'war to end wars', hadn't that been the hope in 1918? Homes in the future should be built with plenty of land for self-sufficiency with a future war in mind.

While it is difficult to know how carefully the government read such letters or cared about specific consumer requests, it did establish a sub-committee on Design of Dwellings, chaired by Lord Dudley in 1944 that looked at the findings of several housing surveys and the Burt committee letters. The Dudley report made recommendations that echoed concerns voiced in these letters asking for private, quiet, light, simple single-family homes. It recommended various types of homes – semi-detached and three-bedroomed, as well as terraced homes and flats. Town planners and architects, though wary of public opinion and the incursion into their professional scope of practice, 'produced plans on post-war housing in tune with the public's needs and tastes'.[65] While plans did not always translate into reality, the provision of post-war housing became a central pillar of the post-war welfare state.[66]

Although the wartime letter-writing demonstrated participatory democracy, the content of the letters to the Burt Committee also supports James Hinton's contention that the 'longer-term effect of wartime mobilization may well have been to provoke a retreat into the private sphere'.[67] But the return to domesticity did not necessarily lead to a consumer boom in the way that Lizabeth Cohen has proposed for the US. Post-1945 politics in the US encouraged the development of suburbs and with it the mass consumption of consumer durables, especially home appliances and automobiles.[68] In Britain, the first wave of suburbanization took place in the 1930s within a wider context of economic depression and was not, therefore accompanied by the mass consumption of durable goods. In the post-war years suburbanization increased as slum clearance continued and re-housing multiplied the vast council estates on the periphery of bombed-out city centres. Post-war austerity and rationing again prevented the immediate mass consumption of home appliances, automobiles and luxury goods. Thus home building was an engine of economic growth but it did not occur in the same way everywhere as Kenneth Mouré argues in this volume. Yet the letters from the war years also suggest that consumer desire centred around privacy, domestic comfort, and women especially wanted less housework rather than simply 'things' for personal pleasure. Indeed, social class does not appear to have significantly influenced the yearning for more efficient space and a private front door. The wartime letters to the

Burt Committee suggest the state was concerned with consumer opinion but, more significantly, they illuminate the expectation of British consumers that the post-war state, not the market, would help them achieve a better way of life.

Those who wrote to the Burt Committee believed post-war reconstruction should take place according to their wartime longings. By destroying people's homes and their contents, the war provided a moment for individuals to consider an 'ideal' lifestyle and a house that would best incorporate that way of life, even as they imagined the possibility of a post-war existence. By rethinking their belongings and things even as they were destroyed by the enemy's bombs, Britons constructed, if only on paper, proposals for a suitable standard of living in the post-war nation. Their letters give a sense of the dreams of average Britons during a time of intense stress and austerity as well as the expectation that the state would help them attain those dreams. Thus for these individuals, the welfare state was as much about rebuilding consumer society as it was about rebuilding homes.

ACKNOWLEDGEMENTS

A version of this chapter was presented at the North American Conference on British Studies in Portland, Oregon, November 2013. I am grateful for the comments of the audience in Portland as well as the generous insights from Erika Rappaport and Mark Crowley. Special thanks to Russell Trudgen for identifying inter-war homes and to Rosie Trudgen for taking the photographs for this chapter.

NOTES

1. The Interdepartmental Committee of the Ministries of Health and Works and Planning was formed in April 1942 and chaired by Sir George Burt, hereafter the Burt Committee.
2. *John Bull*, 9 January 1943, clipping in the files of the Burt Committee, The National Archives (hereafter TNA) HLG 94/3.
3. Mrs Georgina K Meyor, York, to Burt Committee, 21 December 1942, TNA HLG 94/3.
4. Mrs F. Wilkins, Brixton, to Burt Committee, 24 January 1943, TNA HLG 94/3.
5. Burt Committee files contain over 140 handwritten letters and typed letters from individuals as well as building companies and architects.
6. *Daily Telegraph*, 12 December 1942 and *Star*, 17 December 1942.

7. Approximately 460,000 homes were destroyed and approximately 4 million were damaged during the war. *Housing* Cmd 6609 (London: HMSO, 1945), p. 2.
8. Martin Bulmer, Kevin Bales and Kathryn Kish Sklar, eds, The Social Survey in Historical Perspective, 1880–1940 (Cambridge: Cambridge University Press, 1991), Chapter 1. See also Nick Hubble, *Mass Observation and Everyday Life: Culture, History, Theory* (New York: Palgrave Macmillan, 2006).
9. Peter Scott, *The Making of the Modern British Home: The Suburban Semi and Family Life between the Wars* (Oxford: Oxford University Press, 2013), Chapter 5; Sandra Trudgen Dawson, 'Working Class Consumers and the Campaign for Holidays with Pay', *Twentieth Century British History*, 18:3 (2007) pp. 277–305.
10. Mass Observation conducted several surveys asking the same question of service personnel in wartime. See Tatsuya Tsubaki, 'Planners and the Public: British Popular Opinion on Housing During the Second World War', *Contemporary British History* 14:1 (Spring 2000), pp. 81–98.
11. Paola Messana, *Soviet Communal Living: An Oral History of the Kommunalka*, (London: Palgrave Macmillan, 2011) and Peter Galison, 'Aufbau/Bauhaus: Logical Positivism and Architectural Modernism', *Critical Inquiry* 16:4 (1990), pp. 709–52.
12. Paul Overy, *Light, Air and Openness: Modern Architecture between the Wars* (London: Thames & Hudson, 2008).
13. Scott, *Modern British Home*, p. 51.
14. Mark Swenarton, *Building the New Jerusalem: Architecture, Housing and Politics, 1900–1930* (London: IHS BRE Press, 2010) and his earlier book, *Homes Fit for Heroes* (London: Heinemann, 1981).
15. Alison Ravetz, *Council Housing and Culture: The History of a Social Experiment* (London: Routledge, 2001), Chapter 1.
16. Scott, *Modern British Home*, p. 37.
17. Matthew Hollow, 'Suburban Ideals on England's Interwar Council Estates', *Journal of the Garden History Society* 39:2 (2011), pp. 203–17. Thirty per cent of the 4.3 million homes built were council houses. Scott, *Modern British Home*, p. 43. See also, A. Olechnowicz, *Working-class Housing in England between the Wars: The Becontree Estate* (Oxford: Clarendon, 1997).
18. This was an international movement. See Bianca Murillo, 'Ideal Homes and the Gender Politics of Consumerism in Postcolonial Ghana, 1960–70', *Gender and History* 21:3 (November 2009), pp. 560–75.
19. Deborah S. Ryan, '"All the World and her Husband": The *Daily Mail* Ideal Home Exhibition, 1908–39', in *All the World and Her Husband: Women in Twentieth-century Consumer Culture*, eds Maggie Andrews and Mary M. Talbot (London: Cassell, 2000), pp. 10–22.
20. Ibid., p. 11. See also Ina Zweiniger-Bargielowska, *Managing the Body: Beauty, Health, and Fitness in Britain 1880–1939* (Oxford: Oxford University Press, 2011).

21. Selina Todd, *Young Women, Work and Family in England, 1918–1950* (Oxford: Oxford University Press, 2005).
22. Deborah S. Ryan, *The Ideal Home through the 20th Century: 'Daily Mail' Ideal Home Exhibition* (London: Hazar, 1997), p. 34.
23. Ibid., p. 59. See also Mark Crowley, this volume.
24. Ibid., p. 56.
25. Peter Scott, 'Marketing Mass Home Ownership and the Creation of the Modern Working-class Consumer in Inter-war Britain', *Business History* 50:1 (2008), pp. 4–25.
26. Ryan, *Ideal Home Exhibition*, p. 21.
27. T. Chapman and J. Hockey, 'The Ideal Home as it is Imagined and as it is Lived', in *Ideal Homes? Social Change and Domestic Life*, eds Tony Chapman and Jenny Hockey (London: Routledge, 1999), p. 8.
28. Scott, *Modern British Home*, p. 121.
29. Robert Mackay, *Half the Battle: Civilian Morale in Britain during the Second World War* (Manchester: Manchester University Press, 2002).
30. Mrs M. M. Hooper, Cardiff, to Burt Committee, 22 December 1942, TNA HLG 94/3.
31. Scott, *Modern British Home*, p. 121.
32. Jose Harris, 'War and Social History: Britain and the Home Front during the Second World War', *Journal of European History* 1:1 (1992), pp. 17–35. See also, Lucy Noakes, *War and the British: Gender, Memory and National Identity* (London: I. B. Tauris, 1998).
33. Sandra Trudgen Dawson, 'Busy and Bored: The Politics of Work and Leisure for Women Workers in WWII British Government Hostels', *Twentieth Century British History* 20:1 (2010), pp. 30–49.
34. G. Falstead, Ilford, to Burt Committee, 7 January 1943, TNA HLG 94/3.
35. Unsigned postcard postmarked 13 January 1943, TNA HLG 94/4. In Scotland some tenement blocks did not have indoor toilets until the 1970s. Raymond Young, *Annie's Loo: The Govan Origins of Scotland's Community Based Housing Associations* (Glendaruel: Argyll Publishing, 2013), Chapter 1.
36. Mass Observation, *An Enquiry into People's Homes* (London: John Murray, 1943), pp. 67–8.
37. Scott, *Modern British Home*, p. 59.
38. Elizabeth Wilton, Bristol, to Burt Committee, 5 June 1943, TNA HLG 94/3.
39. M. F. Whelan to Burt Committee, 22 July 1943, TNA HLG 94/3.
40. John G. Watson, Harrogate, to Burt Committee, 28 December 1942, TNA HLG 94/3.
41. Men were often in charge of planning contraceptive use in a marriage see Kate Fisher, *Birth Control, Sex, and Marriage in Britain, 1918–1960* (Oxford: Oxford University Press, 2006), pp. 189–237.

42. Simon Szreter, *Fertility, Class and Gender in Britain, 1860–1940*, 2nd edn. (Cambridge: Cambridge University Press, 2000), p. 1.
43. Mrs M. Black, Edmonton London, to Burt Committee, 18 December 1942, TNA HLG 94/3.
44. Gail Braybon and Penny Summerfield, *Out of the Cage: Women's Experiences in the Two World Wars* (London: Pandora Press, 1987).
45. Mrs A. Tempest, Harrogate, to Burt Committee, 25 December 1042, TNA HLG 94/3.
46. Mr M. B. Ashton, Middlesex, to Burt Committee, 30 December 1942 TNA HLG 94/3.
47. Miss L. M. Barker, Harrow, to Burt Committee, 3 January 1943, TNA HLG 94/3.
48. Katharine Holden, 'Imaginary Widows: Spinsters, Marriage, and the "Lost Generation" in Britain after the Great War', *Journal of Family History* 30:4 (2005), pp. 88–409 and 'Personal Costs and Personal Pleasures: Care and the Unmarried Woman in Inter-war Britain', in Janet Fink, ed. *Care: Personal Lives and Social Policy* (Milton Keynes: Open University Press, 2004), pp. 43–76.
49. Mrs H. E. Hambly, Barnstable, to Burt Committee, 1 March 1943, TNA HLG 94/1.
50. Sandra Trudgen Dawson, *Holiday Camps in Twentieth-century Britain: Packaging Pleasure* (Manchester: Manchester University Press, 2011).
51. Ina Zweiniger-Bargielowska, *Austerity in Britain: Rationing, Controls, and Consumption 1939-1955* (Oxford: Oxford University Press, 2000); Peter Hennessy, *Never Again: Britain 1945-51* (Pantheon, 1994) and *Having it So Good: Britain in the Fifties* (London: Penguin, 2007).
52. Arthur L. Henry, Dumbartonshire, to Burt Committee, 11 January 1943, TNA HLG 94/3.
53. G. F. Hunneyberry, Huddersfield, to Burt Committee, 20 December 1942, TNA HLG 94/3.
54. S. Cannon to Burt Committee, 17 December 1942, TNA HLG 94/3.
55. Mrs Marie B. Budd, Sidmouth, to Burt Committee, 12 February 1943, TNA HLG 94/4 and Ryan, *Ideal Homes*, p. 58.
56. Mrs P. Harrison, Hammersmith, to Burt Committee, 17 December 1942, TNA HLG 94/4.
57. Zweiniger-Bargielowska, *Managing the Body* and in this volume.
58. Harrison, 17 December 1942.
59. H. L. White, Exeter, to Burt Committee, 28 December 1942, TNA HLG 94/3. Ryan, *Ideal Homes*, p. 58.
60. Arthur L. Henry, Dumbartonshire, to Burt Committee, 11 January 1943, TNA HLG 94/3.
61. W. Page Edwards to Burt Committee, 18 December 1942, TNA HLG 94/3.

62. Ryan, *Ideal Homes*, p. 58.
63. Sean O'Connell, *The Car in British Society: Class, Gender and Motoring, 1896–1939* (Manchester: Manchester University Press, 1998).
64. White, 28 December 1942.
65. Tsubaki, 'Planners and the Public', p. 96.
66. Peter Malpass, 'The Wobbly Pillar? Housing and the British Postwar Welfare State', *Journal of Social Policy* 32:4 (2003), pp. 589–606.
67. James Hinton, *Nine Wartime Lives: Mass Observation and the Making of the Modern Self* (Oxford: Oxford University Press, 2010), p. 13.
68. Lizabeth Cohen, *A Consumers' Republic: The Politics of Mass Consumption in Postwar America* (New York: Alfred A. Knopf, 2003), pp. 194–6.

CHAPTER TWELVE

Saving for the Nation: The Post Office and National Consumerism, c. 1860–1945

MARK J. CROWLEY

This chapter examines the development of the Post Office Savings Bank (POSB) from its beginnings in the mid-nineteenth century to an unparalleled position in Britain's consumer society by the first half of the twentieth century. The 'marketing' of thrift and saving to the working classes created a patriotic link between saving and national strength: a governmental desire, galvanized by the patriotism of the Napoleonic Wars and finally realized in 1861 through the establishment of a savings bank specifically for the working and middle classes as a branch within the General Post Office (GPO). Scholars have argued that the POSB, especially with the growth of tariff reform at the beginning of the twentieth century, reinforced a neo-mercantilist relationship that sought to boost domestic consumption and encourage people to save and invest their scarce resources in the event of a future economic slump.[1] Other plans included streamlining POSB banking processes to maximize efficiency. This chapter will examine how debates over these issues and the resulting decisions culminated in the presentation and preservation of the POSB as a key component of British consumer culture in the first half of the twentieth century.

Britain's banking system was not well-organized. Throughout the nineteenth century it remained largely the domain for the wealthy. The poor relied on a vast array of voluntary organizations, some completely unregulated by government (such as pawnbrokers) to meet the strains of daily life. Friendly societies, supported by charities, provided some financial insurance in the absence of a welfare state, although access to resources depended on their reserve and the individual's relationship with its officers. Remaining unregulated until 1875, societies retained limited control over their membership and executive composition, with no legal basis to enforce the return of funds.[2] The 1875 Friendly Society Act, passed by Disraeli's Conservative government, gave societies more control over their management, while ensuring 'the adoption of sound rules, effective audit, and rates of payment sufficient to maintain solvency' that put 'people's savings on a satisfactory basis'.[3] The establishment in 1844 of the co-operative movement in Rochdale by a collection of workers seeking cooperation to ensure lower prices, fairer competition and a distribution of profits according to purchases (known as the 'divi') was instrumental to these changes. However, while the success of the co-operative movement as a local and later national force helped rationalize savings, it did not signal a significant move towards a distinctly working-class savings movement. In 1872, the Loan and Deposit department of the Co-operative Wholesale Society was established (renamed the CWS Bank in 1876) primarily as a business bank for co-operative societies, and did not become a registered company offering clearing services for personal customers until 1971.[4] In the nineteenth century, in the absence of unemployment insurance and the relative infancy of the co-operative movement, there were still few safe havens for working-class savings.[5]

The Liberal Government created the POSB in 1861 in response to this void in the financial system. The aim was to integrate those in manual and low-paid occupations who were ineligible or reluctant to open a private bank account, and to encourage thrift among the lower classes. The Palmerston government supported this, as did the Postmaster General Sir Rowland Hill, creator of the Penny Post, and then-Chancellor of the Exchequer, William Gladstone, who, as Prime Minister, described the POSB as 'the most important institution which has been created in the last fifty years for the welfare of the people and the State'.[6] Despite no explicit political connection, the Liberal Party remained staunchly in favour of the POSB. Indeed, the POSB proved to be a vital institution that helped poorer citizens deposit and invest (with a nominal 2.5 per cent interest payment) their money in a government-backed establishment. Thus, even before gaining the right to vote, the poor became integrated stakeholders in the nation. By opening an account with the POSB, individuals were told they could prepare for unforeseen hardships, such as unemployment.[7] However, the largest consumer base for the POSB was initially the lower middle classes, who tended to distrust the unregulated friendly societies and similar institutions. Largely because of growing affluence, this clientele looked to government-backed initiatives, even after the 1875 Act, as a safe haven for their savings.[8] Yet the POSB had a lot of catching up to do to gain ground on the private banks and growing insurance industry. Many people remained tied to the status quo provided by private banks and insurance companies.[9]

The POSB was both conservative and innovative. Although wary to tread into areas hitherto dominated by private sector banks, the POSB did contribute to some major developments in individual savings.[10] Yet the POSB's function was not merely financial, nor was it entirely regressive. It was shaped by a Treasury that wanted to increase the GPO's activity as a major banking institution, as well as a more cautious Post Office with little experience in this arena. Post Office managers did not want to offer the same services as those provided by high street banks. It also had difficulty overcoming working-class perceptions that savings banks were for the wealthy. According to Martin Daunton, savings banks were regarded by the working-class as 'paternalistic rather than democratic, without a sense of collective identity and purpose'.[11] Former economist and banker-turned-MP Thomas Attwood blasted the savings banks as 'a sort of screw in the hands of the Government to fix down the working class to its system'.[12] To a certain extent, Attwood was correct, since the POSB did restrict depositors' activity, believing that controlled withdrawals would stabilize the nation's finances and enforce thrift among a profligate working class.[13] The POSB marketed itself as the 'People's Bank', espousing an anti-consumer message that income should be saved, not spent. By 1870, the POSB had more branches than private banks. Arguably the POSB's long-term aim was to encourage rational spending choices among working-class consumers who were spending their income on new 'luxuries' or 'pleasures', such as alcohol and tobacco. It was unclear, however, how the Post Office hoped, or indeed believed that it could successfully regulate consumer habits in a way that would enforce thrift and discourage spending.[14]

In 1904 the Postmaster General claimed:

> It is the object of the Post Office Savings Bank to provide a safe place of deposit with a moderate rate of interest for the savings of the working classes as a provision, not only against old age or death, but also for other contingencies of life, such as sickness, want of employment etc.[15]

In this sense, the POSB operated as a state-controlled friendly society offering welfare services in the absence of a formalized welfare state. In so doing, the government also hoped to educate the working classes on the value of thrift and financial planning. Daunton argues that the government had 'no intention of converting it [the POSB] into a banking institution', the aim rather was to encourage saving and thrift by controlling withdrawals.[16] Naturally, the meaning of 'thrift' differed across social classes. Many middle-class consumers considered cash saved in a bank as testimony of hard work and frugality.[17] Working-class perceptions saw savings as insurance against future emergencies, such as unemployment, sickness, or health problems, while investing in trade-union membership as protection from employer bullying.[18] No doubt men and women perceived thrift differently and there is evidence to suggest that families often quarrelled about how to spend the family finances.[19] However, the POSB was built on middle-class perceptions first theorized in the late-eighteenth and early-nineteenth century. Political economists such as Jeremy Bentham and utopian socialist Robert Owen contemplated how to encourage the working classes to save rather than spend their scarce resources.[20] Nearly a century later, GPO managers were still trying to encourage savings without violating Gladstonian notions of thrifty government. The POSB fulfilled this dream since it required very little additional investment – Post Office clerks could use existing Post Office counters for POSB transactions.[21]

The onset of the First World War gave new urgency to the importance of thrift and the securities offered by a government-backed bank. The war also secured the POSB's future. While the POSB was built on Victorian liberal ideas about the morality of spending and the value of frugality, it was also a flexible modern institution. As early as the First World War, the POSB used modern commercial techniques to transform thrift from an individual to a national duty. From 1914, it correlated the purchase of government bonds with national duty. These bonds, later re-named War Savings Certificates in 1916, helped the country invest in the required machinery and weaponry for war, with the public, for the first time, expected to contribute to wartime costs.[22] By 1918, £207 million in certificates were purchased, largely as the result of modern advertising techniques and wartime propaganda.[23] The Post Office thought these investments would cease at the end of the war, but enthusiasm to continue investing was so great that in 1920 the bonds were re-named National Savings Certificates. These certificates continued to sell until after the Second World War, as many citizens now used the POSB as their primary savings bank.[24]

But not everyone wanted to save after the First World War. Many consumers wanted to spend, and the Post Office adapted to the changing consumer needs. This in turn ensured the continued growth of the POSB and the need to improve services for its large consumer base.[25] Originally the POSB system was set up so that deposits and withdrawals could only be made at the branch where the account was held – a policy designed to encourage savings and thrift by developing a system of regular, small deposits through steady visits to the same Post Office branch. It also made policies about limiting withdrawals easier to monitor. Officials hoped this would prevent consumers from making unnecessary withdrawals from POSB accounts. In 1919, judging it as restrictive and overly intrusive for consumers, the Post Office abandoned the policy, liberalizing its financial system. Restrictions limiting depositors to an annual balance of £30 were abolished. Savers could now deposit a maximum of £150 per day, with no limit on the account's balance. Additionally, savers could now withdraw funds from any Post Office branch in the network which provided customers with greater flexibility for personal transactions.[26]

Official estimates indicated those with annual incomes under £250 had, by 1928/9, saved £40–50 million.[27] By the end of the 1920s, 25 per cent of Britons had a POSB account, amounting to twelve million accounts with £283 million in deposits.[28] Following the shake of public confidence in private banks after the 1929 Wall Street crash, consumers felt even more strongly that investing in an institution not so prone to bankruptcy was safer.[29] Nevertheless, the failure to invest in infrastructure and new machinery reduced the Post Office's effectiveness in the long term.[30] Frequent reports noted long queues at Post Office counters, especially Crown offices in larger cities like London. Additionally, cumbersome ledger and book-keeping methods reduced efficiency and made the banking process more complex. Furthermore, the reliance on London storage of ledgers increased waiting times for those in more remote areas.[31]

During the 1930s, in an attempt to inspire the confidence of a sceptical public who now mistrusted private banks, the POSB became a kind of hybrid institution – a 'commercialized' state department. The POSB was the first government agency to open a Public Relations Department in 1933. Relying on new technologies, such as the poster and innovations in colour printing techniques, POSB propaganda emphasized prudence and thrift, saving and making do rather than spending on consumer goods that were in short supply.[32] Under the leadership of former secretary to the Empire Marketing Board (EMB), Sir Stephen Tallents, the POSB illustrates the way the state attempted to mould consumer ideologies and behaviours.[33] These government agencies encouraged investing in the nation rather than spending on individual pleasures and pastimes. At the same time, like the most advanced private businesses, these agencies relied on clear and cogent marketing strategies to gain the interest of consumers. As Erika Rappaport demonstrates in this volume, the creation of the EMB sought to stimulate demand for British products through imperial purchases. Tallents brought his EMB experience to the Post Office, but rather than focus on promoting an imperial nation, he now fostered consumer interest and demand in distinctly 'British' products, creating a correlation between investment, civic duty and national pride. However, the growth of Fascism in Europe changed perceptions about 'the nation' and the type of products requiring commoditization and consumption. Fostering 'Britishness' and national unity in the face of Fascist aggression replaced the previously dominant concerns of achieving national unity to combat economic and imperial decline. Here, Tallents believed the Post Office could be an essential component in a movement to secure the commoditization of savings products as a means of promoting patriotism.

The Poster Advisory Group, established in 1934 under Tallents's leadership, provided guidance on using modern art to publicize Post Office products and services.[34] This was the heyday of the poster as modern media, and Tallents believed consumers could be convinced to invest in the POSB, just as they could be persuaded to buy soap or sugar or any other commercial product. Just as during a war, the Post Office could expand its consumer base through advertising.[35] Tallents specifically discussed art in his proposals to enhance the POSB, and in later initiatives, a wide body of experts and ordinary members of the public, including children, were asked to contribute. Ironically, as Radice has argued, the success of the savings movement depended heavily on the government's effectiveness and the POSB's ability to demonstrate the necessity for thrift.[36]

Government estimates indicated that savings held by the working- and lower-middle classes would, by 1937, total between £100–120 million because of the increase in working-class incomes. Faced with more income, the working classes were expected to choose to save. The increasing number of new POSB accounts suggested that they did so.[37] This, together with the healthier economic conditions by the late 1930s, prompted government predictions of surpluses in the unemployment insurance fund. Reduced expenditure on unemployment, and a rise of £223 million in consumer spending, produced indirect taxes of around £10 million. Consequently, the British economy was in a relatively healthy position by 1938.[38] Additionally, reduced spending on foreign travel and private transportation caused by fears of international hostilities after 1938, meant that people now not only had more disposable income, but were developing a strong tendency to save in preparation for war, the hardships it would bring and the potential difficulties, such as unemployment, of the post-war world.[39] Furthermore, as

Sandra Dawson argues in this volume and elsewhere, the Holidays with Pay Act (1938) and the increased marketing of mortgages to the working classes illustrates the way working families emerged as a significant consumer group.[40] The value of savings held in the POSB by 1938 was £1,057,101,000.[41]

The POSB thus was well-positioned to play a vital role in the maintenance of morale and preservation of the nation's financial and moral fabric during the Second World War. Indeed, immediately after the Munich crisis in September 1938, the Post Office began to prepare for war.[42] It spent more than any government department (£11,600) on poster design (before printing) to publicize their services and their envisaged role in a future conflict, thus making the efforts of the Ministry of Labour (who spent £3,300 on poster production and printing) the National Milk Publicity Council (who paid £100 to an agency to produce 10,000 posters) and HM Office of Works (who spent £150 on 5,000 posters publicizing the importance of protecting ancient and historic monuments) almost pale into insignificance.[43] Nevertheless, this is much less than private businesses spent on advertising. For example, Selfridge's spent £30,000 on their 1909 opening day campaign alone.[44] However, the Post Office sustained its pre-war advertising expenditure throughout the war.

At the outbreak of war in 1939, the Post Office was not classified as an 'essential industry'. As conscription depleted the GPO workforce, the Post Office became feminized as women responded to the call for workers and took 'female only' positions such as typists and clerks. Women filled more than 100,000 jobs, a third of its workforce.[45] By January 1940, 54,000 skilled men had left to join the forces. 26,000 women undertook counter work, with another 25,000 on various telephone duties. There were 1,600 female engineers, 23,000 postwomen, 500 in the stores departments, 17,000 clerks and typists with over 3,000 cleaners. Of the 23,000 sub-post offices in the country, 8,700 were controlled by women.[46] At the same time, the Post Office was expected to do more. As the official publication of the Association of Head Postmasters trade union commented 'August, 1939, saw the Post Office as a mighty machine doing its job uncommonly well. Its task of providing communications had shrunk the world, and its help in administering social services had expanded the life of the individual.'[47] The public was becoming more accustomed to and dependent on its efficient postal and telegraph services, public telephones and banking facilities.[48]

The ability to maintain communication with friends and family and the facilities to send money to people's accounts certainly helped to unify the nation and provide some solace for those worried about loved ones. However, the effectiveness of the Post Office was heavily influenced by several internal ideological battles. Modernization, not only in the technological sense, but also in societal attitudes, was a key component of this teleology – a situation that ran contrary to conventional wisdom, and was largely influenced by necessity.[49] There were a number of significant attitudinal changes in the Post Office during the interwar years that improved staff relations and consumer services, and as the Association of Head Postmasters commented in 1941: 'The Post Office shed many of its less pleasant characteristics after the last war, and took on a different outlook towards public and staff.'[50] For women, the war and the POSB provided greater opportunities for employment and advancement. In terms of services, and despite the exigencies of war, Treasury officials continued to emphasize the importance of separation between the public and private sectors, and were keen not to encroach on the domain of the private sector.

Pressure on the Post Office remained intense. As a result, officials considered curbing general business to offer a better service to the armed forces at home and abroad.[51] Reductions affected the POSB and the telegram service.[52] Managers went to great lengths to maintain Post Office services and kept changes and any reduction of services carefully concealed from the public to maintain civilian morale. For example, by 1942, the records of 13,000,000 National Savings Certificate holders were guarded by women fire fighters rather than men.[53] Over 100 trained women from the ages of 16 to 50 worked in this area to protect the savings of its depositors, and manned their posts from the outbreak of the war.[54] Very few men worked as guards. Conscription reduced the number of male postal workers, and those who remained were transferred to areas such as Post Office engineering or telephones in the interest of maintaining the country's communications.[55]

The task to maintain the savings movement was herculean. The war and the appearance of stalemate as experienced in the First World War made disseminating and encouraging the message of thrift much more difficult. This was particularly the case for women expected to survive on low wages and limited army pensions. To overcome these difficulties, Post Office officials considered it essential to change the presentation of thrift from a personal or individual quality to a collective characteristic, and to emphasize the idea that wise spending and investment would help the national interest.[56] Although the benefit of individual thrift was not ignored, it was secondary to the wider propaganda of sustaining civilian morale and ensuring much-needed funds for the war machine. [57]

Despite the message shift, the POSB continued to disseminate government propaganda in a similar fashion to that in the First World War. The POSB Marketing Department launched several campaigns that helped solidify the position of the POSB into the people's national consciousness, such as the

'Saving for the Nation' campaign.[58] This made the POSB a key component of the war effort and Britain's wartime consumer society, as well as a vital element in what Angus Calder and others have termed 'the People's War'.[59] Post Office activities were applauded by the public and the popular press. The *Observer* stated on 5 December 1938 that 'the praise of the Post Office is nowadays in everybody's mouth; its efficiency, its courtesy and humanity', and by 1939, *The Penrose Annual* acknowledged that 'the press praises more often than it blames', and 'generally speaking, the public regards the Post Office as a friend'.[60] As the war progressed, so did Post Office efforts to integrate into the rest of society. The Postmaster General, W. S. Morrison, met weekly with BBC officials to write press releases extolling the work of the Post Office to the public. One major emphasis was the convergence of male and female roles. In 1940 the *Daily Mirror* exclaimed, 'The War is making things happen that never did happen before. Here is one – Mr. and Mrs. Postman.'[61] By 1942, 26,000 women were employed as POSB clerks out of an overall 113,000 women. This represented a 100 per cent increase from pre-war female employment figures.[62] These numbers helped create the image of the war as a collective effort where not only men and women were expected to 'do their bit', but also that all resources should be recycled or used intelligently to aid the war effort.[63]

The close connection between the War Office, especially the Ministry of Information, and the Post Office proved influential in disseminating the propaganda message. Posters created an inextricable link between investment in the POSB and the nation's efforts to win the war.[64] Slogans like 'Money is Power' and 'Make your Money provide the driving power – put it into the Post Office Savings Bank' made the Post Office a key component of the war effort.[65] Images of army ships, aeroplanes, power stations and munitions factories reinforced the heavily masculinised notion of power, military might and solidarity symbolic of the defiance and will emphasized through Winston Churchill's speeches. Accompanying slogans, by default, condemned personal spending in favour of thrift in the national interest. Furthermore, images of men in war factories reinforced the idea of physical strength and brawn in the face of Nazi aggression, but also reminded consumers that this strength was a collaborative national effort from both men and women. POSB posters illustrated the way every citizen could take an active part in the war effort.[66] Although not explicit, the focus on women workers in the labour market, particularly the Post Office, reinforced the nature of the war effort as one requiring strength, cooperation and national solidarity.

At the early stages, posters were sent to schools, both so that children could understand the role of the Post Office and to gauge the effectiveness

Figure 12.1. 'Make Your Money Provide the Driving Power, Put it into the Post Office Savings Bank', 1942 (Austin Cooper). BPMA, POST 110/3189. Reproduced with the permission of the British Postal Museum and Archive. © Royal Mail Group 2014, courtesy of The British Postal Museum & Archive.

of propaganda on children. The posters were primarily the works of those charged with designing posters for the Post Office, including Frank Newbould, Austin Cooper and Eric Fraser. Those featured in Figures 12.1 and 12.2, along with others, were sent for initial reaction. This came in the wake of the failure of the Ministry of Information's red poster propaganda campaign to encourage national solidarity, which, according to Mass Observation (MO) created hostility among women.[67] More than 27,000 posters were sent to the 28,000 schools on the Post Office's mailing list, as well as to magazine editors and several local and regional art councils. Embracing all areas and cohorts of society, it generated a sense of inclusiveness that was perhaps absent in other propaganda messages. These various initiatives aimed to persuade Britons of all ages that participating in a POSB scheme was a valid contribution to the war effort, and that every penny invested would help the British Army defeat the enemy. Yet getting agreement on 'taste' was difficult. Tallents left the Post Office to work for the BBC as Public Relations Controller in 1936, and his replacement, E. T.

Figure 12.2. 'Make Your Money Provide the Driving Power, Put it into the Post Office Savings Bank', 1942 (Eric Fraser) BPMA, POST 110/3191. Reproduced with the permission of the British Postal Museum and Archive. © Royal Mail Group 2014, courtesy of The British Postal Museum & Archive.

Crutchley, streamlined resources and disbanded the poster department at the end of the Second World War.[68]

Establishing a link between the propaganda drive and the success of the POSB is difficult to quantify. Certainly the images associated with the wartime campaign were not unique: rather they were very similar to other state-funded propaganda and private advertising. Additionally, with no end to the war in sight, public scepticism about propaganda increased.[69] MO revealed that many people remained unsure about the government's propaganda messages. As the war progressed, communicating with women especially through propaganda became increasingly difficult and MO concluded:

> She is thus not likely to go out of her way to meet any propaganda. It must come to her. The main opinion-forming factors are her everyday life and needs, the views of her friends, and especially her husband. ... The housewife reacts more readily to the propaganda of advertising, prices,

shop windows, which she sees every day; the cost of living against which she must always battle.[70]

The POSB helped bridge the gender and class gap as it explained to both male and female consumers that by putting their savings in the Post Office they were part of the national community. Indeed even small accounts collectively would win the war. Such ideas were not new. In fact they were part of the POSB message from its inception in the 1860s when the Liberal government sought to control what workers did with extra cash.

The POSB revolutionized the way many citizens managed their savings, even if the overall development was slow. According to Daunton, the slow development of the POSB in Britain compared to its European and worldwide counterparts in the same period was heavily influenced by the limitations placed upon it as a public enterprise.[71] Yet it shaped and facilitated Britain's consumer society in the first half of the twentieth century, especially in wartime. As Robinson has argued, the Post Office made 'an extraordinary contribution to the war effort through the numerous ways in which it touched the life of every citizen, for it was better able than ever to meet its responsibilities'.[72] This, through the POSB and its other agency services, was to prove the enduring impact of the Post Office for the remainder of the century.

ACKNOWLEDGEMENTS

This research was carried out thanks to the generous financial support of the Arts and Humanities Research Council (Award 2006/128080). A version of this chapter was presented at the Economic and Business History Society Conference in Manchester (May 2014). I would like to thank Peter Wardley and the other participants and audience members for their helpful comments. I am also grateful to the numerous scholars who commented on earlier versions of this work, including Pat Thane, Mark Billings, Mitch Larson, Bernado Batiz-Lazo, Martin Daunton, Sally Alexander and Helen Glew, together with my co-editors, who have been insightful and supportive throughout.

NOTES

1. See Samuel Graveson, ed., *Penny Post Centenary: An Account of Rowland Hill's Great Reform of 1840 and of the Introduction of Adhesive Postage Stamps, with Chapters on the Birth of the Postal Service* (London: Postal History Society, 1940).

2. See Paul Johnson, *Saving and Spending: the Working-Class Economy in Britain 1870–1939* (Oxford: Clarendon, 1985) and Anna Davin, *Growing Up Poor: Home, School and Street Children in London 1870-1914* (London: Rivers Oram Press, 1996). See also Margaret Fuller, *West Country Friendly Societies: An Account of Village Benefit Clubs and their Brass Pole Heads* (Oakwood Press & University of Reading, 1964) and Simon Cordery, *British Friendly Societies, 1750–1914* (Basingstoke: Palgrave Macmillan, 2003).
3. William Flavelle Monypenny and George Earle Buckle, *The Life of Benjamin Disraeli, Earl of Beaconsfield. Volume II. 1860–1881* (London: John Murray, 1929), pp. 704–5.
4. See 'Our History: The Co-operative group' for a detailed chronological account. http://www.co-operative.coop/corporate/aboutus/ourhistory/ [accessed 29 July 2014].
5. This was introduced with the Unemployment Insurance Act (1934).
6. Thomas H. Carter, 'The Post-Office as a Depository for Savings', *The North American Review*, 191:653 (April 1910), pp. 449–55.
7. See John Stevenson, *Social Conditions between the Wars* (Harmondsworth: Penguin, 1977), John Stevenson & Chris Cook, *Britain in the Depression: Society and Politics 1929–1939* (London: Longman, 1994), Sidney Pollard, *The Development of the British Economy, 1914-1990*, 4th edn. (London: Longman, 1992) and T. O. Lloyd, *Empire, Welfare State, Europe: English History 1906–1994*, 4th edn. (Oxford: Oxford University Press, 1993).
8. Jose Harris, 'Political Ideas and the Debate on State Welfare, 1900-45' in *War and Social Change: British Society in the Second World War,* ed. Harold L. Smith (Manchester: Manchester University Press, 1986), p. 235. See also Helen Glew, 'Women Workers in the Post Office, 1914–1939'. (Unpublished PhD thesis, University of London, 2010).
9. Martin Daunton, *Royal Mail, The Post Office Since 1860* (London: Athlone Press, 1984), p. 106.
10. Alan Booth and Mark Billings, 'Techno-nationalism, the Post Office and the creation of Britain's National Giro' in *Technological Innovation in Retail Finance: International Historical Perspectives*, ed. B. Bátiz-Lazo, J. C. Maixé-Altés and P. Thomes (Abingdon: Routledge, 2011).
11. Daunton, *Royal Mail*, p. 93.
12. Ibid.
13. Donald Tucker, *The Evolution of People's Banks* (New York: Columbia University, 1922).
14. Alan Clinton, *Post Office Workers: A Trade Union and Social History* (London: Allen & Unwin, 1984).
15. Daunton, *Royal Mail,* p. 113.
16. Ibid.
17. On shifting perceptions of affluence, see John Benson, *The Rise of Consumer Society in Britain: 1880–1980* (London & New York: Longman, 1994), Chapter 3.

18. Alan Booth and Sean Glynn, 'Unemployment in the Interwar Period: A Multiple Problem', *Journal of Contemporary History*, 10:4 (October 1975), pp. 611–36 and Chris Cook & John Stevenson, *The Slump: Society and Politics during the Depression* (London: Jonathan Cape, 1977).
19. Ellen Ross, *Love and Toil: Motherhood in Outcast London, 1870–1918* (Oxford: Oxford University Press, 1993), Elizabeth Roberts, *A Woman's Place: An Oral History of Working Class Women, 1890–1940* (Oxford: Wiley-Blackwell, 1995); Anna Clark, *The Struggle for the Breeches: Gender and the Making of the British Working Class* (University of California Press, 1997); and Erika Rappaport, *Shopping for Pleasure: Women in the Making of London's West End* (Princeton, NJ: Oxford: Princeton University Press, 2001).
20. J. C. Moody and G. C. Fite, *The Credit Union Movement: Origins and Development 1850 to 1980* (Lincoln: University of Nebraska Press, 1971).
21. R. H. Coase, 'Rowland Hill and the Penny Post', *Economica* 6:24 (November 1939), pp. 423–35.
22. See David Edgerton, *Britain's War Machine: Weapons, Resources and Experts in the Second World War* (London: Allen Lane, 2012).
23. British Postal Museum and Archive (hereafter BPMA), POST 75/95, War Savings Certificates, 1916.
24. For statistics and analysis of Post Office Savings Bank accounts opened after the First World War, and the Post Office's response see BPMA, POST 56/22, A report by Sir Thomas Gardiner, Director General of the Post Office, 1936–45.
25. Daunton, *Royal Mail*, p.112.
26. E. A. Radice, 'Consumption, Savings, and War Finance', *Oxford Economic Papers* 4 (September 1940), pp. 1–14.
27. Mark J. Crowley, 'Women Post Office Workers in Britain: The Long Struggle for Gender Equality and the Positive Impact of World War Two', *Essays in Economic and Business History* XXX (2012), pp. 89–97.
28. Radice, p. 5.
29. Margaret Ackrill and Leslie Hannah, *Barclays: The Business of Banking, 1690–1996* (New York: Cambridge University Press, 2001).
30. Martin Campbell-Kelly, 'Data Processing and Technological Change', *Technology and Culture* 39:1 (January 1998), pp. 1–32.
31. Clinton, *Post Office Workers*.
32. Daunton, *Royal Mail*, Duncan Campbell Smith, *Masters of the Post: The Authorized History of Royal Mail* (London: Penguin, 2011); Glew, 'Women Workers in the Post Office, 1914–1939' and Mark J. Crowley, 'Women Workers in the General Post Office, 1939–1945: Gender Conflict or Political Emancipation?' (Unpublished PhD thesis, University of London, 2010).
33. Daunton, *Royal Mail*, p. 354. Scott Anthony, *Public Relations and the Making of Modern Britain: Stephen Tallents and the Birth of a Progressive Media Profession* (Manchester: Manchester University Press, 2013).

34. Michael T. Saler, *The Avant-Garde in Interwar England* (Oxford: Oxford University Press, 2009), p. 9.
35. Yasuko Suga, 'State Patronage of Design? The Elitism/Commercialism Battle in the General Post Office's Graphic Production', *Journal of Design History* 13:1 (2000), p. 23.
36. Radice, p. 6.
37. The National Archives, Public Record Office (hereafter abbreviated TNA: PRO), CAB 27 / 575: 13 Nov. 1934, Oliver Stanley, Minister of Labour.
38. Arthur Marwick, 'The Labour Party and the Welfare State in Britain, 1900–1948', *The American Historical Review* 73:2 (December 1967), pp. 380–403. Subsequent debates on this argument found in Paul Addison, *The Road to 1945: British Politics and the Second World War* (London: Cape, 1975) and Max Beloff, *Wars and Welfare, Britain 1914–1945* (London: Edward Arnold, 1984), among others.
39. Keith Laybourn, *Unemployment and Employment Policies Concerning Women in Britain, 1900–1951*, (Lewiston, NY: Edwin Mellen Press, 2002) and 'Waking Up to the Fact that there are any Unemployed: Unemployment and the Domestic Solution in Britain, 1918–39', *History* (2003), pp. 607–23.
40. See Sandra Trudgen Dawson, 'Working Class Consumers and the Campaign for Holidays with Pay', *Twentieth Century British History* 18:3 (2007), pp. 277–305 and also in this volume.
41. Cited in BPMA, POST 56/96, 'The First Hundred Thousand: How Women are Helping the Post Office', 6 November 1941.
42. The Women's Library, London Metropolitan University (hereafter abbreviated WL), 6NCS/1/A/6, Post Office Liaison Committee, 16 December 1935.
43. Suga, p. 24.
44. London Retail Businesses, *Journal of the Royal Society of Arts* 67: 3475 (27 June 1919), p. 525.
45. Ibid.
46. Ibid.
47. BPMA, POST 115/699, *The Organ of the Association of Head Postmasters* (UK) April 1941, p. 14.
48. See Mark J. Crowley, 'Reducing, Re-defining and Retaining: The Struggle to Maintain a Stable Workforce and Service in the British Post Office during the Second World War', *Essays in Economic and Business History* XXXI (2013), pp. 53–77.
49. BPMA, *Post Office Magazine*, 3:1, (January 1936), p. 2.
50. BPMA, POST 115/699, *The Organ of the Association of Head Postmasters* (UK) April 1941, p. 14.
51. BPMA, POST 56/110, Man and Woman Power: General Review, 9 December 1942.
52. Howard Robinson, *Britain's Post Office: A History of Development from the Beginnings to the Present Day* (Oxford: Oxford University Press, 1953), p. 275.

One of the latest major analyses of the Second World War, Edgerton's, *Britain's War Machine* acknowledges but does not examine in detail the role of the POSB.

53. BPMA, POST 56/99, Post Office Women fire fighters – they protect over 580,000,000 war savings certificates, 7 February 1942.
54. Ibid.
55. Ibid.
56. BPMA, POST 56/96, Restrictions on Telegraph and Telephone Services, 31 Aug. 1939.
57. The Parliamentary Archives (hereafter abbreviated PA), Thomas Balogh, 'Industrial Conscription and Democracy' (undated).
58. Ivor Halstead, *Post Haste: The Story of the Post Office in Peace and War* (London: Lindsay Drummond, 1944).
59. See Angus Calder, *The Myth of the Blitz* (London: Pimlico, 1992) and his *The People's War: Britain 1939-45* (London: Pimlico, 1992); Addison, *The Road to 1945*; and Gail Braybon and Penny Summerfield, *Out of the Cage: Women's Experiences in the Two World Wars* (London: Pandora Press, 1987).
60. Suga, p. 33.
61. *Daily Mirror*, 17 December 1940.
62. BPMA, POST 56/99, Half of Post Office Workers are Women, 28 January 1942.
63. Peter Thorsheim, 'Salvage and Destruction: The Recycling of Books and Manuscripts in Great Britain during the Second World War', *Contemporary European History* 22:3 (2013), pp. 431–52.
64. Caroline Levine, 'Propaganda for Democracy: The Curious Case of *Love on the Dole*', *Journal of British Studies* 45:4 (October 2006), pp. 846–74.
65. This formed part of 4 major artworks in this period, including 'Make Your Money Provide the Driving Power, Put it into the Post Office Savings Bank', 1942 (Austin Cooper), 'Money is Power: Save through the Post Office Savings Bank', c. 1940, (Artist unknown), 'Save for National Safety, Bank with the Post Office Savings Bank', c. 1939, (Frank Newbould) and 'Make Your Money Provide the Driving Power, Put it into the Post Office Savings Bank' 1942 (Eric Fraser). See the collections in BPMA, POST 110/3193.
66. Crowley, 'Reducing, Redefining and Retaining', p. 57.
67. Mass Observation Archive, University of Sussex (hereafter MO), 25 July, 1940: Mass Observation Report 290, p. 52.
68. Suga, pp. 27–8.
69. Nicoletta F. Gullace, 'Allied Propaganda and World War I: Interwar Legacies, Media Studies, and the Politics of War Guilt', *History Compass* 9 (September 2011), pp. 657–759.
70. MO, Report 290, 25 July 1940, p. 153.
71. Daunton, *Royal Mail*, p.112.
72. Robinson, *Britain's Post Office*, p. 263.

CHAPTER THIRTEEN

Prosperity for All? Britain and Mass Consumption in Western Europe after World War II

KENNETH MOURÉ

'Why', asked a League of Nations study in 1943, 'has society been so organized that all can find work to do when the object of that work is destruction, but men and women are unable to find employment when they desire to work to satisfy their own wants? Why can society be so elaborately and so efficiently organized to lower but not to raise the standard of living?'[1] Millions suffered unemployment in the 1930s, and human and material losses in World War II left Europe devastated. The war restored full employment with new output dedicated to destruction. Would it be possible to avoid mass unemployment and economic contraction, employing labour for constructive purposes when peace was restored?

Most belligerents suffered a net loss of wealth and reduced civilian consumption. Although the main belligerent powers' total gross domestic product (GDP) increased by 34.7 per cent from 1938 to 1943,[2] widespread destruction and deprivation were the war's immediate impacts. The European reconstruction and economic boom from 1950 to the mid-1970s built on an exceptional conjunction of increased demand and new productive potential for consumer goods. The spread of mass consumption marked a major transition in Western Europe; in Britain, the 'nation of shopkeepers' became a nation of shoppers.

Reconstruction needs were vastly greater than in 1918, owing to the larger geographic reach and physical destruction wrought by World War II. The need to reconstruct and modernize productive capacity left ordinary consumers with little benefit in the first post-war years. The wartime sacrifices and the obvious lesson that American economic power had been essential to victory prompted hopes for a better world. But the remarkable post-war growth recorded in aggregate statistics can mislead us concerning when and how consumption by individuals, families and communities improved, with their daily needs and frustrations with continuing shortages being lost in national rates of growth. Private needs and desires were fundamental to the growth of new consumption. This chapter addresses two issues: first, the explanations for the European economic miracle and how British experience compares to that on the Continent, and, second, how this era fostered the development of a modern 'consumer society' in Britain and Western Europe.

Europe's post-war 'economic miracle' marked a distinct break in the rate of long-term growth, measured as the annual percentage increase in national output (GDP) (see Table 13.1). This rate had averaged less than 2 per cent in the nineteenth century, and slowed to barely 1 per cent in Western Europe from 1913 to 1950. The average annual growth of real GDP (corrected for inflation) from 1950 to 1973 was 4.5 per cent for Western Europe, 3.6 per cent for the United States and 9.3 per cent for Japan. Real GDP growth per capita (to remove the increase from population growth) was 4.0 per cent for Western Europe, 2.2 per cent for the US and 8.0 per cent for Japan. Britain lagged in both measures: 3.0 per cent growth for real GDP, 2.5 per cent for real GDP per capita.[3]

Table 13.1. Growth of real GDP, 1950–73 (average annual compound growth rate).[4]

	Real GDP growth (1913–50)	*Real GDP growth (1950–73)*	*Real GDP per capita (1950–73)*
Western Europe	1.1	4.5	4.0
France	1.1	5.0	4.0
Germany	1.3	5.9	4.9
Italy	1.5	5.6	5.0
UK	1.3	3.0	2.5
US	2.8	3.6	2.2
Japan	2.2	9.3	8.0

Two underlying trends produced this rapid growth. The first was the push to 'catch up' the growth foregone since 1929. In 1945, after 16 years of depression and war, Western European economies were producing well below their growth path of the 1920s. Investment to catch up explains part of the robust record, particularly in the 1950s. The second trend was 'convergence' – the adoption of new technologies and management practices in order to raise European productivity relative to the US, where mass production methods had transformed manufacturing, distribution and consumption. Technological gaps had widened in wartime. New investment in the US was in contrast to the destruction of productive capacity in Europe.[5] For Britain, the milder Depression and stronger wartime growth limited the potential for 'catch-up', and British technology and management were closer to US standards, reducing the opportunity for 'convergence'.

In contrast to policies following World War I, when governments ended controls quickly and retreated from economic direction, governments were more successful in wartime management and remained active in economic management after 1945. The peacetime transition dealt with a greater mobilization of resources and more extensive war damage, and sought to assure domestic recovery, full employment and modernization.[6] Many states promised to maintain full employment and improve social security, with labour deferring wage demands and new consumption in the interests of national recovery.[7] In Britain, Labour governments tried to avoid cycles of boom and slump by encouraging investment and modernization with 'cheap money' (historically low interest rates) and counter-cyclical fiscal policy (increased spending when the economy slows, cutting back in boom periods).[8] European labour relations benefited from cooperative institutional structures to resolve labour conflict and foster wage restraint, with less strike activity in all of Western Europe except Italy.[9]

This cooperation was made possible by the new commitments to social welfare, full employment and state-organized social insurance. In Britain, the Beveridge Report (1942) provided an influential programmatic statement of the need for comprehensive insurance against illness, injury, old age and unemployment. Full employment was the essential foundation for a secure social order and the achievement of Beveridge's ultimate objective, 'the abolition of Want'.[10] In January 1941 Franklin Roosevelt had proposed four freedoms for all people, one of which was freedom from want. The Atlantic Charter in August 1941 included freedom from want and freedom from fear. Organizing a better economic world was a fundamental objective for Allied states.[11]

Labour migration increased productivity. Low productivity labour moved from rural to urban areas and from agriculture to manufacture (France and Austria). Refugees came from Eastern Europe, particularly skilled workers moving to West Germany. Workers moved from slower-growth Mediterranean countries to Northern and Western Europe. The return of Europeans and educated elites from colonies during decolonization added to supplies of skilled labour. Britain already had low employment in agriculture (5 per cent in 1945, compared to 25 per cent in Germany, and more than 30 per cent in France), and experienced net emigration of people often better educated than the new immigrants. Traditional craft unions maintained their bargaining power and government policy focused on short-run objectives to win electoral support. The result was less pressure for productivity improvement or wage restraint, with Britain lagging in growth of worker productivity.[12]

New international institutions to provide exchange-rate stability and increase trade and capital movements included the International Monetary Fund, the European Payments Union and the General Agreement on Tariffs and Trade negotiations.[13] This institutional network encouraged investment and trade by offering greater assurance that investment in trade-based specialization at home would not be frustrated by protectionist policies and exchange-rate instability. Intra-European trade became a major engine of economic growth, with the European Payments Union (1950–8) and the European Coal and Steel Community (1951–67) leading to the European Common Market in 1958.[14] Britain stood aloof, participating in the US-led international organizations but not wishing to compromise its Commonwealth trade in European institutions. It joined the European Community in 1973.

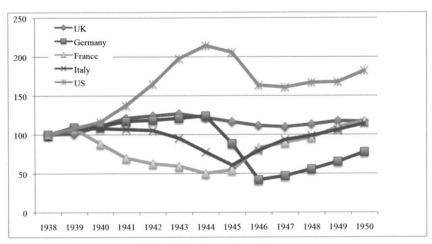

Figure 13.1. Indexed real GDP 1938–50, 1938–100[15]

The US led international developments from a position of unrivalled economic and financial power. Real GDP doubled from 1938 to 1945 (see Figure 13.1). In 1945 the US produced 50 per cent of the world's manufactured goods and was the only significant source for international financial assistance. Conscious of the need to support a global transition to peace, the US worked to develop an international system of stable exchange rates and free trade without becoming 'Santa Claus to the world'.[16] The US unemployment rate had fallen to less than 2 per cent (from 18 per cent in 1938), and exports had increased by 400 per cent.[17] Industry and business leaders pushed for a rapid end to economic controls and opposed social welfare measures and state commitment to full employment.[18] But authorities were worried how full employment could be maintained when government wartime purchasing ended. The Pabst Brewing Company sponsored an essay contest seeking solutions to the post-war employment challenge: it offered $50,000 in prizes and attracted over 35,000 entries.[19] Developing international trade and finance would provide vital markets for US goods.

In the post-war era the British economy had less to gain from catch-up and convergence, and little benefit from labour migration. The need for recovery from war damage and economic decline was less significant, and Britain considered itself a victor in need of transitional assistance, not a defeated power desperately needing aid.[20] Efforts to restore the pound sterling and maintain imperial and international prestige came at a high cost. Britain borrowed $5 billion from the US in 1945. Funds intended to last four years were gone in two, and the attempt to restore sterling convertibility in July 1947 lasted only a few weeks. Despite success in stabilizing prices and increasing exports, Britain needed American financial help, including Marshall Plan funds, which Britain used to import food and raw materials.[21] But continuing shortages, pent-up consumer demand and the need for modernization offered opportunities that differed from those in Continental Europe by degree, not in their essential character.

The 1950s opened a period of transition in Western Europe, with the mass consumption of manufactured goods as the key change in a major shift in European consumption.[22] Victoria de Grazia defines the change as the replacement of a European regime of class-demarcated 'bourgeois consumption' with one of mass consumption in a 'consumer society'. She stresses retail distribution and advertising as the keys to this change. Traditional family firms and small-scale, individual retailers with an outmoded model for selling gave way to a normative American model of mass marketing, chain retailing and commercial advertising – 'modern commerce'. This transformation brought greater efficiency, higher consumption, freer trade and more democratic values.[23] De Grazia gives little attention to the impact of the war on consumption beyond its disrupting the flow of American influence, the defeat of Nazi Germany and Fascist Italy and containment of Communist regimes opposed to the American model.

'Mass consumption' and 'consumer society' were not new. Depending on the definitions chosen, their onset can be traced back to the seventeenth and eighteenth centuries,[24] and they were clearly present as broader class-based consumption in urban Western Europe in the nineteenth and early twentieth centuries. The growth of department store sales and cultures extended the purchase of standardized goods to less affluent consumers and refashioned the spaces and the practices of retailing, selling ways of life rather than the means to live, and changing access and attitudes toward consumption in the second half of the nineteenth century.[25] New retailing practices extended consumption beyond the bourgeois customers expecting to be waited on by clerk-servants. Consumer cooperatives provided new retailing structured to protect working-class members against predatory retail practices. The cooperatives focused on essentials, food and clothing, and offered innovative retailing that expanded as consumption increased, leading the way in the development of self-service retail outlets.[26] New consumer practices and values spread to urban families with rising disposable income, and to workers and farmers as their incomes grew and access to goods improved. It was a process of incremental expansion, with inconsistencies in where, why and how fast it spread. The changes were more urban than rural, more regional than national, and had significant gender, racial and generational inequities. But the breadth and variety of change are of more interest than the delays, as the changes developed a cumulative momentum.

Europe after 1945 is striking for the accelerated rate of change and the surge in growth. Interpreting the post-war era as one of 'regime change' poses problems of defining distinct 'regimes' in a complex and varied system of changes in production, distribution and retailing practices. The development of consumer societies was neither linear, nor geographically uniform, nor unitary in form. The US model for mass production had been fostered in the nineteenth and early twentieth centuries by unique circumstances of industrial production based on an exceptionally large, unified national market, large firms, corporate ownership, competitive oligopolies and government intervention to limit the acceptable forms of industrial organization (cartels and trusts). Its consumer society developed with a dynamic for mass production and consumption based on market size, wealth and labour scarcity that encouraged investment in equipment, product standardization and mass retailing, and an ideal of acquisition and consumption as the keys to personal fulfilment.[27] The adaptation of the US pattern of mass production and consumer desire to Western Europe varied from country to country, with a clear trend towards larger firm size and similar management practices,[28] but significant differences in adapting to consumer expectations.

For European consumers, deprivation in depression and war combined with the example of US abundance to fuel desires for new consumption, plus resentments when material conditions slowly improved. Nella Last recorded the frustrations with material shortages as a Mass Observation diarist in Cumbria, England. In September 1945 she noted that 'America again has emerged unscathed, her people at home unaware there has been a war, except for a little rationing and of course those who have had men in the Forces'. At the turn of the year, she observed, 'All the brave talk of a "new world" seems to be dying slowly. People have not changed one bit. Many in fact have turned selfish and self-seeking, and grown hard and bitter.' How could the younger generation grow up unselfish, she wondered, when there was so little to share? In October 1947 she wrote, 'Never in the worst of the war did I see so many queues – or such long ones.'[29] Conditions on the Continent were yet more forbidding. French rationing was stricter after Liberation, with fraying tolerance for restrictions that had been blamed on the Germans, but then increased in the post-Liberation years.[30] In Italy, the first two years after the war were 'two years of hunger', with notable improvement coming only in 1949/50.[31] In Germany, shortages after the defeat were far worse than those during the war.

Consumer deprivation affected popular attitudes, expectations and actions, and thus the potential for new growth. The Depression in the 1930s and government success in mobilizing for war offered new hopes that state direction could promote full utilization of a nation's productive resources. The Beveridge commitment to social welfare and full employment met with widespread approval in Europe for a stronger state role to manage the economy.[32] Frank Trentmann observes that war experience changed the state's role for consumers as well: 'it was the need to rationalize scarce resources in war-time or to boost demand to overcome economic depression that made states identify consumers as a core target of public policy'.[33] Post-war policy agendas paid greater attention to effective demand, investment and the need for full employment.[34]

West Germany's economic miracle displayed the most vivid change from deprivation to abundance. Nazi policy had sustained civilian consumption in the first half of the war, exploiting and plundering defeated enemies. But physical destruction and the choking off of resources as German forces retreated had reduced German consumers to a subsistence level in

1945. The worst years of deprivation followed the defeat, from 1945 to 1948, with widespread hunger, shortages of clothing and fuel, and reliance on Allied relief, consumer improvisation and black markets to survive.[35] Recovery was slowed by the extensive damage to housing and transport, Allied policy disputes, Soviet reparation demands and the administrative division of the country. West Germany regained its 1938 level of output in 1951, with rapid growth thereafter based on a social market economy that encouraged the production of consumer goods. Ludwig Erhard stressed 'the basic democratic right of consumer freedom' as a path to 'Prosperity for All'.[36] He based his programme on the rapid growth of a consumer economy that would give new meaning and purpose to a society whose values and activities had been warped in the Third Reich.[37] East Germany, in contrast, structured its planned economy with a Stalinist emphasis on producer goods and a consumer goods deficit economy. The West German market economy rewarded labour with consumer goods, stimulating higher productivity and income growth to three times their levels in the East when the two Germanies reunited in 1990.[38]

To European states rebuilding their economies, the US offered, advertised and exported a consumption model based on mass production, democratic choice and an affluent society stressing quality of life as measured by material abundance. Before 1914, 'Taylorist' American production methods interested Europeans for their potential to increase productivity, and in the 1920s 'Fordism' added higher wages to the American model to increase consumer demand.[39] Economies of scale, price competition and the rationalization of production process on which these were based had no distinctly 'American' identity. European economies lacked the same opportunity and incentive to move rapidly to this scale of mass production in the inter-war years, and while efficiency and affluence were desirable ends, their American version seemed to threaten fundamental values of caution and thrift, craftsmanship, individualism and social responsibility. Many European visitors found the US example alarming for its standardization,[40] seeing the US as 'a cultural wasteland, pandering to the lowest common denominator through its mass media'.[41] Fascist critics of capitalist market economies envied US mass production for its ability to deliver goods, but condemned the selfish nature of individual consumption.[42]

The importance of US power for the Allied victory, post-war reconstruction and peace-keeping, as well as the presence of abundantly supplied US troops in Britain and Continental Europe, brought home to Europeans the tremendous gap between material wealth and living standards in Europe and in the US.[43] But the differences in material wealth, the US propaganda for the Marshall Plan (often ill-adapted to European audiences who equated propaganda with fascism),[44] and the obvious self-interest in US lending to extend advantages in global financial and trading power all gave cause for suspicion. Americanization was easily conflated with any modern practice that seemed foreign and potentially damaging to traditional values, hierarchies and aesthetics. In the context of Cold War politics and the pressure to take sides, the US offered an attractive model for increasing productivity, wealth and private consumption. The term 'Americanization' is simplistic in relation to the complexity of political, economic and cultural changes that were not exclusively or consistently of US origin, but clearly carried 'American' influence.[45]

'Westernization' may better capture the process of exchange that reconstruction and modernization encouraged.[46] The flow of transatlantic goods and ideas was neither one way nor consistent in impact. The process involved selective adaptations, with choices and changes to suit local and national needs and cultures, and to build on European foundations. The transfer of goods, methods and ideas offered significant opportunities for Europeans to make choices, to resist and to develop their own alternatives and innovations. Transatlantic influence was an exchange, a set of borrowings in which US wealth and power provided resources, ideas and opportunities, and from which European countries could select, adapt and exchange what they bought and borrowed to suit their own needs.

Britain experienced austerity with less post-war trauma from physical devastation and war refugees than the battlegrounds in Continental Europe. Its intermediate status between the US and Europe provides an opportunity to understand the post-war development of consumer society under less extreme conditions. The 'age of austerity' was imposed by the balance of payments deficit, the need for resources from abroad, and the Labour government's use of austerity to develop a mixed economy with greater state ownership and a commitment to maintain full employment.[47] Consumption, deferred in wartime by taxation and government borrowing, was further delayed. For consumers, this meant unwelcome restraint and restrictions. Britons engaged in more black market activity and showed less willingness to tolerate hardship or to support the Labour agenda for continued controls.[48] The Council of Industrial Design's 'Britain Can Make It' exhibition in 1946, intended to show off the quality of British manufactures, was dubbed 'Britain Can't Have It' by the press, as many goods on display were not yet available for purchase.[49] The 1951 Festival of Britain, intended to celebrate 'British achievement' 100 years after the Great Exhibition of 1851, was scaled back from the original intention to be an international showcase to a celebration of British accomplishment and designs for the future. The Skylon, an illuminated, aluminium-clad, steel-frame sculpture 300 feet high, suspended by cables, was likened to the British economy, suspended in mid-air with 'no visible means of support'.[50] Wartime rationing and food subsidies ended in 1954.[51] Consumer expenditure, which had increased significantly for food, drink and durable goods in 1946 and for clothing between 1946 and 1948, slowed significantly in the late 1940s, and regained strength only after 1952.[52]

The importance of new consumption after the war is clearest in the purchases of durable goods, household appliances and automobiles. Britain clearly lagged behind the US. The percentage of households wired for electricity was similar in both countries in 1946 (slightly more than 75 per cent), but in the US housing size and quality was much better, with higher percentages of households owning clothes washers, refrigerators and automobiles.[53] Continental Europe was further behind, with a clear surge in appliance purchases from the mid-1950s through the 1960s. In West Germany, Ludwig Erhard, Minister of Economics, and the German trade union federation both called for 'A Refrigerator in Every Household' in 1953, when households with refrigerators numbered less than one in ten.[54] In Table 13.2a the statistics for households owning durable appliances show the substantial US lead in consumer goods ownership after 1945 and the speed with which that gap narrowed, for England and Wales beginning in the 1950s, for France and West Germany much more rapidly in the 1960s, overtaking Britain. For televisions, the emblematic new article of mass consumption, US ownership surged in the 1950s, and maintained a significantly higher level (Tables 13.2a and b). The increase in television ownership shows the greater speed in diffusion of goods for pleasure rather than for saving time. Increased household consumption lay at the heart of the growth of mass consumerism, and these figures show changes only at the aggregate level, without distinguishing the major disparities within nations according to class, employment, community, age and gender.

Consumer values and practices were not imported uncritically with new finished goods. European practices took what was most enticing and adapted it to local cultures and practices. In terms of US products and values after 1945, studies specific to Britain demonstrate the adaptation of American influences in the British adoption of products ranging from household appliances to juke boxes.[57] Consumer society emerged from existing social and economic organizations and behaviour. The growing choice of goods in the 1950s relied on a new willingness to purchase based on changing attitudes toward the use of new income. Recent historical work provides examples of strong continuities in the selective adoption of new goods and practices.

The Marshall Plan financed 'technical assistance programs' to introduce European businessmen, engineers and workers to the best in American

Table 13.2a. % Households with domestic appliances.[55]

Item	Year	US	England & Wales	France	W. Germany	E. Germany
Clothes washers	1948	71	6.3			
	c1955	77.1	17.5	(1954) 8.4		0.5
	c1960	85.4	35.8	24.8	(1962) 9	6.2
	1970	92.1	63	56.7	38	53.8
	1975	n.a.	70.1	72	84	73
Refrigerators	1948	76.6	2.1			
	c1955	94.1	8.1	(1954) 7.5	10	0.4
	c1960	98.2	18.2	26.8	(1962) 51.8	6.1
	1970	99.8	57.6	79.5	94	56.4
	1975	99.9	75.1	91	93	84.7
Televisions (b/w)	1948	2.9	0.5			
	c1955	76.1	34.7	(1954) 1.0	(1953) 0.3	1.2
	1960	89.4	73.7	13.6		18.5
	1970	98.7	93.4	69.5		73.6
	1975	99.9	*75.1	83.9	70	87.9

* British households with black and white (b&w) televisions decline as the number of households with colour televisions increase.

Table 13.2b. Televisions.[56]

Item	Year	US	UK	France	W. Germany	E. Germany	Italy
Televisions per 1000 inhabitants	1955	227	105	6	5	0.8	4
	1960	310	211	41	83	60	43
	1965	362	248	131	200	201	117
	1970	412	293	201	272	282	181
	1975	571	316	268	306	307	217

technology, management and labour relations. Managers in Britain and France selected what impressed them, and judged much of what they observed to be foreign, unnecessary or undesirable.[58] Retailing innovations such as the spread of 'self-service' shops for durable goods and groceries were often greeted with scepticism. Greater choice, less reliance on the shopkeepers' knowledge trusted by local consumers, and standardized packaging to provide customers with product information took hold gradually, and cultural expectations influenced the pace and extent of changes. European food retailing adopted self-service and supermarkets, but the timing and manner varied to fit national and local geographies and cultures. It did not follow the US model marked by a growing preference for huge outlets, malls and one-stop shopping for suburbanites driving cars. Higher population density, limited space in stores and homes, and different food cultures produced adaptations to modernize practices within the constraints of space, time, income and expectations.[59] Even in the US, local ethnic and working-class communities resisted standardization by chain grocery retailing.[60]

Cooperative movements, not chain retailing, led the way in the spread of self-service grocery stores. Cooperatives had developed in a period of limited choice and great distrust of product quality and retailer profiteering. Like early consumer associations, they were concerned by the labour conditions of workers producing the goods they bought. With more disposable income and competition in a growing market for retail goods, the original needs met by cooperatives to protect their members were less urgent, whereas the need to invest in stock and retail space rose with the increase in consumer goods and choices. Britain's strong cooperative movement lost momentum after the war as political parties and consumer organizations marginalized the cooperatives' efforts to advance consumers' interests, and shoppers sought greater choice and lower prices. Although they lost market share, cooperatives remained significant in Britain and continued to be strong in Finland, Norway, Sweden and Denmark.[61]

Advertising and market research are key components of the American model that conquered Europe. But advertising innovation, too, involved selective adaptation rather than conquest, and developed from a transatlantic exchange of ideas and personnel. Many early advertising entrepreneurs and theorists came from Europe, and the interchange of personnel and ideas constantly adapted to cultural expectations.[62] Many Europeans were sceptical of new advertising after the war as 'a massive confidence trick on the public', a legal deception that added cost but no value to the goods they might purchase. In Britain, Lord Leverhulme claimed that half of all advertising cost was wasted, and that nobody knew which half.[63] In inter-war Germany, US firms offered advanced practices in selling mass consumption that influenced Weimar era businesses and Nazi propaganda.[64] In the words of American ad writer E. B. Weiss in 1941, 'Propaganda and advertising have the same goal – moulding the minds of millions of people.'[65] The similarities would be troubling for Europeans manipulated and alienated by wartime political propaganda.

Consumers needed guidance and protection in a world of increasing choice. More consumption was not a necessary consequence of rising income, which might go instead to investment and savings. Wage earners needed persuasion to purchase more, and education on how to make wise choices and protection against fraud. Consumer groups promoted new consumption with magazines to inform buyers, such as the Consumer Association's *Which?* and the British Standards Association's *Shopper's Guide*.[66] State regulation was needed to guard against misrepresentations, fraud and unsafe merchandise.[67]

There was nothing essentially democratic about advertising, but disposable income and choice in how to spend it were fundamental to the spread of mass consumption, and market activity was more compatible with democratic than authoritarian politics. In the US, war experience produced a commitment to make mass consumption and consumer freedom central to US culture and political economy, 'a Consumer's Republic that entrusted the private mass consumption marketplace, supported by government resources, with delivering not only economic prosperity but also loftier social and political ambitions for a more equal, free and democratic nation'.[68] Erica Carter and Michael Wildt see consumption and democratic choice closely linked to refashioned West German consumer practices and national identity in the 1950s. New purchasing opportunities after years of shortages identified democratic practice and citizenship with consumer freedom in the marketplace.[69] Rebecca Pulju links the development of mass consumption in France to women's role as citizen consumers.[70] In Britain, a longer tradition had linked consumption, citizenship and democratic choice in the nineteenth century. The battle for free trade established a system of beliefs about what constituted legitimate politics, the public interest and national identity.[71] British consumers obtained representation and a public voice through organizations like the Consumers' Association (1956) and the National Consumer Council (1975), with a tension between the 'rights' of the individual consumer seeking to maximize satisfaction and broader collective and social rights.[72] In the Cold War context of the 1950s, those who advocated for economic development and increased consumption did so with political and cultural views that attached political meanings and public importance to consumer choices. The choices and the political meanings varied by country and appeared strongest in the US.[73]

The resistance to new products, self-service retailing, aggressive advertising and the use of credit for purchasing suggest the 'unnatural' quality to the dynamics creating mass consumption. Critics in the 1950s and 1960s deserve more attention for the concerns they raised about the nature and the adverse consequences of mass consumption and the future problems they foresaw. The public notice their work attracted indicates broadly shared intuitions and anxieties about the consequences of mass consumerism. Understanding how their voices were heard and why they had so little influence is important in assessing the dynamic for change and its force and consequences. E. J. Mishan, critical of economic growth as the means to a better future, observed that leaders had 'a propensity to keep their eyes glued to the speedometer without regard to the direction taken'.[74] Mishan was the most forceful of several European critics who questioned 'the price of economic progress' in paying attention to the negative consequences of 'growthmania'. These included the growing evidence of environmental damage, social atomization and isolation, the breakdown of communities and collective commitments to public goods, and the cultural trend toward conformity as the combination of competition and the need for economies of scale reduced the diversity, independence and freedom for controversial work in cultural and intellectual life.[75] Mishan argued that economic growth in Britain was reducing social welfare, its adverse impact on quality of life outweighing its material benefits. Similar critiques called attention to the excesses and limitations of growth in the 1970s, particularly E. F. Schumacher's *Small is Beautiful*,[76] without altering the faith in economic growth as essential and increased consumption as its purpose. In the US, critics achieved best-seller status with works demanding public notice of the adverse impacts of advertising (Vance Packard), underinvestment in public goods (Galbraith) and environmental damage (Rachel Carson).[77] European critics questioning the purpose of increased consumption and the cultural changes it fostered included Roland Barthes, Umberto Eco and Jean Baudrillard. Baudrillard saw the traffic accident as the most spectacular 'happening' in consumer society, 'by which it gives, in the ritual destruction of matter and life, the proof of its material excess'.[78]

The public attention and the high sales of work by these critics suggest that mass consumption and the emphasis on growth deserve more research to understand how mass consumption practices spread in spite of or alongside such critiques. Was their lack of impact a consequence of the inherent weakness of consumer politics' 'single-issue campaigns, fragile alliances and ever-changing agendas',[79] or is that very fragmentation and weakness a consequence of human vulnerability to the attractions of material comfort and pleasure? If goods do provide such comfort, does the desire for 'more' win out inevitably over alternatives? The variety of the cultural adaptations to mass consumption, the flexibility of markets and marketing to acknowledge and exploit difference, and the ready acceptance of more as better in choices about income, development and consumption, merit exploration not just for where economic development and consumerism take us, but how we construct identities through our practices as consumers. And the views of the critics must be balanced by attention to the opportunities offered for creative expression and resistance to conformity in the popular culture fostered by new consumption.[80]

The seductive power of material wealth is obvious, as is the power of the promise that more consumption will bring a better life. Stefan Zweig's *The Post-Office Girl* recorded this power of attraction and its destructive force in inter-war Europe, in his character Christine's response to the new clothes, hair and cosmetics bought for her by her aunt (married to a wealthy American): 'smitten with herself, unable to have enough of this alluring new self that smiles as it approaches from the mirror, beautifully dressed, young, and re-made'.[81] Carolyn Steedman observes this longing for transformation in her mother's aspirations: 'From a Lancashire mill town and a working-class twenties childhood she came away wanting: fine clothes, glamour, money; to be what she wasn't.'[82] For both, the longing for transformation was not fulfilled. The development of consumer society depends upon ever increasing demand for goods that are desired, not needed. Satisfaction is then gauged through what is purchased, with employment increasingly seen as only a means to that end. This opens immense potential for disappointment. Material goods accumulate in ever greater quantities without providing the satisfaction or the transformation they were purchased to attain, just the evidence of disappointment.[83]

Robert Nathan, recovering from wounds in Walter Reed Army Hospital in 1943, wrote that the war was not just against aggression and dictatorship, but also against 'depression, unemployment, and economic chaos'. Pensions or returning to their old jobs after the war would not compensate the veterans' sacrifices: 'Much more essential is prosperity and jobs for all.'[84] Post-war economic growth created full employment, prosperity for many (not all), and the output and purchasing power for a transition to economies of mass consumption. Unemployment did not become a serious problem until the 1970s; in the UK, it first exceeded 2 per cent in 1965. In *The Transition from War to Peace Economy*, the League of Nations had called for an economy that would satisfy the wants of ordinary consumers. The post-war economy did so, gradually but abundantly increasing employment, income and consumer desire and transforming the world of goods, marketing, consumption and consumer culture.

British experience differed from Western Europe in degree rather than in kind. Britain's greater urbanization and industrialization reduced the opportunity for growth through catch-up and convergence, while the constraints of the labour market, the balance of payments and social welfare costs slowed the growth of private consumption. But the British transition to mass consumption for this reason offers an opportunity to analyse the adaptations and resistance to mass consumption under calmer circumstances than elsewhere. The slower pace of change and the 'special relationship' with the US made the changes and the resistance in Britain less dramatic, less urgent and less politically charged, allowing clearer analysis of the values, practices and beliefs that were challenged and changed by new income, access to goods and consumption practices. The adaptations and resistances add to our understanding of the alternatives chosen or rejected in adopting and adapting new cultures of purchasing. How and why new goods and marketing seemed threatening and 'American', and how practices were altered to temper change and preserve traditions, can tell us more about the longer-term transformation of European economies and consumer cultures. The path of consumer society in terms of choice, affluence and purpose was not predetermined. The years after 1945 marked a key transition in which increasing affluence and consumer choice reduced resistance to a world focused increasingly on consumption as the source for meaning and identity. The resistances, their persistence, and their lack of persuasive power against the seduction of increased consumption, are particularly important for the values they reveal in relationships and behaviours not yet commodified. They anticipate problems that persist, in more urgent form, today.

NOTES

1. League of Nations, *The Transition from War to Peace Economy* (Geneva: League of Nations, 1943), p. 9.
2. Mark Harrison, 'The Economies of World War II: An Overview', in *The Economics of World War II: Six Great Powers in International Comparison*, ed. Mark Harrison (Cambridge: Cambridge University Press, 1998), p. 10. The countries included are Germany, Italy, Japan, Austria, France, the UK, the USSR and the USA. In 1990 prices, their combined output increased from $2315 billion (US, one-thousand millions) in 1938 to $3118 billion in 1943.
3. Angus Maddison, *Dynamic Forces in Capitalist Development: A Long-Run Comparative View* (Oxford: Oxford University Press, 1991), pp. 50–1, and discussion of these factors in Barry Eichengreen, *The European Economy since 1945: Coordinated Capitalism and Beyond* (Princeton, NJ: Princeton University Press, 2007), pp. 16–18.
4. Sources: Eichengreen, *The European Economy since 1945*, pp. 16–17 and Maddison, *Dynamic Forces*, pp. 50–1.
5. Eichengreen, *The European Economy since 1945*, pp. 20–31.
6. Charles S. Maier, 'The Two Postwar Eras and the Conditions for Stability in Twentieth-Century Western Europe', *In Search of Stability: Explorations in Historical Political Economy* (Cambridge: Cambridge University Press, 1987)

pp. 153–84; Andrea Boltho, 'Reconstruction after Two World Wars – Why the Differences?', *Journal of European Economic History* 30:2 (2001), pp. 429–56.

7. Maier, 'The Two Postwar Eras', pp. 176–7 and 'The Politics of Productivity: Foundations of American International Economic policy after World War II', *In Search of Stability*, pp. 121–52.

8. Susan Howson, *British Monetary Policy 1945–1951* (Oxford: Oxford University Press, 1993).

9. Boltho, 'Reconstruction', p. 439. See also Eichengreen, 'Institutions and Economic Growth: Europe after World War II', in *Economic Growth in Europe since 1945*, eds Nicholas Crafts and Gianni Toniolo (Cambridge: Cambridge University Press, 1996), pp. 38–72.

10. Inter-Departmental Committee on Social Insurance and Allied Services, *Social Insurance and Allied Services*, (London: HMSO, 1942); Jose Harris, 'Beveridge's Social and Political Thought', in *Beveridge and Social Security: An International Retrospective*, eds John Hills, John Ditch and Howard Glennerster (Oxford: Clarendon Press, 1994), pp. 23–36.

11. On advertising the war as a defence of the American way of life based on consumption, Charles F. McGovern, *Sold American: Consumption and Citizenship, 1890–1945* (Chapel Hill, NC: University of North Carolina Press, 2006), pp. 327–65. The Hoover Vacuum Cleaner Company added a fifth freedom to Roosevelt's four in 1944: freedom of choice (especially choice of vacuum cleaners); Richard Wightman Fox and T. J. Jackson Lears, 'Introduction', *The Culture of Consumption: Critical Essays in American History, 1880–1980* (New York: Pantheon Books, 1983) p. ix.

12. Charles P. Kindleberger, *Europe's Postwar Growth: The Role of Labor Supply* (Cambridge, MA: Harvard University Press, 1967), pp. 76–86; Eichengreen, *The European Economy*, pp. 88 and 122–6; and Charles Bean and Nicholas Crafts, 'British Economic Growth since 1945: Relative Economic Decline … and Renaissance?' in *Economic Growth in Europe since 1945*, eds Nicholas Crafts and Gianni Toniolo (Cambridge: Cambridge University Press, 1996) pp. 132–3, 139–42.

13. Harold James, *International Monetary Cooperation since Bretton Woods*, (New York and Washington, DC: IMF and Oxford University Press, 1996); Douglas A. Irwin, 'The GATT's Contribution to Economic Recovery in Postwar Western Europe', in *Europe's Postwar Recovery*, ed. Barry Eichengreen.

14. Alan S. Milward, *The Reconstruction of Western Europe, 1945–1951* (London: Methuen, 1984); John Gillingham, *European Integration 1950–2003: Superstate or New Market Economy?* (Cambridge: Cambridge University Press, 2003).

15. Source: Calculated from Angus Maddison, *The World Economy: Historical Statistics* (Paris: Development Centre of the Organization for Economic Cooperation and Development, 2003), pp. 50–1, 85.

16. William Adams Brown Jr and Redvers Opie, *American Foreign Assistance* (Washington, DC: The Brookings Institution, 1953).

17. Hugh Rockoff, 'The United States: From Ploughshares to Swords', in *The Economics of World War II*, ed. Harrison, pp. 82–111.
18. Nelson Lichtenstein, *Labor's War at Home* (Cambridge: Cambridge University Press, 1982); Robert M. Collins, *The Business Response to Keynes, 1929–1964* (New York: Columbia University Press, 1981); Elizabeth A. Fones-Wolf, *Selling Free Enterprise: The Business Assault on Labor and Liberalism, 1945–60* (Urbana, IL: University of Illinois Press, 1994); Kim Phillips-Fein, *Invisible Hands: The Making of the Conservative Movement from the New Deal to Reagan* (New York: W. W. Norton, 2009).
19. Collins, *Business Response*, pp. 99–100.
20. Correlli Barnett has argued vigorously that poor policy in the war years and after, based on illusions that included an 'outward façade of victory' and over-reliance on US aid, failed to meet the need for fundamental reforms in industry and education. Correlli Barnett, *The Audit of War: The Illusion & Reality of Britain as a Great Nation* (London: Macmillan, 1986).
21. Milward, *The Reconstruction of Western Europe*; Alec Cairncross, *Years of Recovery: British Economic Policy 1945–51* (London: Methuen, 1985); Bean and Crafts, 'British Economic Growth', p. 142.
22. Frank Trentmann provides a thorough historiographical guide and conceptual critique in 'The Long History of Contemporary Consumer Society: Chronologies, Practices, and Politics in Modern Europe', *Archiv für Sozialgeschichte* 49 (2009), pp. 107–28.
23. Victoria de Grazia, with Ellen Furlough, eds, *The Sex of Things: Gender and Consumption in Historical Perspective* (Berkeley, CA: University of California Press, 1997), p. 4, elaborated in idem, 'Changing Consumption Regimes in Europe, 1930–1970: Comparative Perspectives on the Distribution Problem', in *Getting and Spending: European and American Consumer Societies in the Twentieth Century*, eds Susan Strasser, Charles McGovern and Matthias Judt (Cambridge: Cambridge University Press, 1998), pp. 59–83, and *Irresistible Empire: America's Advance through 20th-Century Europe* (Cambridge, MA: Belknap Press, 2005), pp. 4–9.
24. Joan Thirsk, *Economic Policy and Projects: The Development of a Consumer Society in Early Modern England* (Oxford: Clarendon Press, 1978); John Brewer and Roy Porter, eds, *Consumption and the World of Goods*, (London: Routledge, 1993).
25. Michael B. Miller, *The Bon Marché: Bourgeois Culture and the Department Store, 1860–1920* (Princeton, NJ: Princeton University Press, 1981); Rosalind H. Williams, *Dream Worlds: Mass Consumption in Late Nineteenth-Century France* (Berkeley, CA: University of California Press, 1982); Geoffrey Crossick and Serge Jaumain, eds, *Cathedrals of Consumption: The European Department Store 1850–1939* (Farnham: Ashgate, 1998); Erika Rappaport, *Shopping for Pleasure: Women and the Making of London's West End* (Princeton, NJ: Princeton University Press, 2000).
26. Ellen Furlough and Carl Strikwerda, eds, *Consumers Against Capitalism? Consumer Cooperation in Europe, North America, and Japan, 1840–1990* (New York: Rowman & Littlefield, 1999).

27. William Leach, *Land of Desire: Merchants, Power, and the Rise of a New American Culture* (New York: Random House, 1993); Kathleen G. Donohue, *Freedom from Want: American Liberalism and the Idea of the Consumer*, (Baltimore, NJ: Johns Hopkins University Press, 2003); Daniel Horowitz, *The Morality of Spending: Attitudes toward the Consumer Society in America, 1875–1940* (Baltimore, NJ: Johns Hopkins University Press, 1985).

28. For national adaptations in France, Germany and Italy see Marie-Laure Djelic, *Exporting the American Model: The Postwar Transformation of European Business* (Oxford: Oxford University Press, 1998).

29. Patricia and Robert Malcolmson, eds, *Nella Last's Peace: The Post-war Diaries of Housewife 49* (London: Profile Books, 2008), pp. 18, 63, 84, 198. On Mass Observation observers see James Hinton, *The Mass Observers: A History, 1937–1949* (Oxford: Oxford University Press, 2013).

30. Dominique Veillon, *Vivre et Survivre en France 1939–1947* (Paris: Payot, 1995).

31. R. Volpi, quoted by Vera Zamagani, *The Economic History of Italy 1860–1990* (Oxford: Clarendon Press, 1993), p. 323.

32. Peter Baldwin, 'Beveridge in the *Longue Durée*', in *Beveridge and Social Security*, pp. 37–55.

33. Frank Trentmann, 'Knowing Consumers – Histories, Identities, Practices: An Introduction', in *The Making of the Consumer: Knowledge, Power and Identity in the Modern World*, ed. Frank Trentmann (Oxford and New York: Berg, 2006), p. 12.

34. On the impact of the Keynesian Revolution and demand management, see, G. C. Peden, *The Treasury and British Public Policy, 1906–1959* (Oxford: Oxford University Press, 2000); Michel Margairaz, *L'État, les Finances et l'Économie: Histoire d'une Conversion 1932–1952* (Paris: CHEFF, 1991); and for Europe more broadly Peter A. Hall, ed., *The Political Power of Economic Ideas: Keynesianism Across Nations* (Princeton, NJ: Princeton University Press, 1989).

35. Willi A. Boelcke, *Der Schwarzmarkt 1945–1948. Vom Überleben nach dem Kriege* (Braunschweig: Westermann, 1986); Paul Steege, *Black Market, Cold War: Everyday Life in Berlin, 1946–1949* (Cambridge: Cambridge University Press, 2007); Malte Zierenberg, *Stadt der Schieber: Der Berliner Schwarzmarkt 1939–1950* (Göttingen: Vandenhoeck & Ruprecht, 2008).

36. Erica Carter, 'Alice in Consumer Wonderland: West German Case Studies in Gender and Consumer Culture', in *West Germany under Construction: Politics, Society, and Culture in the Adenauer Era*, ed. Robert G. Moeller (Ann Arbor, MI: University of Michigan Press, 1997), p. 353; Anthony James Nicholls, *Freedom with Responsibility: The Social Market Economy in Germany, 1918–1963* (Oxford: Clarendon Press, 1994).

37. Konrad H. Jarausch and Michael Geyer, *Shattered Past: Reconstructing German Histories* (Princeton, NJ: Princeton University Press, 2003), pp. 269–314; and Carter, 'Alice in the Consumer Wonderland', pp. 351–2.

38. Konrad H. Jarausch, *After Hitler: Recivilizing Germans, 1945–1995* (Oxford: Oxford University Press, 2006), p. 94.

39. Charles S. Maier, 'Society as Factory', in *In Search of Stability: Explorations in Historical Political Economy*, pp. 19–69; Mary Nolan, *Visions of Modernity: American Business and the Modernization of Germany* (Oxford: Oxford University Press, 1994).
40. David Strauss, *Menace in the West: The Rise of French Anti-Americanism in Modern Times* (New York: Greenwood Press, 1979); Nolan, *Visions of Modernity*; Stefan Schwarzkopf, 'Who Said "Americanization"? The Case of Twentieth-Century Advertising and Mass Marketing from a British Perspective', in *Decentering America*, ed. Jessica C. E. Gienow-Hecht (New York: Berghahn Books, 2007), pp. 26–30.
41. S. Jonathan Weisen, *Creating the Nazi Marketplace: Commerce and Consumption in the Third Reich* (Cambridge University Press, 2011), p. 141.
42. Weisen, *Nazi Marketplace*, pp. 34–41; R. J. B. Bosworth, *Mussolini's Italy: Life Under the Fascist Dictatorship, 1915–1945* (New York: Penguin Press, 2005), pp. 409–10; Victoria de Grazia, *How Fascism Ruled Women: Italy, 1922–1945* (Berkeley, CA: University of California Press, 1992), pp. 207–10.
43. David Reynolds, *Rich Relations: The American Occupation of Britain, 1942–1945* (New York: Random House, 1995); Peter Schrijvers, *Liberators: The Allies and Belgian Society, 1944–1945* (Cambridge: Cambridge University Press, 2009); Régine Torrent, *La France américaine: Controverses de la Libération* (Brussels: Éditions Racine, 2004).
44. Brian Angus McKenzie, *Remaking France: Americanization, Public Diplomacy, and the Marshall Plan* (New York: Berghahn Books, 2005); Reinhold Wagnleitner, *Coca-Colonization and the Cold War: The Cultural Mission of the United States in Austria after the Second World War* (Chapel Hill, NC: University of North Carolina Press, 1994); Alexander Stephan, ed., *The Americanization of Europe: Culture, Diplomacy, and Anti-Americanism after 1945* (New York: Berghahn Books, 2006).
45. Mary Nolan, 'Americanization as a Paradigm of German History', in *Conflict, Catastrophe and Continuity: Essays on Modern German History*, eds Frank Biess, Mark Roseman and Hanna Schissler (New York: Berghahn Books, 2007), pp. 200–18; and the detailed studies of change to retail practice in Ralph Jessen and Lydia Langer, eds, *Transformations of Retailing in Europe after 1945* (Farnham: Ashgate, 2012).
46. Jarausch, *After Hitler*, pp. 99–101, and Schwarzkopf, 'Who Said "Americanization"?'
47. Jim Tomlinson, 'Marshall Aid and the "Shortage Economy" in Britain in the 1940s', *Contemporary European History* 9:1 (2000), pp. 137–55.
48. Ina Zweiniger-Bargielowska, *Austerity in Britain: Rationing, Controls, and Consumption, 1939–1955* (Oxford: Oxford University Press, 2000); Mark Roodhouse, *Black Market Britain, 1939–1955* (Oxford: Oxford University Press, 2013).
49. Becky E. Conekin, *The Autobiography of a Nation: The 1951 Festival of Britain* (Manchester: Manchester University Press, 2003), p. 50. In France the

1948 *Salon des Arts Ménagers* displayed household appliances that would not be available for from six months to two years; see Rebecca J. Pulju, *Women and Mass Consumer Society in Postwar France* (Cambridge: Cambridge University Press, 2011), p. 184.

50. Conekin, *Autobiography of a Nation*, p. 55. Churchill's Conservative government scrapped the Skylon and bulldozed most of the Festival site in 1952.

51. Zweiniger-Bargielowska, *Austerity in Britain*, pp. 29–31.

52. Howson, *British Monetary Policy*, pp. 182, 212; C. H. Feinstein, *National Income, Expenditure and Output of the United Kingdom 1855–1965* (Cambridge: Cambridge University Press, 1976), Table 5.

53. Sue Bowden and Avner Offer, 'Household Appliances and the Use of Time: The United States and Britain since the 1920s', *Economic History Review* 47:4 (1994), pp. 725–48.

54. Erhard cited in Axel Schildt and Arnold Sywottek, '"Reconstruction" and "Modernization": West German Social History during the 1950s', in *West Germany under Construction*, ed. Moeller, p. 429; the union quote cited in Michael Wildt, '"Wohlstand für alle": Das Spannungsfeld von Konsum und Politik in der Bundesrepublik', in *Die Konsumgesellschaft in Deutschland 1890–1990: Ein Handbuch*, eds Heinz-Gerhard Haupt and Claudius Torp (Frankfurt: Campus Verlag, 2009), p. 309.

55. Sources: United States, England and Wales: Sue Bowden and Avner Offer, 'Household Appliances', Table A1, 745–6; France: Jean Fourastié, *Productivité et richesse des nations* (Paris: Gallimard, 2005), p. 317; W. Germany: for appliances in 1975, *Consumer Europe 1982* (London: Euromonitor Publications, 1982), pp. 429, 436, 533; for figures in the 1950s and 1960s for washing machines and refrigerators, Victor Fast, 'Die Technisierung der Hausarbeit von 1950 bis 1970', Universität Bielefeld, 2006; for washing machines and refrigerators in 1970, Heinrich Weiler and Fritz Homann, *Wirtshaftspartner DDR: Wirtschaftsstruktur, Recht, Steuern, Fördermaßnahmen, Ansprechpartner* (Bonn: Economica, 1990), p. 21; E. Germany: Stephan Merl, 'Staat und Konsum in der Zentralverwaltungswirtschaft: Rußland und die ostmitteleuropäischen Länder', in *Europäische Konsumgeschichte: Zur Gesellschafts- und Kulturgeschichte des Konsums*, eds Hannes Siegrist, Hartmut Kaelble and Jürgen Kocka *(18. Bis 20. Jahrhundert)* (Frankfurt: Campus Verlag, 1997), p. 227.

56. Source: A. S. Deaton, 'The Structure of Demand in Europe 1920–1970', in *The Fontana Economic History of Europe*, Vol. 5, *The Twentieth Century -1*, ed. Carlo M. Cipolla (London: Fontana Books, 1976), p. 125; UNESCO, *Statistics on Radio and Television 1950–1960* (Paris: UNESCO, 1963), pp. 80–2; UNESCO, *Statistical Yearbook* (Paris: UNESCO, 1968), p. 489; *United Nations Statistical Yearbook*, various years.

57. Adrian Horn, *Juke box Britain: Americanisation and Youth Culture, 1945–60* (Manchester: Manchester University Press, 2009) and Conekin, Mort and Waters, *Moments of Modernity: Reconstructing Britain, 1945–1964* (London and New York: Rivers Oram Press, 1999).

58. Nick Tiratsoo, 'Limits of Americanisation: The United States Productivity Gospel in Britain', in *Moments of Modernity*, eds Conekin, Mort and Waters, pp. 96–113; Richard F. Kuisel, *Seducing the French: The Dilemma of Americanization* (Berkeley: University of California Press, 1993), pp. 70–102.

59. De Grazia, *Irresistible Empire*; Ralph Jessen and Lydia Langer, eds, *Transformations of Retailing in Europe after 1945* (Farnham: Ashgate, 2012), for essays on supermarkets in Britain, Italy and West Germany.

60. Lizabeth Cohen, *Making a New Deal: Industrial Workers in Chicago, 1919–1939* (Cambridge: Cambridge University Press, 1990), pp. 109–20; Tracey Deutsch, *Building a Housewife's Paradise: Gender, Politics, and American Grocery Stores in the Twentieth Century* (Chapel Hill, NC: University of North Carolina Press, 2010).

61. See John K. Walton, 'The Post-war Decline of the British Retail Co-operative Movement: Nature, Causes and Consequences', in *Consumerism and Co-operative Movement in Modern British History*, eds Lawrence Black and Nicole Robertson (Manchester: Manchester University Press, 2009), pp. 13–31, and the essays in that collection; Peter Gurney, 'The Battle of the Consumer in Postwar Britain', *Journal of Modern History* 77:4 (2005): 956–87; and *Consumers Against Capitalism? Consumer Cooperation in Europe, North America and Japan, 1840–1990*, eds Ellen Furlough and Carl Strikwerda.

62. Stefan Schwarzkopf, 'Managing the Unmanageable: The Professionalization of Market and Consumer Research in Post-War Europe', in *Transformations*, eds Jessen and Langer, pp. 164–78; Schwarzkopf, 'Who Said "Americanization"?'

63. Robert Millar, *The Affluent Sheep* (London: Longman, 1963), pp. 61 and 63.

64. Corey Ross, 'Visions of Prosperity: The Americanization of Advertising in Interwar Germany', in *Selling Modernity: Advertising in Twentieth-Century Germany*, eds Pamela E. Swett, S. Jonathan Wiesen and Jonathan R. Zatlin (Durham, NC: Duke University Press, 2007), pp. 52–77; Hartmut Berghoff, 'Enticement and Deprivation: The Regulation of Consumption in Pre-War Nazi Germany', in *The Politics of Consumption: Material Culture and Citizenship in Europe and America*, eds Martin Daunton and Matthew Hilton (Oxford: Berg, 2001), pp. 165–84.

65. Quoted in McGovern, *Sold American*, p. 334.

66. Millar, *Affluent Sheep*, pp. 5–6; Lawrence Black, *Redefining British Politics: Culture, Consumerism and Participation, 1954–70* (Basingstoke: Palgrave Macmillan, 2010); Matthew Hilton, *Consumerism in Twentieth-Century Britain: The Search for a Historical Movement* (Cambridge: Cambridge University Press, 2003).

67. The classic from this era is Ralph Nader, *Unsafe at Any Speed: The Designed-In Dangers of the American Automobile* (New York: Grossman, 1965); for the need for regulation in the US and deregulation since the 1970s, Thomas O. McGarity, *Freedom to Harm: The Lasting Legacy of the Laissez Faire Revival* (New Haven, CT: Yale University Press, 2013).

68. Lizabeth Cohen, *A Consumers' Republic: The Politics of Mass Consumption in Postwar America* (New York: Vintage Books, 2003), p. 13; Meg Jacobs, *Pocketbook Politics: Economic Citizenship in Twentieth-Century America* (Princeton, NJ: Princeton University Press, 2005); and McGovern, *Sold American*.
69. Erica Carter, *How German Is She? Postwar West German Reconstruction and the Consuming Woman* (Ann Arbor, MI: University of Michigan Press, 1997); Michael Wildt, 'Changes in Consumption as Social Practice in West Germany During the 1950s', in *Getting and Spending*, eds Strasser, McGovern and Judt, pp. 301–16.
70. Pulju, *Women and Mass Consumer Society*.
71. Frank Trentmann, *Free Trade Nation: Commerce, Consumption, and Civil Society in Modern Britain* (Oxford: Oxford University Press, 2008), pp. 69–80.
72. Matthew Hilton, 'The Fable of the Sheep, or, Private Virtues, Public Vices: The Consumer Revolution of the Twentieth Century', *Past and Present* 174 (2002), pp. 222–56.
73. Sheryl Kroen, 'La Magie des Objets, le Plan Marshall et l'Instauration d'une Démocratie de Consommateurs', in *Au nom du Consommateur: Consommation et Politique en Europe et aux États-Unis au XXe Siècle*, eds Alain Chatriot, Marie-Emmanuelle Chessel and Matthew Hilton (Paris: Éditions La Découverte, 2004), pp. 80–97.
74. E. J. Mishan, *Growth: The Price We Pay* (London: Staples Press, 1969), p. 8.
75. Mishan, *Growth*. John Kenneth Galbraith raised similar concerns in *The Affluent Society* (New York: Houghton Mifflin, 1958), posing the problem as one of a 'social imbalance' between the ever greater abundance of private goods and the greater need for public goods, including education, health care, environmental protection, reduced crime, better transportation. See also Tibor Scitovsky, *Papers on Welfare and Growth* (London: Allen & Unwin, 1964).
76. E. F. Schumacher, *Small is Beautiful: A Study of Economics as if People Mattered* (London: Blond & Briggs, 1973).
77. Galbraith, *The Affluent Society*; Vance Packard, *The Hidden Persuaders* (New York: D. McKay, 1957); and Rachel Carson, *Silent Spring* (New York: Houghton Mifflin, 1962); discussed in Daniel Horowitz, *The Anxieties of Affluence: Critiques of American Consumer Culture, 1939–1979* (Amherst, MA: University of Massachusetts Press, 2004).
78. Jean Baudrillard, *La Société de Consommation, Ses Mythes, Ses Structures* (Paris: Denoël, 1970), pp. 55–6.
79. Matthew Hilton and Martin Daunton, 'Material Politics: An Introduction', in *Politics of Consumption*, p. 3.
80. Daniel Horowitz, *Consuming Pleasures: Intellectuals and Popular Culture in the Postwar World* (Philadelphia, PA: University of Pennsylvania Press, 2012).
81. Stefan Zweig, *The Post-Office Girl*, trans. Joel Rotenberg (New York: NYRB, 2008), p. 55.

82. Carolyn Steedman, *Landscape for a Good Woman* (London: Virago Press, 1986), p. 6.
83. Tibor Scitovsky, *The Joyless Economy* (Oxford: Oxford University Press, 1976); Albert O. Hirschman, *Shifting Involvements: Private Interest and Public Action* (Princeton, NJ: Princeton University Press, 1982).
84. Robert R. Nathan, *Mobilizing for Abundance* (New York: McGraw-Hill, 1944), pp. ix, xi.

CHAPTER FOURTEEN

A House Divided: The Organized Consumer and the British Labour Party, 1945–60

PETER GURNEY

The development of a 'consumer society' in post-war Britain was not a smooth, inexorable process facilitated merely by changes in supply and demand. Without rising real incomes, particularly among the working class, greater availability of credit and an increasing propensity to consume a range of new commodities, this major watershed would not have been possible.[1] Transformations were no doubt also facilitated by the expanding reach of advertising agencies that, according to one recent study of the London office of the American firm J. Walter Thompson, played a vital role in 'assembling' and 'mobilizing' the post-war housewife-consumer in a specifically national context.[2] However, the argument of this chapter is that such changes involved profound political choices and struggles that continue to be largely overlooked by historians. The focus below is on the fraught relationship between the institution which represented organized working-class consumers, the cooperative movement, and the Labour Party during the Attlee years and beyond. The chapter demonstrates how the organized consumer was almost completely marginalized by the Labour government and goes on to suggest that the continued subordination of the cooperative alternative meant that the Labour Party, like the Conservatives, increasingly embraced an individual, competitive model of consumption and the consumer during the second half of the 1950s. This was a crucial decade, for it was during this period that the atomized figure of the individual consumer began to exert a hegemonic influence across both polity and civil society, shaping both the epistemologies and languages through which the political and economic domains were thought and represented. The conclusion stresses how Labour's marginalization of the cooperative alternative has left an important legacy for the continuing critique of capitalist forms of consumerism.

The most important body of organized consumers in Britain, the retail cooperative movement, was in a buoyant mood at the end of World War II. It had worked closely with government during hostilities and its contribution to the home front was widely recognized. On paper it looked impressive. In 1946, the movement could claim more than 9.7 million members and 1037 retail societies. Annual trade of these societies stood at over £402 million, while annual trade of the English and Scottish Cooperative Wholesale Societies (CWS and SCWS) amounted to £249 million. Most important, the movement continued to expand in the immediate post-war period. By 1958, membership had reached 12.5 million, although the number of societies had been reduced to 918 through a process of amalgamation. The annual trade of retail societies was now nearly £998 million, while the annual trade of the CWS and SCWS was well over £550 million.[3] The movement was in the vanguard of retail transformations during and after the war. For example, it opened the first self-service grocery store in the country in 1942, and its leaders studied and were also fascinated by frozen foods and out-of-town supermarkets, changes that were transforming food shopping in the US.[4]

Despite the coop's continued centrality to British retailing after the war, it became less of a factor in British politics during Attlee's post-war Labour government. This was not because consumer issues had diminished. Working people still organized around consumption and articulated an alternative vision of how the market should be regulated. British cooperators had developed, from the early nineteenth century onwards, a democratic, ethical model of consumption which privileged an associated, active membership rather than the gullible, individual consumer frequently imagined by capitalist advertisers.[5] Moreover, recent work by a growing number of scholars has demonstrated how the cooperative movement continued to play a crucial role in defining working-class community and culture during the inter-war years and beyond.[6] Many cooperators in the first half of the twentieth century continued to look forward to the creation of a 'Cooperative Commonwealth', when social production as well as distribution would be entirely owned and controlled by the people. This radical alternative diverged from (but also intersected with) competitive paths to mass consumption and by the mid-twentieth century the state exerted a shaping influence on both.

The cooperative movement had a long-standing relationship with the Labour Party, with a formal agreement dating back to 1927 that was renegotiated in 1946. Under these agreements local Cooperative parties could affiliate to divisional Labour parties with representation and voting rights in proportion to numbers affiliated, but it was voluntary and did not replace existing local arrangements. In other words, difficult issues were fudged: the agreements were regarded as both a step towards absorption by the Labour Party and as an assertion of independence, for they helped defeat those cooperators who wanted direct affiliation.[7] Nevertheless, both organizations shared a commitment to the creation of a more egalitarian society, even a 'Cooperative Commonwealth', although this suitably vague term often concealed profound differences. Many cooperators believed a strengthened alliance with Labour to be vital after the war, given increased capitalist pressure on the consumer. The concentration of industry was a major worry. Before the war was over an editorial in the *Co-operative News* asked; 'Are we to have Government control, or are we to have our economic life controlled by private monopolies, combines, cartels and trade associations?' There were 2500 trade associations in Britain by this time and it seemed probable that their influence on Government would increase in the future. This critique was a staple of cooperative discourse going back at least to the 1890s, though a new urgency can be discerned at this time. Labour's promise to establish public supervision of monopolies and cartels in industries not yet ripe for public ownership was considered evasive at the very least.[8] Meanwhile, the capitalist press, exemplified by the *Daily Sketch*, described the cooperative movement as 'the largest and most ruthless combine-cartel in the country', A. V. Alexander, leader of the cooperative group in the Commons, pointed out that for many commodities the only alternative to the 'giant trusts' was the coop – 'the people's main defence against monopoly'. He went on to list some key antagonists: 'For soap, it is the only effective competitor of the Unilever combine; Co-op tobacco and cigarettes are almost the sole challenge to the Imperial Tobacco Co.; Co-op milling is the single alternative to the Rank and Spiller combines.'[9] Founded towards the end of World War I to represent cooperators in parliament, the Cooperative Party won 23 seats in the 1945 general election, so it was hoped that calls for protection against private capital would be taken seriously. After all, the Labour Party depended upon the movement to make its policy of 'austerity' acceptable to many working-class consumers.[10]

The cooperative movement achieved considerable success here. The cooperative press educated members about the problems of post-war dislocation, for example arguing in favour of rationing as a means to evenly distribute the burden of reconstruction across classes and an aid to building up manufacturing and exports. The movement supported Food Minister, John Strachey, and denounced Conservatives for exploiting the situation for narrow political ends.[11] However, cracks began to appear from the autumn of 1946. C. W. Fulker, Secretary of the Parliamentary Committee of the Cooperative Union, pointed out that enforcement of the bread rationing scheme was 'largely non-existent', divisional food offices were, 'out of touch with women with the basket', and that consequently the measure should be scrapped immediately. At meetings throughout the country, others were even less polite. When the Central Board of the Cooperative Union met in October it was apparent that rationing was causing serious friction. Harold Taylor criticized the lack of consultation with the organized consumer and cautioned, 'We are anxious that the Government should not be drawn into the wilderness again either because of the egotistical attitude of some Ministers or because of their attitude to the Co-operative movement.'[12]

Disaffection was clearly increasing, not with rationing *per se* but with the operation of the various schemes. Datum line distribution and points allocation caused most complaint; under the 'straight' rationing scheme that determined allocation of basic foodstuffs, such as butter, bacon, sugar and meat, goods were distributed to retailers based on the number of customers registered with them (the so-called datum line, which had been established at the start of the war), while other goods such as canned foods, fresh fruit, fish and many other commodities whose supply was more variable were rationed using a points system, with individual consumers receiving a specified allocation of points.[13] The Parliamentary Committee met Strachey in November 1946 and pressed for allocation of points based on customer registration. Strachey unhelpfully admitted that he would 'have to do something about it, but it was very difficult to see just what'.[14] The datum line issue worsened as membership had increased by at least one million since the line had been calculated and thus points goods were allocated on the basis of information that was now woefully out of date.

Nevertheless, many sections of the movement continued to rally to the government's cause, especially when provoked. The Women's Cooperative Guild, for instance, repudiated claims by the Housewives' League and the Conservative Party that Britain was starving and placed on record the appreciation of 62,000 Guildswomen for the Government's efforts to maintain price controls and rationing in the context of world food shortages at its Annual Congress in 1947. Despite grumblings at both the local and national level, the editor of the *News* also continued to back Strachey and remained sanguine about the morale of the majority: 'The British people, although weary of restrictions and queues, are still prepared to accept rationing schemes that provide fair shares for all.' The first real indication that people's patience had been stretched to the limit was provided by the municipal elections in November 1947 when Labour lost 652 seats, nearly half the gains made two years earlier.[15]

The Government's taxation and housing policy also caused concern. The profits tax was doubled to two shillings in the pound but the increase in purchase tax caused most resentment, falling heavily as it did on the poorest members. Although the Chancellor, Stafford Cripps, depended on the movement to support anti-inflationary measures like price controls, no attempt was made to meet their criticisms.[16] Moreover, the allocation of shops on new council estates caused serious conflict. Societies were awarded too few shops on new developments, or else were excluded altogether, undermining the movement's local roots. Under pressure from the Parliamentary Committee of the Cooperative Union, Labour issued a letter signed by the Party Secretary, Morgan Phillips, urging local authorities to ensure that cooperators received fair consideration in the allocation of new sites, but this was too little, too late. At the Labour Party Conference in 1952 the Cooperative MP, Will Coldrick, reminded delegates that, 'these new estates require shops and we often found that the Labour movement was treating the co-operative movement in the same way as private enterprise and multiple shops'.[17] Overall, it was the general lack of consultation that so infuriated cooperators. They were excluded from the Economic Planning Board and although some had mixed feelings about joining 'a national body formed by capitalist enterprise', cooperators were deeply concerned that, 'the organised consumers of this country have no voice in the planning of our economic affairs'.[18]

Most damaging of all were disagreements over the issue of public ownership. Trouble had been brewing for years over preferred forms but Labour's plans to nationalize industrial insurance brought things to a head in 1949. At the Labour Party Conference that year, relations had reached breaking point because of the widespread belief within the movement that Labour's enthusiasm for nationalization would make it difficult for cooperators to retain their 'own form of economic organisation'. Herbert Morrison, who drew up Labour's draft election programme, *Labour Believes in Britain*, lavished praise on the movement, especially for its efforts to curb inflation, but this did little to impress the Secretary of the Cooperative Party, Jack Bailey, who argued for 'socialisation' rather than nationalization. The Co-operative MP Percy Davies also urged the conference to support the

'Third Way' represented by cooperation. Other Cabinet Ministers, including Hugh Dalton, strongly backed the movement in public, which only fuelled suspicions of a serious rift.[19]

It seemed that relations could not degenerate any further when Lord Shepherd, Labour Chief Whip in the House of Lords, revealed that the Government was considering plans to establish state shops – an idea that had been discussed in Labour circles at the end of the war – in order to increase competition in retailing. Such action would have threatened the very existence of independent cooperative societies. Strachey quickly issued a denial and expressed his support for the form of 'social production and distribution' represented by co-operation, but the damage had been done.[20] At the root of the problem lay the strategy of nationalization itself. Many cooperators were highly critical of the undemocratic and ineffective Consumer Councils attached to nationalized industries and agreed with the Walsall cooperator Fred Abbotts that 'the multiplication of state boards would lead to a totalitarian and not a socialist State'. Reports of this serious confrontation appeared in the press, and populist Tories, such as Lord Woolton, made rather lame attempts to appeal to cooperative voters.[21] A compromise was eventually reached over insurance, with Labour adopting plans to 'mutualize' rather than nationalize the industry, leaving untouched most of the field already occupied by the Cooperative Insurance Society. The *News* had claimed victory in advance, wryly concluding that 'the Labour Party fears the effect of this campaign on its pool at the next election'.[22]

Although the precise effects of worsening relations between cooperators and the Labour Party on the general election in February 1950 are difficult to gauge, it seems unlikely that public controversy would have helped Labour. The electoral gains achieved five years before were almost completely wiped out (the number of Cooperative Party MPs fell to 17), and this lent a new urgency to the debate over public ownership and Labour strategy. Cooperators thereafter made repeated demands for an explicit declaration from Labour regarding the role of their movement within the socialist society of the future; a policy statement issued by the Cooperative Union, *The Co-operative Movement in a Collectivist Economy*, put the case for cooperative rather than state ownership most forcefully. Exasperation with Labour was reinforced by the leadership's commitment to nationalization 'as an end in itself', as Gordon Schaffer pointed out at a meeting of the Croydon Men's Guild in March.[23]

There is some evidence to suggest that the Labour Party made an effort to appease the consumer interest following its setback at the polls. *Labour and the New Society* advocated a Consumers' Charter which guaranteed the maintenance of price controls and food subsidies, recommended the establishment of consumer advice centres, and legislative action against manufacturers which boycotted price-cutting retailers: 'the socialist aim must be to supplement the democracy of workers with a democracy of consumers'. Even Herbert Morrison admitted that, 'nationalisation is only one of several possible ways of working together', and promised to deliver a Consumers' Charter before the next election. At the Labour Party conference in October, he declared: 'We seek to establish a live democracy of consumers … We must let the consumer make his voice heard more than in the past. We have a wonderful democracy in the great consumer Co-operative movement.'[24] Many cooperators remained unconvinced by all this and treated Morrison's conversion with a good deal of scepticism.

Perhaps one of the most forthright denunciations of the policy of the Attlee Government was made by Donald Dow, a director of the SCWS, at a conference at Galashiels in February 1951. Dow expressed his amazement at the docility with which the movement had accepted a subordinate role in post-war Britain: 'Having to a large extent created the present Government, the co-operative movement is being led, by deference to the Government, to soft pedal on some of its principles and allow itself to be pushed into a back seat – a situation which the most intense efforts of capitalist monopolists and enemies of co-operation could not accomplish in days gone by.' Relations remained extremely volatile up until the general election in October. After the narrow defeat of the Labour Party the editor of the *News* called for a complete rethink of nationalization, which he condemned as an undemocratic policy that bred disillusionment and apathy among the working class and which had thus contributed, in no small measure, to Labour's eventual defeat.[25]

With Labour out of office and relations between the cooperative movement and the Labour Party strained to the limit, cooperators had to face the challenges posed by the power of the monopolies and trade associations on their own. A critical stage in the contest was reached by the early 1950s. For example, 'the unabated war' between rival producers in the soap trade, characterized by massive advertising campaigns, aggressive marketing strategies and generous discounts, made it difficult for CWS soap factories to compete. The movement lacked technological expertise and the necessary plant to produce the new synthetic detergents pushed by competitors like Unilever. Moreover, cooperative brands were only sold in one shop out of every 15 and it therefore proved very difficult to maintain, let alone increase, the existing market share of less than 20 per cent. Despite such problems, the movement engaged in the struggle and consequently secured supplies from private manufacturers.[26] The CWS pinned its hopes on 'Spel', a new washing powder launched in the summer of 1952. Its advertising portrayed capitalist manufacturers as the enemy of the movement and working-class consumers more generally and described the contest in almost apocalyptic terms: 'What would any of the private makers give to have "Spel" out of the way? ... This battle is too big to lose', warned an editorial in the *News*. 'If we fail here it is going to be a tragedy for us all', declared Robert Deans at a meeting of CWS directors at Leicester. It soon became apparent that the odds were stacked against the CWS and although activists made determined efforts to educate members about 'the gigantic financial and industrial organizations which work behind the simple product names which have been given to the competitive powders', recalcitrant shoppers continued to demand brands such as 'Persil' at the stores and sales of 'Spel' plummeted.[27]

Heightened competition intensified pressure to increase expenditure on advertising in the press, radio and television. Over £15,000 was spent promoting 'Spel' the year it was introduced, although this was a paltry sum compared to the well over £320,000 spent advertising 'Persil' over the same period. The CWS sponsored a quiz show in the autumn of 1954 on the commercial station Radio Luxembourg, aimed specifically at, 'the younger engaged or married couples whose tastes and buying habits are just being formed'. The following year the CWS also bought air time on commercial television.[28] Many cooperators may have agreed with left wing Labour MP Aneurin Bevan, who once described advertising as, 'one of the evil consequences of a society which is itself evil', but the movement had little choice but to take up the weapons of its adversaries. Overall, however, cooperative advertising remained small-scale as the movement still spent less than £1 million annually, compared to the £200 million expended by capitalist companies.[29] Such initiatives did little to remedy the stagnation of cooperative trade, particularly in 'dry goods'. Cooperators tended to collapse together the threat posed by monopolies with the rapid expansion of multiple stores, particularly Marks and Spencer, a company that managed to project both a 'classless' and 'moralized' vision of consumer modernity in which quality, style and value were for the first time within reach of the majority of shoppers.[30]

Many cooperators had hoped that public ownership and legislative regulation would check the monopolies. They also campaigned vigorously for the abolition of resale price maintenance – a form of price fixing used by private manufacturers to protect their profit margins – which had been effectively used to boycott the coop and shut it out of important markets for decades. The movement was to be acutely disappointed here as Helen Mercer has shown in her valuable study.[31]

Ominously enough, leading Labour Party revisionists, including Hugh Gaitskell and Anthony Crosland, openly rejected the cooperative alternative and enthusiastically welcomed the 'embourgeoisement' of the working class, purportedly brought about by rising levels of consumption.[32] Generational factors were undoubtedly of some importance here. A younger generation of 'modernizers' rejected the ascetic 'Labour Socialism' of the inter-war years.[33] The editor of the *New Statesman* issued the following warning in the run up to the 1959 general election: 'Mr Gaitskell ... sees the coming election as a contest in publicity techniques ... Someone has to tell the electorate the truth, to treat the voter as a citizen and not as a consumer ... This is a task that can best be accomplished by Socialist methods – and it is the real alternative to the ad-man's appeal to the ad-mass.' This new generation of Labour leaders were following the Conservative Party, which at least since the 1920s had established electoral successes by appealing to the female consumer. The Conservatives spent nearly £0.5 million on the 1959 election, making extensive use of billposters, newspapers and television, and even hired a public relations firm to improve its image. Influential left intellectuals concluded that Labour had to adopt similar methods, which their critics believed could only happen if the party 'completely surrendered to Mr Crosland's philosophy of Revisionism'.[34] The influential Conservative Research Department, for example, published a pamphlet entitled, *Choice: A Report on Consumer Protection* in 1961, which argued that the individual 'discriminating consumer is in fact the key figure in the competitive system'.[35] Powerful interest groups including constituency party members, the trade unions and of course the cooperative movement continued to speak in a different idiom, but the shift at the centre was surely significant. The tendency was to follow the lead of the Conservative Party, which claimed insistently to both champion and speak on behalf of the acquisitive individual consumer.

The Labour Party certainly began to take the interest of the consumer more seriously during its long period in opposition but the organized working-class consumer was not the preferred point of reference. An article in the *New Statesman* that canvassed the idea of a Charter for Consumers, for example, conceded that what Labour lacked was, 'an appealing alternative to the free market', and observed that historically the party had sought to safeguard the interests of those groups in society (trade unionists and the poor, for example), most easily victimized or exploited. Now it was the turn of the consumer and this provided an excellent opportunity to attack the party, which now dominated political discourse:

> When they talk of the 'sovereignty of the consumer', what they really mean is the inalienable right of manufacturers and merchants to control the market. For 'free enterprise' is full of snares for the simple shopper,

and not the least of them is the delusion that he is master of the market. In fact, capitalism is a vast conspiracy against the consumer.[36]

Duplicitous advertising, the persistence of resale price maintenance and confusion produced by a dizzying array of goods, now made action imperative. Although the writer grudgingly acknowledged the Cooperative Party's proposal for a Ministry of Consumers' Welfare, the potential role of the movement was completely overlooked. Whereas the Cooperative Party was calling for a Consumers' Ministry that would serve to empower the wider movement by the mid-1950s, Labour backed the idea of a Consumers' Advisory Service which, as the Labour MP Elaine Burton remarked would be 'a permanent and *reasonably ferocious* watchdog of consumer interests'.[37] Not something, in other words, that big capitalists like Unilever or international advertising agencies like J. Walter Thompson needed to be much concerned about. Paternalism characterized Labour's approach and the party preferred to offer 'protection' to the isolated consumer rather than collective empowerment.

Again, Labour differed little from the Conservatives in this respect. When the 1946 agreement between the Labour Party and the Cooperative Union came to an end in 1957, reconciliation seemed further away than ever, prompting G. W. Rhodes to warn that, 'the Labour Movement may well be heading for a disastrous split which will make the 1950–1 episodes appear mild in retrospect'. The breakdown in communication between cooperators and their Labour allies was now almost irrevocable. The editor of the *News*, for example, had to remind fellow journalists on the labour periodical, the *Daily Herald*, that although the Consumer Advisory Service had proven to be a lamentable failure, consumers were not completely 'forgotten', as the paper had recently suggested, for more than 12 million of them were associated in the cooperative movement.[38] This inability to take the organized consumer seriously and develop more democratic representations of the consumer was highly disabling and surely helped to undermine Labour's potential to effect a major transformation of British society in the second half of the twentieth century.

The decline of the British cooperative movement after World War II was due in large measure to structural economic and political constraints. The movement received no help from the state regardless of which party was in power. It was also actively marginalized by a political ally that had traditionally prioritized production and was beginning to internalize a competitive model of consumption and adopt the language of consumer 'choice' and individual rights. In short, far from seeing the emergence of a consumer movement, as scholars such as Matthew Hilton have proposed, this period instead witnessed the effective marginalization of the one significant consumer movement Britain ever had.[39] Political marginalization and the fact that many cooperative ideologues were locked into a nineteenth-century aesthetic that prioritized utility and value over style also led to the decline of cooperative retailing. Unlike savvy advertising agencies the leaders of the cooperative movement did not listen carefully enough to the voices of working-class consumers.[40] Although the movement appeared healthy in terms of membership figures, the stores began to lag seriously behind in post-war Britain, especially in the sale of clothes and home furnishings, and lost the custom of young fashion-conscious buyers in particular. Working-class consumers who desired the 'New Look' increasingly voted with their pocketbooks and shopped elsewhere.[41]

In a review article, Frank Trentmann has called for us to be more cautious about using general terms such as 'consumer society' and 'consumerism' as they are often freighted with pejorative, moral implications.[42] There is something in this, certainly; middle-class intellectuals have been too quick to denounce the materialism of the 'masses', easy to do when one has enough of the good things in life oneself, as some anthropologists have reminded us.[43] Nevertheless, this is no reason to jettison critical thought entirely. For questions about consumption inevitably raise questions to do with politics, power and morality. We might reject 'consumer society' and 'consumerism' as analytical tools, but we nevertheless still need concepts to think with, for, as Douglas has insisted: 'There is no serious consumption theory possible that avoids some responsibility for social criticism. Ultimately, consumption is about power.'[44] Since the onset of the capitalist golden age, most professional economists and politicians have understandably shirked this subject, because of the moral and ideological pitfalls involved. However, Marx, John Stuart Mill and Alfred Marshall all distinguished between 'good' and 'bad' forms of consumption and understood that consumption necessarily raised questions of morality.[45] Nearer to our own time, John Maynard Keynes optimistically speculated that the economic problem, the problem of scarce resources, 'may be solved, or be at least within sight of solution, within a hundred years', and that scarcity therefore did not constitute 'the permanent problem of the human race'. But this would only be possible, Keynes believed, if we concentrated on meeting our vital or 'absolute' needs and subordinated 'relative' needs, the satisfaction of which 'lifts us above, makes us feel superior to, our fellows'.[46] Whatever their shortcomings, many cooperators would have agreed with Keynes and that is why the history and practice of cooperation has continuing value.

NOTES

1. An overview that adopts this approach is John Benson, *The Rise of Consumer Society in Britain, 1880–1980* (London: Longman, 1994).

2. Sean Nixon, *Hard Sell. Advertising, Affluence and Transatlantic Relations, c. 1951–69* (Manchester: Manchester University Press, 2013).

3. Arnold Bonner, *British Co-operation. The History, Principles, and Organization of the British Co-operative Movement* (Manchester: Cooperative Union, 1961), pp. 209–29, 251–9; Johnston Birchall, *Co-op: The People's Business* (Manchester: Manchester University Press, 1994), pp. 136–46.

4. Barbara Usherwood, '"Mrs Housewife and Her Grocer": The Advent of Self-Service Food Shopping in Great Britain', in *All the World and Her Husband: Women in 20th Century Consumer Culture*, eds Margaret Andrews and Mary Talbot (London: Cassell, 2000); Andrew Alexander, 'Format Development and Retail Change: Supermarket Retailing and the London Co-operative Society', *Business History* 50:4 (2008), pp. 489–508; and for the US experience Tracey Deutsch, *Building a Housewife's Paradise: Gender, Politics, and American Grocery Stores in the Twentieth Century* (Chapel Hill, NC: University of North Carolina Press, 2010).

5. Peter Gurney, *Co-operative Culture and the Politics of Consumption in England, 1870–1930* (Manchester: Manchester University Press, 1996).

6. See, *inter alia*, Alan Burton, *The British Consumer Co-operative Movement and Film, 1890s to 1960s* (Manchester: Manchester University Press, 2005); Lawrence Black and Nicole Robertson, eds, *Consumerism and the Co-operative Movement in Modern British History* (Manchester: Manchester University Press, 2009); Martin Purvis, 'Retailing and Economic Uncertainty in Interwar Britain: Co-operative (mis)fortunes in North-west England', in *English Geographies 1600–1950: Historical Essays on English Customs, Cultures and Communities in Honour of Jack Langton*, eds Elizabeth Baigent and Robert J. Mayhew (Oxford: St John's College Research Centre, 2009); Nicole Robertson, *The Co-operative Movement and Communities in Britain, 1914–1960: Minding Their Own Business* (Farnham: Ashgate, 2010); Peter Gurney, 'Co-operation and the "New Consumerism" in Interwar England', *Business History* 54:6 (2012), pp. 905–24; John F. Wilson, Anthony Webster and Rachel Vorberg-Rugh, *Building Co-operation: A Business History of The Co-operative Group, 1863–2013* (Oxford: Oxford University Press, 2013). There is also burgeoning interest in the history of co-operation in the wider European and global context. See, for example, Ellen Furlough and Carl Strikwerda, eds, *Consumers against Capitalism? : Consumer Cooperation in Europe, North America, and Japan, 1840–1990* (Lanham, MA: Rowman and Littlefield, 1999); Patrizia Battilani and Harm G. Schröter, eds, *The Cooperative Business Movement, 1950 to the Present* (Cambridge: Cambridge University Press, 2012).

7. G. W. Rhodes, *Co-operative-Labour Relations 1900–1962* (Loughborough: Cooperative Union, 1962), pp. 30–2, 75–9; T. F. Carbery, *Consumers in Politics. A History and General Review of the Co-operative Party* (Manchester: Manchester University Press, 1969).

8. *Co-operative News*, 31 March 1945, p. 8; 28 April 1945, p. 8.
9. Ibid., 16 June 1945, p. 1. For the growth of monopolies see Leslie Hannah, *The Rise of the Corporate Economy* (Baltimore, NJ: Johns Hopkins University Press, 1983).
10. G. D. N. Worswick, 'Economic Policy and the Co-operative Movement', in *The Co-operative Movement in Labour Britain*, ed. Noah Barou (London: Gollancz, 1948), pp. 14–29.
11. *Co-operative News*, 14 July 1945, p. 8; 21 July 1945, p. 8; 22 June 1946, p. 8; 6 July 1946, p. 8.
12. Ibid., 5 October 1946, p. 2; 12 October 1946, p. 1; 19 October 1946, p. 1; 26 October 1946, p. 5.
13. *How Britain was Fed in War Time. Food Control 1939–1945* (London: HMSO, 1946), pp. 56–60.
14. *Co-operative News*, 28 December 1946, pp. 1, 8; 10 May 1947, p. 8.
15. Ibid., 28 June 1947, p. 14; 8 November 1947, p. 8; 15 November 1947, p. 8. Zweiniger-Bargielowska has argued that rationing was a major vote loser for Labour, especially amongst women, a claim disputed by Hinton who maintains that working-class women became more favourable to Labour between 1945 and 1951. See Ina Zweiniger-Bargielowska, 'Rationing, Austerity and the Conservative Party Recovery after 1945', *Historical Journal* 37:1 (1994), pp. 173–97; James Hinton, 'Militant Housewives: The British Housewives' League and the Attlee Government', *History Workshop Journal* 38 (1994), pp. 128–56. Evidence from the cooperative movement supports Hinton.
16. *Co-operative News*, 22 November 1947, pp. 1, 8; 29 November 1947, p. 3; 16 April 1949, pp. 1, 8.
17. Ibid., 17 January 1948, pp. 2, 8; 4 June 1949, p. 1; 19 November 1949, p. 5; 11 November 1950, p. 1; 4 October 1952, p. 1; 12 November 1952, p. 7.
18. The Economic Planning Board was recruited from the Federation of British Industry, the British Employers' Confederation and the TUC. See ibid., 6 December 1947, p. 1; 20 December 1947, p. 8.
19. Ibid., 4 June 1949, p. 1; 18 June 1949, pp. 1, 7–8; 2 July 1949, p. 5; Bernard Donoughue and G. W. Jones, *Herbert Morrison, A Portrait of a Politician* (London: Weidenfeld and Nicolson, 1973) pp. 211–12.
20. *Co-operative News*, 15 October 1949, p. 1; 22 October 1949, p. 1; Kevin Manton, 'The Labour Party and Retail Distribution, 1919–1951', *Labour History Review* 73:3 (2008), pp. 269–86.
21. *Co-operative News*, 22 October 1949, p. 7; 5 November 1949, p. 7.
22. Ibid., 29 October 1949, p. 1; 3 December 1949, p. 1; Rhodes, *Co-operative-Labour Relations*, pp. 87-90.
23. *Co-operative News*, 18 March 1950, p. 1; 25 March 1950, p. 3; 15 April 1950, pp. 3–4, p. 14.

24. Ibid., 26 August 1950, pp. 1–2; 6 May 1950, p. 1; 7 October 1950, p. 1; 14 October 1950, p. 5. For later attempts by Morrison to woo the movement see ibid., 4 May 1957, p. 2.
25. Ibid., 3 March 1951, p. 1; 7 April 1951, p. 3; 3 November 1951, pp. 2, 16; Robert Millward and John Singleton, *The Political Economy of Nationalisation in Britain, 1920–1950* (Cambridge: Cambridge University Press, 1995).
26. *Co-operative News*, 26 January 1952, p. 4; 16 February 1952, p. 2.
27. Ibid., 27 December 1952, p. 2; 25 July 1953, p. 2; 5 September 1953, p. 2.
28. Ibid., 5 September 1953, pp. 2, 10; 15 May 1954, p. 1; 9 October 1954, p. 9; 17 September 1955, p. 1.
29. Ibid., 20 June 1953, p. 2. For contrasting assessments of the movement's use of advertising see my article, 'The Battle of the Consumer in Postwar Britain', *Journal of Modern History* 77:4 (2005), pp. 956–87; and Stefan Schwarzkopf, 'Innovation, Modernisation, Consumerism: the Co-operative movement and the Making of British Advertising and Marketing Culture, 1890s–1960s', in *Consumerism and the Co-operative Movement*, ed. Black and Robertson.
30. Marks and Spencer increased its annual turnover from just over £34 million in 1948 to well over £130 million in 1958. Goronwy Rees, *St Michael. A History of Marks and Spencer* (London: Weidenfeld & Nicolson, 1969), pp. 142–5, 180–94.
31. Helen Mercer, *Constructing a Competitive Order: The Hidden History of British Anti-Trust Policy* (Cambridge: Cambridge University Press, 1995).
32. See C. A. R. Crosland, *The Future of Socialism* (London: Jonathan Cape, 1956), p. 112. Crosland's work was hotly debated in the *Co-operative News* when it was published. See 10 November 1956, p. 10; 17 November 1956, p. 8; 1 December 1956, p. 9; 15 December 1956, p. 9.
33. Steven Fielding, 'Activists against "Affluence": Labour Party Culture during the "Golden Age," c. 1950–1970', *Journal of British Studies* 40:2 (2001), pp. 247, 251.
34. *New Statesman and Nation*, 1 November 1958, p. 1; 11 June 1960, p. 866. For Conservative appeals to the female consumer see Erika Rappaport's chapter in this volume and Ina Zweiniger-Bargielowska, *Austerity in Britain. Rationing, Controls, and Consumption, 1939–1955* (Oxford: Oxford University Press, 2000).
35. Original draft of the pamphlet written by the Conservative Research Department, 'Report of the Policy Committee on Consumer Protection', June 1961, 1:3, paragraph 13.
36. *New Statesman and Nation*, 1 January 1955, pp. 3–4.
37. Elaine Burton, *The Battle of the Consumer* (London: Labour Party, 1955), p. 10. My emphasis.
38. *Co-operative News*, 2 February 1957, p. 2; 4 May 1957, p. 3. The Labour Party tried, unsuccessfully, to get the movement to affiliate nationally to Labour at this time.

39. Matthew Hilton, *Consumerism in Twentieth-century Britain: The Search for a Historical Movement* (Cambridge: Cambridge University Press, 2003).
40. See Nixon, *Hard Sell*.
41. For the debate on Dior's New Look within the movement see my article, 'The Battle of the Consumer', pp. 962–3.
42. Frank Trentmann, 'Beyond Consumerism: New Historical Perspectives on Consumption', *Journal of Contemporary History* 39:3 (2004), pp. 373–401.
43. See Mary Douglas and Baron Isherwood, *The World of Goods. Towards an Anthropology of Consumption* (London and New York: Routledge, 1978).
44. Mary Douglas, 'Why do People Want Goods?', in *Understanding Enterprise Culture: Themes in the Work of Mary Douglas*, eds Shaun Hargreaves Heap and Angus Ross (Edinburgh: Edinburgh University Press, 1992), p. 30.
45. Matthew Hilton, 'The Legacy of Luxury: Moralities of Consumption Since the 18th Century', *Journal of Consumer Culture* 4:1 (2004), pp. 101–23.
46. J. M. Keynes, *Essays in Persuasion* (1931; New York: Classic House Books, 2009), p. 197.

CHAPTER FIFTEEN

Early British Television: The Allure and Threat of America

KELLY BOYD

In May and June of 1951, the BBC Controller of Television Programmes, Cecil McGivern, travelled to Washington and New York to survey the way television worked in the US.[1] He spent time at the four existing networks (ABC, CBS, NBC and Dumont), talked to fellow broadcasters, trudged through studios, watched productions in progress and generally meditated on what American television had to teach his department, as well as highlighting the things the BBC were already doing well. On return, McGivern wrote an extensive memo (over 50 pages, typed, single-spaced) sharing his observations and analysis. Marked 'private and confidential', the memo was circulated widely to the upper echelons of BBC management, including the Director-General, for discussion. The memo provides a window into the impact of American network television on McGivern, who didn't pull any punches. A brief series of vignettes captured the vibrancy of the new medium in New York. There was the network executive who 'wistfully' desired to offer educational programmes – but was kept from doing so because they didn't 'make a dime'. There was the commercial for the deodorant that goes 'POOF!' and the overheard pitches, complaints and comments, some bullying, others comic, but all demonstrating the active engagement of both professionals and the public with the new medium. McGivern stressed the complexity of the industry: even the heads of networks were uncertain what would happen next. Most importantly, he rejected the opportunity to sneer at the way commercial imperatives dictated network schedules. His introduction closed on a ruminative note: 'in some important aspects [American TV] is superior to British Television and is worthy of considerable respect. In some ways, American TV makes us, I regret to say, look very like amateurs.'[2]

McGivern was not saying that American television had got everything right. He was deeply committed to establishing a dynamically creative 'British' system. Rather than genuflecting to American television, McGivern's account reflected his sense of what it meant to produce 'British television'. The BBC would treat television as a new and different art form, worthy of its role in reinforcing British national identity and culture. While McGivern's ideas of British culture resembled Victorian notions of placing a high value on education, hard work and restrained emotions, he reworked these characteristics to fit the age of austerity following World War II. In a post-war world where American global power seemed to know no bounds, BBC television carved a pathway that incorporated American products and ideas in ways that also reinforced British national identity. BBC executives welcomed a certain degree of American ideas and content. Nevertheless, they shared many of the fears of British cultural critics like Richard Hoggart that American culture posed a distinctive threat to a unified British identity. Transnational exchanges as well as a wariness of those exchanges shaped the technological and cultural history of the new medium in the post-war decades. This chapter explores the contested transatlantic context which influenced the BBC's history.[3]

The resumption and expansion of television broadcasting in Britain after 1945 was warmly greeted by the general population. Politicians, cultural critics and educators, however, viewed it as more problematic. Although the BBC was the first organization in the world to offer regularly scheduled, over-the-air transmissions in the late 1930s, by 1946 US broadcasters had launched their own services. In the decade before commercial television arrived in Britain in 1955, there was a complex relationship between transatlantic television broadcasters.[4] Both systems remained in flux in the 1940s and 1950s and their contexts were vastly different. American broadcasters were locked into a commercial framework where parent companies embraced the new medium and committed capital to their ventures. The challenge was to create a new commercial medium, discover how to develop programming and schedules, wrestle with rapidly evolving technologies, expand across a large continent and make sure no competitor got the upper hand.[5] The post-war BBC television division faced different problems. Like every other organization in Britain, the BBC operated in an age of austerity. Funding was limited to licence fees; its charter encountered frequent review; and finally, the BBC faced the constant question of whether commercial broadcasting would become available.[6] In addition, debates continued about the threat of American influence on British culture. One task for the returning television division was to reinforce British cultural institutions in its offerings, while at the same time profiting from exchanges with its equivalents across the Atlantic. The outcome suggests the extent to which the BBC absorbed, adapted and sometimes ignored American developments.

When the television service restarted in 1946, it had several things working in its favour. First, the BBC gained a great respect during the war years as a unifying influence for a country at war. It was a reliable source of news and support during the conflict, but it also deepened and reinforced the national culture it had defined since its foundation. Second was its experience of programme creation. The regularly scheduled daily shows of the late 1930s suggested what material worked best. Advances in technology could be incorporated immediately, while programme-makers could exploit their experience in wartime radio as well. Third, experiences garnered after 1939 meant that the BBC increasingly supplied programmes calculated to entertain a mass audience. The Forces Programme largely jettisoned the educational shows in favour of more light music, variety and comedy. At the war's end, this became the Light Programme and several of its producers, writers and executives moved directly to the television service.[7] The BBC also faced post-war austerity's greatest challenge: limited financial resources. The capital investment for transmitters and relays needed to make television available throughout England, Wales, Scotland and Northern Ireland was unobtainable immediately after the war, especially as television-viewing was seen as a leisure activity. Furthermore, money and materials were also unavailable to manufacturers to begin the mass production of television sets.[8] Finally, BBC managers were reluctant to expand the television service. Radio's success during the war years meant that it remained the top priority and the first order of business was to establish a third radio network.[9] Until the launch of commercial television in the mid-1950s, television remained a low priority and starved of investment.[10] A reorganization in 1949 demoted the television service.[11] Telecasting was limited to two to three hours daily, and there was little money to pay performers, writers, technicians or administrators. Nevertheless, there was a great deal of enthusiasm for how television programmes could be shaped and developed in the future.

From the beginning, television, like radio, was seen as a live medium.[12] Many shows were broadcast live from a studio, but there were as many outside broadcasts as possible, projecting the modern world straight to the home. Plays, concerts, popular singers, panel discussions, cookery, gardening and some short films were present from the resumption of transmission. Outside broadcasts were, unsurprisingly, the place where television was praised as particularly innovative.[13] The June 1946 launch was timed to broadcast the Victory Parade commemorating the first anniversary of the end of the war in Europe. Wimbledon tennis was shown the same year as well as cricket, rugby and the Lord Mayor's show. Almost everything, barring a few short film inserts, was transmitted live. This gave an immediacy to everything the viewer saw and it meant limited resources were not wasted on film stock, physical editing and the attendant activities these entailed.

The BBC had long-standing relationships with several American counterparts reinforced by personal ties to individuals. During the war, CBS war correspondent Edward R. Murrow used BBC studios for his broadcasts and often spoke on the BBC. After the war the relationship continued as Murrow was appointed Vice-President and Director of Public Affairs at CBS in 1946. He regularly exchanged programme notes and matters of interest with the BBC.[14] The frustrations he experienced with American commercial television are legendary, but in the context of the BBC serves to illustrate that on neither side of the Atlantic was television's shape preordained. The two structures emerged from a series of institutional arguments affected by radio traditions, the availability of investment (in the UK), the need to recoup that investment and generate profits (in the US), and cultural attitudes towards leisure. In the US, the emphasis on profit generation meant that daily broadcasting hours were long and programming ideas were in demand. Murrow urged others to cultivate links to the BBC to profit from their experience.

There was a steady flow of information across the Atlantic throughout these early years as each set of broadcasters moulded the form television would take for their own culture. George Moskovics, General Manager of WCBW (later to become WCBS) in New York, requested details about the BBC weekly 30-minute show *Picture Page*, noting its similarities to WCBW's *Saturday Evening Spotlight*. A stalwart of the pre-war schedule, *Picture Page* was revived immediately in 1946. Maurice Gorham, Head of the Television Service, responded with an extensive list of this magazine programme's guest list. They included Dominion and Colonial troops in town for the Victory Parade, American movie star Lizbeth Scott, a demonstration of the about-to-be-tested ejection seat for jet pilots, a South African journalist passing through who reported on a recent American prize fight, and the American Wightman Cup tennis team as well as outside broadcasts. He closed with a request for more information about *Saturday Evening Spotlight*.[15]

Driven by advertising and commercial considerations, American executives were especially concerned about viewers' likes and dislikes. American television pitched to the multiethnic urban audience of New York, and ultimately was dominated by its goal of reaching a mass viewership.[16] The BBC, on the other hand, retained its Reithian ethic – to entertain, enlighten and educate.[17] Rather than giving audiences what they wished to see, the balance of programmes would be what the BBC thought they ought to see. The list of who appeared on one day of *Picture Page* reinforced Britain's place as a world hub. The BBC welcomed troops, journalists and performers with additional material stressing Britain's technological advances.[18] In these early years the audience was a metropolitan one. The expense of purchasing a television meant the audience was perceived as middle-class, a segment of the population generally believed to support Reithian goals.[19] Yet there were other reasons for planning programmes that emphasized the pleasures of well-made plays, literary panel discussions or a peek at a new addition to the London Zoo. Through their programming choices, the BBC hoped to successfully resist the threat of Americanization, a regularly articulated fear of post-war elites. This was not a new fear, but one that had concerned the BBC since its foundation in the 1920s.[20]

Worries about American influence abroad had grown throughout the century as the US expanded its commercial presence around the world, but particularly in Europe.[21] This continued during World War II when the general population received its first mass exposure to Americans stationed in Britain.[22] Some Britons within broadcasting range of the American Armed Forces Radio Network sampled American radio culture without commercial interruption. Surveys, however, suggested that while audiences enjoyed American entertainers, home-grown artists were more popular.[23] Everywhere, American culture competed with other international influences.[24] Dick Hebdige reminds us that British society in the 1950s was attracted to European fashions and products as often as to American ones.[25] Italian fashion and motorbikes enthralled the adolescents of that era. Similarly, in his exploration of American advertising agencies in Britain and Germany, Stefan Schwarzkopf argues that the idea of Americanization ignores the extent to which the US was 'Europeanized' in the early twentieth century, particularly admiring many facets of British life, but also seeing it as the mother country. More importantly, American manufacturers wishing to sell in Europe had to pay attention to a transatlantic modernity that recognized the inherent attributes of European culture that enticed consumers to buy new goods.[26] This often meant playing down a product's American origin.

The post-war worries were a continuation of an elite distrust of American culture dating back to Matthew Arnold and gathering momentum in the inter-war writings of F. R. Leavis, George Orwell and most memorably articulated by Richard Hoggart in the 1950s.[27] Cultural elites at institutions like the BBC were torn between wishing to maintain what they perceived to be a common British culture – constructed in elevated terms as the appreciation of art, music and literature – and the recognition that many listeners enjoyed rather lighter fare. This culture was elite and often required a degree of education or familiarity that the bulk of the population did not have. Although the BBC tried to supply this education, by the early 1930s it was clear that many in the audience preferred jazz and dance music to opera and symphonies. In the face of competition from commercial continental broadcasters like Radio Luxembourg, schedules were reshaped to include lighter fare at times when more people would be likely to tune in.[28]

Importantly, there was a long history of British performers reworking American musical forms and translating them to appeal to British listeners.[29] BBC television continued this, often extending the appeal of an earlier mediated form as new ones emerged. British dance bands and popular performers from overseas dotted early television schedules and the likes of Henry Hall and Jack Payne helped to prolong their popularity into the 1950s.[30] As is well known, the BBC resisted rock 'n' roll, which instead found its audience through juke boxes in arcades, cafés and milk bars. American culture was almost by definition exuberant and by practice consumerist. Neither behaviour was encouraged in Britain in the late 1940s and early 1950s.[31] The BBC instead constructed a British national culture that valued self-control and thrift, making and promoting a culture of austerity.

This was the context for dealing with American cultural products in the post-war decade and the one faced by Cecil McGivern in 1950. McGivern had worked for the BBC from 1936 to 1945. He wrote and directed radio documentaries, but in 1945 he left to work as a scriptwriter for the Rank Organization. After contributing to the screenplays of David Lean's *Great Expectations* (1946) and Marc Allégret's *Blanche Fury* (1948), he returned to the BBC as Head of Television Programmes, becoming Controller of Television Programmes in 1950. McGivern was centrally concerned with developing, making and scheduling programming for the network, ranking second below the Director of Television in the BBC television hierarchy. He held this post for six key years that paralleled the founding of commercial television in Britain.[32] McGivern's leadership crucially established the underlying ideals for the rapidly expanding output in these years. His post-America-visit memo illustrates his underlying philosophy of what television might become.

Television had to highlight the Britishness of the medium while both exploring the new technology and learning from the successes and failures of its American cousin. For example, McGivern enviously noted the technical innovations that were quickly integrated into American productions and the willingness of cameramen and others to increase productivity. This flexibility contrasted with the rigidity he often experienced in London.[33] Yet McGivern preferred the BBC's use of on-screen announcers which he believed gave 'a humanity, a warmth and an intimacy' that was missing from American television, which filled all interstitial moments with advertising.[34] His assessment of the technical side of American television ended on a note of approbation, emphasizing that 'it was impossible not to be impressed by the efficiency, the flexibility and the speed of the Americans ... They enjoy their job and tackle it enthusiastically. They are also, of course, highly paid and well fed.'[35]

McGivern's initial impression was that American television was positive, accentuating the exciting nature of the programmes. He also noted that pressure on individual shows was lessened because other channels provided alternative options. Nevertheless, McGivern thought American shows included 'too much talking': 'Talking at you, selling you aprons, refrigerators, telling you about the Korean War ... giving you advice, telling you about themselves, about other people, telling you funny stories. There is far too much talking, and not nearly enough of showing you things, objects, dances, happenings.' But he also recognized that this was because 'American TV programmes are based on personalities'. While seeing the perils of personality-driven television, McGivern believed the BBC should develop more personalities than they already had but warned against too much talk.[36]

Individuals were already at the centre of cinema and radio.[37] The American film industry developed the star system early in the century and radio networks followed the same path. In Britain, the BBC had long employed individuals who deployed their personalities and knowledge to steer the audience through an evening's listening.[38] As was the case in music hall, television employed a master of ceremonies to introduce acts and smooth over the rough edges.[39] Whether focusing on continuity between programmes, contextualizing a foreign film, revealing new species on *Zoo Quest*, or chairing a discussion, personalities were at the centre of a successful evening's viewing. The Director General, Sir William Haley, agreed in a memo to the Programme Board: 'PERSONALITIES. TV must be built around personalities.' He noted that 'Film stars were built up and made for films.' They also made things cheaper, he continued, for 'If you build up personality you send down costs – chorus-girls, settings, designs are not needed to the same extent.' Of course, it was not cheap to develop a personality, but as Haley explained, 'Americans are prepared to keep on that person for an intensive period. Say twelve consecutive evenings. Therefore we must find our own artists and groom them only for TV.'[40] Furthermore, Haley argued that using 'personalities' was a frugal measure in the long run because it was a means to control talent.[41]

Another aspect of American television that McGivern enthused over was 'programme flexibility'. By this, he did not mean responding to technical challenges, but the way relaxed hosts like Kate Smith or Arthur Godfrey could turn from selling goods to interviewing atypical guests about serious matters.[42] McGivern witnessed Godfrey chair a discussion about the Korean Conflict with four undergraduates who 'gave their views pointedly and well'.[43] What impressed him most was that this 'was completely unrehearsed, and was excellent. Such an item was not lowered in dignity by its setting – the rest of the programme gained.' McGivern admired Godfrey's skills and believed it 'made our sharp division of programme categories seem over-rigid and stiff'. McGivern believed it would benefit the BBC to occasionally 'take this particular leaf out of the American book in all its categories'. Similarly, he praised the American ability to time their programmes consistently, which was an unresolved topic of debate within the television service.[44]

In terms of the quality of American television programmes and their lessons for the BBC, McGivern was very judicious, crediting the hard work of all involved. Interestingly, his visit was probably at the height of live television in the US. McGivern witnessed the production of *Your Show of Shows* with Sid Caesar, *Star Theatre* featuring Milton Berle and *Four Star Revue* with Jimmy Durante. All were performed and broadcast live in New York, but filmed for later transmission elsewhere as there was no direct link between East and West Coasts. He also watched *You Bet Your Life* with Groucho Marx, a new type of show that had transferred from radio. It was filmed live in Los Angeles using six cameras, edited together, then flown to New York for broadcast and depended only on Groucho's wit.[45] The last was, of course, a harbinger of the shift from live to pre-recorded American television. *I Love Lucy* debuted later that year, and in less than a decade the world McGivern outlined in his memo was gone.

On returning to England, McGivern admitted he found British television 'small, meagre', 'dull'. Although he 'switched off in dismay', McGivern did not despair but thought the BBC could 'do better'. Musing on the 'big difference between the two operations', he wrote that 'We think all the time ... of the television medium, how it is different from radio, from the theatre, from films. We try all the time to produce *television* programmes. We are purists. Consequently, we have become slow, extravagant in some ways, over-conscious of the art potentially in the medium.' In contrast, 'The

Americans think of television as a piece of mechanics and treat it with the familiarity they treat the telephone. We regard it as a sculptor regards his clay. The correct answer is probably – as often – a compromise.'[46]

McGivern's compromise, however, was not to make BBC television more like its American counterpart. Each had different aims and each culture valorized different things. BBC television managers did not reject American work practices. Whether emphasizing efficiency or the constant evolution in search of large audiences, these transcended nationality. Rather, they perceived a danger within the far more slippery ideas of quality and taste. Seeing themselves as guardians of 'quality', the Programme Board constantly discussed matters of taste. They rejected proposals for topics that did not seem to reach a certain standard and were especially critical of programmes that failed to achieve this goal. The Programme Board eagerly examined reports from the BBC's Audience Research Unit, congratulating themselves on the good taste of the viewers who preferred the best shows.[47] Notions of taste reinforced ideas of Britain as a respectable, ordered nation that rejected the 'shiny barbarism' of America, in Hoggart's memorable phrase.[48]

Yet American cultural products were incorporated into early television schedules. During the war there was a brief period when BBC radio services reversed their long-standing policy of minimizing if not excluding American popular culture.[49] US radio networks generously provided popular American programmes featuring stars like Jack Benny and Bob Hope at little or no cost. These were popular and also filled gaps in BBC schedules as performers and programme makers were called up for service. By 1944 – with the end of the war in sight – the policy was reversed. When Jack Benny's agent offered his latest radio series, edited, free of commercial advertisements and at no cost to the BBC in 1945, he was rebuffed.[50] Debates about the inclusion of American material for radio that surged after the end of the war influenced television managers. Most had been party to these discussions as part of radio's senior management.[51] McGivern's desire was to create the best programmes possible for a British audience, striving for excellence. Television was a unique art form that deserved the care given to any cultural production.

Some 'quality' American content was shown from 1947 with BBC productions of respected American playwrights like Eugene O'Neill or Elmer Rice, and from 1948 children could enjoy an increasing number of western films.[52] Until 1951, however, very little other American content was available.[53] Film distributors were wary of television and only a few independents were willing to make their inventory available. From 1951 there was a shift. In the US the filmed series became the norm. By 1954 the

BBC began to include a few American series on a weekly basis. Interestingly, these were by and large series made by independent producers in the US, not for network television, but for syndication outside primetime hours.[54]

With the launch of commercial television imminent, the BBC increased its American offerings including episodes from ongoing American drama anthologies (although often featuring a British star) and, when possible, something from Edward R. Murrow. Several *See It Now* programmes were broadcast, including Murrow's condemnation of Senator Joseph McCarthy and the latter's reply. The BBC wished to include more of Murrow's shows, the files indicate, had funds been available. Additionally, the BBC licensed and adapted several panel shows that were popular in the US. For example, *What's My Line?* launched in 1951, ran for over a decade, making Gilbert Harding a celebrity. *Animal, Vegetable, Mineral* elevated archaeologist Sir Mortimer Wheeler to TV Personality of the Year in 1954.[55] The latter, in particular, neatly integrated entertainment with information, inspiring a generation of archaeologists. These were also the prototypes of the amusing panel show that would become a mainstay of BBC programming to the present day.[56] These programmes provided a venue for clever interaction between witty members of the educated elite. In their British iteration they invoked Boxing Day parlour games or scintillating dinner parties, rejecting the earnestness of the American originals.[57]

In his six years as Controller of Television Programmes, McGivern was dedicated to delivering a quality service to the increasing numbers of television viewers. Swirling around him were the debates about commercial television, the perils it posed and the degradation of American culture it would inject into Britain. American and British broadcasting had traditionally utilized each other to highlight the perils they wished to avoid.[58] This 'historic dualism' allowed them to sketch a Manichean vision of the broadcasting terrain, with one espousing quality over chaos and the other independence from the state in order to pursue the profit merited in a capitalist society. The early BBC television service successfully navigated this peril, leaving itself in a position to continue to focus on the maintenance and strengthening of British culture when its commercial rival launched. And through its response to the challenge of Americanization it helped set the terms for its rival as well. The debate did not end with the coming of independent television, rather it intensified.

McGivern, however, was effectively demoted in 1956, and after a series of indignities eventually resigned in 1961. His successors were far more focused on increasing viewer numbers than he had been, but McGivern's legacy was often brought up. Norman Collins, who preceded McGivern at the BBC (but subsequently moved on to be a key player in commercial television), invoked his successor to challenge a comment made in the *Encyclopaedia Britannica Book of the Year for 1960* that 'during the year BBC and ITV output became increasingly difficult to distinguish'. Although he recognized that the BBC had changed since the launch of commercial television, Collins noted that 'throughout the whole of the BBC programme structure can be seen the legacy of those high artistic standards nurtured over the years by Mr Cecil McGivern'. In the face of competition, the BBC 'continued to put such energy, resource and expenditure into their major documentary and other informative programmes'.[59] A decade later, during another period of criticism, two of the men newly appointed to top jobs at the BBC mentioned McGivern's teachings as keys to their own points of view. Bryan Cowgill (Controller of BBC1) stressed the importance of 'editorial judgment (by which I suppose you could say *value* judgment and *independence*)', while Aubrey Singer (Controller of BBC2) zeroed in on McGivern's command to 'Remember we're a social organization, more concerned with serving society than with serving ourselves.'[60] The society served was Britain, and, increasingly, the rest of the world, as BBC programmes swiftly became amongst the most widely viewed across the globe.

Singer commissioned such prestigious programmes as *Civilisation* with Sir Kenneth Clark (1969) and *The Ascent of Man* with Jacob Bronowski (1973) while at the BBC. These American-funded co-productions marked a new phase in the 'special relationship'.[61] The productions emphasized quality, employing experts to guide viewers through complex ideas, accompanied by stunning visual images. They also helped establish the central role Britain continued to play in disseminating culture around the world. Perhaps the best evidence of this was another series commissioned by Singer at the suggestion of *Civilisation*'s producer, Michael Gill. In 1972, *America: A Personal History of the United States* debuted to critical praise on both sides of the Atlantic.[62] Its presenter, Alistair Cooke, spent much of his career as a journalist contributing to the BBC through what eventually became known as his weekly radio programme, *Letter from America* (1946–2004). Cooke's knowledge of America was deep. He first arrived in 1932 on a Commonwealth Fund fellowship and eventually settled in the US. *America* was, however, a thoroughly British cultural production and the first television series to explore the history of the US. It is the best evidence that McGivern's emphasis on television as an art form, and his dedication to quality and taste continued to animate programme makers at the BBC long after his departure. The emphasis on value and taste eventually allowed the BBC to export its interpretation of American history not just to the US, but around the world. Rather than a parochial outlook, the BBC championed engagement with television and employed it to situate Britain at the centre of Anglophone culture worldwide.

NOTES

1. McGivern Report, 20 June 1951. British Broadcasting Corporation Written Archive Centre (hereafter WAC) T8/88/2 TV Foreign Countries: USA Television Development; File 2 (1951–2) (hereafter McGivern). My thanks to Mark Crowley, Sandra Dawson, Rohan McWilliam and Erika Rappaport for their thoughtful comments. I would also like to acknowledge the help given to me at the BBC Written Archives Centre by their archivists, particularly Erin O'Neill, who guided me through the available documents there.
2. McGivern, p. 2.
3. American television did not face an influx of television from around the world. Until the establishment of the Public Broadcasting Network in 1970 acquisition of foreign-produced programmes was rare. The exceptions were series like *The Adventures of Robin Hood* (ITV 1955–9), which was syndicated by CBS, but not shown across the network. ABC did broadcast several series of *The Avengers* (ITV/Thames, 1961–9) in a primetime slot, but this was a very rare example of an American network venturing outside of Hollywood for its programming. *The Saint* (1962–9) was also syndicated and ran as a summer replacement on NBC. See James Chapman, *Saints and Avengers: British Adventure Series of the 1960s* (London: I. B. Tauris, 2002).
4. Erik Barnouw, *Tube of Plenty: The Evolution of American Television* (New York: Oxford University Press, 1975); James Baughman, *Same Time Same Station: Creating American Television, 1948–1961*, Baltimore, NJ: Johns Hopkins University Press, 2007).
5. William Boddy, *Fifties Television: The Industry and Its Critics* (Urbana, IL: University of Illinois Press, 1990), pp. 15–65.
6. The early BBC struggled to establish autonomy under the threat of government interference. See Asa Briggs, *The History of Broadcasting in the United Kingdom*, 5 vols (Oxford: Oxford University Press, 1961–5); Paddy Scannell and David Cardiff, 'Serving the Nation: Public Service Broadcasting before the War', in *Popular Culture: Past and Present*, eds Bernard Waites, Tony Bennett and Graham Martin (London: Croom Helm, 1981), pp. 166–88.
7. David Cardiff and Paddy Scannell, '"Good luck war workers!": Class, Politics and Entertainment in Wartime Broadcasting', in *Popular Culture and Social Relations*, eds Tony Bennett, Colin Mercer and Janet Woollacott (Milton Keynes: Open University Press, 1986), pp. 93–116.
8. Jack Williams, *Entertaining the Nation: A Social History of British Television* (London: Sutton, 2004), pp. 45–6.
9. Briggs, *History of Broadcasting*, Vol. 4, pp. 60–9, 192–4.
10. The expansion in order to televise the coronation in 1953 also forced more investment, which the BBC took advantage of: Briggs, *History of Broadcasting*, Vol. 4, pp. 420–35.

11. Briggs, *History of Broadcasting*, Vol. 4, p. 461.
12. Rob Turnock, *Television and Consumer Society: Britain and the Transformation of Modernity* (London: I. B. Tauris, 2007), pp. 75–106. Briggs quotes Director of Television George Barnes as stating that 78 per cent of its broadcasts in 1954 were live, *History of Broadcasting*. Vol. 4, p. 897.
13. Briggs, *History of Broadcasting*, Vol. 4, pp. 250–2.
14. WAC T8/74/1 TV Foreign Countries/USA/Columbia Broadcasting System/File 1 (1936–47).
15. Letter from Maurice Gorham, Head of the Television Service, to George Moskovic, Commercial Manager, WCBW, 18 June 1946 (WAC T8/74/1 TV Foreign Countries/USA/Columbia Broadcasting System/File 1 (1936–47).
16. Initially the US audience was chiefly located in a few large urban areas. More markets were served by the early 1950s but regulatory issues meant much of the country only slowly gained access. Denver was the last major metropolitan area to begin broadcasting in 1958. See Barnouw, *Tube of Plenty*.
17. Sir John Reith was the Corporation's first director general and his emphasis on education, information and entertainment (in that order) have informed the BBC since its foundation.
18. The segment on the prototype ejector seat is notable as it would not be tested in flight for another month. Although there had been some work in this field before, the model developed by Sir James Martin at Martin-Baker led to their being one of the leading manufacturers of the technology.
19. Audience research figures showed that television ownership was a bit more complex. See Chris Hand, 'The Advent of ITV and Television in Lower Income Households: Correlation or Causation?' *Journal of British Cinema and Television* 4 (2007), pp. 67–79 and Deborah Chambers, 'The Material Form of the Television Set', *Media History* 17:4 (2011), pp. 359–75.
20. Briggs, *History of Broadcasting*; Paddy Scannell and David Cardiff, *A Social History of British Broadcasting, Volume 1: 1922–1939 Serving the Nation* (Oxford: Oxford University Press, 1991); Valeria Camporesi, *Mass Culture and National Traditions: The BBC and American Broadcasting, 1922–1954* (Florence: European University Institute, 1990).
21. Victoria de Grazia, *Irresistible Empire: America's Advance Through Twentieth-Century Europe* (Cambridge, MA: The Belknap Press of Harvard University, 2005). In Britain the Americanization debate often revolved around cinema. See, for example, Mark Glancy, 'Temporary American Citizens? British Audiences, Hollywood Films and the Threat of Americanization in the 1920s', *Historical Journal of Film Radio and Television* 26 4 (2006), pp. 464–84; and Paul Swann, *The Hollywood Feature Film in Postwar Britain* (London: Croom Helm, 1987).
22. David Reynolds, *Rich Relations: The American Occupation of Britain, 1942–45* (London: HarperCollins, 1995); Sonya Rose, *Which People's War?: National Identity and Citizenship in Britain, 1939–1945* (Oxford: Oxford University Press, 2003).

23. Camporesi, *Mass Culture and National Traditions*, pp. 185–6.
24. Rob Kroes, Robert W. Rydell and D. F. J. Bosscher, eds, 'Introduction', *Cultural Transmissions and Receptions: American Mass Culture in Europe* (Amsterdam: VU University Press, 1993); Richard Pells, *Not Like Us: How Europeans Have Loved, Hated, and Transformed American Culture since World War II* (New York: Basic Books, 1998); de Grazia, *Irresistible Empire*.
25. Dick Hebdige, 'Towards a Cartography of Taste', *Block* 4 (1981); reprinted in his *Hiding in the Light: On Images and Things* (London: Comedia, 1988), pp. 45–76.
26. See de Grazia, *Irresistible Empire*; James Obelkovich, 'Americanisation in British Consumer Markets, 1950–2000', in *Americanisation in 20th-Century Europe: Business, Culture, Politics*, eds Matthias Kipping and Nick Tiratsoo (Lille: Centre de Recherche sur l'Histoire de l'Europe du Nord-Ouest, n.d. (2001)), pp. 61–74; Stefan Schwarzkopf, 'Who Said "Americanization"? The Case of Twentieth-Century Advertising from a British Perspective', in *Decentering America*, ed. Jessica Gienow-Hecht (New York: Berghahn Books, 2007), pp. 23–72.
27. For a concise introduction see Chris Waters, 'Beyond "Americanization": Rethinking Anglo-American Cultural Exchange between the Wars', *Cultural and Social History* 4:4 (2007), pp. 451–9.
28. D. L. LeMahieu, *A Culture for Democracy: Mass Communications and the Cultivated Mind in Britain Between the Wars* (Oxford: Clarendon Press, 1988).
29. John Baxendale, '"… into Another Kind of Life in Which Anything Might Happen …": Popular Music and Late Modernity, 1910–1930', *Popular Music* 14:2 (1995), pp. 137–54; Peter Bailey, 'Fats Waller Meets Harry Champion: Americanization, National Identity and Sexual Politics in Inter-War British Music Hall', *Cultural and Social History* 4:4 (2007), pp. 495–509; James J. Nott, 'Contesting Popular Dancing and Dance Music in Britain During the 1920s', *Cultural and Social History* 10:3 (2013), pp. 439–56. See also James J. Nott, *Music for the People: Popular Music and Dance in Interwar Britain* (Oxford: Oxford University Press, 2002).
30. Joe Moran, *Armchair Nation: An Intimate History of Britain in Front of the TV* (London: Profile Books, 2013), pp. 99–100.
31. Adrian Horn, *Juke Box Britain: Americanisation and Youth Culture, 1945–60* (Manchester: Manchester University Press, 2009), p. 41; Michelle Jones, 'Design and the Domestic Persuader: Television and the British Broadcasting Corporation's Promotion of Post-war "Good Design"', *Journal of Design History* 16:4 (2003), pp. 307–18.
32. Briggs, *History of Broadcasting*, Vol. 4, pp. 205–6.
33. McGivern, p. 10. See also WAC TV Policy T16/154/2. Memo dated 20 July 1949.
34. McGivern, p. 10.
35. McGivern, p. 11.

36. The BBC was initially ambivalent about the development of personalities. Briggs, *History of Broadcasting*, Vol. 4, p. 284. Also see Su Holmes, '"Whoever Heard of Anyone Being a Screaming Success for Doing Nothing?" "Sabrina", the BBC and Television Fame in the 1950s', *Media History* 17:1 (2011), pp. 33–48.

37. Richard Dyer, *Stars* (London: BFI, 1979); Christine Gledhill, ed., *Stardom: Industry of Desire* (London: Routledge, 1991).

38. On the role of announcers in radio, see Simon Frith, 'The Pleasures of the Hearth: The Making of BBC Light Entertainment', in *Formations of Pleasure* (London: Routledge and Kegan Paul, 1983), pp. 107–9; and Scannell and Cardiff, 'Serving the Nation', p. 182.

39. John Langer, 'Television's "Personality System"', *Media, Culture and Society* 4:4 (1981), pp. 351–65.

40. Programme Board Meeting 20 (28 June 1951). Addenda headed 'D.G.'s comment at Programme Board, 28th June 1951' (WAC TV Policy T16/105/1). Capitalization and punctuation as in the original.

41. The BBC also wanted to sustain the development of British talent in what they recognized to be the rise of American performers controlled from outside the UK. See Briggs, *History of Broadcasting*, Vol. 2, pp. 87–9; Frith, 'Pleasures of the Hearth', pp. 118–19; and Scannell and Cardiff, 'Serving the Nation', pp. 178–9.

42. Susan Murray, 'Our Man Godfrey: Arthur Godfrey and the Selling of Stardom in Early Television', *Television & New Media* 2:3 (2001), pp. 187–204. Marsha F. Cassidy, *What Women Watched; Daytime Television in the 1950s* (Austin, TX: University of Texas Press, 2005), pp. 49–74.

43. McGivern, p. 17.

44. Discussions of time overruns dot the minutes of Programme Board meetings: see for example, TV Policy; Meetings; Programme Board WAC T16/105/2 File 1B 1952 (2nd of 2 files).

45. McGivern, p. 24.

46. McGivern, p. 54. Emphasis in the original.

47. Minuted Programme Board Meeting 49 (14 February 1952) Lime Grove, Item 442: Viewer Research Figures: 'It was encouraging that highest appreciation figures were for the more intelligent performances.' These included 'Noah Gives Thanks', a fantasy by Eric Crozier; 'Ballet for Beginners: Les Sylphides'; 'Music for You'; *Science Newsreel*; and an outside broadcast: 'Other People's Jobs: The Silica Screen' (WAC TV Policy T16/105/2 TV Policy Meetings: Programme Board).

48. Richard Hoggart, *The Uses of Literacy* (London: Chatto and Windus, 1957), p. 160.

49. Michele Hilmes, 'Front Line Family: "Women's Culture" Comes to the BBC', *Media, Culture and Society* 29:1 (2007), pp. 5–29.

50. Camporesi, *Mass Culture and National Traditions*, p. 171.

51. Norman Collins joined the BBC in 1935; after the war he was appointed Controller of the Light Programme, the network that had served as the Forces

Network during the conflict. In 1947, he became Controller of Television, succeeding Maurice Gorham, who, after a long career at the BBC, briefly got television up and running after the war. Cecil Madden had been television's first programme organizer and returned to the job in 1946.

52. Kelly Boyd, 'The Western and British Identity on British Television in the 1950s', in *Leisure and Cultural Conflict in Twentieth-Century Britain*, ed. Brett Bebber (Manchester: Manchester University Press, 2012), pp. 109–28.

53. Kerry Segrave, *American Television Abroad: Hollywood's Attempt to Dominate World Television* (Jefferson, NC: McFarland, 1998).

54. Kelly Boyd, 'Cowboys, Comedy and Crime: American Programmes on BBC Television, 1946–1955', *Media History* 17:3 (2011), pp. 233–51.

55. Andy Medhurst, 'Every Wart and Pustule: Gilbert Harding and Television Stardom', in *Popular Television in Britain: Studies in Cultural History*, ed. John Corner (London: BFI, 1991), pp. 60–74.

56. The best example today is *QI* (2003–present).

57. Su Holmes, '"The Question is – Is It All Worth Knowing?" The Cultural Circulation of the Early British Quiz Show', *Media, Culture and Society* 29:1 (2007), pp. 53–74, explores the wider cultural debates over the game show.

58. From the birth of radio, the BBC and the American networks had used each other to illustrate what they did not wish to become; this continued with the arrival of television. See Michele Hilmes, 'British Quality, American Chaos: Historical Dualisms and What They Leave Out', *The Radio Journal: International Studies in Broadcast and Audio Media* 1:1 (2003), pp. 13–27. This is more fully developed in Michele Hilmes, *Network Nations: A Transnational History of British and American Broadcasting* (London: Routledge, 2012).

59. Norman Collins, 'Like – But Oh How Different!', *The Times*, 20 November 1961, p. iv. It was probably Collins, identified only as N.C., who contributed an addenda to McGivern's obituary two years later. Recalling his subject's dedication, he stressed McGivern's emphasis on 'values' and principles, but particularly the way people were 'immediately invigorated by McGivern's deep and underlying sense of moral responsibility for the job in hand'. See 'Mr Cecil McGivern', *The Times*, 4 February 1963, p. 14. Malcolm Muggeridge's similar obituarial addenda echoed this, recalling 'He believed utterly, perhaps excessively in the artistic and instructional possibilities of television, and dedicated all his time and energy to it', *The Times*, 6 February 1963, p. 15.

60. Willard De'Ath, 'The New TV Toppers', *The Times*, 7 July 1974, pp. 46[S]–7[S]. Italics in the original.

61. Hilmes, *Network Nations*, pp. 291–7.

62. Alistair Cooke, *Alistair Cooke's America*, revised edn. (London: BBC Books, 2003 (1973)).

SELECT BIBLIOGRAPHY

Abrams, Mark. *The Teenage Consumer*. London: London Press Exchange, 1959.
—*The Teenage Consumer Part II*. London: London Press Exchange, 1961.
Addison, Paul. *The Road to 1945: British Politics and the Second World War*. London: Cape, 1975.
Aldridge, Alan. 'The Construction of Rational Consumption in *Which?* Magazine: The More Blobs the Better', *Sociology* 28 (1994), 899–912.
Alexander, Andrew. 'Format Development and Retail Change: Supermarket Retailing and the London Co-operative Society', *Business History* 50:4 (2008), 489–508.
Andrews, Maggie and Mary M. Talbot, eds. *All the World and Her Husband: Women in Twentieth-Century Consumer Culture*. London: Cassell, 2000.
Anthony, Scott. *Public Relations and the Making of Modern Britain: Stephen Tallents and the Birth of a Progressive Media Profession*. Manchester: Manchester University Press, 2012.
Appadurai, Arjun. 'Introduction: Commodities and the Politics of Value'. In *The Social Life of Things: Commodities in Cultural Perspective*. Edited by Arjun Appadurai. Cambridge: Cambridge University Press, 1988.
Bailey, Peter. *Leisure and Class in Victorian England: Rational Recreation and the Contest for Control 1830–1885*. London: Methuen, 1987.
—'Jazz at the Spirella – Coming of Age in 1950s Coventry'. In *Moments of Modernity? Reconstructing Britain 1945–64*. Edited by Becky E. Conekin, Frank Mort and Chris Waters. London: Rivers Oram Press, 1998.
—'Fats Waller Meets Harry Champion: Americanization, National Identity and Sexual Politics in Inter-War British Music Hall', *Cultural and Social History* 4:4 (2007), 495–509.
Balnave, Nikola and Greg Patmore. 'The Politics of Consumption and Co-Operation: An Overview', *Labour History* 91 (2006), 1–12.
—'The Politics of Consumption and Labour History', *Labour History* 100 (2011): 145–66.

Barnouw, Erik. *Tube of Plenty: The Evolution of American Television*. New York: Oxford University Press, 1975.
Barr, Andrew. *Drink: A Social History*. London: Pimlico, 1998.
Baudrillard, Jean. *The Consumer Society: Myths and Structures*. Translated by Chris Turner. London: Sage, 2004.
Baxendale, John. *Priestley's England: J. B. Priestley and English Culture*. Manchester: Manchester University Press, 2007.
Bean, Charles and Nicholas Crafts. 'British Economic Growth since 1945: Relative Economic Decline ... and Renaissance?' In *Economic Growth in Europe since 1945*, edited by Nicholas Crafts and Gianni Toniolo. Cambridge: Cambridge University Press, 1996.
Beaujot, Ariel. *Victorian Fashion Accessories*. London: Berg, 2012.
Beaven, Brad. *Leisure, Citizenship and Working-Class Men in Britain, 1850–1945*. Manchester: Manchester University Press, 2009.
Bebber, Brett. *Violence and Racism in Football: Politics and Cultural Conflict in British Society, 1968–98*. London: Pickering & Chatto, 2012.
Beers, Laura. *Your Britain: Media and the Making of the Labour Party*. Cambridge, MA: Harvard University Press, 2010.
Belich, James. *Replenishing the Earth: The Settler Revolution and the Rise of the Anglo-World, 1783–1939*. Oxford: Oxford University Press, 2009.
Belisle, Donica. *Retail Nation: Department Stores and the Making of Modern Canada*. Vancouver: University of British Columbia Press, 2011.
Bengry, Justin. 'Courting the Pink Pound: *Men Only* and the Queer Consumer, 1935–39', *History Workshop Journal* 68 (2009), 122–48.
—'Peacock Revolution: Mainstreaming Queer Styles in Post-War Britain, 1945–1967', *Socialist History* 36 (2010, 55–68.
Benson, John. *The Rise of Consumer Society in Britain, 1880–1980*. Harlow: Longman, 1994.
Benson, John and Laura Ugolini. *A Nation of Shopkeepers: Five Centuries of British Retailing*. New York: I. B. Tauris, 2003.
Berg, Maxine. *Luxury and Pleasure in Eighteenth-Century Britain*. Oxford: Oxford University Press, 2005.
Bermingham, Ann and John Brewer, eds. *The Consumption of Culture, 1600–1800: Image, Object, Text*. London and New York: Routledge, 1995.
Bingham, Adrian. *Gender, Modernity, and the Popular Press in Inter-War Britain*. Oxford: Oxford University Press, 2004.
—*Family Newspapers? Sex, Private Life, and the British Popular Press, 1918–1978*. Oxford: Oxford University Press, 2009.
Birchall, Johnston. *Co-op: The People's Business*. Manchester: Manchester University Press, 1994.
Black, Lawrence. *The Political Culture of the Left in Affluent Britain, 1951–64: Old Labour, New Britain?* Basingstoke: Palgrave Macmillan, 2003.
—*Redefining British Politics: Culture, Consumerism and Participation, 1954–70*. Basingstoke: Palgrave Macmillan, 2010.
Black, Lawrence and Hugh Pemberton, eds. *An Affluent Society: Britain's Post-War 'Golden Age' Revisited*. London: Aldershot, 2004.
Black, Lawrence and Nicole Robertson, eds. *Consumerism and the Co-Operative Movement in Modern British History: Taking Stock*. Manchester: Manchester University Press, 2009.

Bocock, Robert. *Consumption*. London: Routledge, 1993.
Boddy, William. *Fifties Television: The Industry and Its Critics*. Urbana, IL: University of Illinois Press, 1990.
Boltho, Andrea. 'Reconstruction after Two World Wars – Why the Differences?', *Journal of European Economic History* 30 (2001), 429–56.
Bourke, Joanna. 'The Great Male Renunciation: Men's Dress Reform in Interwar Britain', *Journal of Design History* 9 (1996), 23–33.
Bowden, Sue and Avner Offer. 'Household Appliances and the Use of Time: The United States and Britain Since the 1920s', *Economic History Review* 47:4 (1994), 725–48.
Bowlby, Rachel. *Just Looking: Consumer Culture in Dreiser, Gissing and Zola*. London: Methuen, 1985.
Boyce, David. 'Coded Desire in 1920's Advertising', *The Gay and Lesbian Review* 7:1 (2000), 26–30.
Boyd, Kelly, *Manliness and the Boys' Story Paper in Britain, 1855–1940*. London: Palgrave Macmillan, 2003.
—'The Western and British Identity on British Television in the 1950s'. In *Leisure and Cultural Conflict in Twentieth-Century Britain*, edited by Brett Bebber. Manchester: Manchester University Press, 2012.
Bradley, Kate. *Poverty, Philanthropy and the State: Charities and the Working Classes in London. 1918–1979*. Manchester: Manchester University Press, 2009.
Brady, Sean. *Masculinity and Male Homosexuality in Britain, 1861–1913*. Basingstoke: Palgrave Macmillan, 2005.
Breen, Timothy H. *The Marketplace of Revolution: How Consumer Politics Shaped American Independence*. Oxford: Oxford University Press, 2004.
Breward, Christopher. *The Culture of Fashion: A New History of Fashionable Dress*. Manchester: Manchester University Press, 1995.
—*The Hidden Consumer: Masculinities, Fashion, and City Life, 1860–1914*. Manchester: Manchester University Press, 1999.
Brewer, John and Roy Porter, eds. *Consumption and the World of Goods*. London: Routledge, 1993.
Brewer, John and Frank Trentmann, eds. *Consuming Cultures: Global Perspectives: Historical Trajectories, Transnational Exchanges*. Oxford: Berg, 2006.
Briggs, Asa. *The History of Broadcasting in the United Kingdom* (5 Vols). Oxford: Oxford University Press, 1961–95.
—*Victorian Things*. Chicago, IL: University of Chicago Press, 1989.
Burke, Timothy. *Lifebuoy Men, Lux Women: Commodification, Consumption and Cleanliness in Modern Zimbabwe*. Durham, NC: Duke University Press, 1996.
Burnett, John. *Liquid Pleasures: A Social History of Drinks in Modern Britain*. London: Routledge, 1999.
Buzzard, James. 'Mass Observation, Modernism, and Autoethnography', *Modernism/Modernity* 4 (1997), 93–122.
Cairncross, Alec. *Years of Recovery: British Economic Policy 1945–51*. London: Methuen, 1985.
Campbell, Colin. *The Romantic Ethic and the Spirit of Modern Consumerism*. Oxford: Blackwell, 1987.
Camporesi, Valeria. *Mass Culture and National Traditions: The BBC and American Broadcasting, 1922–1954*. Florence: European University Institute, 1990.

Carden-Coyne, Ana. *Reconstructing the Body: Classicism, Modernism, and the First World War*. Oxford: Oxford University Press, 2009.

Carter, Erica. *How German Is She? Postwar West German Reconstruction and the Consuming Woman*. Ann Arbor, MI: University of Michigan Press, 1997.

Cassidy, Marsha F. *What Women Watched: Daytime Television in the 1950s*. Austin, TX: University of Texas Press, 2005.

Casson, Mark and Lopes, Teresa da Silva. 'Imitation, Brand Protection and Globalization of British Business', *Business History Review* 86:2 (2012), 287–310.

Chambers, Deborah. 'The Material Form of the Television Set', *Media History* 17:4 (2011), 359–75.

Chapman, Tony and Jenny Hockey. 'The Ideal Home as it is Imagined and as it is Lived'. In *Ideal Homes? Social Change and Domestic Life*, edited by Tony Chapman and Jenny Hockey. London: Routledge, 1999.

Chasin, Alexandra. *Selling Out: The Gay and Lesbian Movement Goes to Market*. Basingstoke: Palgrave, 2000.

Chatterjee, Piya. *A Time for Tea: Women, Labor and Post/Colonial Politics on an Indian Plantation*. Durham, NH: Duke University Press, 2001.

Church, Roy. 'Advertising Consumer Goods in Nineteenth-Century Britain: Reinterpretations', *Economic History Review* 53:4 (2000), 621–45.

Clark, Gracia. *'Onions are my Husband': Survival and Accumulation by West African Market Women*. Chicago, IL: University of Chicago Press, 1994.

Clarke, B. *From Grub Street to Fleet Street: An Illustrated History of English Newspapers to 1899*. Aldershot: Ashgate, 2004.

Cocks, H. G. *Nameless Offences: Homosexual Desire in the Nineteenth Century*. London: I. B. Tauris, 2003.

—*Classified: The Secret History of the Personal Column*. London: Arrow Books, 2009.

Cohen, Deborah. *Household Gods: The British and their Possessions*. New Haven, CT: Yale University Press, 2006.

Cohen, Lizabeth. *A Consumer's Republic: The Politics of Mass Consumption in Postwar America*. New York: Knopf, 2003.

Cohen, Stanley. *Folk Devils and Moral Panics: The Creation of the Mods and Rockers*. Oxford: Basil Blackwell, 1990.

Cole, Shaun. *'Don We Now Our Gay Apparel': Gay Men's Dress in the Twentieth Century*. Oxford: Berg, 2000.

Collins, Robert M. *The Business Response to Keynes, 1929–1964*. New York: Columbia University Press, 1981.

Comaroff, John L. and Jean Comaroff. *Of Revelation and Revolution: Christianity, Colonialism, and Consciousness in South Africa*, 2 Vols. Chicago, IL: Chicago University Press, 1991.

Conekin, Becky E. *The Autobiography of a Nation: The 1951 Festival of Britain*. Manchester: Manchester University Press, 2003.

—*Lee Miller in Fashion*. New York: Monacelli, 2013.

Constantine, Stephen. '"Bringing the Empire Alive": The Empire Marketing Board and Imperial Propaganda, 1926–33'. In *Imperialism and Popular Culture*, edited by John M. MacKenzie. Manchester: Manchester University Press, 1986.

Cook, Chris and John Stevenson. *The Slump: Society and Politics during the Depression*. London: Jonathan Cape, 1977.

Cook, Matt. *London and the Culture of Homosexuality, 1885–1914*. Cambridge: Cambridge University Press, 2003.

Coopey, Richard, Sean O'Connell and Dilwyn Porter. *Mail Order Retailing in Britain: A Business and Social History*. Oxford: Oxford University Press, 2005.

Corrigan, Peter. *The Sociology of Consumption: An Introduction*. London: Sage, 1997.

Cowan, Brian William, *The Social Life of Coffee: The Emergence of the British Coffee House*. New Haven, CT: Yale University Press, 2005.

Crary, Jonathan. *Suspensions of Perception: Attention, Spectacle and Modern Culture*. Cambridge, MA: MIT Press, 2001.

Crawford, Robert. *But Wait, There's More! A History of Australian Advertising, 1900–2000*. Melbourne: Melbourne University Press, 2008.

Crossick, Geoffrey and Serge Jaumain, eds. *Cathedrals of Consumption: The European Department Store 1850–1939*. Brookfield, VT: Ashgate, 1999.

Cunningham, Hugh. *Leisure in the Industrial Revolution, c. 1780–c. 1880*. London: Croom Helm, 1980.

Cutlip, Scott M. *The Unseen Power: Public Relations, A History*. New York: Routledge, 1994.

D'Emilio, John. 'Capitalism and Gay Identity'. In *The Powers of Desire: The Politics of Sexuality*, edited by Ann Snitow, Christine Stansell and Sharon Thompson. New York: Monthly Review Press, 1983.

Daly, Suzanne. *The Empire Inside: Indian Commodities in Victorian Domestic Novels*. Ann Arbor, MI: University of Michigan Press, 2011.

Daunton, Martin and Matthew Hilton, eds. *The Politics of Consumption: Material Culture and Citizenship in Europe and America*. Oxford: Berg, 2001.

Dauvergne, Peter. *The Shadows of Consumption: Consequences for the Global Environment*. Cambridge, MA: MIT Press, 2010.

Davidoff, Leonore and Catherine Hall. *Family Fortunes: Men and Women of the English Middle Class, 1780–1850*. Chicago, IL: University of Chicago Press, 1987.

Davies, Andrew. *Leisure, Gender, and Poverty: Working Class Culture in Manchester and Salford 1900–1939*. Buckingham: Open University Press, 1992.

Dawson, Sandra Trudgen. *Holiday Camps in Twentieth-Century Britain: Packaging Pleasure*. Manchester: Manchester University Press, 2011.

—'Busy and Bored: The Politics of Work and Leisure for Women Workers in WWII British Government Hostels', *Twentieth Century British History* 20:1 (2010), 29–49.

—'Working Class Consumers and the Campaign for Holidays with Pay', *Twentieth Century British History* 18 (2007), 277–305.

—'Selling the Circus: Englishness, Circus Fans and Democracy in Britain'. In *Leisure and Cultural Conflict in Twentieth-Century Britain*, edited by Brett Bebber. Manchester: Manchester University Press, 2012.

de Grazia, Victoria. *How Fascism Ruled Women: Italy, 1922–1945*. Berkeley, CA: University of California Press, 1992.

—'Changing Consumption Regimes in Europe'. In *Getting and Spending: European and American Consumer Societies in the Twentieth Century*, edited by Susan Strasser, Charles McGovern and Matthias Judt. Cambridge: Cambridge University Press, 1998.

—*Irresistible Empire: America's Advance through Twentieth-Century Europe.* Cambridge, MA: The Belknap Press of Harvard University, 2006.
—'Foreword'. In *Selling Modernity: Advertising in Twentieth-Century Germany,* edited by P. E. Swett, S. J. Wiesen and J. R. Zatlin. Durham, NH: Duke University Press, 2007.
Decker, Stephanie. 'Corporate Legitimacy and Advertising: British Companies and the Rhetoric of Development in West Africa, 1950–1970', *Business History Review* 81 (2007), 59–86.
Deslandes, Paul. 'The Cultural Politics of Gay Pornography in 1970s Britain'. In *British Queer History*, edited by Brian Lewis. Manchester: Manchester University Press, 2013.
Deutsch, Tracey. *Building a Housewife's Paradise: Gender, Politics, and American Grocery Stores in the Twentieth Century.* Chapel Hill, NC: University of North Carolina Press, 2012.
Djelic, Marie-Laure. *Exporting the American Model: The Postwar Transformation of European Business.* Oxford: Oxford University Press, 2001.
Donajgrodzki, A. P., ed. *Social Control in Nineteenth-Century Britain.* London: Croom Helm, 1977.
Donohue, Kathleen G. *Freedom from Want: American Liberalism and the Idea of the Consumer.* Baltimore, NJ: Johns Hopkins University Press, 2005.
Douglas, Mary. 'Why Do People Want Goods?' In *Understanding Enterprise Culture: Themes in the Work of Mary Douglas,* edited by Shaun Hargreaves Heap and Angus Ross. Edinburgh: Edinburgh University Press, 1992.
Douglas, Mary and Baron Isherwood. *The World of Goods: Towards an Anthropology of Consumption.* London: Allen Lane, 1979.
—, ed. *Production of Culture/Cultures of Production.* London: Sage, 1997.
Dunbar, D. S. *Almost Gentlemen: The Growth and Development of the Advertising Agent, 1875–1975.* London: J. Walter Thompson, 1976.
Dyer, Gillian. *Advertising as Communication.* London: Routledge, 1982.
Dyhouse, Carol. *Glamour: Women, History, Feminism.* London: Zed Books, 2010.
Edgerton, David. *Britain's War Machine: Weapons, Resources and Experts in the Second World War.* London: Allen Lane, 2012.
Edwards, Tim. *Contradictions of Consumption: Concepts, Practices and Politics in Consumer Society.* Maidenhead: Open University Press, 2000.
Eichengreen, Barry. *The European Economy since 1945: Coordinated Capitalism and Beyond.* Princeton, NJ: Princeton University Press, 2007.
Esty, Jed. *A Shrinking Island: Modernism and National Culture.* Princeton, NJ: Princeton University Press, 2004.
Ewing, Elizabeth. *History of Twentieth Century Fashion.* London: Batsford, 1992.
Faulconbridge, J. R. *et al.*, eds. *The Globalization of Advertising: Agencies, Cities and Spaces of Creativity.* London: Routledge, 2011.
Featherstone, Mike. *Consumer Culture and Postmodernism.* Los Angeles, CA: Sage, 2007.
Featherstone, Simon. *Englishness: Twentieth-Century Popular Culture and the Forming of English Identity.* Edinburgh: Edinburgh University Press, 2009.
Fieldhouse, David Kenneth. *Merchant Capital and Economic Decolonization: The United Africa Company 1929–1987.* Oxford: Clarendon Press, 1994.

Fielding, Steven. 'Activists against "Affluence": Labour Party Culture during the "Golden Age," circa 1950–1970', *Journal of British Studies* 40:2 (2001), 241–67.

Fielding, Steven, Peter Thompson and Nick Tiratsoo. *England Arise! The Labour Party and Popular Politics in 1940s Britain*. Manchester: Manchester University Press, 1995.

Fletcher, Winston. *Powers of Persuasion: The Inside Story of British Advertising, 1951–2000*. Oxford: Oxford University Press, 2008.

Fones-Wolf, Elizabeth A. *Selling Free Enterprise: The Business Assault on Labor and Liberalism, 1945–60*. Urbana, IL: University of Illinois Press, 1994.

Forrest, Katherine, ed. *Lesbian Pulp Fiction: The Sexually Intrepid World of Lesbian Paperback Novels, 1950–1965*. Berkeley, CA: Cleis Press, 2005.

Fowler, David. *The First Teenagers: The Lifestyle of Young Wage-Earners in Interwar Britain*. London: Woburn Press, 1995.

—*Youth Culture in Modern Britain, c. 1920–c.1970*. Basingstoke: Palgrave Macmillan, 2008.

Fox, Richard Wightman and Lears, T. J. Jackson, eds. *The Culture of Consumption: Critical Essays in American History, 1880–1980*. New York: Pantheon Books, 1983.

Fox, Stephen R. *The Mirror Makers: A History of American Advertising and its Creators*. Urbana, IL: University of Illinois Press, 1997.

Fraser, W. Hamish. *The Coming of the Mass Market, 1850–1914*. London: Macmillan, 1981.

Frith, Simon. *Sound Effects. Youth, Leisure and the Politics of Rock 'n' Roll*. London: Constable, 1983.

Fromer, Julie E. *A Necessary Luxury: Tea in Victorian England*. Athens, OH: Ohio University Press, 2008.

Furlough, Ellen and Carl Strikwerda, eds. *Consumers Against Capitalism? Consumer Cooperation in Europe, North America, and Japan, 1840–1990*. London: Rowman & Littlefield, 1999.

Gagnier, Regenia. *Idylls of the Marketplace: Oscar Wilde and the Victorian Public*. Stanford, CA: Stanford University Press, 1986.

Gay, Paul du. *Consumption & Identity at Work*. London: Sage, 1995.

Giles, Judy. *The Parlour and the Suburb: Domestic Identities, Class, Femininity and Modernity*. Oxford: Berg, 2004.

Gillingham, John. *European Integration 1950–2003: Superstate or New Market Economy?* Cambridge: Cambridge University Press, 2003.

Glancy, Mark. 'Temporary American Citizens? British Audiences, Hollywood Films and the Threat of Americanization in the 1920s', *Historical Journal of Film Radio and Television* 26 (2006), 464–84.

Gledhill, Christine, ed. *Stardom: Industry of Desire*. London: Routledge, 1991.

Gluckman, Amy and Betsy Reed, eds. *Homo Economics: Capitalism, Community, and Lesbian and Gay Life*. New York: Routledge, 1997.

Graeber, David. 'Consumption', *Current Anthropology* 52:4 (2011), 489–511.

Grazia, Victoria de with Ellen Furlough, eds. *The Sex of Things: Gender and Consumption in Historical Perspective*. Berkeley, CA: University of California Press, 1996.

Groot, Joanna de. 'Metropolitan Desires and Colonial Connections: Reflections on Consumption and Empire'. In *At Home with the Empire: Metropolitan*

Culture and the Imperial World, edited by Catherine Hall and Sonya O. Rose. Cambridge: Cambridge University Press, 2007.

Greenfield, Jill, Sean O'Connell and Chris Reid. 'Fashioning Masculinity: *Men Only*, Consumption and the Development of Marketing in the 1930s', *Twentieth-Century British History* 10:4 (1999), 457–76.

Gunn, Simon. *The Public Culture of the Victorian Middle Classes: Ritual and Authority and the English Industrial City, 1840–1914*. Manchester: Manchester University Press, 2000.

Gunn, Simon and James Vernon, eds. *The Peculiarities of Liberal Modernity in Imperial Britain*. Berkeley, CA: Berkeley University Press, 2011.

Gurney, Peter. *Co-operative Culture and the Politics of Consumption in England, 1870–1930*. Manchester: Manchester University Press, 1996.

—'The Battle of the Consumer in Postwar Britain', *Journal of Modern History* 77:4 (2005), 956–87.

—'"Rejoicing in Potatoes": The Politics of Consumption in England during the "Hungry Forties"', *Past and Present* 203 (2009), 99–136.

Hall, Peter A., ed. *The Political Power of Economic Ideas: Keynesianism Across Nations*, Princeton, NJ: Princeton University Press, 1989.

Hall, Stuart, ed. *Representation: Cultural Representations and Signifying Practices*. London: Sage, 1997.

Hall, Stuart and Tony Jefferson, eds. *Resistance through Rituals: Youth Subcultures in Post-War Britain*, 2nd edn. London: Routledge, 2006.

Hannah, Leslie. *The Rise of the Corporate Economy*. 2nd edn. London: Methuen, 1983.

Harrison, Mark. 'The Economies of World War II: An Overview'. In *The Economics of World War II: Six Great Powers in International Comparison*, edited by Mark Harrison. Cambridge: Cambridge University Press, 1998.

Haynes, Douglas E., Abigail McGowan, Tirthankar Roy and Haruka Yanagisawa, eds. *Towards a History of Consumption in South Asia*. New Delhi: Oxford University Press, 2010.

Hebdige, Dick. *Subculture: The Meaning of Style*. London: Methuen, 1979.

—*Hiding in the Light: On Images and Things*. London: Routledge, 1988.

Hennessey, Peter. *Having It So Good: Britain in the Fifties*. Harmondsworth: Penguin, 2007.

Hennessy, Rosemary. *Profit and Pleasure: Sexual Identities in Late Capitalism*. New York: Routledge, 2000.

Hesmondhalgh, David. *The Cultural Industries*. London: Sage, 2007.

Hilton, Boyd. *The Age of Atonement: The Influence of Evangelicalism on Social and Economic Thought, 1785–1865*. Oxford: Oxford University Press, 1991.

Hilton, Matthew. 'The Fable of the Sheep, or, Private Virtues, Public Vices: The Consumer Revolution of the Twentieth Century', *Past and Present* 174 (2002), 222–56.

—*Consumerism in Twentieth Century Britain: The Search for a Historical Movement*. Cambridge: Cambridge University Press, 2003.

—'The Legacy of Luxury: Moralities of Consumption since the 18th Century', *Journal of Consumer Culture* 4:1 (2004), 101–23.

Hinton, James. *Nine Wartime Lives: Mass Observation and the Making of the Modern Self*. Oxford: Oxford University Press, 2010.

—*The Mass Observers: A History, 1937–1949*. Oxford: Oxford University Press, 2013.
Hirschman, Albert O. *Shifting Involvements: Private Interest and Public Action*. Princeton, NJ: Princeton University Press, 1982.
Hoffenberg, Peter H. *An Empire on Display: English, Indian, and Australian Exhibitions from the Crystal Palace to the Great War*. Berkeley, CA: University of California Press, 2001.
Hoganson, Kristin L. 'Stuff It: Domestic Consumption and the Americanization of the World Paradigm', *Diplomatic History* 30:4 (2006), 571–94.
—*Consumers' Imperium: The Global Production of American Domesticity, 1865–1920*. Chapel Hill, NC: University of North Carolina Press, 2007.
Hoggart, Richard. *The Uses of Literacy: Aspects of Working-Class Life with Special References to Publications and Entertainments*. London: Chatto and Windus, 1957.
Holt, Richard. *Sport and the British: A Modern History*. Oxford: Oxford University Press, 1989.
Horn, Adrian. *Juke Box Britain: Americanisation and Youth Culture, 1945–60*. Manchester: Manchester University Press, 2009.
Hornsey, Richard. *The Spiv and the Architect: Unruly Life in Postwar London*. Minneapolis, MN: University of Minnesota Press, 2010.
Horowitz, Daniel. *The Morality of Spending: Attitudes toward the Consumer Society in America, 1875–1940*. Baltimore, NJ: Johns Hopkins University Press, 1985.
—*The Anxieties of Affluence: Critiques of American Consumer Culture, 1939–1979*. Amherst, MA: University of Massachusetts Press, 2004.
—*Consuming Pleasures: Intellectuals and Popular Culture in the Postwar World*. Philadelphia, PA: University of Pennsylvania Press, 2012.
Horwood, Catherine. *Keeping Up Appearances: Fashion and Class between the Wars*. Stroud: The History Press, 2005.
Houlbrook, Matt. *Queer London: Perils and Pleasures in the Sexual Metropolis, 1918–1957*. Chicago, IL: University of Chicago Press, 2006.
Hubble, Nick. *Mass-Observation and Everyday Life: Culture, History, Theory*. Basingstoke: Palgrave Macmillan, 2006.
Humphries, Jane. 'Household Economy'. In *The Cambridge Economic History of Britain, Volume I: Industrialisation, 1700–1860*, edited by Roderick Floud and Paul Johnson. Cambridge: Cambridge University Press, 2004.
Ingebretson, Edward. 'Gone Shopping: The Commodification of Same Sex Desire', *Journal of Gay, Lesbian, and Bisexual Identity* 4:2 (1999), 125–48.
Jackson, Louise A. '"The Coffee Club Menace": Policing Youth, Leisure and Sexuality in Post-War Manchester', *Cultural and Social History* 5:3 (2008), 289–308.
Jacobs, Meg. *Pocketbook Politics: Economic Citizenship in Twentieth-Century America*. Princeton, NJ: Princeton University Press, 2005.
James, Harold. *International Monetary Cooperation since Bretton Woods*. New York and Washington: IMF and Oxford University Press, 1996.
Jennings, Rebecca. *Tomboys and Bachelor Girls: A Lesbian History of Post-war Britain*. Manchester: Manchester University Press, 2007.
Jeremy, David J. *A Business History of Britain, 1900–1990s*. Oxford: Oxford University Press, 1998.

Jessen, Ralph and Lydia Langer, eds. *Transformations of Retailing in Europe after 1945*. Farnham: Ashgate, 2012.

Jobling, Paul J. *Man Appeal: Advertising, Modernism and Men's Wear*. Oxford: Berg, 2005.

Johnson, Paul. *Saving and Spending: The Working-Class Economy in Britain 1870–1939*. Oxford: Clarendon, 1985.

Jones, Michelle. 'Design and the Domestic Persuader: Television and the British Broadcasting Corporation's Promotion of Post-war "Good Design"', *Journal of Design History* 16: 4 (2003), 307–18.

Kates, Steven M. *Twenty Million New Customers! Understanding Gay Men's Consumer Behavior*. New York: Haworth Press, 1998.

Keynes, John Maynard. *Essays in Persuasion* (1933). New York: Classic House Books, 2009.

Kowaleski-Wallace, Elizabeth. *Consuming Subjects: Women, Shopping and Business in the Eighteenth Century*. New York: Columbia, 1997.

Kroen, Sheryl. 'La Magie des Objets, le Plan Marshall et l'Instauration d'une Démocratie de Consommateurs'. In *Au Nom du Consommateur: Consommation et Politique en Europe et aux États-Unis au XXe Siècle*, edited by Alain Chatriot, Marie-Emmanuelle Chessel and Matthew Hilton. Paris: Éditions La Découverte, 2004.

Kroes, Rob, Robert W. Rydell and D. F. J. Bosscher, eds. *Cultural Transmissions and Receptions: American Mass Culture in Europe*. Amsterdam: VU University Press, 1993.

Kuisel, Richard F. *Seducing the French: The Dilemma of Americanization*. Berkeley, CA: University of California Press, 1993.

L'Etang, Jacquie. *Public Relations in Britain: A History of Professional Practice in the Twentieth Century*. Mahwah, NJ: Lawrence Erlbaum Associates, 2004.

Langhamer, Claire. *Women's Leisure in England, 1920–60*. Manchester: Manchester University Press, 2000.

Lawrence, Jon. 'Class, "Affluence" and the Study of Everyday Life in Britain, c. 1930–64', *Cultural and Social History* 10:2 (2013), 273–300.

Leach, William. *Land of Desire: Merchants, Power, and the Rise of a New American Culture*. New York: Random House, 1993.

Lee, Martyn J. *The Consumer Society Reader*. Oxford: Blackwell, 2000.

Leiss, William, Stephen Kline, Sut Jhally and Jackie Botterill. *Social Communication in Advertising: Consumption in the Mediated Marketplace*. New York: Routledge, 2005.

LeMahieu, D. L. *A Culture for Democracy: Mass Communications and the Cultivated Mind in Britain Between the Wars*. Oxford: Clarendon Press, 1988.

Leslie, D. A. 'Global Scan: the Globalisation of Advertising Agencies, Concepts and Campaigns', *Economic Geography* 71:4 (1995), 402–26.

Levy Peck, Linda. *Consuming Splendor: Society and Culture in Seventeenth-Century England*. Cambridge: Cambridge University Press, 2005.

Lewis, B. *So Clean: Lord Leverhulme, Soap and Civilization*. Manchester: Manchester University Press, 2008.

Loeb, Lori Anne. *Consuming Angels: Advertising and Victorian Women*. New York: Oxford University Press, 1994.

Lowe, Rodney. *The Welfare State in Britain since 1945*, 3rd edn. London: Palgrave Macmillan, 2005.

Lugosi, P., 'Queer Consumption and Commercial Hospitality: Communitas, Myths and the Production of Liminoid Space', *International Journal of Sociology and Social Policy* 27:3/4 (2007), 163–74.

Lury, Celia. *Consumer Culture*, 2nd edn. New Brunswick, NJ: Rutgers University Press, 2011.

Lysack, Krista. *Come Buy, Come Buy: Shopping and the Culture of Consumption in Victorian Women's Writing*. Athens, OH: Ohio University Press, 2008.

MacKay, Hugh, ed. *Consumption and Everyday Life*. London: Sage, 1997.

MacKenzie, John M. *Propaganda and Empire: The Manipulation of British Public Opinion, 1880–1960*. Manchester: Manchester University Press, 1984.

—ed. *Imperialism and Popular Culture*, Manchester: Manchester University Press, 1986.

Magee, Gary B. and Andrew S. Thompson. *Empire and Globalization: Networks of People, Goods and Capital in the British World, c. 1850–1914*. Cambridge: Cambridge University Press, 2010.

Maier, Charles S. 'The Two Postwar Eras and the Conditions for Stability in Twentieth-Century Western Europe'. In *In Search of Stability: Explorations in Historical Political Economy*, edited by Charles S. Maier. Cambridge: Cambridge University Press, 1987.

Manton, Kevin. 'The Labour Party and Retail Distribution, 1919–1951', *Labour History Review* 73 (2008), 269–86.

Martin, M. *Trois Siècles de Publicité en France*. Paris: Odile Jacob, 1992.

Marwick, Arthur. *The Home Front: The British and the Second World War*. London: Thames & Hudson, 1976.

Mathias, Peter. *Retailing Revolution: A History of Multiple Retailing in the Food Trades Based upon the Allied Suppliers Group of Companies*. London: Prentice Hall Press, 1967.

Maynard, Steven. '"Without Working?": Capitalism, Urban Culture, and Gay History', *Journal of Urban History* 30 (2004), 378–98.

McDevitt, Patrick F. *May the Best Man Win: Sport, Masculinity and Nationalism in Great Britain and the Empire, 1880–1935*. New York: Palgrave Macmillan, 2004.

McFall, L. *Advertising: A Cultural Economy*. London: Sage, 2004.

McGarity, Thomas O. *Freedom to Harm: The Lasting Legacy of the Laissez Faire Revival*. New Haven, CT: Yale University Press, 2013.

McGovern, Charles F. *Sold American: Consumption and Citizenship, 1890–1945*. Chapel Hill, NC: University of North Carolina Press, 2006.

McKendrick, Neil, John Brewer and J. H. Plumb. *The Birth of a Consumer Society in England*. Bloomington, IN: Indiana University Press, 1982.

McKibbin, Ross. *Classes and Cultures: England 1918–1951*. Oxford: Oxford University Press, 1998.

McRobbie, Angela. *In the Culture Society: Art, Fashion and Popular Music*. Abingdon: Routledge, 1999.

Miller, Andrew H. *Novels Behind Glass: Commodity Culture and Victorian Narrative*. Cambridge: Cambridge University Press, 1995.

Miller, Daniel, ed. *Acknowledging Consumption: A Review of New Studies*. London: Routledge, 1995.

—*Material Cultures: Why Some Things Matter*. Chicago, IL: Chicago University Press, 1998.
—*Consumption: Critical Concepts in the Social Sciences*. London: Routledge, 2001.
—*Consumption and its Consequences*, London: Polity, 2012.
Miller, Michael B. *The Bon Marché: Bourgeois Culture and the Department Store, 1860–1920*. Princeton, NJ: Princeton University Press, 1981.
Millward, Robert and John Singleton. *The Political Economy of Nationalisation in Britain, 1920–1950*. Cambridge: Cambridge University Press, 1995.
Mintz, Sidney. *Sweetness and Power: The Place of Sugar in Modern History*. Harmondsworth: Penguin, 1985.
Moran, Joe. 'Milk Bars, Starbucks and *The Uses of Literacy*', *Cultural Studies* 20:6 (2006), 552–73.
—*Armchair Nation: An Intimate History of Britain in Front of the TV*. London: Profile Books, 2013.
Mort, Frank. *Cultures of Consumption: Masculinities and Social Space in Late Twentieth Century Britain*. London: Routledge, 1996.
—*Capital Affairs: London and the Making of the Permissive Society*. New Haven, CT: Yale, 2010.
Mowatt, Simon and Howard Cox. *Revolutions from Grub Street: A History of Magazine Publishing in Britain*. Oxford: Oxford University Press, 2014.
Murillo, Bianca. 'Ideal Homes and the Gender Politics of Consumerism in Postcolonial Ghana, 1960–70', *Gender and History* 21:3 (2009), 560–75.
—*Conditional Sales: Global Commerce and the Making of an African Consumer Society*. Athens, OH: Ohio University Press, forthcoming, 2015.
Murton, James. 'John Bull and Sons: The Empire Marketing Board and the Creation of a British Imperial Food System'. In *Edible Histories, Cultural Politics: Towards a Canadian Food History*, edited by Franca Iacovetta, Valerie J. Korinek and Marlene Epp. Toronto: University of Toronto Press, 2012.
Nava, Mica. *Changing Cultures: Feminism, Youth and Consumerism*. London: Sage, 1992.
Nava, Mica, Andrew Blake, Iain MacRury and Barry Richards, eds. *Buy This Book: Studies in Advertising and Consumption*. Abingdon: Routledge, 1997.
Nevett, T. R. *Advertising in Britain: A History*. London: Heinemann, 1982.
—'American Influences on British Advertising before 1920'. In *Historical Perspectives in Marketing*, edited by Terence R. Nevett and Ronald Fullerton, Lexington, MA: Lexington Books, 1988.
Nicholas, Siân. *The Echo of War: Home Front Propaganda and the Wartime BBC, 1939–45*. Manchester: Manchester University Press, 1996.
Nixon, Sean. *Hard Sell: Advertising, Affluence and Transatlantic Relations, c. 1951–69*. Manchester: Manchester University Press, 2013.
Nolan, Mary. *Visions of Modernity: American Business and the Modernization of Germany*. Oxford: Oxford University Press, 1994.
Nott, James J. *Music for the People: Popular Music and Dance in Interwar Britain*. Oxford: Oxford University Press, 2002.
Nützenadel, Alexander and Frank Trentmann, eds. *Food and Globalization: Consumption, Markets and Politics in the Modern World*. Oxford: Berg, 2008.

Nym Mayhall, Laura. 'The Prince of Wales *Versus* Clark Gable: Anglophone Celebrity and Citizenship Between the War', *Cultural and Social History* 4:4 (2007), 529–43.
O'Connell, Sean. *The Car and British Society: Class, Gender and Motoring 1896–1939*. Manchester: Manchester University Press, 1998.
—*Credit and Community: Working-Class Debt in the UK since 1880*. Oxford: Oxford University Press, 2009.
Offer, Avner. *The Challenge of Affluence: Self-Control and Well-Being in the United States and Britain since 1950*. Oxford: Oxford University Press, 2006.
Osbergy, Bill. *Youth in Britain*. Oxford: Blackwell, 1998.
Overton, Mark, Jane Whittle, Darron Dean and Andrew Hann, eds. *Production and Consumption in English Households, 1600–1750*. London: Routledge, 2004.
Pashupati, Kartik and Subir Sengupta. 'Advertising in India: The Winds of Change'. In *Advertising in Asia: Communication, Culture and Consumption*, edited by Katherine T. Frith. Ames, IA: Iowa State Press, 1996.
Pedler, Frederick. *The Lion and the Unicorn in Africa: A History of the Origins of the United African Company 1787–1931*. London: Heinemann, 1974.
Pells, Richard. *Not Like Us: How Europeans Have Loved, Hated, and American Culture since World War II*. 3rd edn. New York: Basic Books, 1998.
Pollard, Sidney. *The Development of the British Economy, 1914–1990*, London: Hodder and Stoughton, 1973.
Pomeranz, Kenneth. *The Great Divergence: China, Europe, and the Making of the Modern World Economy*. Princeton, NJ: Princeton University Press, 2000.
Prestholdt, Jeremy. *Domesticating the World: African Consumerism and the Genealogies of Globalization*. Berkeley, CA: University of California Press, 2008.
Pulju, Rebecca J. *Women and Mass Consumer Society in Postwar France*. Cambridge: Cambridge University Press, 2011.
Ramamurthy, Anandi. *Imperial Persuaders: Images of Africa and Asia in British Advertising*. Manchester: Manchester University Press, 2003.
Rappaport, Erika. *Shopping for Pleasure: Women in the Making of London's West End*. Princeton, NJ: Princeton University Press, 2000.
—'Packaging China: Foreign Articles and Dangerous Tastes in the Mid-Victorian Tea Party'. In *The Making of the Consumer: Knowledge, Power and Identity in the Modern World*, edited by Frank Trentmann. Oxford: Berg, 2006.
—'Consumption'. In *The Ashgate Companion to Modern Imperial Histories*, edited by Philippa Levine and John Marriott. Farnham: Ashgate, 2012.
—'Sacred Tastes and Useful Pleasures: The Temperance Tea Party and the Creation of a Sober Consumer Culture in Early Industrial Britain', *Journal of British Studies* 52 (2013), 990–1016.
—'The Senses in the Marketplace: Stimulation and Distraction, Gratification and Control'. In *Senses in the Nineteenth-Century Marketplace*, edited by Constance Classen. London: Berg, 2014.
Rich, Rachel. *Bourgeois Consumption: Food, Space and Identity in London and Paris, 1859–1914*. Manchester: University of Manchester Press, 2011.
Richards, Jeffrey. *Films and National Identity: From Dickens to Dad's Army*. Manchester: Manchester University Press, 1997.

Richards, Thomas. *The Commodity Culture of Victorian England: Advertising and Spectacle, 1851–1914*. London: Verso, 1991.
Roodhouse, Mark. *Black Market Britain, 1939–1955*. Oxford: Oxford University Press, 2013.
Ross, Ellen. *Love and Toil: Motherhood in Outcast London, 1870–1918*. Oxford: Oxford University Press, 1993.
Ryan, Deborah S. *The Ideal Home through the 20th Century: 'Daily Mail' Ideal Home Exhibition*. London: Hazar, 1997.
Sassatelli, Roberta. *Consumer Culture: History, Theory and Politics*. London: Sage, 2007.
Savage, Jon. *Teenage: The Creation of Youth 1875–1945*. London: Chatto and Windus, 2007.
Schröter, H. *Americanization of the European Economy: A Compact Survey of American Economic Influence in Europe since the 1880s*. Dordrecht: Springer, 2005.
Schwarzkopf, Stefan. 'Transatlantic Invasions or Common Culture? Modes of Cultural and Economic Exchange between the American and the British Advertising Industries, 1951–1989'. In *Anglo-American Media Interactions, 1850–2000*, edited by M. Hampton and J. Wiener. London: Palgrave, 2007.
—'Who said "Americanization"? The Case of Twentieth-Century Advertising and Mass Marketing from a British Perspective'. In *Decentering America*, edited by Jessica Gienow-Hecht. New York: Berghahn, 2007.
—'Innovation, Modernisation, Consumerism: The Co-operative Movement and the Making of British Advertising and Marketing Culture, 1890s–1960s'. In *Consumerism and the Co-operative Movement in Modern British History*, edited by Lawrence Black and Nicole Robertson. Manchester: Manchester University Press, 2009.
—'The Subsiding Sizzle of Advertising History: Methodological and Theoretical Challenges in the Post-Advertising Age', *Journal of Historical Research in Marketing* 3 (2011), 528–48.
—'The Statisticalization of the Consumer in British Market Research, c. 1920–1960'. In *Statistics and the Public Sphere: Numbers and the People in Modern Britain, c. 1800–2000*, edited by T. Crook and G. O'Hara. New York: Routledge, 2011.
—'Managing the Unmanageable: The Professionalization of Market and Consumer Research in Post-War Europe'. In *Transformations of Retailing in Europe after 1945*, edited by Ralph Jessen and Lydia Langer. Farnham: Ashgate, 2012.
—'From Fordist to Creative Economies: The de-Americanization of European Advertising Cultures since the 1960s', *European Review of History* 20 (2013), 859–79.
Scott, Peter. *The Making of the Modern British Home: The Suburban Semi and Family Life between the Wars*. Oxford: Oxford University Press, 2013.
Segrave, Kerry. *American Television Abroad: Hollywood's Attempt to Dominate World Television*. Jefferson, NC: McFarland, 1998.
Sender, Katherine. *Business, Not Politics: The Making of the Gay Market*. New York: Columbia University Press, 2004.
Shammas, Carole. *The Pre-Industrial Consumer in England and America*. Oxford: Figueroa Press, 1990.

Shannon, Brent. *The Cut of His Coat: Men, Dress, and Consumer Culture in Britain, 1860–1914*. Athens, OH: Ohio University Press, 2006.
Slater, Don. *Consumer Culture and Modernity*. Cambridge: Polity Press, 1997.
Smart, Barry. *Consumer Society: Critical Issues and Environmental Consequences*. London: Sage, 2010.
Smith, Woodruff D. *Consumption and the Making of Respectability, 1660–1800*. New York: Routledge, 2002.
Steele, Valerie. *The Corset: A Cultural History*. New Haven, CT: Yale University Press, 2001.
Stephen, Daniel. *The Empire of Progress: West Africans, Indians and Britons at the British Empire Exhibition, 1924–25*. New York: Palgrave Macmillan, 2013.
Stockwell, Sarah. *The Business of Decolonization: British Business Strategies in the Gold Coast*. Oxford: Oxford University Press, 2000.
Stoler, Ann Laura. *Along the Archival Grain: Epistemic Anxieties and Colonial Common Sense*. Princeton, NJ: Princeton University Press, 2009.
Strasser, Susan. 'The Alien Past: Consumer Culture in Historical Perspective', *Journal of Consumer Policy* 26:4 (2003), 375–93.
Styles, John. *The Dress of the People: Everyday Fashion in Eighteenth-Century England*. New Haven, CT: Yale University Press, 2007.
Styles, John and Amanda Vickery, eds. *Gender, Taste, and Material Culture in Britain and North America, 1700–1830*. New Haven, CT: Yale Center for British Art, 2006.
Suga, Yasuko. 'State Patronage of Design? The Elitism/Commercialism Battle in the General Post Office's Graphic Production', *Journal of Design History* 13:1 (2000), 23–37.
Summerfield, Penelope. 'Women, Work and Welfare: A Study of Child Care and Shopping and Britain in the Second World War', *Journal of Social History* 17 (1983), 249–69.
Susman, Warren I. *Culture as History: The Transformation of American Society in the Twentieth Century*. New York: Pantheon Books, 1984.
Sussman, Charlotte. *Consuming Anxieties: Consumer Protest, Gender, and British Slavery, 1713–1833*. Stanford, CA: Stanford University Press, 2000.
Tebbutt, Melanie. *Being Boys: Youth, Leisure and Identity in the Inter-War Years*. Manchester: Manchester University Press, 2012.
Thackeray, David. *Conservatism for the Democratic Age: Conservative Cultures and the Challenge of Mass Politics in Early Twentieth-Century England*. Manchester: Manchester University Press, 2013.
Thirsk, Joan. *Economic Policy and Projects: The Development of a Consumer Society in Early Modern England*. Oxford: Clarendon Press, 1978.
Thompson, Noel. 'Socialist Political Economy in an Age of Affluence: The Reception of J. K. Galbraith by the British Social-Democratic Left in the 1950s and 1960s', *Twentieth Century British History* 21 (2010), 50–79.
Thornton, Sarah. *Club Cultures: Music, Media and Subcultural Capital*. London: Polity Press, 1995.
Throsby, David. *The Economics of Cultural Policy*. Cambridge: Cambridge University Press, 2010.
Tickner, Lisa. *The Spectacle of Women: Imagery of the Suffrage Campaign, 1907–1914*. London: Chatto and Windus, 1987.

Tinkler, Penny. *Smoke Signals: Women, Smoking and Visual Culture in Britain*. Oxford: Berg, 2006.
—*Using Photographs in Social and Historical Research*. London: Sage, 2013.
Tiratsoo, Nick. 'Limits of Americanisation: The United States Productivity Gospel in Britain'. In *Moments of Modernity, Reconstructing Britain, 1945–1964*, edited by Becky Conekin, Frank Mort and Chris Waters. London: New York: Rivers Oram Press, 1999.
Todd, Selina. *Young Women, Work, and Family in England, 1918–1950*. Oxford: Oxford University Press, 2005.
Topik, Steven C. and Allen Wells, 'Commodity Chains in a Global Economy'. In *A World Connecting: 1870–1945*, edited by Emily S. Rosenberg, Akira Iriye, Jurgen Osterhammel *et al*. Cambridge, MA: Harvard University Press, 2012.
—*Global Markets Transformed, 1870–1945*. Cambridge, MA: The Belknap Press of Harvard University Press, 2012.
Treasure, John. *The History of British Advertising Agencies, 1875–1939*. Edinburgh: Scottish Academic Press, 1976.
Trentmann, Frank. 'Beyond Consumerism: New Historical Perspectives on Consumption', *Journal of Contemporary History* 39 (2004), 373–401.
—'Knowing Consumers – Histories, Identities, Practices: An Introduction'. In *The Making of the Consumer: Knowledge, Power and Identity in the Modern World*, edited by Frank Trentmann. Oxford: Berg, 2006.
—*Free Trade Nation: Commerce, Consumption, and Civil Society in Modern Britain*. Oxford: Oxford University Press, 2008.
—'The Long History of Contemporary Consumer Society: Chronologies, Practices, and Politics in Modern Europe', *Archiv für Sozialgeschichte* 49 (2009), 107–28.
—'Crossing Divides: Consumption and Globalization in History', *Journal of Consumer Culture* 9:2 (2009), 187–220.
—ed. *The Oxford Handbook of the History of Consumption*. Oxford: Oxford University Press, 2012.
Trivedi, Lisa. *Clothing Gandhi's Nation: Homespun and Modern India*. Bloomington, IN: Indiana University Press, 2007.
Tungate, Mark, *Adland: A Global History of Advertising*. London: Kogan Page, 2007.
Turnock, Rob. *Television and Consumer Society: Britain and the Transformation of Modernity*. London: I. B. Tauris, 2007.
Ugolini, Laura. *Men and Menswear: Sartorial Consumption in Britain, 1880–1939*. Aldershot: Ashgate, 2007.
Vernon, James. *Hunger: A Modern History*. Cambridge, MA: The Belknap Press of Harvard University Press, 2007.
Vries, Jan de. *The Industrious Revolution: Consumer Behavior and the Household Economy, 1650 to the Present*. Cambridge: Cambridge University Press, 2008.
Wagner, Tamara S. and Narin Hassan, eds. *Consuming Culture in the Long Nineteenth Century: Narratives of Consumption, 1700–1900*. Lanham, MD: Lexington Books, 2007.
Wagnleitner, Reinhold. *Coca-Colonization and the Cold War: The Cultural Mission of the United States in Austria after the Second World War*. Chapel Hill, NC: University of North Carolina Press, 1994.

Wakeman, Rosemary. 'The Golden Age of Prosperity, 1953–73'. In *Themes in European History since 1945*, edited by Rosemary Wakeman. London: Routledge, 2003.

Walkowitz, Judith R. *Nights Out: Life in Cosmopolitan London*. New Haven, CT: Yale University Press, 2012.

Walton, John K., 'The Post-war Decline of the British Retail Co-operative Movement: Nature, Causes and Consequences'. In *Consumerism and Co-operative Movement in Modern British History: Taking Stock*, edited by Lawrence Black and Nicole Robertson. Manchester: Manchester University Press, 2009.

Walvin, James. *Leisure and Society 1830–1950*. London: Longman, 1978.

Wardlow, Daniel L. *Gays, Lesbians, and Consumer Behavior: Theory, Practice, and Research Issues in Marketing*. New York: Haworth, 1996.

Waters, Chris. 'Beyond "Americanization": Rethinking Anglo-American Cultural Exchange between the Wars', *Cultural & Social History* 4:4 (2007), 451–9.

Weatherill, Lorna. *Consumer Behaviour and Material Culture in Britain, 1660–1760*. London: Routledge, 1996.

Weeks, Jeffrey. 'Capitalism and the Organization of Sex'. In *Homosexuality: Power and Politics*, edited by Gay Left Collective. London: Allison and Busby, 1980.

—'Queer(y)ing the "Modern Homosexual"', *Journal of British Studies* 51:3 (2012), 523–39.

Weinbaum, Alys Eve, Lynn M. Thomas, Priti Ramamurthy, Uta G. Poiger, Madeleine Yue Dong and Tani E. Barlow, eds. *The Modern Girl Around the World: Consumption, Modernity, and Globalization*. Durham, NH and London: Duke University Press, 2008.

Weisen, S. Jonathan. *Creating the Nazi Marketplace: Commerce and Consumption in the Third Reich*. Cambridge: Cambridge University Press, 2011.

West, Douglas. C. 'From T-Square to T-Plan: The London Office of the J. Walter Thompson Advertising Agency, 1919–1970', *Business History* 29 (1987), 199–217.

—'Multinational Competition in the British Advertising Agency Business, 1936–87', *Business History Review* 62:3 (1988), 467–501.

Williams, Jack. *Entertaining the Nation: A Social History of British Television*. London: Sutton, 2004.

Williams, Rosalind H. *Dream Worlds: Mass Consumption in Late Nineteenth-Century France*. Berkeley, CA: University of California Press, 1982.

Wilson, Elizabeth and Lou Taylor. *Through the Looking Glass: A History of Dress from 1860 to the Present Day*. London: BBC Books, 1989.

Zukin, Sharon and Jennifer Smith Maguire. 'Consumers and Consumption', *Annual Review of Sociology* 30 (2004), 173–97.

Zweiniger-Bargielowska, Ina. *Austerity in Britain: Rationing, Controls, and Consumption, 1939–1955*. Oxford: Oxford University Press, 2000.

—*Managing the Body: Beauty, Health, and Fitness in Britain 1880–1939*. Oxford: Oxford University Press, 2011.

Zweiniger-Bargielowska, Ina and Rachel Duffett and Alan Drouard, eds. *Food and War in Twentieth Century Europe*. Farnham: Ashgate, 2011.

INDEX

2 I's Coffee Bar 2

Abrams, Mark 72, 79, 88
Accra Government Girl's School 166
Accra 165, 169, 170
Adler, Alfred 63
adolescent bricolage 90
advertising 122, 123
    advertising agencies, 9, 123
        Auguste Havas 125
        C. Mitchell (1837) 124
        C. Vernon & Sons (1884) 124
        Charles Barker & Sons 123
        Charles (Karl) Holzer and Henri Henrion 125
        Frederick Potter (1897) 124
        G. Street (1830) 124
        George Reynell 123
        Gordon & Gotch 124
        Hémet, Jep et Carré 125
        Henry Sell 124, 125
        J. Walter Thompson (JWT) 125, 129, 130, 132
        Mather & Crowther (1850) 124
        Saatchi & Saatchi 130, 132
        S. H. Benson (1893) 124, 130
        Samson Clark (1896) 124
        Scripps 123
        Sell's Advertising Agency 127
        Smith's (1878) 124
        T. B. Browne (1880) 124, 130
        T. R. Gourvish 109
        Thomas Brooks Browne 124
        Volney B. Palmer 125
        William Tayler 123
    advertising agent, 123
    advertising industry, 122
aegis 133
aerial bombing 180
affluence 3, 8
    affluent society 10, 180
    age of affluence 103
African Empire 4
Akuse 164
A-levels 98
American 1, 2
    Americana 76
    American Beat 94
Americanization 11, 12, 122, 221, 133
Anglo-American 134
Anglo-American consumer culture 11
Appadurai, Arjun 4
Artist and Journal of Home Culture, The 25
Asatsu 133
Assam Legislative Council 146
Association of West African Merchants (AWAM) 162

austerity 8, 221, 254
Austin, Bunny 43
Ayer, Francis Wayland 125

Baden-Powell, Robert, Sir 41, 42
Badgett, M. V. Lee 31
Baghdad 133
Baiden, Mary 165, 169
Bailey, Peter 89
Bakelite Kodak Brownie 127, 90
Baldwin, Stanley 142
Barbera, Joseph 2
Bars 8
Baxter, A. C. C. 170
BBC orchestra 46
Beatles 95
    Beatniks 96
    Beatlemania 90
Belich, James 11
Bengry, Justin 65
Benson & Hedges 132
Benson, John 4
Bentine, Michael 94
Bethnal Green 79
Beveridge Report 215
Birds Eye 132
Black and White Milk Bars 74
Black market 221
Board of Trade 143
Boase Massimi Pollitt 130
Bohemian 94
    Bohemians 96, 97
Bombay 162
Boston Tea Party 140
Botchway, Catherine 165
Bowie, David 3
Boy Scouts 41, 143
Boyce, David 27
Boye, Beauty 166
Brake, Laurel 25
Branckik, Blaine 24, 27
Brand New Cadillac 2
Breward, Christopher 26, 38
Brighter Football Campaign 111
Brighton 77
British Airways 132
British Broadcasting Corporation (BBC) 11, 143

British East Africa 140
British Empire 132
British Empire Producers' Organization 143
British European Airways 125
British identity 10
British Institute of Public Opinion (Gallup) 180
British Rail 107, 108, 109, 110, 112, 113
    British Rail Special trains 104
British Restaurants 77
British-American Tobacco 167
Britishness 11
Brooke Bond 150
Brummell Beau 21
Brussels 162
Brylcreem 56, 58
Burke, Timothy 162
Burt Committee 179, 180, 182, 184, 185, 191
Butlin's 93
Buy Empire Tea campaign 144

Cadbury's 128
café 72, 76 78, 79, 82
    cafés 71, 72
    café culture 9, 81
Cambridge 47
canteens 71
Cape Coast 165
Carden-Coyne, Ana 55
Carnaby Street 27, 73
Carpenter, Edward 39
Cartland, Barbara 41
Central Mission, 150
Ceylon 140, 141, 146
Ceylon Association 145
Chamberlain, Joseph 142
Chamberlain, Neville 140
Chasin, Alexandra 31
Chaudhury, Rai Bahadur Nagendra Nath 146
Chauncey, George 29
Chelsea 30
Chicago World's Fair (1893) 144
China 144
Church, Roy 128

INDEX

Churchill, Stella 41
Churchill, Winston 139
City of London College 171
Clark, Jessica 32
Clarke, John 105
clubs 8
Cocks, H. G. 28
coffee bar 2, 9, 95, 97, 98, 99
   coffee houses 123
   coffee shop 96
   coffee stall project 81
   coffee stalls 71
Cohen, Lizabeth 25
Cole, Sean 27
Collett Dickenson Pearce (CDP) 130, 131
Colman Prentis & Varley 130
Colonial Development Act (1929) 162
Colonial Office 162
commodities 2, 4
Cone and Belding 129
Connell, R. W. 38
conscription 185
Conservative Party 9, 10, 140, 142
Conservative Women's Society 150
Conservatives 141
Consumer Advisory Service 246
consumerism 3, 6
   consumer affluence 11
   consumer behaviours 4, 6, 7, 9, 12
   consumer culture 2, 11, 12
   consumer society 3, 7, 8, 214, 218
   consumption 3
Consumers' Association 225
Cook, Matt 25, 26, 28
Co-operative movement 5, 151, 198, 224, 237
   Cooperative commonwealth 238, 239
   Cooperative Insurance System 242
   Cooperative Party 239
   Co-operative Society 143, 151
   Cooperative Union 246
   Co-operative Wholesale Society 146, 198
Cornell University 145
Crane, Lionel 22
Crawford, W. S. 130

credit 10, 159, 160, 162, 163, 164, 165, 166, 167, 170
Criminal Law Amendment Act (1885) 25
Cunliffe-Lister, Philip, Sir 140

D. J. Trevelyan 111
D'Emilio, John 22
Dadzie, Martha Sylvia 169
Daily Mirror 76, 79
Daily Sketch 45
Daily Telegraph 121
Daily Worker 56
decolonization 7, 216
Dentsu 133
Department of the Environment 104, 105, 109
Department stores 6
Derrick, Paul E. 125
Deslandes, Paul 26, 28, 38
deviant 89
Dillon, Michael 66
Directory Services Inc. (DSI) 28
Doan, Laura 23
domestic sphere 6
dominions 140
Donnelly 88
Dorland 129
Dosse, Philip 28
Double Diamond 93
Drink Empire Tea campaign 139, 140, 142, 144, 145, 151
Duchess of York 143
Duggan, Lisa 31
Duke of York 41, 46
Dulwich College Mission 78
Dunkwa 165
Dunlop 128

Early Modern 12
East African 141
East End 73
Eden, Anthony 53-4
Edwardian 1
Edwardian Tariff Reform League 142
Eisenhower, Dwight D. 145
Eleven Plus 90
emigration 216

Empire 3, 5, 7, 8, 9, 10, 11, 122, 133, 139, 140, 141, 142, 144, 145, 151, 167
  Empire Buying 151
  Empire Crusade 142
  Empire Crusaders 152
  Empire Day Medal Association 143
  Empire Grown Tea 146
  Empire-Grown Tea (1934) 147
  Empire Marketing Board 10, 140, 143, 144, 151, 152, 201
  Empire Tea 145, 146
  Empire Tea campaign 150
  Empire Tea Exhibition 1932, 146
Erwin, Wasey & Co. 129
Esso petrol 129
Esty, William 145
European Coal and Steel Community 216
European Common Market 12, 216
European Community 216
European Payments Union 216
evangelicalism, 4
Evening Standard 40, 41, 42
exhibitions 6
Ezer, Daisy 133

F. & A. Swanzy 163
Fashion 26
Federation of British Industries 143
Federation of Gold Coast Women 165
femininity 7
Festival of Britain (1951) 221
Fiat 132
Films & Filming 28
Fitz-Gerald, Patrick 169
Flame Trees of Thika, The (1959), 145
Fleet Street 74, 75, 123, 125
Flugel, John Carl 41, 42, 43, 54
football 7, 9, 103
  clubs 104
  hooliganism, 103, 112
  specials 109, 112
  stadium 105
  violence 103. 104, 113
Football League 111, 112
Forces Programme 255
Ford 132

Fortes, Charles 74
Forum Club 143
Fowler, Mark 72
Free Market 5
Freud, Clement 106
Friendly societies 198
  Friendly Society Act (1875) 198
Frigidaire refrigerators 129
Fry's 128
full employment 213, 215, 217, 219, 221

Gaggia, Achille 72
Garnier, Charles 124
Gay Liberation 24
Gay News 28
G. B. Ollivant Limited (GBO) 168
Gellhorn, Martha 73
General Agreement on Tariffs and Trade Negotiations 216
General Motors cars 129
George VI 47
Germain, Conrad 28
Ghana 147, 160, 162, 164, 171
Ghana National Trading Corporation 172
Gillette disposable razor 64
Girls' Life Brigade 98
Gladstone, William 198
Glasgow 150
global trade 122
globalization 12
Good Housekeeping 183
Goon Show 94
Goons 93, 95 98
Gorman, Paul 27
Gosling, Ray 79
Great Depression 10, 12
Grocer, The 146
Gropius, Walter 181
Gold Coast 162, 169
Goodyear tyres 129
Grant, Elspeth 145
Great Exhibition 1851, 141
Grey Global 132
Guinea Times 159
Gunn, Simon 134
Gurney, Peter 141, 152

INDEX

Hackenschmidt, George 39
Hadley, Hopton 40
Hairdressers' Weekly Journal 59
Haire, Norman 41
Hakuhodo 133
Haley, Bill 88
Hamburg 162
Hamlet cigars 132
Hanna-Barbera Studios 2
Hardaker, Alan 112
Hardy, Rick 2
Harper, John 144
Harper's Bazaar 183
Havas 133
Health and Strength 39, 42, 46
Hebdige, Dick 4
Hegarty, John 131
hegemonic' masculinity 38
Heineken 132
Hill, Rowland, Sir 198
Hillyard, Brame 43
Hoggart, Richard 1, 2, 73
Holden, Brian Maurice 2
holiday camps 188
holidays with pay 71
Home and Colonial Stores 146
Home front, 180, 238
Home Office 104, 105, 110, 111
Homes and Garden 183
Homes Fit for Heroes 181
homonationalism 31
Honey 95
hooligan 105
Horn, Adrian 72
Horniman's 128
Hornsey, Richard 26, 28
Horwood, Catherine 47
Houlbrook, Matt 23, 24, 26, 29, 65
Housing and Town Planning Act (1919) 181
Housing design 179
Howell, Denis 112, 113
Hoxton Café 81
    Hoxton Café Project 80
Hudson's 128
Huxley, Aldous 145
Huxley, Gervas 144, 151
Huxley, Julian 145

Ideal Home 183
Ideal Home Exhibition 182, 183, 184, 186, 189
Ifeoma Chuku, Gloria 166
Igbo 166
immigrants 216
Imperial consumer 9
imperial protectionism 140
imperialism 4, 12
in loco parentis 93
India 139, 140, 144
Indian Tea Association 139, 144
Indian Tea Cess Committee 141, 145
industrialization 5
Inge, Dean 41
Ingebretson, Edward 31
Inner London Education Authority grant 80
International Exhibition, Wembley (1924) 140
International Hygiene Exhibition, Dresden 43
International Males Advertiser, The 28
International Monetary Fund 216
Interpublic 133
Inter-war 10
Iraq 133

Java 146
Jennings, Rebecca 30
Jeremy 28
Jobling, Paul 27
John Bull 21
Johnson, David 28
Jordan, Alfred 37, 41, 45
Juke box 2, 76, 81

Kates, Stephen 31
Kellogg's cereals 129
Kenya 145
Kodak camera 89, 129
Kotalko's True Hair Grower 57, 58
Ku-Bist Hair Fixative 58, 59
Kumasi 165, 168, 169
Kwa Kwa, Agnes 165

Labouchère Amendment 25
Labour Government 10

Labour 141
Labour Party 237, 239
Labour's Youth Commission and the Albemarle Report 73
Laite, Julia 32
Lancashire Cotton Fair 43
Lane, William Arbuthnot, Sir 37
Le Corbusier 181
League Liner 111
League of Empire Housewives 143
Lean, David 258
Leo Burnett agency 130
lesbian 29, 30
Leslie, Deborah 132
Letter from America 263
Lever Brothers 125, 128
Lewis, Brian 32
Lewis's department store 146, 147
Leyendecker, J. C. 27
Lidderdale, Mrs. 150
Light Programme 255
Lipton's 128, 146
Liverpool 108
London 122, 162, 171
   London Calling 3
   London County Council (LCC) 77, 78
   London Gazette 123
   London Parochial Charities Foundation 78–9, 80
   London Press Exchange (LPE) 124, 130
   London School of Economics 133
   London Stock Exchange 132
   London Times 129
   London Youth Committee 79
Loos, Adolf 181
Lord & Thomas 129
Lord Beaverbrook 142, 143, 152
Los Angeles 133
Louisiana Purchase Exhibition, St Louis (1904) 144
Love Me Do 95
Lowe Howard Spink 130
Lux soap 125
Lyle 128
Lyons 150
   Lyons Corner Houses 72, 76

MacDonald, Ramsay 140
Mackenzie, John 152
Madison Avenue 129, 132, 133
Makola 165
male beauty 7, 8
Man Alive 27
Man, Vince 27
Manchester 146, 147, 162
Manchester United 108
market halls 6
Market Traders' Association 165
marketplace 3
Marshall Plan 217, 222
Martin, Richard 27
Marwick, Arthur 10
masculinity 7, 8
mass consumerism 10, 180, 213, 217, 218
   mass culture 1
   Mass Observation (MO) 8, 53, 54, 55, 56, 61, 62, 64, 66, 89, 180, 186, 206, 219
   mass politics 3
   mass production 218, 220
Maypole 146
Mazawattee Tea Co. 125
McCann Erickson 129, 130
McGivern, Cecil 253, 254, 258, 259, 260, 261, 262, 263
McIntosh, Hugh D. 74
McKibbin, Ross 55, 89
McLeod, Charles C. Sir 145
Meadow Milk Bars 74
Memoirs of the Unemployed 63
Men Only 24, 26, 60
Men's Dress Reform Party (MDRP) 8, 37, 38, 39, 41, 42, 43, 44, 45, 46, 47, 48
Men's Wear 42, 43, 44
Mensah, Esther 165, 166, 169
Milan 162
Milk bar 72, 75, 81
Milk Marketing Board 74
Miller, David 4
Milligan, Spike 94
Ministry of Agriculture 143
Ministry of Food 77
Ministry of Information 206
Modern Man, The 26

modernization 215, 221
Mods 73, 95
Mort, Frank 23, 38
Mosse, George 38
Müller, Jørgen Peter 39
Mumbai 133
Murillo, Bianca 32, 147

National Consumer Council 225
National Federation of Merchant Tailors 43
National Milk Bars 74
National Savings Certificates 200
National Temperance League 74
Netherlands East Indies 140, 144
New Health 39, 45, 47
New Health Society (NHS) 37, 39, 41
New York 133, 162
Newsom, Earl 145
Nigeria 166
nineteenth century 123, 124
Nixon, Richard 145
Nkrumah, Kwame, President 172
Non-governmental agencies 12

Obuasi 165
Ogilvy group 132
Omnicom 133
O'Neill, Alistair 27
Opoku, Mary 159, 161
Osaka 162
Orwell, George 1, 2, 43, 258
Osgersby 89
Oxford 47, 63

Palmolive soap 129
Parker Pens 132
participatory democracy 10
Party of Empire Crusaders 142
passbook 163, 165, 166, 171, 172
pawnbrokers 198
Pax Americana 134
Pax Britannica 134
Pears soap 125, 128
Permissive Society 8
Perry, Fred 47
Philadelphia 133
Philosophy of Advertising 128

photograph 163
Picture Page 55, 59, 256, 257
Playboys, The 2
political economy 4
political reform 4
Post Office 143, 151
Post Office Savings Bank (POSB) 10, 197, 200, 201, 206
Poster Advisory Group 202
Postmaster General 199
post-war, 104
post-war reconstruction 11, 180
Power, Lisa 24
Presbyterian Church 165
Presley, Elvis 2, 76
Primrose League 143
Prince of Wales 41
print media 123
Psychology of Clothes, The 42
Puar, Jasbir 31
Publicis 133
Punch 39, 44, 47

Quaker Oats 125, 129
queer consumption 7
queer market 8

Radio Luxembourg 244, 258
Rappaport, Erika 74, 128, 162
Rational Recreation 5, 71, 81, 98
Ready Steady Go 95
recreation 9
restaurants 6
retail 8
Rex, Stewart 130
Road to Wigan Pier, The 43
Robert Otto Inc. 130
Rock Around the Clock 88, 94
Rockers 95
Rolfe, Frederick 26
Rolling Stones 95
Roper, Elmo 145
Rotary Clubs of America 78
Rowntree's 128
Royal Empire Society 145
Royal Geographical Society 125

Saatchi, Charles 131, 132, 133

Saatchi, Maurice 132, 133
Saatchi, Nathan 133
Safety at Sports Ground Bill 106
Saleeby, Caleb Williams 37, 40, 41, 45
Samson Clark 130
Saturday Evening Spotlight 256
saving 197
    savings banks 197
Schiess, H. 169
school leaving age 88
Schulman, Sarah 30
Schwarzkopf, Stefan, 144
Secombe, Harry 94
Sekondi 169
Sellers, Peter 94
sex appeal 54, 55
Shanghai 133
Shanks, Edward 40
Shannon, Brent 26
Shaw, George Bernard 39
Sheppard, Dick, Canon 74
Shopper's Guide 225
Sigel, Lisa 56
Silk Cut cigarettes 132
Sinatra, Frank 76
Smith, Charles 32
Snowden, Philip 139
social welfare 10, 215, 217, 219, 226, 227
Socialist 6
socialization 9
Société Générale des Annonces (SGA) 125
Soho 2, 74
Song of Ceylon (1934) 147
Sorrell, Martin 132, 133
Spartacus 28
Spender, Humphrey 89
Spinar, Lloyd 28
standard of living 6
Standard Oil 145
State welfare 12
Steel, Tommy 2
Stephen, John 27
St. Johnston, Eric 111
Stock Market Crash 1929, 140
Stoke City 108
Stoler, Anne 167

Stonewall Riots 24
Strand Milk Bars 74
Strasser, Susan 134
Studio: An Illustrated Magazine of Fine and Applied Art, The 26
Styles, John
Sumatra 146
Sunlight 39
Sunlight League 39
Sunlight soap 125
Swiss African Trading Company (SAT) 168

Tailor and Cutter 43, 44
Taj Mahal 147
Tallents, Stephen 141, 143, 151
Tate 128
Taylor, Vince 2, 4
tea 7
Tebbutt, Melanie 72
Teddy Boys 73
Teddy Girls 94
teenage consumer 72
television 11, 94, 95
Temperance 4
Temperance Friendly Society 63
The Clash 2
Thesiger, Ernest 41, 44
thrift 197, 198, 200
thug 105
Times, The 74
TIMM: The International Male Magazine 28
Tit-Bits 57, 59, 60
transnational 3
Trentmann, Frank 3, 142
Tudor Walters Committee 181
Turbin, Carole 27
Turnbull, Hugh, Sir 75

Ugolini, Laura 28, 43
unattached youth 78
unemployment insurance 198, 202
unemployment 213
Union Jack 146
United Africa Company (UAC) 159, 160, 162, 163, 164, 165, 166, 167, 169, 170

United Nations 12
University of Reading 145

vandalism 107, 112
Vassall, John 21
Vernon, James 5, 77, 134
Vickers 130
Vickery, Amanda 55
Victorian 4, 9, 12
Vinolia 57
voluntary organisations 198
Von Gloeden, Wilhelm 26

Wall Street Crash 10
War Savings Certificates 200
Wedgewood, Josiah 5, 6
Weeks, Jeffrey 22
Welfare state, 5, 180, 190, 198, 200
West End 74, 75
Which? 225
White, James, 123
Wilde, Oscar 26
Wilkinson disposable razor 64
Williams, Leonard 41, 45
Williamson, H. S. 147
Wimbledon 47
Wimpy 76

Winch, N. 40
Winterbottom, Walter 106
Wolverhampton 150
Woman & Home 183
Woman's Own 184
Women's Conservative and Unionist Association 150
Women's Guild of Empire 150
Women's Institute 145
World War I (see also First World War) 1, 6, 7, 39, 55, 71, 123, 129, 134, 141, 181, 200, 215, 239
World War II 7, II, 12, 28, 30, 47, 55, 56, 75, 76, 77, 129, 162, 169, 213, 246, 257
Wrigley's chewing gum 129

Young & Rubicam 129, 132
Young Women's Christian Association (YWCA) 73, 150
   YWCA Coffee Stall 80
   YWCA London Coffee Stall Project 78
youth culture 4, 7, 8, 12, 72
Youth Ventures Limited 79

Ziggy Stardust 3